AFRICAN ETHNOGRAPHIC STUDIES
OF THE 20TH CENTURY

I0027972

Volume 56

STANLEYVILLE

STANLEYVILLE

An African Urban Community Under Belgian Administration

VALDO PONS

R Routledge
Taylor & Francis Group

LONDON AND NEW YORK

First published in 1969 by Oxford University Press for the International African Institute.

This edition first published in 2018
by Routledge
2 Park Square, Milton Park, Abingdon, Oxon OX14 4RN

and by Routledge
711 Third Avenue, New York, NY 10017

Routledge is an imprint of the Taylor & Francis Group, an informa business

British Library Cataloguing in Publication Data
A catalogue record for this book is available from the British Library

ISBN: 978-0-8153-8713-8 (Set)
ISBN: 978-0-429-48813-9 (Set) (ebk)
ISBN: 978-1-138-59743-3 (Volume 56) (hbk)
ISBN: 978-1-138-59751-8 (Volume 56) (pbk)
ISBN: 978-0-429-48690-6 (Volume 56) (ebk)

Publisher's Note
The publisher has gone to great lengths to ensure the quality of this reprint but points out that some imperfections in the original copies may be apparent.

Disclaimer
The publisher has made every effort to trace copyright holders and would welcome correspondence from those they have been unable to trace.

The members of the committee of an association of *évolués* photographed with their European president. The late Patrice Lumumba, later to become the first Prime Minister of the Democratic Republic of the Congo, is on the extreme right

Stanleyville

AN AFRICAN URBAN COMMUNITY
UNDER BELGIAN ADMINISTRATION

VALDO PONS

University of Manchester

Foreword by
DARYLL FORDE
Director, International African Institute

Published for the
INTERNATIONAL AFRICAN INSTITUTE
by the
OXFORD UNIVERSITY PRESS
1969

Oxford University Press, Ely House, London W.1

GLASGOW NEW YORK TORONTO MELBOURNE WELLINGTON
CAPE TOWN SALISBURY IBADAN NAIROBI LUSAKA ADDIS ABABA
BOMBAY CALCUTTA MADRAS KARACHI LAHORE DACCA
KUALA LUMPUR HONG KONG TOKYO

*The International African Institute and
the author gratefully acknowledge a grant
by the University of Manchester towards
the cost of publication of this volume.*

MADE IN GREAT BRITAIN AT THE PITMAN PRESS, BATH

CONTENTS

PLATES

MAPS AND DIAGRAMS

TABLES

FOREWORD

Dr. Pons's book on the social structure of the African community in Stanleyville (now Kisangani) is the outcome of field research which was undertaken in the fifties as part of a project for the development of studies on the extensive social changes taking place in African towns. The accelerated pace of economic development and the changes in outlook and aspirations among both the administrations and urban populations in African territories after the war had made the need for systematic study of social conditions and trends among urbanized and industrialized African populations increasingly apparent. In the quarter of a century that had elapsed since the publication of Orde Browne's *The African Labourer* (1933) and the pioneer enquiry by J. Merle Davies on *Modern Industry and the African* (1933) conducted on the Northern Rhodesian Copper Belt under the auspices of the International Missionary Council, a number of investigations had been undertaken in various parts of Africa. But they had been uncoordinated efforts, very diverse in scope, a few directed to special sociological problems and others to immediate considerations of social welfare and administration. A number of new studies were now being undertaken in several parts of Africa and there was need both for an appraisal of the results and implications of the work already done and for an exploration of the scope and methods of further research that was called for.

The International African Institute discussed with Unesco in 1950 means for furthering and co-ordinating such studies and was entrusted by it with the execution of a series of projects. These were focused on preparations for an international conference of social scientists and others to review the social effects of industrialization and urban development in Africa. This conference was held at Abidjan from 29 September to 27 October 1954, at the invitation of the French Government and in consultation with the Commission for Technical Co-operation in Africa South of the Sahara. A series of field reports and other studies was prepared in advance, and it provided a first opportunity for a comprehensive exchange of views on the scope, methods and results so far achieved in this field and for the formulation of proposals concerning future research. The preparatory surveys and the papers presented and discussed at this conference were published in *Social Implications of Industrialization and Urbanization in Africa South of the Sahara* (English and French Editions) Unesco, 1956.

The preparatory surveys on the distribution and character of modern forms of production in tropical Africa and on the social effects of economic development, brought out very clearly a number of general consequences of the creation of heterogeneous, largely unskilled wage-earning populations in African towns. They also showed, however, that there were wide differences in the economic conditions and social milieu of such urban populations which had to be taken into account. It was clear that there was very great diversity with regard to such factors as the recency and rate of urban growth, as well as the strength of indigenous patterns of authority and social control; the range and frequency of migration and the degree of ethnic heterogeneity; the character and variety of working situations and levels of income; the premises and practices of administrations and expatriate entrepreneurs.

All of these had far-reaching effects on the patterns and stresses of urban life. But their diversity and variability had by no means been fully recognized in the more generalized accounts of urban conditions in Africa. Moreover their evaluation in a particular study often presented difficult problems of method. With few exceptions, earlier enquiries into African urban conditions had tended—not unnaturally, in view of the complexity of the situation and the very limited facilities for investigation that had been available—to be confined to some restricted aspect such as material conditions with regard to working conditions and standards of living, or the formal organization of industrial activity, welfare services and administration. Many such studies had practical aims, for example the provision of basic information with regard to development programmes and, while some had more theoretical objectives concerning the nature and determinants of social relations, they often suffered from vagueness of definition or a lack of sufficient data to resolve the problems posed. Another frequent limitation, for the purpose of comparative analysis, was inadequacy of methods of investigation. This was particularly apparent in connexion with techniques of intensive enquiry (open interviews, participant observation, case histories, psychological testing, etc.), the importance of which was being increasingly recognized as essential to the elucidation of social processes. It was clearly necessary to supplement 'social surveys', obtained by sampling for specific information by more intensive studies of social structure and of underlying attitudes. For the interpretations of the quantitative data and of the correlations they suggested often depended on knowledge of social processes and attitudes which such a survey could not itself provide. Furthermore, unless the character and probable interconnexions of significant features of social relations and cultural patterning had been previously ascertained, the selection of the data to be secured by a sample survey tended to be indiscriminate or ill-related to basic problems.

These considerations were borne in mind in planning for a field study of an African urban area to be carried out before the Conference was held and an attempt was made to combine as far as possible the different approaches of earlier studies. To achieve results which would be of both theoretical and practical significance provision was made for a small team of research workers, who, while bringing special skills to the tasks of securing and analysing relevant data in different spheres, would maintain a common approach to the enquiry as a whole.

It was desirable that the study should be carried out in a well-established and diversified urban centre with a considerable variety of full-time occupations and levels of skill. It was also important that the community should not be so large that the research team would find it impossible in the time available to comprehend the society as a whole and establish contact with people and social groups throughout the socio-economic range. Stanleyville in the Eastern Province of the Belgian Congo, with an African population of about 40,000, fulfilled most of these requirements. Long established as a trading and transport centre at the head of navigation on the Congo it had been a railway terminal since 1906, became a focus for road transport in the twenties, and there had been a significant development of light industries since the late thirties. From the point of view of extending the range of African urban studies Stanleyville also presented a useful contrast with several other African urban areas in which studies were being pursued at this time. It differed in its economic functions and its local context from both the 'old' trading towns of West Africa and mushroom mining centres such as those of the central African Copperbelt.

The scope and objectives of the enquiry were formulated to include an analysis of the contemporary social structure and the roles of various kinds of social grouping within it as well as an investigation of the range of factors contributing to the salient features and current trends in the social system. Thus the enquiry involved study of household, kinship, neighbourhood organizations, cliques, associations connected with recreational, religious, political and other activities, and of social differentiation and mobility as well as patterns of authority within formal and informal groups. This called for discovery and analysis of a wide range of factors, whether deriving from European initiatives or from African traditions, which might prove significant for the social configurations. In other words the character of the technical, economic, political, educational and other forces at work in Stanleyville, and in the hinterland from which its population was derived was to be determined objectively in terms of the relevant institutions and activities, and enquiry directed to their effects as seen in the patterns of social relations and in the attitudes and achievements of various social groups and categories.

An international team of three field investigators, an ethnographer, a sociologist and a psychologist, was appointed for two years' work on the project. These were respectively: M. Pierre Clément, of the Universities of Brussels and Paris, who had carried out field research at Vienne, France, as a Research Fellow of the C.N.R.S.; Mr. Valdo Pons, of the University of Cape Town, who had carried out sociological field research in Cape Town, Zanzibar, and rural England; Mlle. Nelly Xydias, of the University of Paris, Institut de Psychologie, Directrice de Service Psychotechnique, who had undertaken socio-psychological research at Vienne, France, and in industrial establishments in Paris. After 3 months preparatory work in London and a visit to Brussels for consultation with specialists there the research team worked in Stanleyville for 18 months in 1952–3. A preliminary account of the research procedures and findings was published as Part III, 'Social Effects of Urbanization in Stanleyville', in the volume referred to above (pp. 229–469).

One respect in which the Stanleyville study marked a considerable advance in research on African urban communities was the wide range and thoroughness of the statistically controlled sample surveys which were undertaken with respect to all the main aspects of social and economic life. At the time of the preliminary report the analysis of much of the data and its application for testing hypotheses concerning social processes and categories suggested by more general observation and documentary sources had still to be done. In this book Dr. Pons has now provided one of the very few detailed analyses so far available on the socio-demographic structure of an African urban community. That we have had to wait some time for it and that it relates to the colonial period over a decade ago does not detract from its value. It is not only valuable as a detailed record of the social framework and trends in one Congolese urban community during the later period of Belgian colonial administration. For, despite the new factors that have been introduced into the local situation following political independence and economic dislocation in the Congo, many of the patterns of inter-personal and inter-group relations analysed here have continued to influence the social life of the community. This study also has more than local significance; for the experiments and methods that it records for securing reliable statistical data and analysing these for testing hypotheses concerning social processes in African towns should serve as a model and as a stimulus to further systematic research in this field.

DARYLL FORDE

ACKNOWLEDGEMENTS

This book is based on field investigations conducted in 1952–3 when I was a member of a team of three social scientists appointed by the International African Institute (under the terms of a contract with Unesco) to carry out a wide programme of study in Stanleyville (now Kisangani)* of the former Belgian Congo. I am much indebted to my colleagues Mlle. Nelly Xydias and M. Pierre Clément for the stimulation of daily conversation in Stanleyville as well as for their collaboration and continued interest in my work during the time which has elapsed since we left the field. In Stanleyville we ran a joint household and it gives me pleasure to recall our co-operation as members of the same domestic unit as well as in our roles of colleagues in research. The studies were carried out under the general direction of Professor Daryll Forde who had initiated the project and whose interest and enthusiasm were unfailing throughout. I wish in particular to acknowledge my personal indebtedness to him for his insistence that I write this book at a time when rival interests and pre-occupations were eroding my own enthusiasm for it. The delay in publication is entirely my own responsibility and not that of the International African Institute.

My colleagues and I received hospitality and valuable advice in Belgium from Professor Guy Malengreau then of the University of Louvain, and in the Congo from officials of the Belgian Administration as well as from many private individuals both African and European. In acknowledging their help I wish in particular to record my indebtedness to Monsieur H. Ledoux of the then *Section Statistique du Secrétariat Général* in Leopoldville for advice in planning the social survey and for later supervising the punching and sorting of the Hollerith cards used for the statistical analysis. I also wish to record my thanks to my wife, Ruth, for undertaking a great deal of the day-to-day work involved in supervising the social survey and in checking and coding the schedules as they came into our office.

The tragic events that have taken place in Stanleyville since the time of the study render it impolitic for me to name the seven African clerks who did the interviewing, but I wish to stress that the success of the survey owed a great deal to their enthusiasm and efficiency. Apart from the tragedies of the intervening years, the usual field-work ethic prevents me from acknowledging individually any of the inhabitants of Avenue 21 who not only made my work there possible but also rendered it pleasant and enjoyable. (The names used in the text are, of course, fictitious.)

---

* Since Independence Day on 30 June 1966, Stanleyville has been officially known by its long-standing African name of Kisangani. I have retained the name of Stanleyville as the present study is entirely confined to the town under colonial rule.

In the years since the field study I have been successively a post-graduate student at the London School of Economics and a member of staff at Rhodes University (South Africa), at Makerere College (Uganda), and at the University of Manchester. I have benefited from discussions on various aspects of the Stanleyville study with friends and colleagues in each of these universities. It was, however, in Manchester that I wrote the book, and I am glad to have the opportunity to acknowledge the influence on my work of Professor Max Gluckman and of the Manchester Seminars. I had been impressed by 'the Manchester approach' to the study of African towns before joining the department and I was particularly pleased to be able to complete the study here.

The following have at various times offered helpful suggestions on drafts of one or more chapters of this book: M. Pierre Clément, Dr. (now Professor) A. L. Epstein, Professor D. Forde, Dr. (now Professor) R. Frankenberg, Mr. M. Griffen, Mr. B. Kapferer, Professor J. C. Mitchell, Dr. B. Roberts, and Mlle. N. Xydias. I am grateful to Miss E. A. Lowcock for drawing the maps, and to Mrs. M. Dearden, Mrs. R. Pons, Mrs. D. Sansom and Mrs. D. Shelton either for compiling and checking tables or for typing parts of the manuscript. My thanks are also due to the Director of the Documents and Publications Service of Unesco for permission to quote material originally published in *Social Implications of Industrialization and Urbanization in Africa South of the Sahara* (1956).

VALDO PONS
University of Manchester

POSTSCRIPT ON A RETURN VISIT TO KISANGANI IN JULY 1967

(Written in January, 1968)

In writing up this study from 1964 to 1966, I had to decide whether to try to relate any part of the analysis to the subsequent history of Stanleyville, especially since the Congo's independence on 30 June, 1960. I decided against this mainly because I had not been back since 1953, either before or after independence. In view of the troubled situation in the Congo over recent years, and especially on account of the widespread disturbances in the East and North-East during and after the 'Simba' rebellion of 1964, it was quite impracticable to envisage a return trip for research purposes at any time up to the early months of 1966. And in July 1966 the rebellion of Katangese gendarmes in the ranks of the *Armée Nationale Congolaise* in Kisangani brought new disruption to the town. Early in 1967, however, a return trip once again began to seem practicable: the rebellion of Katangese gendarmes had been quelled by the end of September 1966; the remnants of 'Simba' bands still operating in the hinterland were being systematically reduced by the A.N.C. assisted by small contingents of White mercenaries in the service of the Mobutu government; and there were qualified hopes and predictions that the economy of the region might soon begin to revive as main roads were brought back into repair. Having the opportunity to travel in Africa in June and July, I therefore included a short visit to Kisangani in my itinerary.

I flew from Kinshasa to Kisangani in an Air Congo plane on the morning of Tuesday, 4 July. I had lost all contact with friends and acquaintances in the town, and I had been unsuccessful in my attempts to ascertain whether anyone that I had known in the past was still there, but I arrived with a letter of introduction to M. Vital Moanda, the Governor of the Province. I also had introductions to Dr. John Carrington, who, after working in the region as a missionary for over thirty years, had taken a senior appointment on the staff of the Université Libre du Congo in Kisangani, and to Mr. Bill Gilvear who was a well known member of the local Protestant Relief Mission. Both Dr. Carrington and Mr. Gilvear were recommended to me by members of the British Embassy in Kinshasa as persons whom I might appropriately ask to intercede on my behalf in the event of my presence in the town being questioned by the Congolese authorities. I had been firmly warned that daily life in Kisangani was subject to many irritations and difficulties especially for strangers. In particular, I was told that I was very likely to be watched and perhaps picked up by the *sûreté*. To minimize the chances of being accused of spying I was advised to leave my camera and tape-recorder in Kinshasa. I had equally been warned that in the interests of personal security I should not wander away from the town centre on my own, and that I should not in any circumstances leave my hotel at night. The seriousness of such warnings was underlined by the murder of an English missionary living close to the town centre by a band of youths a few days before my arrival.

In view of these advices I was naturally apprehensive as I landed at Kisangani airport and booked into my hotel at noon on 4 July. I soon made my way to the Governor's office but found that he was away in Kinshasa. I was also quite unable to find any responsible official willing to take delivery of my letter of introduction. But both Mr. Gilvear and Dr. Carrington arranged to see me without delay and, during the course of the afternoon, Mr. Gilvear drove me to Avenue 21 in Kadondo (formerly Brussels) and to Mangobo (a residential area developed after 1953 to the west of former Belge I). I was also to see Dr. Carrington at the university before nightfall.

By the time I returned to my hotel room in the late afternoon of 4 July I had, without knowing it, already come to the end of my unrestricted time in Kisangani. All hopes and predictions of a period of peace and stability in the town had been either ill-founded or premature for the White mercenary rebellion, led by Denard and Schramme, broke out at 6.30 a.m. on Wednesday, 5 July. With other captive civilians I was to stay in my hotel (the Congo Palace Hotel) in the town centre for eleven days before being evacuated to Kinshasa in a Red Cross plane on the afternoon of Saturday, 15 July. The battle for the airport and town centre of Kisangani lasted from early morning on Wednesday, 5 July, to the afternoon of Wednesday, 12 July, when the White mercenaries and their Katangese supporters finally withdrew from the town. The A.N.C. re-assumed control of the town centre at dawn on Thursday, 13 July. While effectively ensuring the safety of the White civilian population, who had by then mainly congregated either in the Congo Palace Hotel or in a large block of flats in the same area, the officers of the A.N.C. were unable to prevent widespread looting. The greater part of the town centre was once again ransacked by soldiers and civilians alike, and by the time the last Red Cross evacuation plane took off on 15 July, all but a few—perhaps a dozen—of the White residents had once again left the town. Deprived of all possibility of further pursuing the original objectives of my return visit, I took the opportunity of studying captive civilian reactions in the Congo Palace Hotel. (I am at present engaged in the analysis of my observations which I intend to publish in a separate volume.)

On my eventual return to Britain I was to find that on 14 July, when I was still in the Congo Palace Hotel, the *New Statesman* had published an article entitled 'In the North-East Congo' by Miss Gloria Stewart. Had I read and believed such an account before planning my return visit, I might well have been dissuaded from it. Commenting on the outbreak of the mercenary rebellion, Miss Stewart, an English journalist who had spent six weeks in Kisangani and its region in April and May 1967, wrote in the following terms:

On the surface, the present troubles in the Congo spring from the machina tions of Moise Tshombe and his mercenaries. But the malaise is, of course, much deeper-rooted. . . . Life [in the N.E. Congo], for Europeans and Congolese alike, is desperately difficult and dangerous. It is almost impossible to imagine the extent of mismanagement, corruption and foolishness. . . . While I was in Kisangani I met a French teacher who had not been paid for eight months. Saddest of all, the only person who seemed likely to get his pay was a mercenary. Mercenaries do get paid. They are luckier than the Congolese troops, many of whom have not been paid for four months and longer. . . . The mercenaries, regrettably, are crucial to the continued existence of any kind of law and order. . . . when there is trouble, most of the casualties are caused by random shooting by the Congolese troops, who feel they have to fire their guns. . . . Bullet holes can be found in most unlikely places—at the top of six-storey buildings, as well as in the backs of harmless Congolese citizens. Then the looting starts. . . . The town fills up with hordes of people who break in the steel-barred shop windows and steal whatever is going. The shops nowadays have very small stocks and the bank keeps almost no money on hand. It is strange that there are still Europeans in the North-East. . . . From time to time the Congolese authorities say they intend to confiscate all short-wave transmitters held by foreigners—a serious threat for the telephone rarely works and telegrams have only a 50–50 chance of arriving. Even planes are completely unreliable. Scheduled aircraft may or may not take off; often the time-table has been arbitrarily changed—the plane you expected to catch left yesterday. . . . The actions of the Congolese authorities increase the sense of insecurity and fear. One day your documents are in order and the next, for no discernible reason, they are not. . . .

Without necessarily endorsing any of Miss Stewart's particular claims (some of which strike me as possibly exaggerated and biased), I am in no doubt from my few unrestricted hours in Kisangani, as well as from talking to fellow captives in the Congo Palace Hotel between 5 and 15 July, that the general tone of her comments is fully in keeping with the views and attitudes held by many local Europeans. Most Europeans in the town undoubtedly lived in a constant state of fear and apprehension. The White population, which had risen to over 5,000 before 1960, was only about 400 in mid-1967. Some of the Whites—missionaries in particular—lived there out of a sense of duty and commitment; others were persons who, having spent the greater part of their lives in the town, no longer had roots anywhere else, either in Europe or Africa; others were only there for relatively short periods in the hope of making large and quick profits. One young Greek told me that he and his brother had, in two and a half years in Kisangani, made as much for themselves as they could possibly hope to make in a lifetime of hard work in Greece. 'But', he added, 'we are like mercenaries; it is dangerous to be here'.

My own experience of present-day Kisangani beyond the walls of the Congo Palace Hotel is necessarily very limited. But, meagre as my evidence is, it suggests that despite the impressions of 'chaos' and 'disorganization' understandably created in the mind of a visiting European journalist, there are, within the local African community, important elements of cohesion and even of continuity between the situation of pre-independence years and that of the present time. Driving through Kadondo with Mr. Gilvear on the afternoon of 4 July, I was struck by the familiarity of the scene. I was told that Kadondo had been the scene of a great deal of fighting on several occasions since 1960, but the scars of battle were not visible on the native-type houses in this area as they were on the large modern buildings of the town centre. More significantly, I did not see any outward signs of general neglect or of dwelling compounds being abandoned by their residents. The avenues of Kadondo seemed to me just as lively and populated as at the time of my study. And I was later to gather several opinions that the African population of the town as a whole had continued to rise throughout the post-independence years. From its total of some 40,000 persons in 1952/53, it had, we know from the statistics of the Belgian administration, risen to over 70,000 by 1959, and it is now undoubtedly well over 100,000. Although some residents have, during the years of upheaval and disruption, fled to their villages, many have not done so, and others have come to Kisangani for the first time finding it more secure than some of the villages in a hinterland that has in many areas been even more disrupted than the town.

Despite the far-reaching damage to the economy of the town, and despite very high unemployment, *some* important avenues of employment have remained open throughout the years of political upheaval and intermittent hostilities. The drastic fall in the number of Europeans in the town cannot be taken as an accurate index of the decrease in local employment opportunities and resources. The army and the cadres of Congo government officials have in themselves continued to create a demand for various goods and services and have brought a steady flow of money to the town from central government funds. Similarly, schools, missions, hospitals, and the newly-established university have up to a point brought in money from foreign sources. *Some* factories, such as the brewery and mineral water company, have never closed for more than a few days at a time; *some* buildings in the town centre have been abandoned and are now derelict, but a surprising number are still occupied, and a few have actually been built since 1960 (e.g. the buildings of the university which first opened in 1963). I do not have the information to sketch, even in the roughest outline, what has happened to the economic structure of the town since 1960. Nor do I deny that some sections of the African community have suffered actual or near starvation at some periods. I merely suggest that an appreciable proportion of the population has manifestly continued to live off wages earned in the town. This point is important in relation to the next.

On my way to Avenue 21, which had been studied in detail in 1952–3, and on finally locating Lusaka whom I had set out to find, I was to gather that, whatever other effects the recent years of strife may have had on Kadondo, the 'community' of the township with its intricate networks of communication and associaton had clearly survived and perhaps even gained in cohesion. Before reaching Avenue 21, Mr. Gilvear introduced me to an elderly resident who is a minor official in the *Commune* of Kadondo. In the course of twenty minutes of conversation and questioning, I was able to gather news of seven or eight former Brussels personalities who were, or had been, common acquaintances of my informant and myself though he and I had never met before. Moreover, when my informant did not personally know individuals of whom I enquired, he undertook to let me have news of them within a few days. His knowledge of the fate of some, and his obvious confidence that he could quickly ascertain news of those not known to him personally, make my point. He had in effect told me that the 'community' I once knew continued to exist. He was, however, unable to give me news about any residents of Avenue 21. I therefore proceeded there in search of Lusaka.

From my knowledge of Lusaka and from the few insights I had just gained into the local situation, I thought it very unlikely that he would have left the town; I felt certain that, if he were still alive, I would be able to find him. On reaching his former compound I was told by the first resident I met that he was now living in Mangobo. The man to whom I spoke obviously knew him very well and immediately offered to guide me to his home. We drove in almost complete silence. I was increasingly confident that I was back in a familiar environment, but I did not wish unnecessarily to question my companion—whom I did not know—about people with whom I had been acquainted long before the strife of recent years. On eventually finding Lusaka, I was able to stay with him for only a few minutes owing to my appointment at the university. I therefore arranged to spend the following day with him but, as things turned out, I was to leave Kisangani eleven days later without seeing him again.

During the quarter of an hour I had with Lusaka, I heard of the death of his mother, Samenyao, of the birth of his first grandchild to his daughter, Safi, and of Safi's own subsequent death. I gathered that his half-brother, Kisubi, had left Kisangani some years ago but was still alive and hoping to return soon. I also gathered that his 'trial marriage' with Bernadette had only lasted about eighteen months. I noticed that Lusaka's house was larger and better furnished than the one he had had in Avenue 21; and he told me, to my surprise, that he was still working for the same firm as at the time I knew him. In these and other ways, I gathered that he had come through the ordeals of recent years more fortunately than most of the former residents of Avenue 21. He told me that 'with all our recent happenings here, you will only find a few men you knew in the avenue.' He added that

Limela had 'died' when Kisangani was retaken from the 'Simbas', and he went on to mention two leading personalities of Avenue 21 who were still there.

The point of general interest is that Lusaka clearly continued to be in close touch with Avenue 21 and that, whatever changes had over-taken the town of Kisangani, his own life was apparently still set, at least in part, within a series of social networks rooted in the past. If I had been able to speak to him at length, I have little doubt that I could easily have ascertained the basic facts required to sketch out the development of his social connexions since 1952–53. I am equally confident that, on the basis of such knowledge for a number of people, it would be possible to formulate working propositions concerning the impact of the drastic changes of the intervening years on the nature of domestic, neighbourhood, and community relations. The 'chaos', the 'disorganization', and the far-reaching changes in the political control of the town may well not have been matched by social dis-organization or even by marked social change at the grass-roots level of the community.

PART ONE

INTRODUCTION

I

SCOPE AND METHODOLOGY

I

For many years interest in the sociology of African towns lagged far behind that accorded to the institutions of African tribes. This was perhaps natural as long as colonial policies tended to restrict the African's role in economic development to peasant agriculture and to low-paid manual work in other industries. African towns remained essentially European—and in some regions partly Asian—centres. They did of course have some permanent African urban-dwellers but in most regions of sub-Saharan Africa the truly permanent townsman was the exception rather than the rule, and the vast majority of new immigrants normally returned to their tribal areas after varying periods of wage-earning in town. Under these circumstances African urbanism attracted little systematic study. A few pioneer urban studies were conducted by social anthropologists in the 1930s and these have often been cited. But they were exceptions.

During and after World War II the situation changed rapidly. By the mid-1950s urbanization was, in the considered opinion of Davis and Golden, 'probably going ahead faster (in Africa) than anywhere else in the world'.[1] Many African urban-dwellers were still essentially migrant labourers, as indeed many are today, but substantial communities of permanent and semi-permanent town-dwellers were growing rapidly at the very time that the African colonial world was becoming increasingly involved in a spiral of economic expansion and momentous political change. This naturally led to a much greater interest in African towns. A number of social anthropologists followed the lead given by the few who had pioneered urban studies in the 1930s, and they were in turn joined by numbers of social surveyors, sociologists, political scientists, labour economists, urban geographers, and others. As a result the literature on African towns grew rapidly in the 1950s and, as early as 1958, it was possible for Denis to compile a bibliography of nearly 400 items on one or other aspect of urbanization in Central Africa alone.[2] Moreover, since the early 1950s we have had periodic attempts to assess the progress made and to compare reports from different regions of the continent.[3]

In spite of this increased interest, however, Epstein's assessment of African urbanism as largely virgin territory is to some intents and purposes almost as valid today as it was ten years ago.[4] There are two

[Footnotes are given at the end of each chapter.]

main reasons for this. The first is simply that Africa is large and diverse. A significant piece of analysis in one region may provide valuable insights and stimulus to research workers in another, but it also often serves to remind us how varied conditions are and how much exploratory work remains to be done. Secondly, progress has often appeared to be slow partly because much of the work conducted in the past consisted of social surveys which were often designed to do little more than gather basic data which sociologists in more 'advanced' countries do not normally have to collect for themselves.[5] Yet there is some definite progress. As the more significant studies make their appearance, particular problem features of African urbanism are more clearly specified. It then becomes possible for investigators to select problems more meaningfully and thus to study problems of general relevance rather than simply to describe particular communities.

The above remarks are directly relevant to the aim and scope of the present study. The original field data used in this book were gathered in Stanleyville in the early 1950s either before or about the same time as researches such as those of Balandier and his associates in parts of French Africa, of Epstein and Mitchell on the Copperbelt of Northern Rhodesia (now Zambia), of Mayer in East London, South Africa, and of Southall in Uganda. The Stanleyville investigations carried out by my colleagues and myself were thus inevitably launched with very limited guidance from past work. We had certain notions of African urbanism derived from a few of the earlier studies such as Hellman's and Wilson's.[6] Valuable as these were, however, they could not in the absence of other studies give us much sense of direction in approaching an urban situation which clearly differed very appreciably from a slum yard in Johannesburg or a mining compound in Northern Rhodesia. Moreover, not only had Stanleyville itself never before been visited by a sociologist, but its immediate hinterland had received virtually no attention from professional social anthropologists. We thus knew little about the main tribes in the town. As can be seen from our early field reports, we reacted to the difficulties confronting us by launching a series of investigations which struck us as obvious starting points.[7] Our principal objective was to conduct a general community study involving research into household, kinship, and neighbourhood groupings, into associations connected with recreational, religious, political, and other activities, into the work situation, and into social mobility and social stratification.[8]

The present volume uses some of the data previously published by my colleagues and myself, but it is not an attempt either to re-analyse or to bring together all our findings. Nor is it an attempt necessarily to fill in any particular gaps. It is, more specifically, a study of the social implications of some prominent features of Stanleyville as it was in the early 1950s and an attempt to interpret these features of Stanleyville under colonial rule in the light of work reported from other regions of the continent since the time of our study. The main features of the town to which the study draws particular attention are its extreme tribal heterogeneity, the rapid growth of its immigrant population, and the system of urban administration established by the Belgians in centres specifically designated as *centres extra-coutumiers*. All three features struck us forcibly as we began our researches and each clearly had far-reaching implications in all spheres of community life.[9]

Though focusing more particularly on the social implications of selected features of Stanleyville, I try throughout this book to maintain the 'community study approach' which was central to the original investigations. Although I do not attempt to give a comprehensive account of the community I constantly relate the observations reported to their overall community context. To enable me to do this, I devote the first chapter of Part II to a general description of the nature and growth of the town with special reference to the conditions under which Africans lived and worked, and in the remaining chapters of Part II, I concentrate on the analysis of a series of social and demographic data drawn from a random sample of the entire African population of the town.

Part III consists mainly of an account of certain aspects of social relations in one corner of the town. This account is in effect a small-scale community study on its own, though even here I do not attempt to give a detailed description of the 'whole' of social life as is commonly attempted in community studies. Instead I dwell primarily on the nature of social relationships *between men*. As explained in Chapter VII, however, relations *between men* were very directly affected by relations *between the sexes*. In Chapter VIII, I therefore analyse the salient features of the way in which men and women were paired in the town. To do this I once again use data gathered from a sample of the entire population and am thus brought back to the community as a whole and to a further comparison of the neighbourhood studied in detail and other parts of the town.

Parts II and III of the book are thus distinct but complementary. They can, I believe, be read independently of each other and in either order. They are linked by their common interest in tribal heterogeneity, in the rapid growth of numbers, and in the system of urban administration, but each is concerned with social phenomena of an intrinsically different kind. Part II is historical, demographic and sociographic; Part III is sociological and it studies aspects of the system of social relations. In Part II we are simply laying bare the way in which certain characteristics of the population were associated with each other; in doing this we are progressively defining the overall situation within which social relations were enacted, but we are not focusing on the nature of urban social relations as such. Data gathered by survey methods do not easily lend themselves to analysis of day-to-day behaviour. To move beyond the sociographic level we have to use field materials of a different kind; we need information not on the characteristics of individuals but essentially on their behaviour and on the

build-up of incidents in day-to-day life. Part III is thus based largely
on direct observations and on case histories, and its focus is not so
much on categories of persons as on categories of social relations and of
situations.

Finally, in Part IV, I attempt to bring together the main findings of
Parts II and III and to assess some of the general features of social
relations in the wider urban community.

II

The starting point of the study lies in the every-day observation that
the population of Stanleyville was extremely heterogeneous in its tribal
composition. At the beginning of the field work it was immediately
apparent that this heterogeneity had a far-reaching influence on the
system of social relations in the community. At the same time it was
equally apparent that this influence was closely interrelated with
other influences, and particularly with social differentiation seemingly
based on education, occupation, and other experiences and achievements in the urban world. Following the usage of Mitchell in *The
Kalela Dance*, I employ the terms 'tribalism' and 'class' to refer to
these two broad principles of differentiation, but it will be seen that in
the course of the study I tend to discard 'class' altogether and in many
instances use 'tribalism' only as an indication of a general kind of
differentiation. At the present stage, however, the use of the two terms
is convenient.

The initial questions which struck me concerning 'tribalism' and
'class' in Stanleyville can be explained very simply by imagining two
observers being conducted on casual visits to two different neighbourhoods in the town. One observer could well have been taken to an
area where there was a marked tendency for members of the same tribe
to live next to each other. Most of his observations here would have
suggested the existence of discrete tribal neighbourhoods each with
a relatively self-sufficient social life. Thus, for example, he might well
have been told that the incidence of 'mixed' or non-tribal marriages in
the area was low and that the inhabitants tended to organize the greater
part of their neighbourhood and other leisure-time activities on a
largely exclusive tribal basis.[10] He might also have noticed that people
habitually conversed in their tribal vernacular, and that at least some
white-collar employees tended to mix casually with illiterate migrants
and to participate with them in a whole series of encounters as diverse
as casual drinking and gossiping in a bar to tribal dancing on the
occasion of a mourning ceremony. On the basis of such observations
our first observer could well have thought that 'tribalism' remained the
predominant influence affecting day-to-day life in town.

The second observer could, however, have been taken to a neighbourhood where there was no readily discernible evidence of ethnic residential concentration, and where members of many different tribes lived

side by side and commonly shared the same dwelling-compounds, and sometimes the same houses. Here he would have heard most inhabitants conversing in one or both of the *linguae francae* of Swahili and Lingala (and occasionally in French) and he would have seen people mixing in public places, such as bars and dance halls, where the use of a tribal vernacular would have sounded quaint. On inquiry he would have discovered that in this area the incidence of non-tribal marriages was high and that informal friendship groups and formal voluntary associations commonly consisted of members of different tribes. Moreover, in such a neighbourhood he might well have encountered a measure of anti-tribal sentiment and perhaps met people ready to argue that in *Kizungu* ('in the place of the Europeans') 'tribe counts for nothing', or that, 'unlike our fathers, we no longer look at tribe nowadays'. This second observer could thus understandably have come away with the impression that the principle of 'tribalism' was no longer of major importance in the community. Indeed, he might well have been struck by quite another feature, namely the differing ways of life of French-speaking *évolués* and of the relatively uneducated masses of manual workers.

In general, then, our two observers might well have formed seemingly contradictory impressions concerning the importance of 'tribalism' and 'class'. Had they been given the opportunity to wander around the town for any length of time, however, they would have been compelled to modify their first impressions. The fact is that the manner and the extent to which 'tribalism' and 'class' operated to bring people together or to set them apart varied markedly within the community. We are thus naturally led to enquire into the nature of these variations and, ultimately, to ask ourselves how the two principles of 'tribalism' and 'class' operated simultaneously within the same community. From the detailed observations reported in Parts II and III, it will be seen that the high rate of immigration and various features of the urban administrative system were important factors influencing the interplay of 'tribalism' and 'class'. The significance of these and other factors influencing social relations can, however, only be assessed through the use of concepts and methods which allow us to distinguish between several different aspects of the processes of association and division.

We may start from the simple notion of approaching the study of 'tribalism' (or, equally, of 'class') by conceiving of the community as made up of a series of individuals each with a unique set of interpersonal relations, and of examining the tribal components of each of these sets of relations. We could then conceivably proceed to classify each member of the community according to the ratio of social relations he or she maintained with fellow-tribesmen to relations maintained with non-tribesmen. If we had been able to gather the requisite information for all the inhabitants of Stanleyville we would certainly have found wide variation from the cases of people with virtually all their social relations within one tribal colony to cases with highly diverse sets of relations. And there can be no doubt that the distribution of persons along this scale or continuum would have been far from random.

There are several factors which even casual observation revealed as being associated with 'pure' and 'mixed' or tribal and non-tribal sets of inter-personal relations. Firstly, as implied in the impressions attributed to our two casual observers, the extent to which an individual was in contact with fellow-tribesmen and non-tribesmen varied appreciably from one area of the town to another. And we shall see in detail in Part II that there were some 'natural areas' in the town whose inhabitants were very heterogeneous in tribal origin, others which were largely homogeneous, and others still—by far the majority— which fell between these two extremes. Secondly, there was marked variation between particular tribes. Some tribal colonies were relatively 'closed'—in the sense that members tended to restrict their personal relations within their own group—while others were by comparison very 'open'. Thirdly, status in terms of age, sex, occupation, and education was commonly associated with lower or higher degrees of tribal or of non-tribal participation. Thus an educated white-collar worker was, other things being equal, more likely to have a non-tribal set of social relations than, say, an illiterate migrant labourer.[11] Similarly, men were likely to maintain more non-tribal relations than women if for no other reason than that their work roles brought them into more frequent contact with people of other tribes than did the domestic roles of their wives. And so on.

In Part II (and also in sections of Part III) I present several sets of sociographic data which confirm the illustrations given above. But even complete information on the affiliations of all the persons with whom each inhabitant of the town was in personal contact would yield only a partial analysis of the interplay between 'tribalism' and 'class'. We have to carry the study beyond the sociographic level to an assessment of the differing significance of tribal and non-tribal relationships in various situations and, equally, to the analysis of various sets of social relations within which tribal and non-tribal contacts took place. From various incidents and situations reported in Part III it will be seen that a man's tribal affiliation may be a decisive factor in leading him to associate with fellow-tribesmen in one situation but not in another. At the same time, even in a situation in which he unhesitatingly opts or, in some cases perhaps simply accepts, to associate with non-tribesmen, his tribal affiliation may affect his behaviour towards those with whom he is in contact. Or again, we have to bear in mind that a man sometimes opted to associate with fellow-tribesmen on one occasion and with non-tribesmen on another somewhat similar occasion, and that on some occasions his behaviour in relation to others was governed by the same set of norms and values and on other occasions by a different set. We thus have to consider a variety of possibilities in numerous differing situations, and we need a conceptual formulation which allows us to focus our analysis while yet being sufficiently flexible to enable us to take account of the wide ranges of variation in day-to-day life.

The conceptual formulations of Mitchell and Epstein in their respective studies on the Copperbelt were devised to deal with this kind of problem. My analysis derives from their work as well as from subsequent related developments in the work of Mayer. In *The Kalela Dance* Mitchell sees 'tribalism' and 'class' as 'categories of interaction' operating 'to mediate social relationships' in a 'predominantly transient society', but he stresses that it is impossible to generalize about the operation of the two principles without reference to the specific social situations in which interactions take place.[12] He is thus inevitably led to be critical of formulations of the problem which tend to assume—often implicitly rather than explicitly—that, as 'class' becomes more important in modern Africa, 'tribalism' must necessarily become less important as if the change from a 'tribal' to a 'class' society were a unilineal process. 'The evidence we have from Northern Rhodesia', Mitchell writes, 'is that in certain situations Africans ignore either class differences or tribal differences (or both), and in other situations these differences become significant.'[13] He therefore suggests that in approaching the interplay of 'tribalism' and 'class' we invoke the principle of 'situational selection' previously applied in studies of modern African society by Gluckman in his analysis of aspects of social relations in Zululand,[14] and subsequently also used by Epstein and Mayer.[15]

In Stanleyville, as on the Copperbelt, much day-to-day behaviour could readily be analysed in terms of Mitchell's formulation. This is, I believe, abundantly illustrated in Part III of this study and especially in Chapter VI. We have made a useful start when we are able to specify the social relations affected by one or other principle and to indicate differences between situations in which different principles of association operate. But the general problem posed by the interplay of 'tribalism' and 'class' does not end there. In a development and elaboration of Mitchell's formulation, Epstein suggests that we must try to go beyond specifying *where* 'tribalism' and 'class' are 'categories of interaction in day-to-day intercourse' to an assessment of the *way in which* the two influences pervade the overall system of social relations. 'In the common connotation', he writes, ' "tribalism" tends to become an unitary concept, and carries the implicit assumption that, because the evidence points to the persistence in the towns of strong tribal loyalties, those loyalties will operate with the same strength over the total field of social relations . . . But this difficulty is avoided if we approach the town as a field of social relations which is made up of sets of social relations of different kinds, each of which covers a distinct sphere of social interaction, and forms a sub-system . . .; each set may have a certain measure of autonomy so that the tempo and character of change are not evenly distributed over the whole field'.[16]

Epstein's elaboration has very clear advantages over any tending to conceive of interactions as taking place within a series of specific situations in which 'tribalism' is sometimes the decisive principle of association with 'class' or some other principle 'taking over' at other times. Firstly, by distinguishing between different sets of social relations we can begin to consider not only whether 'tribalism', or 'class', or another principle, is decisive in particular interactions, but also the extent to which different principles pervade analytically separable systems or sub-systems of social relations. Secondly, the formulation enables us to conceptualize change over time in the influence of 'tribalism' and 'class'. So it is that Epstein suggests that we attempt to look at the possibly changing interrelations between different sets of social relations; that we may for analytical purposes need to regard different sets of social relations as partly autonomous; and that we try to assess whether the tempo and character of change perhaps varies from one set to another. Epstein was led to this elaboration of Mitchell's formulation partly through the need to find a way of analysing *changes over time* in the pattern of African leadership on the Copperbelt.

It will be seen that the main data presented in the present study do not have the same time depth as some of Epstein's recorded historical materials. We are thus not in a position to 'test' or develop some major aspects of his formulation in any direct way. Yet his approach has influenced my interpretation in several general respects. Firstly, his suggestions have led me to pay particular attention to the possibility that differences in the social configuration of various tribes (and, equally, of various 'natural areas') in the town were not basic or essential differences between them but simply manifestations of different stages reached by various tribal colonies (or 'natural areas') which were, and had been, developing over time. Similarly, Epstein's formulation led me to dwell on the evidence I have that the small-group interactions I observed in one neighbourhood were, in effect, embedded in a process of adjustment over time between sets of social relations that existed in an overall context of change.

Secondly, Epstein's elaboration implicitly directs us to examine the content of 'tribalism' as an influence on social relations. Indeed, in parts of his formulation this is explicit, and it is clearly a question which must arise as soon as we lay stress on the tempo and character of change, or when we specifically set out to compare the influence of 'tribalism' on sets of relations enacted in distinctively different spheres of social life.

Finally, Epstein's suggestion that the overall urban system be delineated as a developing set of interrelated, but perhaps partly autonomous sub-systems of social relations, has influenced my approach to the town as a whole. In attempting to order my field observations I came in the first instance to see social relations in the African residential areas as constituting one of three broad sets of relations which together made up the overall urban system. The first major set which can be partially isolated is that of the rural-urban relations in which many of the inhabitants were still directly involved as migrants travelling to and fro from time to time, as traders engaged in commercial relations with countrymen, or simply as people sometimes corresponding with and visiting their rural kinsmen.

The second major set consists of the whole complex of relations between Africans and Europeans in the town. The African community consisted to a large extent of immigrants from the countryside, often illiterate and 'uncivilized', and having little social equipment appropriate to urban life. The Africans inhabited segregated residential areas in a town with a very particular kind of administration, they were employees of limited experience and skill, and they were politically and economically unprivileged members of the total society. The European community, on the other hand, was made up of employers, administrators, teachers, missionaries and, more generally, of 'civilizers' and holders of economic and political influence, power, and authority.

Having isolated the above sets of social relations, we are then left with, to use Mayer's phrase, the 'within-town ties'[17] of the African residential areas of the town. In their residential areas Africans entered into contact with each other as members of families and other domestic units, as neighbours and friends, as landlords and tenants, as small shopkeepers and customers, as men and women, as adults and children, and the like. This third major set of relations is the one on which I focus in my study of one neighbourhood reported in Part III of the present volume. But we cannot proceed with the analysis of 'within-town ties' without constantly referring to rural-urban and African-European relations of the community as a whole. In Part II, I therefore try to bring the three sets of relations into a perspective appropriate to the study of the local African community.

In approaching the town in this way two points must be stressed. Firstly, the dividing lines between the rural-tribal world and the African urban-residential world and between the urban-residential sphere and the sphere of direct relations with Europeans are not arbitrary demarcations. The rural-tribal hinterland, the African residential areas of the town, and the 'European town' were three strikingly different milieux in which various members of the African community were involved in markedly differing degrees. And these 'three worlds' were reflected in different influences, and in different qualities, which the inhabitants themselves recognized quite readily. Thus, they readily drew a distinction between 'civilized' and 'uncivilized' or 'savage' or 'primitive' or 'backward' men. It was common to hear two men discussing a third in terms such as he is 'a very civilized man', he is 'only a little civilized', he is 'not quite civilized', he was 'civilized long ago', and so forth. And this distinction was closely associated to that drawn by the inhabitants between what they referred to as *Kizungu* and *Kisendji*. *Kizungu* and *Kisendji* are difficult to define precisely because they were used in many different contexts. In a general way, however, they

referred to two ways of life. The *Kizungu* way was 'civilized' and the
Kisendji way was 'traditional' or 'backward'. On leaving his village to
seek employment in town a man was said to be 'following *Kizungu*'.
Sometimes people would say that '*Kizungu* has now entered everywhere', but more generally the two terms were used to distinguish
between existing realities.

Like the notions of *Kizungu* and *Kisendji*, those of 'civilized' and
'uncivilized' are also difficult to define precisely because they too were
used in many different contexts. Moreover we shall see that the terms
were also often related to distinctions of moral worth. The fact is, however, that the two terms referred, in one form or another, to the broad contrast between the modern and the traditional, between town and village.

Similarly, notions of *évolué* and non-*évolué* were based on a real
contrast of far-reaching importance: the contrast between the ways of
life of educated white-collar workers and of the ordinary mass of
urban Africans. The *évolué* way of life derived directly from a European
reference group. The *évolué* image was associated with white-collar
occupations in the 'European town', with schools and offices, with face-
to-face interaction in the French-speaking sector of European-African
relations, with markedly higher incomes than those of manual workers,
and thus with very appreciably different levels and styles of consumption. Here, too, however, the notion was a relative one; an *évolué* was
an educated French-speaking man, but not all educated French-
speaking men were regarded as equally *évolué*, and between themselves
évolués constantly drew numerous fine distinctions of more and of less
évolué in much the same way as non-*évolués* drew distinctions between
more and less 'civilized' men. But the distinctions between more and
less *évolué* were not normally drawn by non-*évolués* to whom the criteria
were largely irrelevant, whereas *évolués* were, like non-*évolués*, likely to
be sensitive to grades and shades of 'civilization'. The difference
between the notions of *évolué* and 'civilized' is important in any analysis
of 'class'. It will, however, be seen that I seldom dwell on *évolués* in this
study, whereas I have frequent occasion in Part III to discuss the notion
of 'civilized' and 'uncivilized'. The reason for this is simply that the
neighbourhood analysed in Part III had virtually no *évolués* inhabitants.
The systematic study of the social relations of *évolués* thus inevitably
lies beyond the scope of the present study, though I constantly refer to
évolués as an important element in the wider community.

The second general point to note in connexion with the division of
the urban field into three major sets of social relations is that it leads
me to distinguish between aspects of the system of social relations
within the African residential areas which were directly linked to, and
dependent on, relations in the other two sets, and those which can
more fruitfully be analysed as products of the very experience of living
in the African areas of the town. I suggest that certain social relations
in which the African population was involved can be analysed as
aspects or extensions or, in some cases, reflections of rural-urban

relations, while others can in a similar way be viewed as aspects, extensions, or reflections of the European-African complex of relations; and others still, though in some measure influenced by rural-urban and European-African relations, can best be conceptualized as relatively autonomous urban-residential developments. To illustrate this we may consider the wide range of formal and semi-formal voluntary associations encountered in the African community; some of these were associations tending to order, foster, or maintain relations between urban immigrants from a particular tribe or region or perhaps from a particular administrative territory in the hinterland. Such voluntary associations call for analysis as extensions or reflections of the 'tribal' world and, in some cases, as an aspect of rural-urban relations. Similarly, certain associations were closely related to distinctions and interests stemming from, or actually based in, the European-dominated spheres of work, church, and school. And, indeed, some associations of *évolués* even had European presidents (cf. Frontispiece). Finally, there were yet other associations which were essentially products of social interaction within the African urban community and had no direct connexion with either the rural-tribal or the European-African complexes of social relations.

Although I have illustrated the distinction being drawn by reference to voluntary associations, the present study does not dwell on these associations for the same reason as it does not dwell on *évolués*, namely, that voluntary associations were rare in the neighbourhood studied in Part III. But the distinction is equally applicable to other sets of social relations. Thus, for example, I later distinguish between networks of personal social relations confined to the town and those extending to rural areas. There were people in the neighbourhood studied who were in various ways still deeply involved in their home villages and whose actions and behaviour in town were demonstrably affected by this continuing involvement. But there were equally some whose village connexions had either lapsed or were, for other reasons, of very little consequence for them. We therefore have to find a way of analysing and comparing the behaviour of people with widely differing involvements and commitments.

In this regard Mayer's conceptualization of the various ways in which Xhosa participate in town life in East London is of direct relevance. Mayer was led to draw a broad distinction between town-rooted and country-rooted persons, and he shows how 'the fact that some Xhosa in East London are town-rooted while others are country-rooted constitutes a social division of major importance in the town'.[18] But he explains that country-rooted and town-rooted are not exclusive categories; many persons in East London are at one and the same time 'town-rooted immigrants' and 'country-rooted migrants', and are thus 'doubly rooted'.[19] The problem discussed by Mayer in these terms is not in itself new. Participation by African urban-dwellers in 'two worlds' has frequently been noted and the accompanying problems of analysis have attracted the attention of a number of authors who have shown, as Gluckman puts it, 'that it is possible for men to dichotomize their actions in separate spheres' and, indeed, that dual participation 'may be an important contribution to the working of the embracing social field'.[20] The particular aspect of Mayer's work which has affected the ordering and interpretation of my data in the present study lies in his use and development of the notion of social network as a tool in assessing the significance of participation in 'two worlds'. Here, too, however, Mayer is developing a concept previously used by others, and we need to refer briefly to its development.

Some notion of networks of social relations underlies a great deal of past sociological investigation, but the relatively precise meaning given to the term in recent studies of African urbanism stems mainly from Barnes's study of a Norwegian village and Bott's study of families in Britain.[21] The first general distinction to note is between sets and networks of social relations. A person may have numerous face-to-face relations with other people drawn from different categories and sections of a population. As long as we are not concerned to focus on the implications for him of the relations *between* the many people with whom he is in contact, we can refer to the totality of his relations with others as his set of social relations. And, if useful and convenient, we can distinguish between different sets according to the attributes of the persons concerned, as well as according to the nature of the relation of each to the subject whose position we are examining. Thus, for example, we may find it useful to refer to an individual's sets of kinsmen, of friends, of neighbours, and the like. And we may well wish to distinguish between sets of relations which a person has with men as against women, with newcomers as against well-established residents, and so on. But as soon as we become interested in the social relations between the various members of the set or sets of people with whom the individual is in touch, we are dealing with an additional series of facts. It was in considering this additional series of facts that Barnes found it convenient to use the term network.[22]

Defined in this way, the phenomenon of social network has a clear and obvious bearing on the study of problems of communication, socialization, social control, and the like, and as soon as we approach problems of this order we are led to draw distinctions not only between sets and networks of social relations but also between different types of networks. Thus Bott distinguishes between different networks according to their degrees of connectedness. One person may have, in Bott's terms, a 'close-knit' network (i.e. one in which there are many relationships among the component units) and another may have a 'loose-knit' network (i.e. one in which there are few relationships among the component units).[23] Another important variable is, of course, the sheer size and composition of networks. We may find it useful to distinguish between large and small networks, between homogeneous and heterogeneous networks, and so on.

In his work Mayer makes regular use of distinctions of this general kind. Thus he distinguishes between migrants with loose-knit and close-knit networks, and he dwells on the implications for the individual of the difference between having continuous and discontinuous networks of social relations. But he does not confine himself to classification; he proceeds to examine the relations between network connectedness and the differing cultures of 'Red' and 'School' Xhosa. And he suggests that differences in the form of networks are related to the diversity of cultural values and social norms; in particular, he suggests that close-knit networks and cultural uniformity are related parts of a syndrome of features associated with 'Red' Xhosa migrants, whereas loose-knit networks and a measure of diversity in cultural values are related parts of a syndrome associated with 'School' migrants. Mayer's analysis thus implies that 'country-rootedness' and 'town-rootedness' should be studied in relation to degree of 'civilization' and, equally, in relation to 'tribalism'. This is in keeping with one of the directives stemming from Epstein's work[24]. Having conceptualized the overall urban system as made up of various sets or spheres of social relations, we have to devise ways of approaching and observing the manner in which these are related to each other. One way of doing this is to examine the manner in which an individual participates in various spheres of social relations and to analyse the different sets of people with whom he or she associates in the course of this participation; where people forming a set are found to be in contact with each other, there do we have a network which has to be studied both in form and in content.

Of particular interest in Mayer's work is the concept of 'incapsulation'. To appreciate the importance of this we may briefly review Mayer's explicit interpretation of the models available for the analysis of the participation of migrants in African towns.[25] He distinguishes between three types of analytical models. The first type consists of models of 'one-way change' where the central expectation is that the migrant on coming to town abandons his tribal roles and norms altogether and so becomes 'detribalized' and 'urbanized'. The second type he refers to as 'alternation' models. In contrast to models of 'one-way change', the 'alternation' models invite us to see the migrant not as changing his culture, but as participating in both rural and urban social systems; the main example of an explicit formulation of this type of model is found in the work (already referred to above) of Gluckman and others whose studies have suggested how the urban and rural social systems can be related to each other. The third model is, as Mayer puts it, a 'somewhat different alternation model'; it is represented by the work of Epstein and Mitchell. The specific innovation here is that 'the model brings out the fact that a man even while actually in town can still be alternating'.[26] As already seen, this type of model invokes the principle of 'situational selection' to explain how a man may switch from one form of behaviour to another according to the nature and structure of the particular situation in which he finds himself at any given time.

Mayer's analysis of the East London data proceeds partly in terms of both 'alternation' models referred to above, but he is in the particular case of the Xhosa confronted with the phenomenon of a major cultural division between 'Red' and 'School' people and this leads him to lay greater stress on the cultural determinance of behaviour within the urban social system than do either Mitchell or Epstein. He explicitly recognizes that there are some social spheres in which the differences between the 'Red' and 'School' cultures are irrelevant, but suggests that there are others in which they are directly relevant. He thus postulates that in certain situations individuals are compelled to choose between two possible courses of action. And, as a result of the choice they make, 'some of the migrants begin to change, but others voluntarily *incapsulate* [my italics] themselves in something as nearly as possible like the tribal relations from which their migration (to town) could have liberated them'.[27] In the final outcome Mayer's analysis is, in his own estimation, a combination 'of certain features of the "alternation" and the "change" types of model'.[28] This modification of the 'alternation' model of urban behaviour is of direct relevance in the analysis of the Stanleyville material, but it will be seen that the data I have lead me to stress the significance in social behaviour of the 'new' urban 'culture' rather than the significance of incapsulation within the 'old' tribal 'culture'.

In using the work of Mitchell, Epstein, and Mayer, I am applying formulations which were only available to me long after I had conducted the field observations on which the present study is based. My use of these formulations is only possible because my attention was at the time of my field study attracted by phenomena of fundamentally the same order as those investigated by these authors in other African towns. Yet it is well to remember that the observations largely preceded the conceptual formulations now applied to them. This must mean that the analysis given here cannot be regarded as a fully valid 'test' of the formulations. Going into the field with these formulations fully developed beforehand would have led to a more rigorous testing of their validity. On the other hand, the ready applicability of the formulations to the materials gathered in Stanleyville is in itself abundant testimony to their value.

FOOTNOTES TO CHAPTER I

[1] Davis and Golden (1954), p. 135.
[2] Denis (1958), pp. 372–394.
[3] Forde (1956), McCulloch (1956a), United Nations (1957), Southall (1961a), Mitchell (1966), Epstein (1966).
[4] Epstein (1958), p. 224.
[5] For a general discussion on this, see Mitchell (1966), p. 39.
[6] Hellman (1958), Wilson (1941 and 1942).
[7] Clément (1956), Pons (1956a and b), Xydias (1956).

8 The background to the Stanleyville studies is outlined in Forde (1956).

9 One significant implication of the extreme tribal heterogeneity of the population has been emphasized by subsequent political developments in the Congo. Thus Lemarchand (1964) considers that 'the ethnic diversity of the Stanleyville population is certainly the main reason for its conspicuous indifference to the appeals of ethnic nationalism . . .' (p. 99). In the late Patrice Lumumba, Stanleyville produced the leader under whom the *Mouvement National Congolais* was to become a nationalist rather than an ethnic party. This party had its conspicuous electoral successes in 1960 in the Eastern Province where it won 58 out of 70 seats in the Provincial Assembly and filled 21 out of the province's 25 seats in the National Assembly. Lemarchand quotes one African as explaining the relative 'absence of tribalism in Stanleyville' by saying 'Nous avons trop de tribus' (p. 99).

10 Throughout the study I use the terms non-tribal and 'mixed' to refer to marriages or other social relations established between members of different tribes. By the same token I use the terms tribal or 'pure' to refer to marriages or other relations between members of the same tribe. These terms seem preferable to the terms 'inter-tribal' and 'intra-tribal' which tend to carry the connotation of social relations established between or within tribal units.

11 For example, I have elsewhere shown that white collar workers were more frequently neighbours to persons of different tribal affiliations than were specialized manual workers, and that specialized manual workers were in turn more likely to have neighbours of different tribes than were ordinary labourers. See Pons (1956b), pp. 664–665.

12 Mitchell (1953), p. 43.

13 Mitchell (1953), p. 43.

14 Gluckman (1958), first published 1940.

15 Epstein (1958), Mayer (1961).

16 Epstein (1958), p. 232.

17 Mayer (1962).

18 Mayer (1961), p. 68.

19 Mayer (1961), pp. 9–10.

20 Gluckman (1961), p. 81.

21 Barnes (1954), Bott (1957).

22 Barnes (1954), p. 43.

23 Bott (1957), p. 59.

24 In studies subsequent to that of 1958, Epstein has also himself developed the use of networks on these lines (1961 and 1969).

25 Mayer (1962), pp. 579–580.

26 Mayer (1962), p. 579.

27 Mayer (1962), p. 591.

28 Mayer (1962), p. 589.

PART TWO

THE CONTEXT OF SOCIAL RELATIONS

II

THE NATURE OF THE TOWN AND OF ITS AFRICAN COMMUNITY

In 1952–53 Stanleyville was the fifth largest labour centre in the Belgian Congo, and by far the largest urban area in the colony's Eastern Province of which it was the administrative capital and the commercial and industrial centre. The town had between 45,000 and 55,000 inhabitants, depending on how its boundaries were defined. This population included some 4,000 Europeans and a small colony of two to three hundred Asians; the balance of about 90 per cent consisted of Africans drawn from a large number of distinctive tribes. Most of the tribes were Bantu-speaking though a few from the far north and north-east were of eastern Sudanic language groups. The largest single tribe in the town accounted for only 15 to 16 per cent of the total. The ethnic heterogeneity of the African population and the absence of any single dominant tribal group were important features of the urban situation in which new sets of social relations were being forged and developed. (See Chapter IV.)

About 85 per cent of the Africans in the town were natives of the Eastern Province which had a total population of 2¼ millions; of these, 1¾ millions were still living in tribal villages while half a million were to be found in a variety of *non-coutumiers* settlements. The population in these *non-coutumiers* settlements was directly dependent on the wage-earning economy built up in the region during the course of over 50 years of colonial development. The *non-coutumiers* settlements of the province included seven urban areas administered as *centres extra-coutumiers* (C.E.C.s). Apart from the C.E.C. of Stanleyville itself, the largest were at Buta and Aketi which had populations of about 10,000 each; the C.E.C. at Paulis (now Isiro) had about 6,000 inhabitants, and those of Bunia, Niangara, and Watsa had from 2,000 to 4,000 each. Thus the combined population of all C.E.C.s in the province did not exceed 75,000, and over 50 per cent of these lived in Stanleyville. The greater part of the half million persons living away from tribal areas were not in C.E.C.s, but either in smaller *non-coutumiers* settlements on the outskirts of trading centres, administrative outposts, and mission stations, or in labour camps attached to other centres of employment such as mines and plantations. Stanleyville was thus a relatively large town set in a vast region of tribal areas and of numerous but small centres of 'civilization'. About a third of the African population consisted of persons who had come to the town from their villages of origin without spending any time in smaller *non-coutumiers* centres; the remaining two thirds were persons either born outside tribal areas or having spent some time away from their villages before coming to Stanleyville. (See Chapter III.)

Relations between Stanleyville and different parts of its vast hinterland varied considerably with distance and mode of communication and according to the varying nature and extent of economic development in different areas. Various tribal groups had differing modes of urban incorporation and were currently involved in markedly different sets of rural-urban relations. (See Chapter IV.)

HISTORY OF GROWTH

Like many African colonial towns of this period, Stanleyville was caught up in a far-reaching process of economic expansion and social development. But although change and growth were salient features of the local scene, they were not new features. From its earliest beginnings as an administrative outpost, the town had experienced phase upon phase of change.[1]

A permanent outpost was first established at the site of the Stanley Falls in 1883. In 1886 this outpost was ransacked by the Arabs but was re-occupied shortly afterwards, and from 1892 to 1894 it played an important part as a supply base for the military campaigns against Arab slave-traders in the Maniema.[2] These early beginnings were followed by the construction, between 1903 and 1906, of a railway-line from the site of Stanleyville to that of Ponthierville on the Lualaba River. The railway turned Stanleyville into an important centre even before roads had been built through the immediate forest hinterland.

In 1920 the European population of the town consisted of about 80 men and 20 women and children, and the African population had risen to some 7,000. Official policy at this stage was to discourage permanent African settlement in towns, and a large proportion of the African population must have been men who had left their wives and children in tribal areas and who were themselves to return home later. In addition to immigrant Africans, there were in an adjacent village a few thousand *Arabisés* (Islamized Africans, a few of whom could have claimed some Arab descent). They had settled here permanently at the close of the 'Arab wars'. At this period the *Arabisés* were mainly cultivators and traders, though they were later to participate increasingly in the wage-earning economy of the town. There were also large villages of Wagenia tribesmen on both banks of the river at the site of the Stanley Falls. Their economy was based on fish which they trapped in baskets suspended over the rapids from a scaffolding of poles. The Wagenia were scarcely involved in the wage-earning economy and were to remain largely refractory to outside influences up to the time of the present study.[3]

Extensive road building in the town's hinterland in the 1920s, and the general economic development of the inter-war period, led to a steady increase in population. This was checked for a few years by the economic depression of the 1930s, but towards the end of the decade the population was again rising steadily. In 1938 there were about 1,000 Europeans in the town, and these included substantial

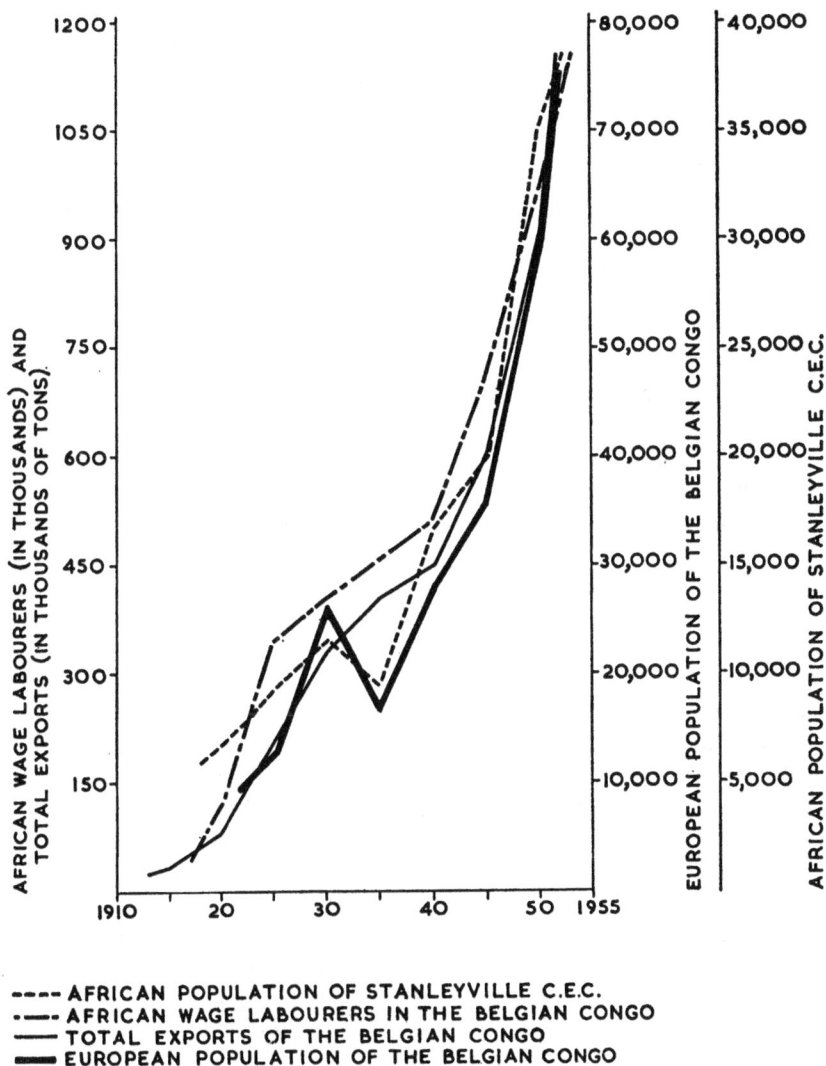

```
----  AFRICAN POPULATION OF STANLEYVILLE C.E.C.
-.--. AFRICAN WAGE LABOURERS IN THE BELGIAN CONGO
----  TOTAL EXPORTS OF THE BELGIAN CONGO
████  EUROPEAN POPULATION OF THE BELGIAN CONGO
```

Fig. I Growth of population in the *Centre Extra-coutumier* of Stanley-ville compared to economic expansion in the Belgian Congo up to 1952

proportions of women and children who were by this time settling there as a matter of course. Immigrant Africans now totalled about 17,000, many of whom must still have been men coming to town for short periods without their families.[4] By now, however, appreciable numbers were settling in the town for longer periods and sometimes on a permanent basis. (See Chapter III.) Together with the local

Arabisés who were participating more and more in the life of the town, the longer-term migrants constituted a small but significant element of stable urban-dwellers.

More rapid economic expansion began late in the 1930's; it continued during World War II, and developed at a greatly increased pace after 1945. By 1945 the immigrant African population had risen to about 20,000, and this total virtually doubled itself between 1945 and 1952. Thus the African population was, during this immediate post-war period, registering a net average increase of about 3,000 persons per year. The continuous influx of immigrants meant that the population always contained a significant proportion of newcomers despite the increasing tendency for families to settle in town on a permanent basis. (See Chapter III.) The European community of the town was equally involved in processes of change and adjustment; most of its new recruits came direct from Europe and were newcomers both to Stanleyville and the Congo.

Despite almost continuous growth in the 1920s and 1930s, Stanleyville had up to the war years remained a quiet and slow-moving colonial town. In the immediate post-war years, however, it rapidly changed into a minor boom-town, with an ever-increasing rate of growth and an ethos of high prosperity and urgent activity. As in many African colonial towns there was during this period a significant measure of industrial development and by 1952 the town had a number of well-established factories. The most important were a brewery, an oil mill, a cigarette factory, and a mineral water factory. In addition, a large hydro-electric plant was under construction. As shown in Table I, industry was now the largest single avenue of employment for Africans, and was followed by building as the second largest. Administration, transport and commerce remained important and continued to develop, but they no longer characterized the town as in earlier periods.

AFRICAN EMPLOYMENT

The economic expansion of the post-war period took place partly through the growth of a few large firms and partly through the proliferation of many small ones. An attempt to enumerate all firms in the town in 1952 revealed 396 for the total European (and Asian) population of under 5,000. Allowing for the fact that the enumeration was not quite complete, the figure suggests that there was one firm for every 10 to 12 members of the non-African population or, roughly, one to every three households. If we then consider that substantial numbers of Europeans were engaged in administration, in educational and missionary work, and in other professional pursuits, the figures point to a business sector with a large proportion of small entrepreneurs. In this setting the few larger establishments stood out sharply. There was one commercial firm with 214 African employees, there were two transport companies with 1,091 and 401 workers respectively, four large building companies with some 4,000 workers between them, and one industrial firm with 1,121 employees. These eight firms employed over a third of the African labour force, the remainder being employed either by the administration in a wide variety of establishments or by the large number of smaller firms.[5]

TABLE I

Fields of employment of wage-earning African men in the Administrative Territory of Stanleyville

FIELD OF EMPLOYMENT	NUMBER	PER CENT
Industry	5,173	23·7
Building	4,381	20·1
Government	3,249	14·9
Commerce	2,735	12·5
Transport	2,671	12·2
Agriculture	1,827	8·4
Private (mainly domestic service)	1,500	6·9
Miscellaneous	298	1·4
Total	21,834	100·1

The table is based on returns for the Territory of Stanleyville within which the town was situated. In 1952 the population of the Territory was 69,875, of whom 48,710 were living outside tribal villages. The figures were drawn from the files of an official inquiry. See Xydias (1956), pp. 285–286.

Most of the larger firms in the town had some European employees, but these constituted a small proportion of the white population. For the most part Europeans were employers and Africans were employees. Close on 90 per cent of African men aged 16 years and over were in European employment, the remainder being evenly divided between the ranks of the non-employed (including boys still at school) and the self-employed. There was virtually no unemployment.

The occupational distribution of African employees and the average earnings of various categories of men are shown in Table 2. White collar workers, who were mainly teachers, clerks, and medical orderlies, earned a mean wage of 2,348 francs per month*. This average was far below the statutory minimum of 9,000 francs for the lowliest of European employees in this colony. A very few African white collar workers reached the statutory minimum for Europeans but all of these were quite exceptional cases. In occupations and earnings, as in all social fields, there was a sharp cleavage between Europeans and Africans. There was, however, a wide range of earnings within the African community, the mean earnings of white collar workers being very much higher than those for all other categories. There were also appreciable differences between various categories of specialized manual workers, and, in turn, between these and ordinary labourers.

* In 1952/53 there were approx. 140 Belgian Congo francs to one pound sterling.

The African labour force thus exhibited very considerable internal differentiation in occupations and in income. These differences were related both to educational achievements and to the varying degrees to which members of the population had previously experienced urban

TABLE 2

Occupational composition and mean wages of African employees

OCCUPATION	PER CENT OF TOTAL WAGE-EARNERS	MEAN WAGE (FRANCS PER MONTH)
White Collar workers (clerks, teachers, medical orderlies and a few others)	10·8	2,348
Specialized manual:		
Car and lorry drivers	5·9	1,102
Carpenters and joiners	11·5	921
Miscellaneous	3·1	907
Mechanics	5·9	882
Masons and painters	11·8	841
Domestic servants (hotels and private houses)	10·6	702
Labourers and others totally unskilled	40·4	583
Total labour force	100·0	959

(Effective sample: 1,682)

and wage-earning conditions. (See Chapter III.) In the eyes of the European community, however, the African labour force appeared as relatively undifferentiated and the main distinction drawn by Europeans was between the few educated French-speaking *évolués* and the mass of the population. With this exception, Europeans were largely unresponsive to differences of status, occupation and education within the African community.

THE NATURE OF WORKING SITUATIONS

Operating mainly with cheap unskilled and semi-skilled labour (and in many cases with hurriedly assembled equipment that was often inadequate in quality or quantity or both), the many small firms in the town employed large numbers of Africans as compared to their small numbers of European managers and supervisors. In 177 commercial firms (many of them no more than family concerns) the mean size of the African pay-rolls was 15·4; in 49 transport companies it was 54·3; in 46 building firms 95·0; and in 47 factories and engineering and other workshops it was 105·5.[6] Thus, although many of the establishments were small in one sense, African workers often found themselves participating in work units that were relatively large. It can be seen from Table 3, for example, that about 60 per cent of wage-earning men were employed in establishments with a labour force of at least 100, while under 20 per cent worked in units of less than 30 men.

TABLE 3

Percentage distribution of African wage-earners according to the number of workers on the pay-rolls of the establishments for which they worked

NO. OF AFRICAN EMPLOYEES PER ESTABLISHMENT	TOTAL NUMBER OF WORKERS IN FIRMS OF A GIVEN SIZE	PER CENT
0–5	1,832	8·4
6–30	2,373	10·9
31–100	4,481	20·5
101–200	4,455	20·4
201–500	5,774	26·4
501–1,200	2,919	13·4
Total	21,834	100·0

As in Table 1, the figures refer to the entire Territory of Stanleyville. The table is based on data given in Xydias (1956), pp. 285–288.

The size of the labour units, the relative lack of skill and experience on the part of the workers, the common absence of stable divisions of labour, and the short periods for which many of the workers had held their present jobs, were all part of a complex of factors with far-reaching implications for social relations between Europeans and Africans as well as between Africans.

Xydias has described aspects of the labour force and working situation in an oil mill employing half a dozen Europeans and about 80 Africans, and processing some 600 tons of cotton seed and 200 tons of palm nuts per month.[7] The mill had started operations in 1949, about three and a half years before Xydias' study. The following extracts from her account convey a vivid impression of the conditions and atmosphere in the mill:

Although the machinery is new, the general conditions are those of an artisan's shop, rather than a modern factory. All internal transport is carried out by hand or in wheelbarrows; the latter can move normally on the concrete floors but outside they run foul of the hummocks and hillocks of the irregular ground; mountains of sacks are heaped up in the yard for want of other storage space. Near the boiler passers-by are forced to paddle their way through oil seeping from a pile of waste which is used as fuel. The workshops are spacious and well ventilated, but always cluttered up; there is no cloakroom for the workers and their outer garments are hung up anywhere on beams or walls.

Men come up to the machines with sacks on their backs, and empty them with a jerk of the shoulders; then they rest until called back to work by one of the whites. Others feed the machines by emptying buckets filled with groundnuts, which are passed from hand to hand; others put the waste back into the sacks and remove it; others are employed sewing up the sacks, sitting in groups on the heaps of material and chatting quietly together. In the yard, one or two workmen are stoking up a fire between three stones. . . . There is constant coming and going, the exact why and wherefore we were never able to fathom. . . .

When we came to hold our interviews, seated in the yard in the shade . . . we had great difficulty in dispersing the groups of workers who thronged around us. . . .

The grounds of the factory border the road; it is easy, without passing through the main doorway, to get across the light fence to go and buy cigarettes or bread or to meet some friend, male or female. . . .

. . . the work . . . is hard, but its rhythm is so little regulated, except at the machines, that there is plenty of opportunity for snatching a rest . . . [and] . . . the whites have a hard task keeping all the workers under their supervision. . . .[8]

Of the mill's 80 African workers, 50 were divided into six teams. Two teams worked together on 8 hour shifts and the mill operated 24 hours a day. Of the remaining men, 15 worked in the store, 10 worked wherever there was an odd job to be done, two were sentries, one a lorry-driver, one the lorry-driver's mate (*aide-chauffeur*), and one a book-keeper. Thirty-three different tribes were represented in the mill. There were 15 Babudu, eight Lokele, and seven Bakusu. Of the remaining tribes, 24 were represented by only one man each. Over two-thirds of the workers were men who had spent their entire childhoods in native villages, and about a third had been in Stanleyville for less than a year. Only three men had worked in the mill since 1949, and 33 had been there for less than two months. Over one three-month period, 41·8 per cent of the employees left the firm.

In addition to the manager and his son, the European staff was supposed to consist of a chemical engineer, an accountant, an overseer-mechanic, and three shift supervisors whose duties were to work round the clock with the teams of African workers. But the recruitment of Europeans, especially shift supervisors, was a constant problem. During the whole period of the study there were never more than two supervisors at any one time. During the same period a total of six men were appointed in succession in abortive attempts to keep the establishment up to strength. One new appointee left, without giving notice, to open a small workshop on his own account; another, recruited from Belgium, was dismissed after three weeks for sleeping on duty; another was dismissed following a violent quarrel with the engineer; and one, who could not keep discipline, left after admitting that 'he was afraid of Congolese'.

Xydias also gives an interesting description of the way in which the work was performed:

At every change of shift an attempt is made to make the best use of the men present . . . subject to this general consideration, the division of labour among the men is arranged very freely. Each man does the job he prefers and agreement is easily reached among the workers; moreover, since some tasks are more tiring than others, they change from one to the other very frequently. There is no need for a white man to give orders to this effect. If he does, he is obeyed, but clearly with bad grace. The men much prefer to be left to arrange things as they think fit.[9]

One instance is recorded of 16 men (including two teams of six) being allocated set tasks in the factory one morning. By the end of the shift eight hours later, only seven of the 16 were still at the posts allocated to them.

This review of conditions in the oil mill illustrates a number of factors in the Stanleyville situation during the post-war period of rapid expansion. 'Ça va trop vite', was a phrase constantly repeated by many Europeans in the town. This was primarily an expression of prejudice and misgiving about Africans and their abilities, but it could also well have been an expression of the irritation and impatience of people in authority as they tried to grapple with innumerable practical problems of development. Although the oil mill cannot be claimed as strictly representative, general observations suggested that it was fairly typical of many firms established since the end of the war and of some older-established ones as well.

Of all African workers in the town, 39·4 per cent had been working at their jobs for less than one year, 33·0 per cent for one or two years, 19·5 per cent for three to nine years and only 8·1 per cent for ten years or more. There was thus a small hard core of workers with long records of work for the same employer, but an expanding economy drawing in large numbers of new recruits inevitably meant that the bulk of the labour force consisted of workers liable to change readily from one job to another and from one employer to another. Impermanence and instability which, as we shall see in Chapters VI and VII, character-ized many social relations in the spheres of domestic and neighbour-hood life, were thus commonly present in the sphere of work as well.

AFRICAN TRADE AND COMMERCE

The commercial and service establishments run and owned by Africans were, with a few striking exceptions, very small, and the income of the majority of self-employed men was often little or no higher—in many cases even lower—than that of wage-earners in European employment.

All persons engaged in providing a regular trade or service from a fixed abode in the C.E.C. were required to obtain licences on the following scale:

The keeper of a bar selling bottled beer   3,000 frs per year
The keeper of a bar selling native drinks   1,500 frs ,,   ,,
A tailor   1,000 frs ,,   ,,
Any artisan other than a tailor   600 frs ,,   ,,
The keeper of a restaurant   500 frs ,,   ,,
A shopkeeper who was not an ex-soldier or a widow   500 frs ,,   ,,
A shopkeeper who was either an ex-soldier or a
    widow   300 frs ,,   ,,

In 1952 there were 591 extant trade or service licences in the C.E.C. which means that a full-time *regular* trade or service was being provided on about one in ten of all dwelling compounds. The nature of business pursued by licence holders is shown in Table 4. Small shop and restaurant keepers were most numerous and, taken together with gardeners, made up over a half of the total. Various dealers in drink constituted the next largest category. Only a small proportion of licences covered a trade or service not connected with food or drink. The few relatively large establishments were principally dance halls selling bottled beer. The many small bars normally sold palm wine and other native drinks. They frequently consisted of no more than a rough open shelter under which a few men would be served by a single person. Most of the shops were also very small and their stocks

TABLE 4

Licensed trade and service establishments in the C.E.C.

TRADE OR SERVICE	NO.	PER CENT	
Shop or restaurant	283	47·9	51·8
Gardener (selling vegetables)	23	3·9	
Retailer of palm wine and other native drinks	147	24·9	
Palm wine gatherer	52	8·8	
Retailer of bottled beer (modern bars usually with dancing premises)	21	3·6	37·3
Shoe repairer	20	3·4	
Ivory worker	19	3·2	
Launderer	8	1·4	
Tailor	6	1·0	10·9
Photographer	5	0·8	
Carpenter	5	0·8	
Misc.	2	0·3	
	591	100·0	100·0

This table is based on figures collated from official files. See Xydias (1956), p. 287.

were usually limited to a narrow range of goods such as bread, sugar, soap, matches, and paraffin. Stocks were commonly kept in the corner of a single room of a private dwelling and were dispensed on the verandah or through an open window.

The total volume of trade and services in the African areas was, however, very much larger than that dispensed from licensed premises. Some women traded in the markets while numbers of wage-earning men provided various part-time services after working hours. Market women dealt mainly in meat and fish and in manioc, rice, fruits, vegetables and other agricultural produce. In addition, numbers of women practised intermittent petty trading on their compounds or on street corners. Some sold bread, cakes, and nuts to passers-by for immediate consumption; others sold small quantities of unprepared foods, such as dried fish, rice, and oil for household consumption. Illicit stocking of a few bottles of beer for sale was also very common and there were numbers of prostitutes and semi-prostitutes.

The volume of part-time services provided by wage-earning men was also appreciable. There were part-time tailors, shoe-repairers, barbers, and bicycle mechanics; there were makers and menders of furniture and of household articles such as brooms, baskets and other containers. There were also men providing a diverse range of services in connexion with the building of houses: some made window frames and doors, some gathered and prepared sticks and leaves for sale as building materials, and others worked as thatchers and builders for owners who could afford to hire their services. Ordinary labourers found occasional work clearing sites for houses or digging wells and latrines on compounds. Detailed investigations revealed that *some* form of trade or service (excluding prostitution) was provided on one compound in every three or four in some localities and on one in two in others.

Africans were thus involved in two distinct sets of economic relations. They worked as employees of Europeans and were largely dependant on European- or Asian-owned shops for a wide range of articles such as clothes, bicycles, and hardware; but they were also involved in wide-spread sets of economic relations with each other as buyers and sellers of produce and of small articles and of various minor services. The far-reaching social significance of the many small trade and service establishments for neighbourhood and community relations is stressed in Chapter VI.

AFRICAN RESIDENTIAL AREAS

The physical lay-out of the town could be seen as both an expression and a symbol of the relations between Africans and Europeans. European residential areas were situated close to, and tended to run into, the area of administrative offices, hotels, shops and other service establishments, while African residential areas were strictly demarcated and well removed from the town centre. The location of African areas contributed to their 'suburban' or dormitory character: from early morning until the night curfew which prohibited African entry to the 'European town' and European entry to African areas, there was a large volume of movement between the 'suburbs' and the centre. Africans left their areas for diverse purposes, primarily to go to work and to shop at the European owned stores and at the morning market in the precinct of the town centre. But there were many additional attractions in the 'European town'. The secondary school and some of the primary schools, the law courts, the labour exchange, the post office, the main African hospital, and most churches were located outside the African areas and all contributed to drawing out most men and numbers of women and children from their residential neighbour- hoods during the day-time. There were a number of social provisions in the African areas (some primary schools and churches, dispensaries, smaller markets, etc.) but European-owned commercial establish- ments were not allowed in the African areas which were strictly reserved for African residence, for such commercial establishments as were run and owned by Africans, and for official and officially- approved welfare activities.

The three African townships of Belge I, Brussels, and Belge II made up the C.E.C., an urban unit described in the next section. There were important differences between the three townships in history of growth, in ethnic and social composition, and in general atmosphere. Belge I was in several senses the principal township. Nearly half of the area of Belge I had been settled before the constitu- tion of the C.E.C. in 1932. At this time, Belge I already had a popula- tion of nearly 6,000 which was to rise to 14,545 by 1952.

The inhabitants of the old-established in-lying area of Belge I had easy access to the shopping centre, the market, the law courts and other services in or near the 'European town'. The area had over the years developed as the most fashionable neighbourhood in the African town as a whole. Most of the leading Congolese *évolués* and nearly all members of the small foreign élite of 'Coastmen' had their homes here.[10] The area was the centre of night-life. It contained most of the modern bars and dance halls in the African town and was the usual meeting place for most of the large voluntary associations of *évolués*. The mass of the population, in the area nonetheless consisted of non- *évolués*. The larger houses of wealthier *évolués* were here often inter- spersed between compounds crowded with dense clusters of small huts and shelters. Towards the northern boundary of Belge I, however, there was a slight fall in population density and the landscape became a little more rural and village-like. The distinctive social atmosphere of Belge I was commonly recognized and commented on by its own inhabitants and others. To many old-established residents, Belge I was a desirable area, but to many newcomers from the countryside it was strange and frightening.

Brussels fell into two parts known as Old Brussels and New Brussels.

New Brussels was an area settled since 1945 and still being extended northwards at the time of the present study. Old Brussels consisted of an area settled either before or at the time of the creation of the C.E.C. when its population was about 3,000. By 1952 there were 11,533 inhabitants in the township. As in Belge I, internal differences were fairly

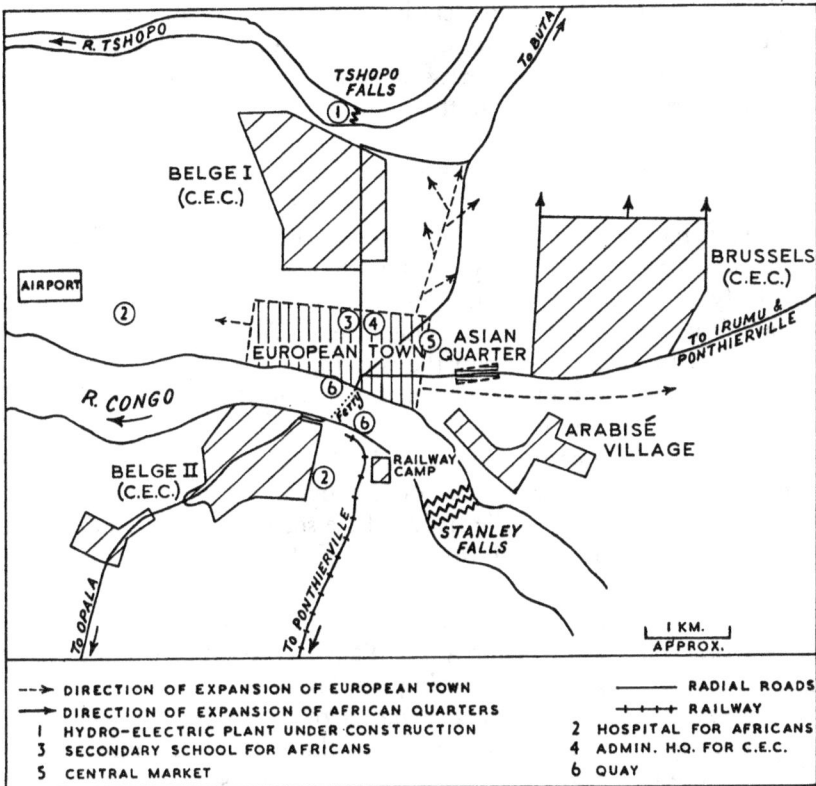

FIG. II   Sketch map of Stanleyville in 1952

marked. The in-lying areas of Brussels were less fashionable (and less slum-like) than those of Belge I, yet more fashionable (and more slum-like) that many neighbourhoods within its own boundaries.

Belge II was on the left or southern bank of the river. It consisted of three fairly distinct parts. The area adjacent to the river had been incorporated into the C.E.C. when already settled as a large riverside village of Lokele tribesmen whose home villages lay a few miles downstream. This part of Belge II remained a predominantly Lokele area. The detached part of Belge II also had a distinctive history of development. At the time of the constitution of the C.E.C. the remnants of an *Arabisé* village situated here were incorporated into the township, and in 1945 a number of newcomers from other *Arabisés* villages in the region had resettled there. The third area of Belge II, lying south of the Lokele area, was thus the only part of the township to have progressively accumulated a markedly mixed ethnic population as had most areas of Belge I and Brussels. At the time of its incorporation into the C.E.C., Belge II had under 2,000 inhabitants. By 1952 it had a population of 11,715 but, unlike Brussels, there were in the township no extensive continuous areas of recently settled compounds.

The location of the three townships of the C.E.C. in relation to each other and to the main roads leading into the town had considerable social significance. Belge I was close to the main road to the north and had always contained a majority of inhabitants from the north of the province; Brussels was close to the main road to the east and north-east and had a majority of inhabitants from those regions; and Belge II had a majority of persons from the south. (See Chapter IV.) The physical separation of the three townships, especially the location of Belge II on the left bank of the river, tended to restrict access to and from each other and this undoubtedly contributed to their development as relatively self-contained communities. Each township had a distinctive social atmosphere, yet the outlying areas of all three had more in common with each other than the in-lying and outlying areas of any one. An analysis of some aspects of the smaller 'natural areas' within the townships is given in Chapter V.

Outside the boundaries of the C.E.C. there were a number of village settlements on the sides of the main roads leading into the town and on the banks of the river. These settlements were not subject to any formal urban administration though they contained varying proportions of wage-earners who came into the town daily. The largest of these settlements were two villages of Wagenia and one of *Arabisés*. The large majority of Wagenia continued as in former years to avoid regular wage-earning employment. They fished for their own needs and for the growing demands of the urban population, but they scarcely participated in the life of the urban community. Their villages were therefore excluded from the present study.

In contrast to the Wagenia, the *Arabisés* were now deeply involved in the life of the town. A few women and old men were still cultivators, working fields on the outskirts of their settlement, but most adult men were wage-earners in the town. (See Chapter IV.) The *Arabisés* village was therefore included in the study despite its separate administration as a rural *chefferie* under a chief responsible not to the C.E.C. but to the Administrator of the Territory. In 1952, the village had a population of nearly 3,000. As far as I could ascertain, the population had been relatively stable for many years.

In addition to the Wagenia and *Arabisés* settlements and to a number of smaller peri-urban villages, there were in the immediate precincts of the town a camp of railway workers, two military camps, a police camp, a mission station with a number of African workers, and a few plantations and workshops with their own small camps of labourers. Except for the railway camp, which had about 1,000 inhabitants, all these smaller settlements were excluded from the study. The town was thus defined as consisting of the three townships of the C.E.C., the *Arabisé* village and the railway camp. The total population of these areas was just over 40,000. The 'urban' population of wage-earners and their dependants in settlements excluded from the study cannot have exceeded 4,000.

THE C.E.C. AND ITS ADMINISTRATION

The C.E.C. of Stanleyville was one of four constituted in the Belgian Congo in 1932 under the provisions of the *Décret sur les Centres Extra-coutumiers* promulgated by the central government in November, 1931. Three more C.E.C.s were created in the colony in 1933, six in 1934, and eight in 1935 by which time this form of urban administration was well established.[11] The decree of 1931 was the outcome of a complete review of urban policy by the central government. Prior to 1931 the administration had taken few positive measures to influence the development of African settlements around the main 'European towns'. The tendency had been to discourage Africans from permanent settlement away from their tribal areas, and to assume that the urban labour force consisted overwhelmingly of migrant labourers who would return to their villages after periods of wage earning.

In fact, however, already in the 1920's significant numbers of migrants were settling in the growing towns as long-term and sometimes as permanent residents. Baumer claims that 'une grande partie' of the men discharged from military service did not return to their villages, and that each contingent of labourers recruited to work in towns left behind 'un grand nombre d'indigènes peu desireux de réintégrer leur milieu coutumier'.[12] Magotte noted in similar vein that African settlements around the towns were by 1930 showing many signs of 'une vie collective propre créant à tous les habitants des intérêts communs', and he claimed that these villages were becoming 'de véritables communes'.[13] Local evidence suggests that such remarks certainly applied to Stanleyville.

The decree of 1931 was the main instrument designed to implement the central government's new urban policy. It was, too, an integral part of a wider set of measures taken at this time to make better use of the colony's limited resources of man-power, and to stabilize and develop the labour force. In sharp contrast to the first thirty years of colonial administration, labour migration was now to be opposed, the perpetuation of 'tribalism' in towns was to be discouraged, and the development of urban communities was to be actively promoted. Under the new decree, the governor of each province was empowered to establish a C.E.C. wherever he considered that an urban settlement of sufficient size and permanence had developed. These urban units were to be semi-autonomous. Each was to be administered by a European official assisted by an African chief, a deputy chief, and a number of councillors. The new C.E.C.s were to deal with a wide range of urban administration. Each was to have its own law courts presided over by the chief and his councillors who were empowered to try a series of minor cases. The C.E.C.s were to be responsible for the maintenance of law and order and were entitled to recruit small police forces for this purpose; they were given powers to control entry into their townships and to allocate dwelling compounds to individual title-holders who were to be responsible for the construction of their own houses; they were to be responsible for the maintenance of roads, cemeteries and other amenities; and they were to set up registration offices keeping records of births and deaths, and of all movements in and out of their areas. Each C.E.C. was to have its own budget and to receive funds from the central administration, while at the same time levying a series of minor rates and taxes.

The *Décret sur les Centres Extra-coutumiers* was hailed by some as a liberal advance. Baumer called it a 'charte communale indigène' for urban-dwellers and did not doubt that the long term legislative intention was to promote urban communities led and administered by Africans.[14] In its application over a period of twenty years, however, the C.E.C. regime had remained a system of close supervision in which the colonial authority retained full control over general policy as well as an over-riding influence in day-to-day administration. The chiefs, their deputies, and their councillors were to remain minor officials carrying out the details of policies which they had little or no power to influence. They were neither traditional representatives of tribal society nor the natural political leaders of any section of the urban communities. They were men chosen by European officials partly for their general competence, and partly for their records of exemplary behaviour. In the particular case of Stanleyville, the position of chief was, and always had been, held by an educated *évolué*, but the councillors were chosen so as to include a majority of non-*évolués*.

CONDITIONS OF ADMISSION TO THE C.E.C.

Persons either born in a C.E.C. or having resided there continuously for ten years were granted the formal status of permanent residents. All others lived in a C.E.C. *à titre précaire* and thus remained subjects of their rural *chefferies* of origin and were liable to expulsion from the C.E.C. in the event of prolonged unemployment or of incapacity or as a disciplinary measure. A migrant seeking to enter a C.E.C. was expected to be in possession of a *passeport de mutation* issued by the rural authority in his *chefferie* and, even if in possession of this document, was only admitted on the approval of the C.E.C. administration. A man who could produce evidence of an offer of employment in the town was normally admitted to the C.E.C. as a matter of course (as were his wife and children) provided that he was monogamous. His admission *à titre précaire* nonetheless meant that he was liable to eviction up to the ten-year limit. If known to be polygynous, he was refused admission even if accompanied by only one wife. A man without an offer of employment was normally admitted to the C.E.C. *à titre temporaire* for one month, at the end of which he would be sent home if he had not found work but allowed to take up residence *à titre précaire* if he had. Women, children, and elderly men unable to work were all normally refused admission (except as visitors) unless they could convince the authorities that they were dependent on a resident of the C.E.C. A married woman who entered the C.E.C. with her husband was only entitled to stay as long as the marriage lasted. If she found herself divorced or widowed within the ten-year limit she was expected to return to her village unless she could show that she was directly dependent on kinsmen in the town. These rules governing residence in the C.E.C. were part of a wider set of regulations which subsumed an entire system of individual registration and control down to the requirement that every inhabitant notify the administration of any change of address *within* the C.E.C.

The system of control over residence and movement in the C.E.C.s was seen by the authorities as essential if health and security were to be maintained, if the labour force was to be stabilized and the growth of slums prevented; it was also seen as an 'educative measure' to promote a sense of order and responsibility, and as part of a more general policy supposedly designed to lead Africans towards *évolution* and a 'civilized' way of life.

Despite the relatively small size of the three townships in Stanleyville at the time of the establishment of the C.E.C., the detailed rules and regulations outlined above were soon found difficult to apply. The annual reports of the C.E.C. repeatedly refer to the enormous difficulties encountered in keeping the population register up to date and, particularly, in enforcing the regulations governing the entry of newcomers. In 1937, for example, the administrator-in-charge wrote:

Le maintain de l'ordre et de la discipline est très ardu . . . par suite de l'affluence de nombreux individus, fuyards des chefferies environantes qui arguent de l'existence d'un contrat de travail pour se faire admettre sans pièces d'identité est sans passeport de mutation. En général, ces contrats de travail ne sont qu'un pretexte pour s'établir au centre extra-coutumier et d'y vivre de resources non-avouables. Après quelques semaines, voires après quelques jours, le contrat est rompu, soit par le maître pour mauvaise volonté de la part de l'engagé, soit par l'abandon du travail par ce dernier.[15]

Comments in similar vein continued to appear in the annual reports of the C.E.C. up to the time of the present study and were frequently linked to assessments, by the administrator-in-charge of the C.E.C., of the social and political climate in the community. The following comment, made in 1945, clearly suggests that the systematic enforcement of the C.E.C.'s controls was felt to be increasingly difficult:

. . . l'esprit de la population est signalé comme satisfaisant mais cette appréciation est évidemment toute relative; ce qui est signalé comme satisfaisant en 1945 eut été taxé de 'déplorable' il y a dix ans d'ici, 'd'étonnant' il y a cinq ans, et de 'digne de retenir l'attention' il y a deux ans seulement.

Cela veut dire tout simplement que la fermentation des idées sociales suit son cours, sans fracas, que il n'y a pas d'attroupements tumultueux, ni de cortèges spectaculaires, ni de grèves sur le tas, ni de mouvements collectifs d'hostilité; cela ne veut pas dire d'avantage. . . .[16]

Despite the difficulties encountered, however, the administration sustained its attempts to apply controls throughout the period under review, and there can be no doubt that, quite apart from any social and political consequences, the demographic composition of the population was much affected. Even if, as seems likely, a certain proportion of the population managed to evade the regulations and controls, a sufficient number were effectively subjected to them to ensure that they could not be openly flouted.[17] The administration thus retained powerful sanctions over the inhabitants and particularly over those who had not yet qualified as permanent inhabitants of the C.E.C.[18]

THE SYSTEM OF ACCOMMODATION

All residents of the C.E.C. were accommodated on dwelling compounds laid out in straight avenues. Compounds had their own latrines to the rear of the dwellings, and a substantial proportion had their own water supplies from wells dug on the sites. In some areas of the town the compounds still had a fair amount of forest vegetation. This was especially marked in the peripheral areas whose general appearance was often more village-like than might have been expected in a town of this size. The C.E.C. regulations required the inhabitants to ensure that fences were erected around their compounds, and that the premises were kept clean and tidy.

Each compound was allocated to a single title-holder who was responsible for building his own dwelling, and who was entitled to accommodate other persons or families on his compound, either in his own buildings or by allowing them to build for themselves. Most dwellings had walls of mud and sticks and roofs of leaves. The dwellings varied in size from small single-room huts to more spacious houses with five or six rooms. Cooking was in most cases done in the open, though some compounds had small separate kitchen buildings. Some higher-paid white-collar workers were often able to afford houses of brick, usually with corrugated iron roofs, but these were found on less than one per cent of over 6,000 compounds in the C.E.C.

Though allocated to individual title-holders, compounds remained the property of the C.E.C. Once established on a compound, a title-holder had virtual security of tenure subject to his conforming with the duties and obligations imposed on him both as a title-holder and as an ordinary resident of the C.E.C. Occupation permits could, however, be cancelled at any time. The sale and purchase of houses was allowed subject to the administration being willing to transfer the occupation permit to the prospective buyer. On the death of a title-holder, his permit was normally transferred to the person inheriting the house.

In New Brussels an overwhelming majority of compounds were held by title-holders to whom they had recently been allocated by the administration, but in the older areas many compounds were held by persons who had either bought or inherited their dwellings. In the in-lying areas of Belge I, for example, about a half of all title-holders had acquired their compounds following on the purchase of a house; between a third and a quarter of the compounds were still held by the title-holders to whom they had initially been allocated; and one in seven was held by a person who had acquired it on the death of a spouse or kinsman.[19]

The distribution of compounds according to the number of households accommodated is shown in Table 5. Over 60 per cent of all compounds had only one household each, a quarter had two, and

TABLE 5

The distribution in the three townships of the C.E.C. of dwelling compounds according to the number of households they accommodated

NUMBER OF HOUSEHOLDS PER COMPOUND	BELGE I		BRUSSELS		BELGE II		TOTAL	
	No.	%	No.	%	No.	%	No.	%
1	109	44·9	229	70·7	153	68·0	491	62·0
2	72	29·6	73	22·5	52	23·1	197	24·9
3	36	14·8	13	4·3	18	8·0	67	8·5
4	19	7·8	6	1·6	2	0·9	27	3·4
5	5	2·1	3	0·9	0	0·0	8	1·0
6	2	0·8	0	0·0	0	0·0	2	0·3
Total samples	243	100·0	324	100·0	225	100·0	792	100·1
Mean number of households per dwelling compound	1·9		1·4		1·4		1·6	

most of the remainder had three or four. Only exceptionally were there as many as five or six households on a compound. In Belge I the mean number of households per compound was 1·9 as against 1·4 in Brussels and Belge II. In Chapter V we shall see that there were also important differences between neighbourhoods within each of the townships.

The proportions of principal households, of subsidiary rent-paying households, and of subsidiary households accommodated free of charge are shown in Table 6. In Belge I there were equal proportions of rent-paying and non-rent-paying tenants and principal households made up only 52·8 per cent of the total. In Brussels and Belge II, on the other hand, principal households accounted for about 70 per cent of the total, and rent-paying households were few compared to those accommodated free of charge. Again, however, we shall see that there

were some important differences in these respects between neighbourhoods within each of the townships.

The social significance of title-holding and house-ownership is
examined in later chapters. We shall see that subsidiary households
were often only temporary residents on a compound. Many tenants
moved frequently from one compound to another. This, combined with
the fact that large numbers of households—whether of title-holders
or of tenants—contained one or more temporary members, contributed

TABLE 6

*Mean numbers of persons and households per compound and proportions of different categories of households
in the three townships of the C.E.C.*

	EFFECTIVE SAMPLE OF DWELLING COMPOUNDS	EFFECTIVE SAMPLE OF HOUSE-HOLDERS	PER CENT PRINCIPAL HOUSE-HOLDS OF TITLE HOLDERS	PER CENT SUBSIDIARY NON-RENT PAYING HOUSE-HOLDS	PER CENT SUBSIDIARY RENT PAYING HOUSE-HOLDS	TOTAL
Belge I	243	461	52·8	23·6	23·6	100·0
Brussels	324	450	72·0	19·6	8·4	100·0
Belge II	226	319	70·2	23·6	6·2	100·0
Total	793	1,230	64·3	22·1	13·6	100·0

to a high rate of residential mobility within the C.E.C.; a vivid impression of this is conveyed by the 1952 Annual Report which states
that some 15,000 changes of address were recorded in the course of
the year. Assuming that every person who moved did so only once,
these figures would suggest movement during the course of the year of
over a third of the total population. But, as we know that not all
residents complied with the requirement of reporting changes of address,
it seems certain that the true proportion of persons moving was higher
than one third. Whatever the exact proportion, a high rate of residential mobility was a marked feature of the social scene and was particularly striking among the more recent immigrants.[20] Different rates of
movement were closely related to various factors affecting the nature of
neighbourhood relations. Title-holders were more stable than tenants;
they were often property-owners and, in many cases, landlords; and
they were for the most part permanent urbanites, well-established members of their neighbourhoods. Many subsidiary householders, whether
or not they paid rent, were so frequently on the move that their relations
with neighbours were commonly of a fleeting and superficial nature.
The full significance of house-ownership as a factor in the process of
urban involvement is revealed in later chapters.

SUMMARY

I have in this chapter attempted to outline a few salient aspects of the overall situation in which Africans found themselves in Stanleyville in 1952–53. The town was set in a vast region of tribal villages and small centres of employment. It was a well-established colonial town in the throes of an economic boom. The population of African wage-earners, like the population of European administrators, missionaries and business men, was growing rapidly and the community as a whole was developing in a very different social atmosphere to that of pre-war days. There was a sharp cleavage between Europeans and Africans in every social field. Europeans were employers and 'teachers'; Africans were employees and 'pupils'. Change and growth were evident on all sides. The largest part of the African population was living in townships under conditions which allowed and promoted the development of a certain range of social relationships while inhibiting—and in some cases prohibiting—the development of others. Thus Africans in the town were often landlords and tenants to each other, but very seldom employers and employees; they were frequently suppliers and consumers of a limited range of goods and services, but very seldom on a large scale. They lived in a situation which, by comparison with that of earlier decades, was highly conducive to the stabilization of urban families and to their permanent involvement in urban life. As is well known, however, they were at this period strictly prohibited from associating for political purposes, and even voluntary associations with social and cultural aims were strictly controlled.[21]

FOOTNOTES TO CHAPTER II

[1] The brief historical sketch given here was compiled from published and unpublished documents available to me in Stanleyville. For a more detailed account than can be given here, see Pons (1956a).

[2] Viscount Mountmorres claims in *The Congo Independent State* (1906), quoted by Lemarchand, that Stanleyville in its short period under Arab influence had developed into 'a large and thriving township' . . . (and presented a scene) 'that might well be laid in Morocco.' This comment was probably a romantic exaggeration. The short Arab intrusion was certainly significant but, as Lemarchand rightly points out, it did not lead to a degree of political and cultural assimilation comparable to that which may be observed among the predominantly Islamized peoples in some other parts of Negro Africa. Lemarchand (1964), p. 30.

[3] The Wagenia's special position among tribes of the region was commented upon from the earliest days of European contact. For example, Livingstone wrote of the Wagenia tribesmen he encountered in the Maniema to the south of Stanleyville that '. . . they are fishermen by taste and profession, and sell the produce of their weirs to those who cultivate the soil. . . .' and that '. . . the Bagenya women are expert in the water as they are accustomed to dive for oysters. . . .'
Extracts from *Last Journals* in Perham, M. and, Simons, J. (1957), pp. 236 and 238.

[4] I was unable to find data on the sex composition of the African population of Stanleyville at this period, but it is of interest to note that in 1928 the central government was concerned about 'la présence de nombreux célibataires ou d'hommes mariés séparés de leurs femmes' in the towns of the Belgian Congo. At this time the adult population of Leopoldville had 40,844 men and only 5,535 women. *Rapport Annuel sur l'Administration de la Colonie du Congo Belge pendant l'année 1928*, Bruxelles, 1929, p. 11.

[5] For a more detailed account of the economic structure of the town see Xydias (1956).

[6] Figures based on official statistical returns. See Xydias (1956).

[7] Xydias (1956), pp. 307–318.

[8] Xydias (1956), pp. 308–309.

[9] Xydias (1956), p. 311.

[10] 'Coastmen' was the term used to refer to clerks recruited from West Africa to work in local English and French firms.

[11] Baumer (1939), p. 66.

[12] Baumer (1939), pp. 16–17.

[13] Magotte (1934), p. 6.

[14] Baumer (1939), p. 58. For other discussions on the system of C.E.C.s see Magotte (1938) and Grévisse (1951).

[15] *Rapport Annuel: Centre Extra-coutumier de Stanleyville*, 1937.

[16] *Rapport Annuel: Centre Extra-coutumier de Stanleyville*, 1945.

[17] In 1952 official permission to enter the C.E.C. was given to 3,860 persons and refused to 268, while 280 persons already living in Stanleyville were ordered to return to their villages of origin. During the same year, 3,252 persons were allowed to enter the C.E.C. as visitors and all but 630 had registered their departure by the end of the year. Figures from *Rapport Annuel: Centre Extra-coutumier de Stanleyville*, 1952.

[18] The attitude of administrators to the residence regulations is well illustrated by the following telling remark in one of the annual reports: 'Une opération d'épurement a éliminé les parasites et les sans travail qui vivent d'expédiants.' *Rapport Annuel: Centre Extra-coutumier de Stanleyville*, 1940.

[19] The exact figures reported from a complete enumeration in two areas were as follows. In an in-lying area of Belge I 27·3 per cent of title-holders were still the original persons to whom they had been allocated by the administration, 51·6 per cent had 'bought' and 12·8 per cent had 'inherited' their compounds, and in 8·3 per cent of the cases the information was not available at the time of interview. In an out-lying area of old Brussels 32·6 per cent of compounds had been allocated, 43·3 per cent 'bought' and 15·4 per cent 'inherited'; there was no information for 8·7 per cent. Pons (1956b), pp. 644–645.

[20] The following is a free translation from Swahili of a song composed by a local guitarist on this theme.
Addressing a lost friend, the guitarist sings:
'Where are you that I see you no more?
I look for you here and there.
I ask all your friends, but no one knows where you are.
They tell me you have gone to the Left Bank, and
there they tell me you have gone to Brussels, and
there they tell me you have gone to Belge . . .,
Where are you that I see you no more?
Come back to your friends.'

[21] All voluntary associations were required to submit their constitutions and annual accounts to the District Commissioner for approval. In fact, Clément found that only 20 out of 65 associations *known to him* had complied with these requirements, and he considers that there were probably many more that had failed to do so. There is, however, no doubt that any association developing a substantial following would have been compelled either to seek authorization or to disband. For detailed information on voluntary associations, see Clément (1956), pp. 469–492.

III

DEMOGRAPHIC AND SOCIAL SELECTION

Like many African towns, Stanleyville had a population with a low proportion of older persons and a substantial excess of men over women.[1] Only 10·6 per cent of the population was over 45 years of age, and the sex ratio over all age groups was 116 males per 100 females. In this chapter I describe the main factors underlying the demographic composition of the population, and I examine some related aspects of social selection in migration and in educational and occupational achievement.

AGE- AND SEX-SELECTIVE MIGRATION

The low proportion of persons over 45 years of age is not surprising if we consider that at this period the town had an intake of some 4,000 new recruits per annum[2] and that these consisted mainly of young adults and children. In 1952–53, for example, 42 per cent of all immigrants were between 16 and 25 years of age, 27 per cent were between 26 and 35, 22 per cent were under 16, and only 9 per cent were over 35.[3] With such an intake, the population of younger adults would have continued to build up out of all proportion to the accumulation of older persons even if there had been no return of the elderly to the countryside. In fact, however, despite an increasing tendency towards permanent settlement in town, it was still common for some immigrants to return to their villages and particularly so in old age.[4] And this outward migration naturally tended to accentuate the disproportion between younger and older inhabitants.

The proportion of males to females varied considerably at different ages (Table 7). Under 11 years of age the two sexes were relatively well balanced, but in the age group 11 to 15 years there was a marked excess of boys over girls. This reflects the greater attraction of the town for boys. Girls did not normally come to town in their early years of adolescence except as members of migrant families, but it was not unusual for boys of this age to seek entry to the C.E.C. on their own, either to attend school or to start work. More significant than the excess of boys over girls, however, was the excess in the in-coming population of adult males over adult females. Large numbers of men coming to town for the first time were unmarried, and many of those who were married left their wives in the countryside for initial periods of several months or even of a year or more.[5] In contrast, women seldom came to town alone; if married, they normally came with or after their husbands, and, if unmarried, they were often prevented or

TABLE 7

Age and sex composition of the African population of Stanleyville

AGE GROUP	MALES (per cent)	FEMALES (per cent)	TOTAL (per cent)	SEX RATIO (males per 100 females)
0–5	7·1	6·7	13·8	107
6–10	3·8	3·8	7·6	100
11–15	4·1	2·8	6·9	146
16–25	10·9	10·7	21·6	102
26–35	13·8	11·6	25·4	119
36–45	8·3	5·8	14·1	143 } 117
46–55	3·6	2·4	6·0	150
56 years and over	2·1	2·5	4·6	84
Total	53·7	46·3	100·0	116

(Effective sample: 4,872)

discouraged from migrating by their parents and kinsmen, and were in any case prohibited from settling in the C.E.C. unless they could show that they were legitimately dependent on a person or family already there.[6] Moreover, unless a woman was a permanent resident of the C.E.C. in her own right, she was liable to eviction in the event of being widowed or divorced.

Wives following their husbands to town, and women newly recruited from the countryside as brides for single men, tended to redress the balance between men and women. But, with the current increase in the total *volume* of immigrants at this period, there was a persistent excess of male over female immigrants. In summary, then, men came to town to work while women came to stay with their menfolk. But an excess of males over females continued to be a prominent feature of the resident population despite the large measure of success attending the official policy of encouraging immigrants to bring their wives and children to town.

The differences in the proportions of the sexes between different adult age categories were mainly due to men marrying, and bringing to town, women younger than themselves. Thus we find that between the ages of 16 and 25 there were 102 males to 100 women, but that 79·7 per cent of the women were married as against only 42·4 per cent of the men. These proportions changed markedly with increasing age until, between the ages of 46 to 55 years, there were as many as 150 men to 100 women but only 45·4 per cent of the women were married as against 66·5 per cent of the men.[7] Above 55 years of age the sex ratio fell appreciably to 84 men per 100 women, but the number of old persons in the population was too small to redress the overall excess of males to any appreciable extent.

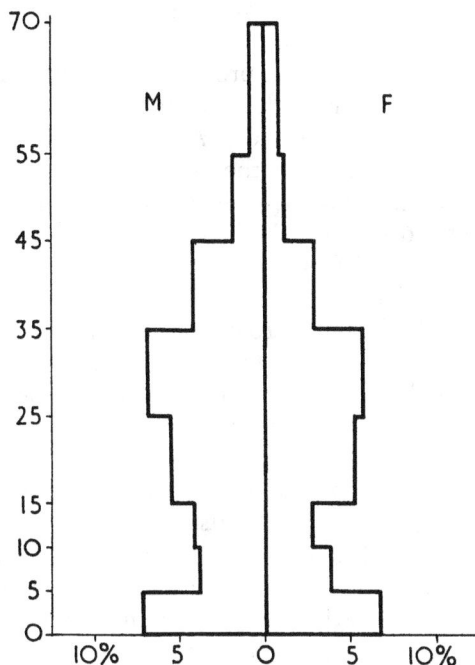

Fɪɢ. III Age and sex structure of the African population of Stanleyville

Comparisons with Other African Urban Populations

While displaying certain characteristic features of African urban populations, Stanleyville stood out as somewhat exceptional in that its demographic disproportions were less acute than those reported from most other medium-sized towns at this period.[8] In Jinja (Uganda), for example, there were in 1951 186 males per 100 females, while only 5·6 per cent of the population was over 45 years of age[9]; Livingstone (in former Northern Rhodesia) had in 1952 a sex ratio of 171, and 7·5 per cent of the inhabitants were 45 and over[10]; Brazzaville (in former French Equatorial Africa) had in 1951 a ratio of 134 males to 100 females while 9·0 per cent of the population was over 43 years[11]; and the Copperbelt towns (of former Northern Rhodesia) had in 1951–54 a mean sex ratio of 129 while only 3·5 per cent of the population was 45 years of age or more.[12]

These comparisons with towns in former French and English territories would suggest that Stanleyville's more 'favourable' demographic structure was, in part at least, a product of the general policies pursued by the Belgians in the 1930s and 1940s to stabilize the wage-earning labour force and to build up well-balanced and permanent urban populations. Such figures as we have for Stanleyville in earlier years are also in keeping with this explanation. In 1938, the earliest year for which I was able to find satisfactory data on the sex composition of the population, the town had a sex ratio of 160 males to 100 females.[13] This had fallen to 125 in 1949 and, as we have seen, to 116 in 1952. The striking fact revealed is that the proportion of men in the town had fallen very appreciably during the very period that the population of the town was increasing most rapidly. And the proportion of males had also fallen in at least three of the smaller C.E.C.s in the Eastern Province; between 1940 and 1949, the sex ratio for Buta (pop. 10,000) had fallen from 110 to 107, for Aketi (pop. 10,000) from 117 to 112, and for Niangara (pop. 4,000) from 135 to 108.[14]

The *relatively* well-balanced sex ratio in Stanleyville and in some smaller C.E.C.s in the Eastern Province was, however, not common to all *non-coutumiers* centres in the Belgian Congo. In the much larger towns of Leopoldville and Elizabethville the disproportions between the sexes continued to be more acute.[15] And in 1952 the total *non-coutumier* population in labour centres (including labour camps) in the Eastern Province had 129 males to 100 females,[16] a ratio very appreciably higher than that in Stanleyville itself. Taking all this evidence into account, it is evident that there were special factors operating to reduce the demographic disproportions in Stanleyville. These lay in the general pattern of rural-urban migration that had developed in the North-Eastern Congo and in the particular relation of Stanleyville to the labour centres of its own hinterland.

The Pattern of Progressive Migration from Village to Town

In a previous analysis I have suggested that migration to Stanleyville was unusually selective of persons who had previous experiences of living away from their tribal villages.[17] The most common pattern of migration from village to town involved one or more periods of living in smaller labour centres in the vicinity of the migrant's village. Hence the move to Stanleyville frequently took place from a small labour centre rather than from a village.[18]

In this connexion, it is revealing to compare the mean ages of migrants at the time of departure from their villages and at the time of arrival in Stanleyville. Adult inhabitants aged 16–25 years reported having first left their villages of origin at the mean age of 13 years, and of having arrived in Stanleyville at the mean age of 16. The mean experience for this age category was thus of having spent three years in small labour centres before moving to Stanleyville. For the age category 26–35, the mean age of departure from the village was 17 years, followed by six years in smaller centres before arriving in Stanleyville at the age of 23 years. And, as explained in Chapter IV, many persons had married for the first time while living in small employment centres.

There was considerable variation in the extent to which smaller centres in different areas of the hinterland sent migrants to Stanleyville. For example, there were in Stanleyville 262 persons born in the Territory of Isangi (close to the town) for every 1,000 persons living *away from native villages in that territory*, whereas many of the further removed territories in the north and north-east of the province had under five persons in Stanleyville for every 1,000 living *away from their tribal villages in those areas*.[19] Migrants from these more distant areas were on average older, and more likely to be married, than were those from the nearer areas.[20] The differences from one area to another were important but should not be allowed to obscure the main observation that the smaller centres of the hinterland contained a high aggregate of wage-earners of whom only a small proportion ever ventured as far as Stanleyville.

SOCIAL SELECTION AND COMMITMENT TO 'CIVILIZED' LIFE

An important measure of social selection took place in the course of progressive migrations to Stanleyville. The many smaller labour centres in the hinterland acted as a population filter: they tended to retain persons who were typically labour migrants seeking short-term employment, and to send out to Stanleyville persons who were, or more readily became, 'civilized' individuals, reluctant to return to their villages and eager to settle their families in town. There is no doubt that in the C.E.C. of Stanleyville there were better opportunities for a man to abandon tribal life, and stronger inducements for him to commit himself permanently to wage-earning, than in the majority of small centres from which a large part of the population came. The overall social context of urban migration had, however, changed appreciably over time, and it is necessary to take note of these changes.

The compulsory recruitment of men to work either for the administration or for private companies had remained overt up to the late 1920s, and probably later in some areas. In reviewing the labour situation in the Eastern Province in 1930–31, Bertrand considered that many wage-earners would not have been in employment at all were it not for the direct pressures put on them by the administration. He wrote:

Il serait vain d'alléguer une exode spontané des hommes. Si l'Administration n'intervenait pas, moins de la moitié de ceux qui sont actuellement en service se trouveraient sur les chantiers miniers et autres.[21] . . . Si, dans beaucoup de territoires, l'autorité administrative ne participe plus en aucune façon aux recrutements de travailleurs pour les entreprises privées, cette heureuse situation n'est pas encore généralisée.[22] . . . S'il est exact, que, souvent . . . les départs sont spontanés, souvent aussi ils sont la conséquence d'opérations de recrutement . . . appuyées fortement par l'Administration.[23] . . . Le rôle de la Colonie ne peut être de rectifier les erreurs commises en faisant peser tout le poids sur les indigènes . . . par une pression exercée sur eux pour les entraîner sur nos chantiers.[24]

An official report written in this vein leaves us in little doubt of the nature of much migration in earlier years. We also know that policies to stabilize and maintain the labour force had not yet been introduced and that the wage-earning section of the population was still made up largely of men who had left their wives and families behind. But we cannot assume that reluctant recruits brought to work in labour centres were invariably eager to return home after their periods of wage-earning. It seems that a large proportion, especially those from labour camps, did in fact return, but as noted in the previous chapter there is also evidence that numbers of others stayed on in peri-urban settlements either out of rank preference to returning home or because a return home was difficult or impossible. Judging from case histories of elderly men in Stanleyville, it would seem that ex-soldiers in particular commonly chose to settle down around the growing towns. Often they had been away from their villages for many years, had travelled to various parts of the Congo, and had been discharged from the *Force Publique* in places far removed from their tribal villages. Ex-labourers perhaps seldom found themselves in quite the same extreme circumstances, but again the evidence both from case histories and from contemporary comments in official reports suggests that *some* were either unable or unwilling to return.

The systematic assessment of factors making for permanent urban settlement in the years prior to the establishment of C.E.C.s lies far beyond the scope of the present study. My impression is, however, that failure to return home in those early days of urban life may be attributed quite as much to the desire to avoid returning to the conditions of rural life that had developed under a forceful colonial administration as to any lure which the limited urban opportunities of the day may have exercised. It is well known that in the early decades of Belgian rule the compulsory cultivation of cash crops and the conscription of men as porters and labourers for the building of roads and for other government projects had caused widespread resentment in tribal areas.[25] Equally it is generally recognized that the methods of rural administration in early days were particularly harsh and oppressive, and that in some areas of the Eastern Province traditional tribal units were almost completely disrupted.[26]

Whatever the case, it is clear that there developed a small but distinct element of townsmen who had, either by choice or by force of circumstances, turned their backs on traditional village life. It was in these early days that there first developed the distinction between *basendji*, who were essentially tribal men, and the new townsmen who came in the course of time to see themselves as 'civilized' persons.

In the 1930s and later the situation changed appreciably in several respects. As seen in Chapter II, there was, first, the development of a positive policy of urbanization leading to the possibility of home-ownership for town-dwellers and to a general improvement in the conditions of urban life. Migrants who were, for whatever reason, disaffected with village life were thus offered a reasonable alternative to returning home after periods of wage-earning. Secondly, the abandonment of large-scale labour conscription in the 1920s was followed by an attenuation of the harsher and more arbitrary methods of administration in rural areas. Some contentious administrative practices, such as the enforcement of compulsory cultivation, were to continue for many years and even, in some measure, up to the time of the present study, but they were increasingly applied selectively as an integral part of a policy specifically intended to mitigate the more disruptive consequences of labour recruitment. Moreover, the general development of the province began to promote greater freedom of movement back and forth between town and country. It was at this period that roads were first built on a large scale and that an extensive transport system was developed throughout the Eastern Province.[27]

These developments, accompanied as they were by steady economic expansion, led to a marked increase in the total number of men entering the labour market and to the growth of a large volume of what Mitchell has described as the *circulation* rather than the migration of labour.[28] Alternate participation in town and village life became the standard pattern of wage-earners, and in the 1950s migrant or '*circulating*' labourers certainly constituted an overwhelming majority of the total population in the employment centres of the region.

In Stanleyville itself, however, the position was appreciably different. Although many of the inhabitants were migrant labourers the town also had a very substantial minority of long-term and permanent urbanites. As Elkan points out, information on the lengths of residence of members of an expanding population does not necessarily tell us very much about their permanence unless we also know the rate of loss through deaths and departures.[29] Yet, if we relate the information on lengths of residence given in Table 8 to other known facts, we can arrive at convincing evidence of a large settled element in the population. In 1952–53 there were about 30,000 *adults* in the town as defined for the purpose of this study and from Table 8 we know that about a quarter of these had been in the town continuously for more than 15 years. Some 7,500 of the 30,000 *adults* of 1952–53 had therefore been in the town since 1937, when, we know, the total population was about 12,000.[30] Thus about 60 per cent of the *total* population of 1937 was still there in 1952–53, and we are left to assume that about 40 per cent (4,500 to 5,000) had either died or emigrated between 1937 and 1952–53. If we now consider that deaths would certainly have accounted for a fair proportion of these 'departures'—an improbably low annual death rate of only 10 per 100 would have accounted for about 1,500 of the original 12,000—it seems that only a minority of the original population of 1937 had emigrated during the 15-year period under review. If we then further consider that a certain proportion of those who had left the town between 1937 and 1952–53 must certainly have gone to other towns and labour centres and not back to their villages, the evidence clearly points to an important nucleus of habitual or permanent wage-earners. Information on the places of birth of the adult population of 1952–53 also supports the view that there was a growing section of permanent urban-dwellers.[31]

TABLE 8

Percentage distributions of persons aged 16 years and over by lengths of residence in Stanleyville and in 'civilized' places

YEARS OF RESIDENCE	PERCENTAGE CONTINUOUSLY RESIDENT IN STANLEYVILLE FOR GIVEN PERIODS	PERCENTAGE RESIDENT IN 'CIVILIZED' PLACES (INCLUDING STANLEYVILLE) FOR GIVEN PERIODS
0–5	47·1	18·4
6–10	19·2	18·5
11–15	9·2	16·4
16–20	6·8	12·8
21–25	5·5	13·7
26 and over	12·2	20·2
Total	100·0	100·0

(Effective sample: 3,491)   (Effective sample: 3,503)

Note: There is an important difference in the basis of the two sets of figures: length of residence in Stanleyville refers to the years of *continuous* residence in the town whereas length of residence in 'civilized' places refers to the total number of years whether continuous or not.

At the same time, however, nearly a half of all adults in the town in 1952–53 had been there for five years or less (Table 8), and a good proportion of these were undoubtedly short-term residents. Taking all the evidence we have into account, we are thus led to the general conclusion that the town had a substantial core of permanent residents but that many of the recent immigrants were there for limited periods.

Permanent Townsmen and Migrant Labourers

The conclusion drawn above is in keeping with evidence gathered through interviews with a small sample of 38 men.[32] Except for a few who could not be contacted, the men made up the total adult male population of 23 dwelling compounds at one end of a single avenue in a poor outlying part of Old Brussels.[33] Exactly 50 per cent were labourers as against 36·7 per cent in the town as a whole, and none held white collar jobs as against 9·5 per cent in the total population.

On the basis of their own assessments only 12 of the 38 saw themselves as 'temporarily urbanized'. The remaining 26 all saw themselves as 'permanently urbanized' and expressed no intention or desire of returning to their villages. Indeed, some of these men were very strongly opposed to the idea of ever returning to tribal life.

Although these 38 men cannot be taken as representative of the town population, their cases clearly illustrate that the population contained elements participating in town life in widely differing ways.

The high incidence of attitudes of 'permanent urbanization' in this sample is particularly significant if we remember that it contained no white collar workers and a disproportionately high number of ordinary labourers.

An analysis of the statements made by the 38 men in explaining their assessments of life in town and in the villages revealed that living in Stanleyville was often seen as a welcome refuge from hardships and difficulties in their home villages. *Kizungu*, or life with the Europeans, offered an escape from the harsh authority of tribal chiefs, from sorcery, from drudgery of work in the fields, from obligations to demanding kinsmen and from the hostilities and jealousies of the village. Their statements also dwelt on the positive attractions of the town which they tended to see as a place holding opportunities of advancement for themselves and their children and offering an enjoyable social life and a material standard of living unattainable in tribal areas.

Counterbalancing the advantages of town life, home villages were often thought of nostalgically for the social and economic security of family life and the abundance of food. But a number of those who stressed attractive aspects of tribal life also explained that, despite the advantages, a return home would involve them in intolerable situations. They considered that after a man had been accustomed to *Kizungu* it was impossible later to accommodate to the 'uncivilized' or *basendji* ways of tribal people. Village people were said to be distrustful and jealous of those who had 'followed the Europeans'. The difficulty of adapting to village ways and people after a spell away was also sensed by some 'temporarily urbanized' men, and this feeling of dislocation partly accounted for their frequently qualified hopes of returning to village life.

The above evidence has, of course, to be evaluated in its correct context. There was at the time very little unemployment in the town, and conditions of life under the C.E.C. regime were increasingly seen as offering an effective alternative to a lifetime of migrating back and forth between village and labour centre. In a general way, too, there had developed in the town a distinctive way of life which contained its own goals, particularly in regard to occupations, to education for boys, to having a dwelling compound both for residence and for small shopkeeping, and to home ownership.

Any deterioration in the relatively favourable urban situation of the times would perhaps have led numbers of seemingly permanent urbandwellers to change their attitudes and their assessments of their own probable futures. But the favourable situation had existed for some years and the current processes of urban selection had already gathered considerable momentum. The views and attitudes of the men opting for town life were not merely the idiosyncratic reactions of individual men. They derived from a developing urban culture which saw tribal life as backward and inferior.

EDUCATIONAL AND OCCUPATIONAL SELECTION

The trends in the demographic and social selection of immigrants coming to town from smaller labour centres and tribal villages illustrate one aspect of the developing processes of differentiation and mobility in the wider African society. Another aspect of these processes manifested itself in competition for educational and occupational opportunities in the urban sphere. In going to school and in going to work, village-born tribesmen were leaving the world of *Kisendji* and entering the world of *Kizungu*. Those who entered *Kizungu* constituted a select group and much larger numbers never actively participated in *Kizungu* at all.[34] And for many who entered *Kizungu*, the move was in the first instance a tentative one. Having taken this first step, some later withdrew permanently, some settled to alternate participation in both spheres over the greater part of a lifetime, and some, as we have seen, abandoned village life altogether. In all cases, however, participation in town life meant entering into competition for a job. I now briefly examine the educational and occupational achievements of the population and the patterns of selection which were developing within the town.

In educational and occupational experiences there were, of course, large discrepancies between the two sexes. Under 2 per cent of the women aged 16 years and over in the town were in wage-earning employment as against nearly 90 per cent of the men; and only 15 per cent of the women had received any kind of formal schooling as against 50 per cent of the men.

Among children being brought up in Stanleyville, the discrepancy was of the same order of magnitude: 34·6 per cent of girls between the ages of 6 and 15 were attending school as against 78·1 per cent of the boys. A few women were entering industrial employment for the first time and this reflected important new trends in urban society but the numbers involved were so small that the development cannot be assessed statistically. I therefore confine myself to examining the educational and occupational achievements of men.[35]

We saw in Chapter II that 10·8 per cent of all male wage-earners were white collar workers, principally teachers, clerks and medical orderlies; 48·8 per cent were specialized manual workers, consisting mainly of drivers, carpenters and joiners, mechanics, masons and painters, and domestic servants; and 40·4 per cent were working as labourers or in other totally unskilled jobs. The educational experiences of men in these three occupational categories varied considerably. With the exception of a few men who had learnt to read and write in the army, all white collar workers had been to school, about 40 per cent had reached secondary schools, and a total of over 80 per cent had spent *at least* four years at school, but none had a university education. Of the specialized manual workers, 43·4 per cent had never attended school, 25·2 per cent had been to school for 3 years or less, 28·8 per cent for 4–6 years, and only 2·6 per cent for more than six years. Of the labourers, 64·7 per cent had never been to school, 21·2 per cent had been for 3 years or less, and only 14·1 per cent for 4 years or more.

The relatively high educational level of the white-collar workers calls for no comment as white collar jobs were by definition closed to illiterates, and we know that a high premium was placed on education in all colonial situations. The figures for specialized manual workers and for ordinary labourers and others totally unskilled show that on the whole men with some education fared appreciably better in finding their way to the more remunerative jobs than did those with no formal education. The degree of overlap was, however, considerable, and there were substantial numbers of men with no schooling who had succeeded in entering even the better specialized manual jobs such as drivers, carpenters, and mechanics, while others with some years of elementary schooling had failed to do so.

In general, then, occupational achievements were associated with schooling even at the level of manual work, but schooling did not account for all the variation. Under local conditions none of the specialized manual occupations normally required that a man should have any or a particular standard of schooling. A very small proportion of carpenters and mechanics had attended vocational schools, but the vast majority of all specialized manual workers had simply picked up their skills in the course of day-to-day life. Thus it is not surprising

TABLE 9

Percentage distribution of wage-earning men in six educational-occupational grades

GRADE	DESCRIPTION	NO. IN SAMPLE	PER CENT
1	White collar workers with over six years schooling*	74	4·4
2	White collar workers with 4–6 years schooling / Specialized manual workers with over 6 years schooling	94	5·6
3	White collar workers with 1–3 years schooling / Specialized manual workers with 4–6 years schooling / Labourers with over 6 years schooling	260	15·5
4	White collar workers with no schooling / Specialized manual workers with 1–3 years schooling / Labourers with 4–6 years schooling	302	18·0
5	Specialized manual workers with no schooling / Labourers with 1–3 years schooling	497	29·6
6	Labourers with no schooling	453	27·0
	Total	1,680	100·1

* Primary schools normally kept children for six years so that most men who had spent more than six years at school had some secondary education.

TABLE 10

Distribution of monthly earnings of wage-earning men in different educational-occupational grades

EARNINGS PER MONTH (FRANCS)	GRADES													TOTAL	
	1		2		3		4		5		6				
	No.	%	No.	%	No.	%	No.	%	No.	%	No.	%	No.	%
350–450	1	1·3	1	1·1	14	5·4	20	6·6	30	6·0	73	16·1	139	8·3
450–649	2	2·7	11	11·7	54	20·8	98	32·5	152	30·6	230	50·8	547	32·6
650–849	3	4·1	16	17·0	70	26·9	91	30·1	161	32·4	79	17·4	420	25·0
850–1,149	5	6·8	17	18·1	57	21·9	44	14·6	92	18·5	22	4·9	237	14·1
1,150–1,749	9	12·2	14	14·9	35	13·5	26	8·6	34	6·8	2	0·4	120	7·1
1,750–2,549	16	21·6	10	10·6	14	5·4	4	1·3	6	1·2	0	0·0	50	3·0
2,550 and over	37	50·0	21	22·3	7	2·7	1	0·3	0	0·0	0	0·0	66	3·9
Earnings unknown or partly in kind	1	1·4	4	4·3	9	3·5	18	6·0	22	4·4	47	10·4	101	6·0
Total	74	100·1	94	100·0	260	100·1	302	100·0	497	99·9	453	100·0	1,680	100·0
Median earnings	2,250		1,150		800		700		700		570		690	
Mean earnings*	3,945		1,495		965		791		770		588		1,008	

* In calculating the means, the upper limit of wages was taken as 10,000 francs for Grade 1 and as 3,000 francs for Grades 2, 3 and 4.

that the proportions of men whose fathers had themselves been wage-earners rose significantly from the lower to the higher occupational categories.[36] In an attempt to establish more homogeneous strata than those of white collar workers, specialized manual workers, and ordinary labourers, all wage-earners were classified into six grades according to the combination of educational and occupational criteria listed in Table 9. The monthly earnings of men in each of the six grades are set out in Table 10. It can be seen that, except for Grades 4 and 5 which had similar income distributions, the grades tend to represent income strata. Men in Grade 1 consisted of white collar workers with a secondary education. They had mean earnings of 3,945 francs per month and accounted for under 5 per cent of the total wage-earning labour force. At the other extreme, men in Grade 6 consisted of labourers with no schooling. They had a mean wage of 588 francs per month and made up 27·0 per cent of all wage-earners.

The social antecedents of men in each of the six grades may be inferred from Tables 11 and 12. Passing from Grade 1 to Grade 6 there is a steady increase in the proportion of men born in native villages and, correspondingly, in the proportion of those whose fathers had not themselves been in European employment. Men in Grade 1 were to an appreciable extent second-generation wage-earners; over a half were born away from rural villages and had fathers who had themselves been wage-earners. In fact, as many as 17·6 per cent were second-generation white collar workers, and 23·0 per cent were sons either of soldiers or of specialized manual workers. These proportions fell appreciably in Grade 2 and continued to do so down to Grade 6 which consisted almost entirely of first generation migrants with fathers who had not themselves 'entered *Kizungu*'. When the proportions in the six grades are compared with each other and with the corresponding proportions for the total labour force, we see, firstly, that men born away from native villages of 'civilized' fathers had

TABLE 11

Types of birthplaces of wage-earning men in different educational-occupational grades

TYPE OF BIRTHPLACE	GRADES												TOTAL	
	1		2		3		4		5		6			
	No.	%	No.	%	No.	%	No.	%	No.	%	No.	%	No.	%
'Towns'	19	25·7	12	12·8	26	10·0	15	5·0	13	2·6	3	0·7	88	5·2
European centres other than 'towns'	27	36·5	26	27·7	40	15·4	27	8·9	33	6·6	16	3·5	169	10·1
Native villages	28	37·8	56	59·6	194	74·6	260	86·1	451	90·7	434	95·8	1,423	84·7
Total	74	100·0	94	100·1	260	100·0	302	100·0	497	99·9	453	100·0	1,680	100·0

Note: 'Towns' were defined as all places where there was an established *centre extra-coutumier* in 1952, but the majority of men classified as born in a 'town' were in fact born in Stanleyville itself.

6

TABLE 12

Fathers' occupations of wage-earning men in different educational-occupational grades

FATHERS' OCCUPATIONS	GRADES												TOTAL	
	1		2		3		4		5		6			
	No.	%	No.	%	No.	%	No.	%	No.	%	No.	%	No.	%
White collar	13	17·6	8	8·5	10	3·8	11	3·6	6	1·2	3	0·7	51	3·0
Specialized manual	8 }	23·0	9 }	19·1	34 }	18·5	23 }	11·9	24 }	9·1	3 }	2·9	177	10·5
Soldier	9 }		9 }		14 }		13 }		21 }		10 }			
Labourer	7	9·5	15	16·0	31	11·9	39	12·9	42	8·5	27	6·0	161	9·6
Rural (peasants, fishermen, etc.)	33	44·6	48	51·1	162	62·3	214	70·9	397	79·9	405	89·4	1,259	74·9
Self-employed and unknown	4	5·4	5	5·3	9	3·5	2	0·7	7	1·4	5	1·1	32	1·9
Total	74	100·1	94	100·0	260	100·0	302	100·0	497	100·1	453	100·1	1,680	99·9

achieved higher occupational positions out of all proportion to their numbers. The advantage they held was significant not only in the struggle for secondary education and the small number of white collar jobs, but also in competition for elementary education and for the large number of good specialized manual jobs, such as driver, carpenter, and mechanic, for which formal schooling was *not* an indispensable pre-requisite.

Secondly, we see that despite the relative occupational success of men with 'civilized' antecedents, the higher grades still contained substantial proportions of sons of rural-tribal fathers. It was only in Grade 1 that village-born men did not constitute a clear majority over all others and here they still made up between a third and half of the total. This reflects an important consequence of the small number of second-generation immigrants in the population. Comparing the number of men who were sons of wage-earners with the numbers in Grades 1, 2, and 3, we see that positions in the three upper strata could only have been filled exclusively by sons of fathers with wage-earning experience if *all* such sons had reached the top.

Table 13 shows the age composition of the six grades of men, and Table 14 gives the educational-occupational composition of different age categories. There was virtually no difference in the age composition of Grades 1 to 4, but the median age rose sharply in the lower grades: from 29 years in Grade 4, to 33 years in Grade 5 and 36 years in Grade 6. Conversely, men over 36 years of age were very largely found in Grades 5 and 6, while men aged 16–25 and 26–35 years were 'over-represented' in Grades 1 to 4.

The relation between age and educational-occupational grade reflects two important trends. First, there was the growth of educational opportunities over time. Very few of the older men had been to school and white collar jobs were thus virtually closed to them. In contrast, the majority of young urban-born men had been to school, while the proportion of young village-born men with some educational experience was also rising rapidly. Secondly, younger men, with or without education, were better able to acquire the skills required for specialized

TABLE 13

Age composition of educational-occupational grades of wage-earning men

AGE GROUP	1		2		3		4		5		6		TOTAL	
	No.	%	No.	%	No.	%	No.	%	No.	%	No.	%	No.	%
16–25	29	39·2	35	37·2	104	40·0	102	33·8	110	22·1	82	18·1	462	27·5
26–35	30	40·5	40	42·6	110	42·3	142	47·0	189	38·0	144	31·8	655	39·0
36–45	11	14·9	16	17·0	38	14·6	48	15·9	121	24·3	137	30·2	371	22·1
46–55	4	5·4	2	2·2	8	3·1	9	3·0	57	11·5	60	13·2	140	8·3
Over 55	0	0·0	1	1·1	0	0·0	1	0·3	20	4·0	30	6·6	52	3·1
Total	74	100·0	94	100·1	260	100·0	302	100·0	497	99·9	453	99·9	1,680	100·0
Median age	29		29		28		29		33		36		32	

manual work such as a lorry-driving, carpentry, and even personal service. With the expansion of jobs requiring *some* skill and the *relative* decrease of jobs requiring no skill, young men were continually finding opportunities to move up the occupational ladder. Large numbers took unspecialized jobs on first coming to town but moved into better positions after acquiring the appropriate skills from friends and kinsmen or from supervisors at their place of work. It was common for chauffeurs,

TABLE 14

Composition of age categories of wage-earning men in terms of educational-occupational grades

GRADES	AGE IN YEARS									
	16–25		26–35		36–45		46 and over		Total	
	No.	%	No.	%	No.	%	No.	%	No.	%
1	29	6·3	30	4·6	11	3·0	4	2·1	74	4·4
2	35	7·6	40	6·1	16	4·3	3	1·6	94	5·6
3	104	22·5	110	16·8	38	10·2	8	4·2	260	15·5
4	102	22·1	142	21·7	48	12·9	10	5·2	302	18·0
5	110	23·8	189	28·9	121	32·6	77	40·1	497	29·6
6	82	17·7	144	22·0	137	36·9	90	46·9	453	27·0
All grades	462	100·0	655	100·1	371	99·9	192	100·1	1,680	100·1

masons, and other specialized workers to have 'pupils' who either paid them fixed sums or gave them regular presents in return for instruction in particular skills.

There was thus a steady flow of young men moving from the ranks of labourers and of *aides-maçons, aides-chaffeurs,* and the like, to specialized jobs. Older men in the labour force consisted partly of those who had tried but failed to enter better jobs, and partly of those who had entered wage-earning too late to attempt to acquire the modest skills required for moving up or who, as labour migrants, were more concerned to earn specific sums of money before returning home than to acquire any working skills.

THE SIGNIFICANCE OF THE DATA

The full significance of the data in this chapter will become apparent as we examine the social configurations of different ethnic colonies and, also, as we proceed to study various aspects of the system of urban relations. At this stage we need only emphasize three general features that distinguished the processes of migration and selection in and around Stanleyville from those in and around other African towns that have been studied systematically. The first feature derives from the distinctive urban policy of the Belgian colonial authority. We saw how this had changed in the early 1930s from an ill-defined negative attitude to a positive policy of promoting a stable urban population. It is abundantly clear that by 1952–53 this policy had achieved some of its general objectives. It was now standard practice for married men to bring their wives and families to town, and home ownership and 'urban careers' were the usual aspirations of a substantial section of the immigrant population. Secondly, the size and nature of the town's hinterland meant that many immigrants had previous experience of 'civilized' life in smaller centres before coming to Stanleyville. Moreover, the location of the town in relation to some tribal areas meant that many immigrants wishing to keep in touch with their villages could only do so every few years rather than every few weeks or months. Home visits were seldom provided for in labour contracts and most immigrants had to plan and finance their own trips home. There was, however, considerable variation in all these respects and the situation of migrants from the immediate hinterland differed markedly from that of persons from further away. Thirdly, wage-earning was far from a standard expectation in the hinterland. *Kizungu* had made deep inroads into the traditional life of all peoples in the region, yet these inroads were limited as compared to many other parts of Southern and Central Africa. In most areas of the North-Eastern Congo there were many men who never embarked on 'urban careers' in the relatively very large town of Stanleyville, or even in lesser towns such as Buta and Aketi; indeed, substantial proportions of tribesmen in the hinterland never left their tribal villages at all, not even for periods of wage-earning on plantations or small centres of employment near to their home villages.

In general, the population of the town consisted of three elements: people who were deeply involved in town life to the total or near-total exclusion of rural involvement, those who were permanent or semi-permanent immigrants but who continued to participate in the rural social system to an appreciable extent despite their urban involvement, and those who, as migrant or 'circulating' labourers, participated in town life despite their continuing deep involvement in village life. All three of these urban elements differed very appreciably from those tribesmen in the region who were not wage-earners or who only ventured to leave their villages for short periods of wage-earning on plantations or in smaller centres lying within or close to their tribal areas.

FOOTNOTES TO CHAPTER III

[1] The main demographic characteristics of African urban populations have often been noted. See, for example, McCulloch's discussion (1956a, pp. 211–212) on the excess of men over women and the low proportion of children and old people.

[2] This estimate is based on the number of migrants in 1952–53 who had been in the town less than one year and is roughly confirmed by the records of admission kept by the C.E.C. Cf. f.n. 17, Chapter II.

[3] The records of admission kept by the C.E.C. did not contain entries on age. The figures given here are estimates based on the ages of persons in the random sample who had been in the town less than one year. See Pons (1956a), p. 262.

[4] African towns have been graphically compared with Army barracks 'accommodating successive waves of National Servicemen, and perhaps some also who have "signed on" for five years, seven or over twenty-one—but sooner or later everybody leaves.' Elkan (1960), p. 4. The weight of the evidence is that in Stanleyville at this period some left 'sooner or later' but others did not.

[5] Men in town without their wives represented 8·0 per cent of all married men falling in the survey sample. Over a third of these had been in town under one year, and over a half under two years. It was exceptional for married men who had been in town several years not to have their wives with them.

[6] Numbers of unmarried women did, however, try to enter the C.E.C. on their own. The administrator-in-charge of the C.E.C. in 1952 complained that keeping unmarried women out was a persistent problem.

[7] Full figures on the marital status of the adult population are given in Chapter VIII, Tables 63 and 64.

[8] Comparing Stanleyville with several other African towns, Denis writes:
'Stanleyville présente une image un peu différente. La population paraît ici notablement plus âgée que dans les autres villes. Les catégories d'âge fécond sont mieux équilibrées . . . Aussi, non seulement la natalité paraît bonne, mais les classes de 5 à 15 ans sont mieux fournies que dans les (autres villes)' Denis (1958), pp. 221–222.

[9] Sofer C. and R. (1955), p.16.

[10] McCulloch (1956b), p. 15.

[11] Balandier (1955), pp. 52–53.

[12] Mitchell (1954), p. 5.

[13] Based on figures from official unpublished records of the C.E.C. Prior to 1938 the population was recorded as consisting of 'men,' 'women,' and 'children,' without distinguishing between boys and girls. Reliable estimates for the early 1930's are therefore difficult to make.

[14] Figures from official unpublished records. I was unable to find adequate data for the remaining C.E.C.s of the province.

[15] In Leopoldville at this period men outnumbered women by 'two to one, although the situation (was) improving,' and in Elizabethville there were about 140 men to 100 women. McCulloch (1956a), pp. 112 and 163.

[16] Figures from official unpublished records.

[17] Pons (1956a).

[18] A similar pattern was at this period reported for Coquilhatville in the Equatorial Province of the Belgian Congo. See Doucy and Feldheim (1956), p. 676.

[19] Corresponding figures for all areas of the Eastern Province are given in Pons (1956a), p. 251.

[20] Cf. the discussion on differences between the nine largest ethnic colonies in Chapter IV.

[21] Bertrand (1931), p. 12.

[22] Bertrand (1931), p. 21.

[23] Bertrand (1931), p. 249.

[24] Bertrand (1931), p. 259.

[25] The conscription of labour and the compulsory cultivation of crops had become the subject of a great deal of discussion within the ranks of the Belgian administration. This is clear from Bertrand (1931) and Magotte (1934), as well as from many other sources.

[26] This was particularly true in the forest regions of the Congo Basin from where the majority of Stanleyville's immigrants came. Weak indigenous political organization and the small size of many traditional groupings were marked characteristics of the peoples in this area. The Belgian recognition of the difficulties of ruling in this area is reflected in the differential arrangements later made for rural administration in the Districts of Kibali-Ituri and Uele (in the north and north-east of the province) and in the District of Stanleyville (which lay entirely within the forest region). In 1951 the District of Stanleyville had 37 *secteurs* (units of administration bringing two or more traditional groupings into one unit with one appointed chief) and only 33 *chefferies* (units based on only one traditional grouping). In contrast the District of Kibali-Ituri had 74 *chefferies* and only 3 *secteurs*, and the District of Uele had 62 *chefferies* and only 6 *secteurs*. For a brief discussion of the extreme difficulties encountered by the administration owing to the fragmentation of tribal entities in the Stanleyville region in earlier years, see Lemarchand (1964), pp. 38–40.

[27] Between 1920 and 1930 the number of kilometres of completed roads in the Eastern Province rose from 350 to over 12,000. Linking up with existing rail and river lines of communication, the new roads had a far-reaching effect on economic development.

[28] Mitchell (1961), p. 232.

[29] Elkan (1960), p. 4.

[30] The C.E.C. records give a population of about 9,500 for 1937, and I am allowing 2,500 to 3,000 for the *Arabisé* village and the railway camp.

[31] The proportion of persons in Stanleyville born outside tribal villages was 25·9 per cent for the age-group 16–25 years, 15·2 per cent for those aged 26–35 years, 14·7 per cent for those aged 36–45 years, 10·9 per cent for those aged 46–35 years, and 3·9 per cent for those aged 56 years and over.

[32] The information is given in greater detail in 'A Note on the Attitudes to Town and Village Life of 38 Men in Stanleyville,' Appendix to Pons (1956b), pp. 667–669.

[33] These men were the inhabitants of Avenue 21 described in Chapter VI.

[34] There was wide variation between tribes of the region in their degree of participation in the wage-earning economy. Thus, for example, there was a striking contrast between the Wagenia, who seldom entered employment even though some of their villages were adjacent to the town, and, say, the Bakumu who tended to enter employment quite readily. But there were also important differences *within* tribal groups, and many of the tribes that were well represented in Stanleyville had large numbers of men who had never been to labour centres. For example, a random sample of 151 Bakumu men in four villages near to the outpost of Wanie Rukula, which was only 60 kilometres away from Stanleyville, gave the following results: 63·6 per cent of men of all ages had never entered employment, 32·5 per cent had worked on plantations and in other small centres of employment, and only 4·0 per cent had worked in Stanleyville itself. Of 23 men in the sample aged 16–25 years, 19 had never been away at all; of 37 aged 26–35 years, 20 had never been away; of 50 aged 36–45, 26 had never been away; and of 41 aged 46 years and over, 31 had never been away. Such figures reveal a sharp contrast to the situation in some areas of Southern and Central Africa where the large majority of all men in tribal villages spend at least a part of their lives earning wages.

[35] Fuller data on the formal schooling of women are given in Pons (1956a), pp. 266–267.

[36] In the population as a whole, 23·5 per cent of wage-earners were sons of fathers who had themselves worked in *Kizungu*, but among labourers the proportion was only 15·6 per cent as against 26·2 per cent for specialized manual workers. For more detailed information, see Pons (1956a), pp. 266–271.

IV

ETHNIC COLONIES

We have so far examined various aspects of the African community in Stanleyville with only a passing reference to its ethnic heterogeneity. The present chapter dwells on this particular feature. I first describe the tribal composition and cultural diversity of the population and analyse the patterns of residential distribution of the nine principal colonies.[1] I then outline the social configurations of three colonies specifically selected to illustrate how a number of inter-ethnic variations were related to different histories and patterns of urban incorporation. After that I compare further social and demographic data for the nine principal colonies. I show that these colonies can be classified into three 'types' of age and sex structure and that each of the three case studies represents one relatively distinct 'type'. Finally, I suggest that although Stanleyville was appreciably different from towns studied in other parts of the continent, inter-ethnic variations of the kind reported in this chapter have commonly been noted in other African settings.

TRIBAL COMPOSITION

It was said in Stanleyville that the town contained representatives of every tribe in the Belgian Congo and of many from beyond the colony's boundaries. This may well have been true but the aggregate of persons from beyond the north-eastern Congo was very small.[2] The tribal composition of a sample of the population is given in Table 15. With an estimated membership of 6,400 the Lokele constituted 15·4 per cent of the total and were the largest single tribe in the town. Next came the *Arabisés* who, though not a tribal group, constituted an equally distinctive ethnic element; they made up 11·8 per cent of the sample and had an estimated population of 4,900. Following the Lokele and the *Arabisés* were seven tribes—the Babua, Bakumu, Topoke, Bambole, Babali, Balengola, and Bamanga—each estimated to have between 1,000 and 4,000 members. Another seven tribes—the Bangelima, Turumbu, Mobango, Basoko, Azande, Mongandu and Bangobango—were estimated to have between 500 and 1,000 members each, and there were many smaller colonies with populations of under 500 each. The nine principal colonies together constituted about two-thirds of the total African population of the town.

The rural areas of origin of the fifteen larger tribal colonies are shown in Fig. IV; with the exceptions of the Azande and Bamanga, all of these were of Bantu stock and were largely recruited within the Congo Basin. In this area, political coherence had in pre-Arab and pre-European days scarcely developed above the level of a few associated groupings of kinsmen which Belgian writers have commonly referred to as 'clans'. The organization of 'clans' in the region was largely dominated by patrilineal principles of succession and kinship and none of the principal tribes was matrilineal. Most of the inhabitants were from forest or river peoples. The scale of political organization in most of the parent populations had remained small, and 'clans' had not normally been distributed over more than a few villages.[3]

Within the town's area of principal recruitment there were important variations between tribes in their histories of urban incorporation and in the current conditions under which rural-urban migration took

TABLE 15

Ethnic composition of the population

TRIBE	EFFECTIVE SAMPLE	PER CENT	ESTIMATED POPULATION
Lokele	752	15·4	6,400
Arabisés	574	11·8	4,900
Babua	427	8·8	3,650
Bakumu	339	7·0	2,900
Topoke	327	6·7	2,800
Bambole	226	4·6	1,900
Babali	205	4·2	1,750
Balengola	194	4·0	1,650
Bamanga	157	3·2	1,350
Total of the nine tribes	3,201	65·7	27,300
Seven tribes estimated each to have a population of 500 to 1,000 in the town	666	13·7	5,700
Upwards of 60 other tribes estimated each to have a population of under 500 in the town	1,007	20·7	8,600
Total	4,874	100·1	41,600

Note: Minor discrepancies between the above and previously published estimates are accounted for by the inclusion here of the *Arabisés* as a tribe. In the previous estimates the *Arabisés* were distributed amongst the tribal groups according to their tribal origins. See Pons (1956a), p. 265.

place. The Lokele came from the densely populated banks of the Congo River close to Stanleyville and, apart from the labour demands of the town, opportunities for wage-earning were more limited in their tribal area than in many further removed areas. Other tribes, like the Bakumu and Bambole, also had villages close to Stanleyville, but came from more sparsely populated areas in parts of which there were greater local demands for labour. Others still came from areas which were less accessible either on account of distance or of other geographical factors. All in all, there was much variation between tribes

in their opportunities for visiting kinsmen at home and for developing
links of trade and exchange between town and village.

For some tribes from beyond the more immediate environs, Stanleyville was not the main centre of employment. The Babua, for example,
tended to look more to the small town of Buta situated in their own
tribal area. Others had no 'principal town' and members of these
tribes were to be found scattered in small centres of employment over
wide areas of the province. Many of the smaller ethnic colonies were
also from forest tribes, but came from much greater distances than most
of the tribes which had large colonies in the town. Others, like the
Azande, came from the open grass-and-tree savanna areas beyond the
forest regions of the Congo Basin. There was also a fair representation
in small colonies of tribesmen from the lake and mountain areas on the
eastern borders of the Congo.

The ethnic heterogeneity of the population was thus accompanied
by highly variable sets of rural-urban relations. Distance from Stanleyville, the kinds of journeys involved, the ease or difficulty with which
migrants could maintain contact with their villages, and varying
opportunities and conditions in different areas and at different times
in the past, had all combined to affect patterns of migration and the
manner in which various tribes had participated in the life of the town.

Variations in modes of urban incorporation and in urban-rural
relations are, however, not our only interest. Equally significant are
the implications for social relations within the town of the large
number and small average size of the ethnic colonies. For many
inhabitants there was little possibility of living within a socially self-
sufficient tribal colony. At work, in the residential neighbourhood, and
in the community at large, most individuals were constantly face to
face with persons who held different tribal loyalties and who had
grown up in cultures which, though basically similar, were sufficiently
distinctive in language and custom to set one man off from another.

Equally, in contrast to many urban African communities, there was
little opportunity for individuals or groups to align themselves socially
and politically with or against any single dominant tribal element.[4]
This was partly because under Belgian colonial administration political
expression was strictly proscribed and partly on account of the very
composition of the population. Nor was there a single cultural current
that might have engulfed a majority of the population. On the contrary,
there were several supra-tribal currents, none of which showed any
clear dominance. The *Arabisés* were the bearers of one distinctive
culture which had in pre-European days affected many tribes from the
south and the east. *Arabisé* influence had, however, made little or no
impact on tribes living to the north, west and south-west of the town.
And, during the period of colonialism, Belgian administration had
effectively checked the possibility of any extension of *Arabisé* influence.
Swahili had become the main *lingua franca* of the region, but its widespread use cannot be taken as a measure of *Arabisé* influence; it was

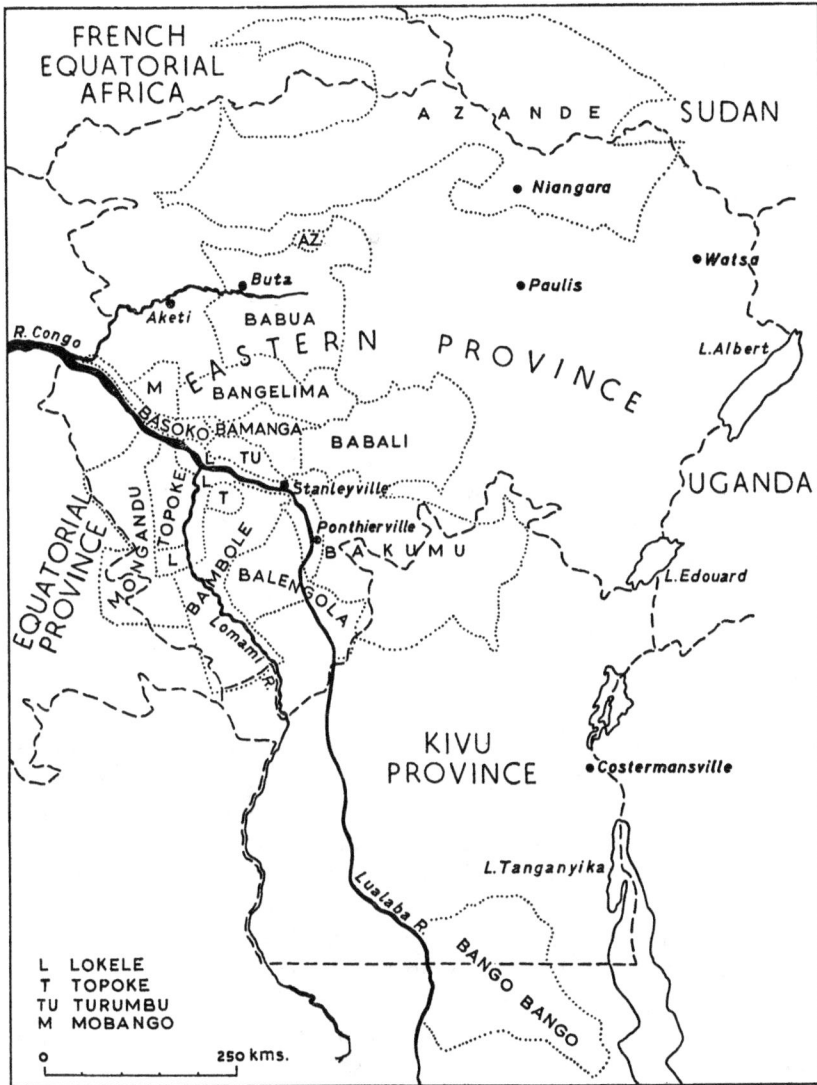

FIG. IV The North-Eastern Congo showing tribal areas of principal tribes
represented in Stanleyville

taught in the schools, and its spread was quite as much a result of European missionary activity and European administration as of the *Arabisé* intrusion of an earlier period. Nor was Swahili the only *lingua franca*. Lingala was used by a number of tribes to the west of Stanleyville, and had also gained fairly general currency as a result of its use in the *Force Publique*. Most persons who had been in town for some years were able to conduct ordinary day-to-day exchanges in both Swahili and Lingala. The law courts of the C.E.C. used either language, according to the preference of the participants in a case before them, but European officials normally expected Africans in the town to respond in whichever of the two languages they themselves happened to know best. Other distinctive cultural influences came from the Azande and Mangbetu, who had in pre-European days been politically dominant in the far north of the Eastern Province, and from the Lokele whose importance in numbers and wealth was in the current situation a significant factor influencing their relations with other tribes. But, in the particular colonial situation of the period, none of the tribal or supra-tribal influences was sufficiently strong or widespread to supersede the basic pattern of multi-group relations, and an individual's tribal affiliation, defined in the most exclusive sense, continued to have significance for him in a wide range of social situations.

RESIDENTIAL CONCENTRATION AND DISPERSION

Some measure of residential concentration was a notable feature of each of the nine principal ethnic colonies, but there was considerable variation in its nature and extent. The basic data from the sample survey are set out in Table 16, and are depicted in Figs. V to XV.[5] Two sets of observations are relevant, the first on differential representation in the three townships of the C.E.C. and in the *Arabisé* village, and the second on patterns of dispersion and concentration *within* the townships.

Some colonies, like the Bamanga and the Bambole, were largely concentrated in one township with no appreciable concentration elsewhere. For example, 89·4 per cent of the Bamanga were in Belge I, and 74·6 per cent of the Bambole in Belge II. Other colonies, like the Babua and the Babali, were found mainly in one township but also had a second smaller, though still substantial, proportion in another. The Babali, for example, had 59·0 per cent of their members in Brussels and 34·1 per cent in Belge I but were scarcely represented elsewhere. Finally, there were colonies with substantial proportions in each of the three townships of the C.E.C. though not in the *Arabisé* village. The Topoke, for example, had 49·5 per cent of their members in Belge I, 25·5 per cent in Brussels, and 23·7 per cent in Belge II.

The tendency for members of a colony to be concentrated in one settlement was in part a function of the geographical position of settlements in relation to routes of access from tribal areas in the countryside. In most cases the main concentration of a tribe was found in the township closest to the roads or—in the case of the Lokele—

to the river of access to the town from various parts of the hinterland. Thus the Bamanga and Babua from the north were mainly settled in Belge I; the Lokele and Bambole, from the west and south-west, lived mainly in Belge II; and the Babali and Bakumu, from eastern areas, were principally in Brussels. This also applied to the *Arabisés* who had over the years drawn the bulk of their immigrants from the south and south-east, either from other *Arabisés* villages along the Lualaba River or from tribes in that region. Out of the nine principal colonies, the Topoke were the only exception in that, though coming from south of the river, they had a majority of their members in Belge I and Brussels. And we shall see that there were special factors in their history of urban incorporation to account for this difference.

The geographical influence on the selection of inhabitants for the townships had an important implication for the development of social relations in the community. It meant that by and large people mingling residentially in any one area of the town were drawn from tribes with long histories of contact as neighbours in the countryside and, in many cases, some cultural affinity. Thus the implications of the high degree of heterogeneity in the population at large were, to some extent, offset in the townships, and the significance of the township as a socially distinctive locality was thereby emphasized. This was particularly noticeable in the case of Belge II where the affinities between the Lokele and tribes like the Bambole and the Topoke contributed to the development of a distinct 'Left Bank' identity.

The second set of observations on the concentration and dispersion of ethnic colonies relates to the patterns of distribution *within* the townships. Here the similarities and differences between colonies emerge more readily if we first relate the proportions of each tribe found in given survey tracts to the proportions of the total population in them. This is done in Table 17 which gives indices of under- and over-representation for the nine ethnic colonies in each of fifteen survey tracts depicted on page 70. As shown in the table, the indices can be used to arrive at an approximate rank order of the nine colonies based partly on their degrees of concentration in one or more tracts, and partly on the converse of the extent of their dispersion in several tracts.

There was no instance of the marked over-representation of a tribe maintained evenly throughout any one of the three townships of the C.E.C. The nearest approach to this was in Belge I, where the over-representation of the Babua was fairly marked in Tract A I, declined gradually on moving outwards through Tracts A II, A III, and A IV, and fell to near-proportional representation in Tract A V. In most other cases, marked over-representation in one or more tracts within a township was accompanied by very much lower representation in others. Although the degrees of dispersion and concentration varied considerably from one tribe to another, the general pattern was one of significant concentrations in small neighbourhoods within the townships. However, despite these concentrations, a high degree of ethnic

TABLE 16

Percentage distributions in residential areas and survey tracts of members of the nine principal ethnic colonies and of 'all other tribes'

(The survey tracts are shown in fig. V, p. 70.)

AREAS AND SURVEY TRACTS	LOKELE %	Arabisés %	BABUA %	BAKUMU %	TOPOKE %	BAMBOLE %	BABALI %	BALENGOLA %	BAMANGA %	ALL OTHER TRIBES %	TOTAL POPULATION %
Belge I											
A I	3·4	0·0	14·2	0·6	4·1	2·1	4·1	4·0	0·0	7·5	5·3
A II	3·6	0·3	12·5	3·1	5·1	2·5	11·4	2·0	0·0	7·4	5·5
A III	5·1	0·6	19·2	2·8	22·2	3·9	5·7	1·0	8·2	11·9	9·4
A IV	5·8	0·5	13·2	4·4	14·0	2·1	6·7	4·0	33·6	8·3	8·2
A V	6·0	1·4	4·5	7·9	4·1	2·5	6·2	4·5	47·6	5·5	6·6
Total	23·9	2·8	63·6	18·8	49·5	13·1	34·1	15·5	89·4	40·6	35·0
Brussels											
B I	1·9	4·5	14·1	6·3	1·9	3·6	6·0	5·0	0·0	13·7	7·3
B II	0·0	3·1	3·5	5·8	0·5	1·8	12·1	2·1	4·2	11·2	5·3
B III	0·0	2·4	4·6	17·6	4·8	0·4	24·1	2·9	0·0	5·7	5·0
B IV	0·8	0·3	10·4	14·4	9·0	4·3	11·6	1·7	0·0	4·7	5·0
B V	0·0	0·0	2·3	10·8	9·3	1·4	5·2	7·0	3·2	5·0	4·0
Total	2·7	10·3	34·9	54·9	25·5	11·5	59·0	18·7	7·4	40·3	26·6
Belge II											
C I	57·8	0·7	0·0	0·0	6·0	13·2	0·5	3·0	0·0	2·7	11·6
C II	10·1	10·2	1·0	11·7	11·7	35·0	2·1	36·8	2·6	10·1	11·8
C III	2·7	23·1	0·0	2·5	6·0	26·4	0·5	5·4	0·6	1·6	5·4
All areas	70·6	34·0	1·0	14·2	23·7	74·6	3·1	45·2	3·2	14·4	28·8
Railway camp	1·8	0·7	0·0	6·3	0·8	0·7	0·4	18·2	0·0	3·5	2·7
Arabisé village	1·1	52·3	0·4	5·8	0·5	0·0	3·5	2·5	0·0	1·4	6·9
All areas	100·1	100·1	99·9	100·0	100·1	99·9	100·1	100·1	100·0	100·2	100·0
Effective sample	754	581	429	360	332	240	218	217	160	1,623	4,914

TABLE 17

Approximate ranking of nine principal ethnic colonies according to indices of over- and under-representation in survey tracts

APPROXIMATE RANK ORDER	BELGE I					BRUSSELS					BELGE II			RAILWAY CAMP	Arabisé VILLAGE	NO. OF TRACTS IN WHICH THERE WAS MARKED OVER-REPRESENTATION	NO. OF TRACTS IN WHICH THERE WAS MARKED UNDER-REPRESENTATION
	A I	A II	A III	A IV	A V	B I	B II	B III	B IV	B V	C I	C II	C III	D	E		
Arabisés	0·0	0·1	0·1	0·1	0·2	0·6	0·6	0·5	0·1	0·0	0·1	0·9	4·3	0·5	7·6	2	12
Bambole	0·4	0·5	0·4	0·3	0·4	0·5	0·3	0·1	0·9	0·4	1·1	3·0	4·9	0·3	0·0	2	11
Bamanga	0·0	0·0	0·9	4·3	7·3	0·0	0·8	0·0	0·0	0·8	0·0	0·2	0·1	0·0	0·0	2	10
Lokele	0·6	0·7	0·5	0·7	0·9	0·3	0·0	0·0	0·2	0·0	5·0	0·9	0·5	0·7	0·2	1	9
Balengola	0·8	0·5	0·1	0·5	0·7	0·7	0·4	0·6	0·3	1·8	0·3	3·1	1·0	6·7	0·4	3	8
Babali	0·8	2·1	0·6	0·8	0·9	0·8	2·3	4·8	2·3	1·3	0·0	0·2	0·1	0·1	0·5	4	6
Topoke	0·8	0·9	2·4	1·7	0·6	0·3	0·1	1·0	1·8	2·3	0·5	1·0	1·1	0·3	0·1	4	6
Bakumu	0·1	0·6	0·3	0·5	1·2	0·9	1·1	3·5	2·9	2·7	0·0	1·0	0·5	2·3	0·8	4	6
Babua	2·7	2·3	2·0	1·6	0·7	1·9	0·7	0·9	2·1	0·6	0·1	0·1	0·0	0·0	0·1	6	6

The index of representation is established by dividing the percentage of *all* inhabitants in a tract into the corresponding percentage for one tribe. For example, 11·6 per cent of all Babali were in Tract B IV, but this contained only 5·0 per cent of the total population of all tribes so that the Babali were over-represented by 2·3. An index of 1·0 indicates even or proportional representation. Indices of 1·4 and over were taken to indicate marked 'over-representation'; indices of 0·7 to 1·3 were taken to indicate near 'proportional representation'; and indices of 0·6 and below to indicate marked 'under-representation'.

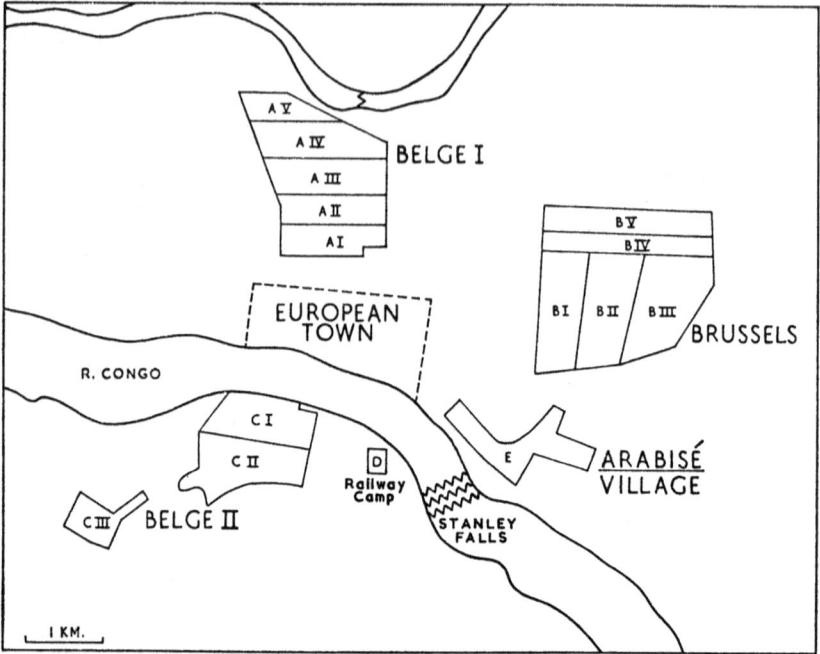

Fig. V Sketch map of Stanleyville showing the survey tracts referred to in the text

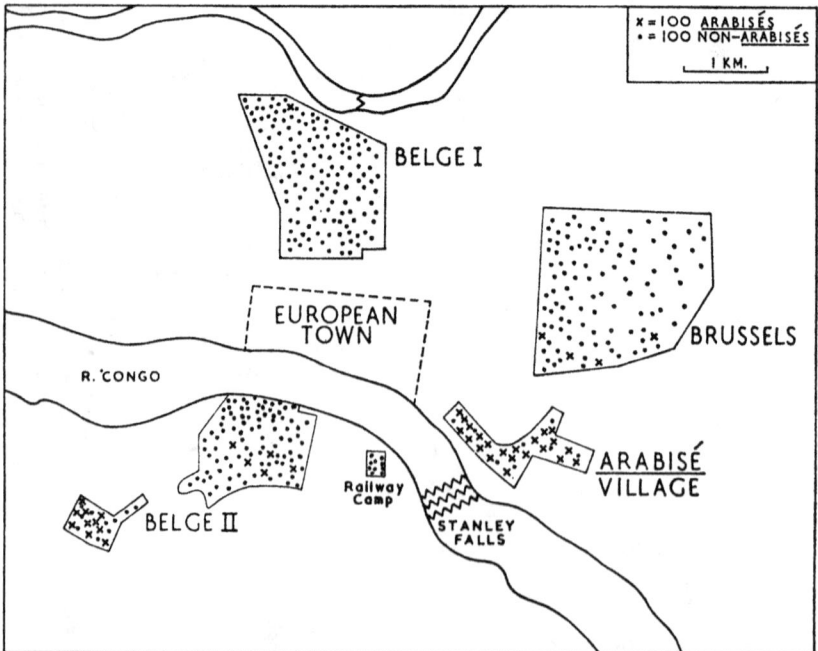

Fig. VI Residential distribution of the *Arabisés*

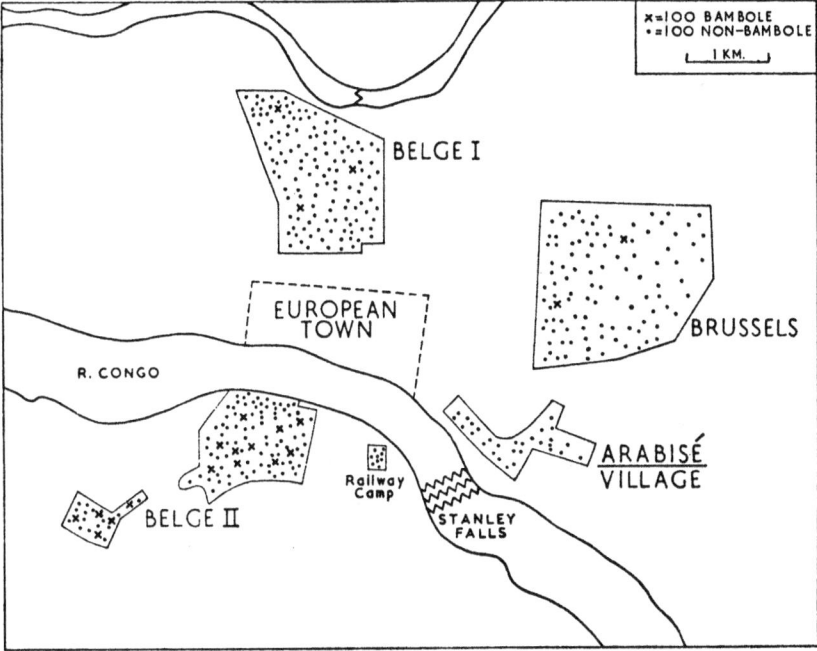

FIG. VII Residential distribution of the Bambole

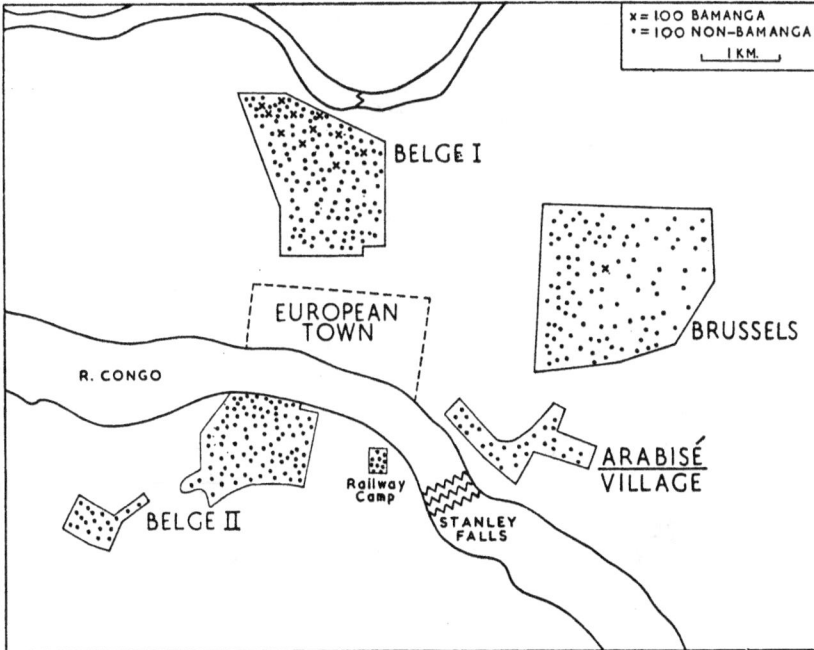

FIG. VIII Residential distribution of the Bamanga

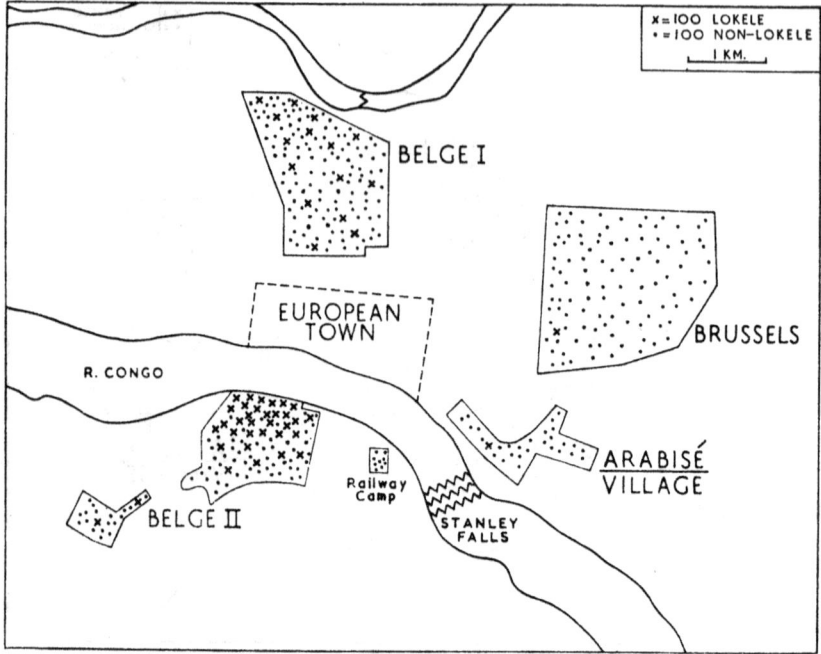

FIG. IX Residential distribution of the Lokele

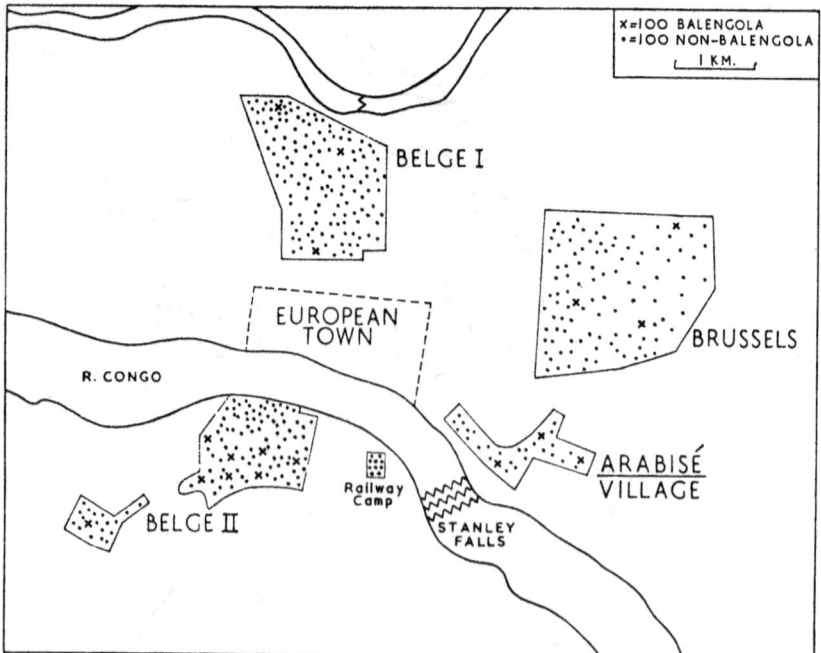

FIG. X Residential distribution of the Balengola

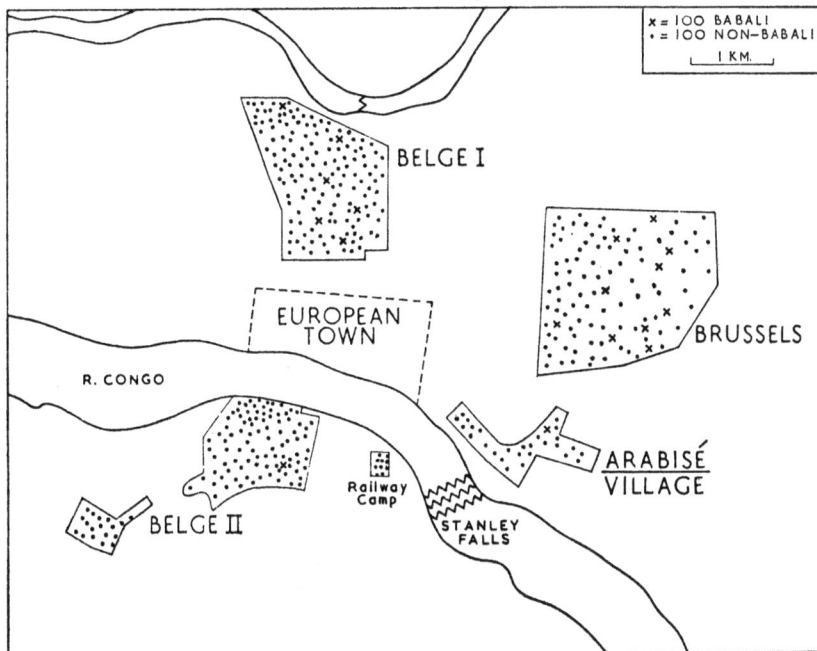

Fig. XI Residential distribution of the Babali

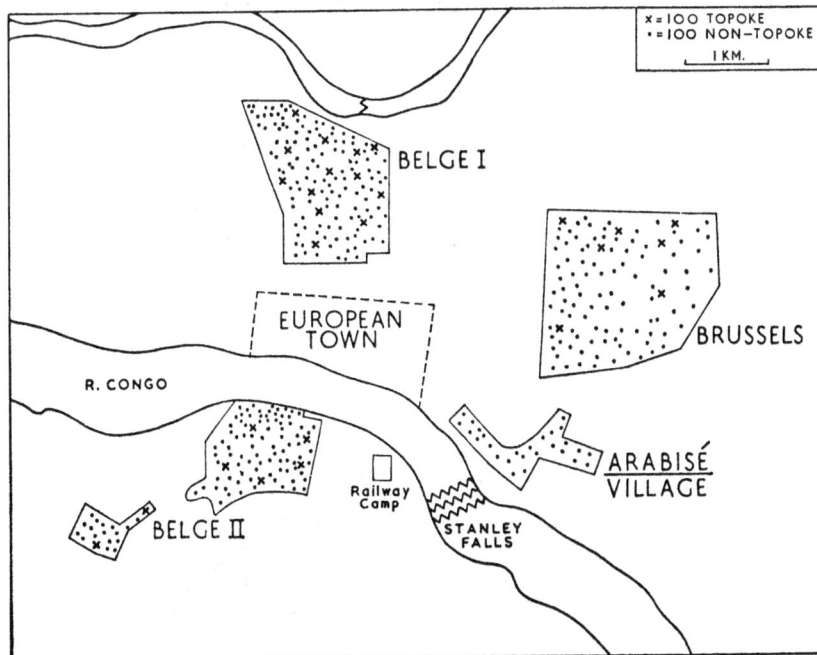

Fig. XII Residential distribution of the Topoke

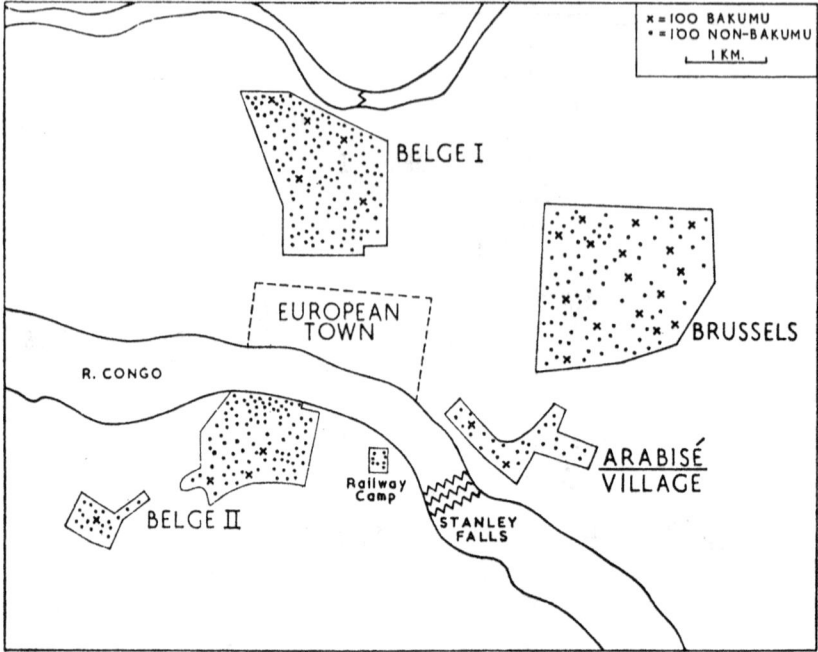

FIG. XIII Residential distribution of the Bakumu

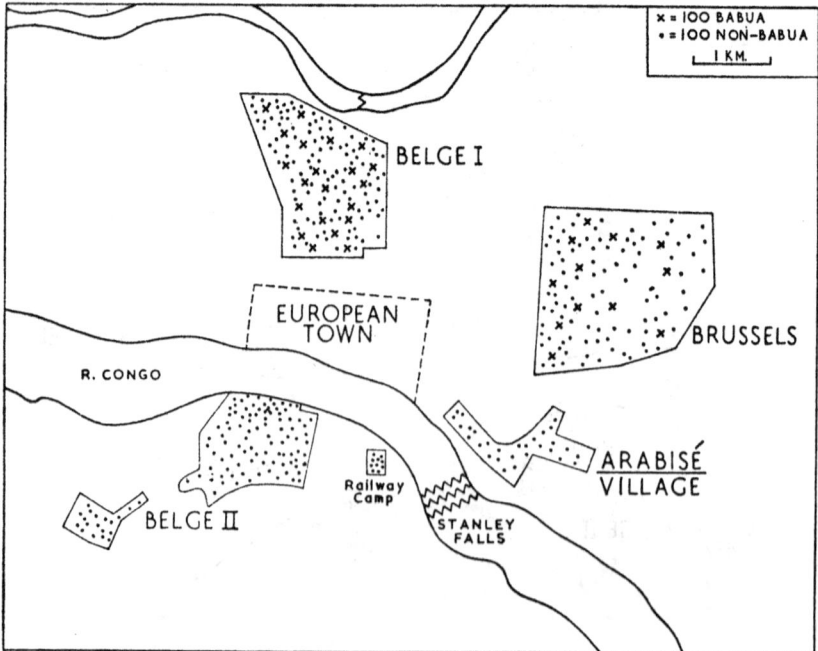

FIG. XIV Residential distribution of the Babua

heterogeneity was a marked feature of most localities. The main exceptions to this were the *Arabisé* village, where 86·7 per cent of the inhabitants were *Arabisés*; the area covered by Tract C II in Belge II, where 80·6 per cent were Lokele; and the detached part of Belge II, where 52·9 per cent were *Arabisés*. No other survey tract had a majority of any one ethnic element. Thus, although 47·6 per cent of the Bamanga were in Tract A V, they constituted only 24·9 per cent of the population there; and while 35·0 per cent of the Balengola were in Tract C II, they accounted for only 13·7 per cent of the total population in the tract. And so on. In some areas there were marked tribal clusters in one or two avenues and, sometimes, in one section of an avenue. For example, a complete enumeration undertaken in Tract B III revealed that in one avenue 34 out of 58 dwelling compounds had Babali title-holders, but the Babali made up only 20 per cent of all the title-holders in the tract. Similarly, in the same area there were clusters of Bakumu and of Barumbi (a tribe that constituted a very small colony in the town).[6] Other marked clusters were of Bambole in Tracts C II and C III, of Bamanga in Tracts A IV and A V, and of Babudu (another small colony) and Babali in Tract B II. Relatively homogeneous clusters were most common in Belge II and in the outer areas of Old Brussels and of Belge I. They had not developed to any extent in New Brussels which had been settled in recent years under the pressure of a much greater demand for dwelling compounds than in earlier years. There is also evidence that tribal clusters had existed in the inner areas of Old Brussels and Belge I in earlier times but that they had largely disintegrated with the growth of economic and status differentiation and with the increasing pressure of demand for accommodation.[7]

THREE TRIBAL CASE HISTORIES

In this section the case histories of the Lokele, Babua, and Topoke are briefly outlined to illustrate the kind of relation that existed between differing modes of urban incorporation and the differing social configurations of various ethnic colonies in the town.

We have seen that the Lokele are a river people, whose tribal homes are situated in a narrow stretch of exceptionally fertile and densely populated land along the banks of the Congo River, starting a few miles downstream from Stanleyville. They had the reputation in the town of being the most skilled fishermen and canoe navigators on the river. They first came to Stanleyville in its earliest days as a small commercial centre and administrative outpost, and they were incorporated into the town in a quite distinctive way.[8] They settled on the left bank of the river where they were for years the only significant colony of immigrants, and where they continued to lead a domestic and neighbourhood life in many ways akin to that in their tribal areas. They were advantageously placed to engage in fishing and in the growing urban trade in articles of native manufacture and in agricultural produce. It seems that in carrying out these functions they strengthened rather than weakened the links with their home villages. Certainly, their early establishment as an urban colony took place without creating any sharp discontinuity between town and village. Over the years, considerable numbers came to settle in Belge I. Many of these were clerks and other better-paid workers who wished to participate in the more fashionable and more 'civilized' life of the urban centre. In moving to the town side of the river, however, the large majority kept in touch with their kinsmen and with the distinctively Lokele 'community' on the left bank.

With easy access to their home areas and with cheap canoe transport on the river, Lokele women found themselves in a very favourable position to compete against women of other tribes for the control of the Stanleyville markets in fish, vegetables and fruits. Over the years they came to be the dominant and most successful group of women traders in the town. Lokele men expected their womenfolk to trade regularly whereas the trading activities of most non-Lokele women were usually casual and intermittent. A Lokele woman brought to her marriage a dowry which she was expected to invest in trade, and there were some cases of Lokele women who made trading profits equal to or higher than the wages earned by their husbands.

The commercial success of Lokele women was a basic factor in the integration of Lokele urban society. It brought to the Lokele a measure of wealth which set them off from other tribes economically and contributed to the maintenance of their ethnic identity. The comparative wealth of Lokele families enabled boys of the tribe to compete with considerable success for education and for white collar jobs. Nearly 20 per cent of Lokele men were white collar workers, a figure significantly higher than for any other tribe; and, conversely, the proportion who were ordinary labourers was considerably lower than average (Table 32). A small but important minority of Lokele men also entered retail trade in non-native goods such as bottled beer, tinned foods, and cigarettes.

The Lokele's achievements in all these respects brought them the reputation of being 'clever' and 'superior' to most other tribes. In casual conversation people frequently named them as the tribe with an ability to get on, and they were sometimes held to rank with well-known tribes of whom the local inhabitants either had no direct experience or whom they only knew through a few inhabitants in the town (e.g. the Baganda, the Hausa, the 'Senegalais', the 'Coastmen', and the Bakongo). At other times they were compared with the *Arabisés* who 'were the rulers here before the Europeans', or with the Azande who were sometimes singled out on account of their legendary military and technological prowess ('they knew how to make guns').

The comparative wealth of the Lokele combined with the success and industriousness of their women had contributed to the stabilization of their bridewealth payments at a very much higher-than-average level for the town. Few men who were not themselves Lokele could hope to marry a Lokele woman. Nor, under normal circumstances, could a Lokele man meet obligations to his wife's family without considerable assistance from his own kinsmen. The women of the tribe had the reputation of being particularly virtuous and the surveillance of Lokele parents over their daughters was claimed by some to be as strict in town as in their tribal villages. This was in turn related to the fact that the Lokele continued in their changing urban situation to attach exceptionally high value to the continuity of family life. As shown in Table 18, it was rather exceptional for a Lokele woman to be unmarried. At the same time, there was, in sharp contrast to many other tribes, notably the Babua referred to below, a strong emphasis on the preservation of traditional values relating to a man's role as husband, father, and kinsman. This is reflected in the figures on the marital status of Lokele men (Table 19).

We have already seen that the Lokele remained residentially concentrated on the left bank of the river in an area of Belge II where there were few non-Lokele. It was largely to this area that new Lokele immigrants turned to find accommodation and other assistance from kinsmen and friends on their first arrival in town. Thus, in the case of the Lokele, there was a whole complex of relations in which rural and urban life were intimately interwoven, while marriage, the rearing of children, and other aspects of domestic and neighbourhood life, continued in town, as in the country, to be largely enacted within a distinctively Lokele setting.

TABLE 18

Marital status of a sample of 187 Lokele women

| STATUS | AGE CATEGORIES | | | | | | | | | |
| | 16–25 | | 26–35 | | 36–45 | | 46 and over | | Total | |
	No.	%	No.	%	No.	%	No.	%	No.	%
Married	65	83·3	57	89·1	27	81·8	6	50·0	155	82·9
Living with a man to whom not married	0	0·0	0	0·0	1	3·0	0	0·0	1	0·5
Widowed, living singly	0	0·0	0	0·0	1	3·0	4	33·3	5	2·7
Divorced, living singly	2	2·6	6	9·4	4	12·1	2	16·7	14	7·5
Never married, living singly	11	14·1	1	1·5	0	0·0	0	0·0	12	6·4
Total	78	100·0	64	100·0	33	99·9	12	100·0	187	100·0

Note: This table excludes seven married women under 16 years of age.

TABLE 19

Marital status of a sample of 215 Lokele men

STATUS	16–25		26–35		36–45		46 and over		Total	
	No.	%	No.	%	No.	%	No.	%	No.	%
Married	38	44·7	63	90·0	40	90·9	13	81·3	154	71·6
Living with a woman to whom not married	2	2·4	0	0·0	2	4·5	0	0·0	4	1·9
Widowed, living singly	0	0·0	1	1·4	0	0·0	1	6·3	2	0·9
Divorced, living singly	0	0·0	3	4·3	2	4·5	1	6·3	6	2·8
Never married, living singly	45	52·9	3	4·3	0	0·0	1	6·3	49	22·8
Total	85	100·0	70	100·0	44	99·9	16	100·2	215	100·0

In sharp contrast to the Lokele, the Babua were said to have a weak sense of tribal solidarity associated with a relative indifference about the continuity of family life. They came from an area some 300 kilometres to the north of Stanleyville and, on leaving their villages, they normally migrated to Buta in the first instance. In the early days of European colonization, they had acquired the reputation of making good soldiers. Substantial numbers had been drafted into the *Force Publique*, and the first settlement of Babua in the early days of Stanleyville's growth was made up of discharged soldiers. In more recent years, they had acquired a similar reputation as good lorry drivers, a skill which they tended to pass on to new arrivals in the town. The survey sample of Babua wage-earners in fact contained 16 per cent of lorry drivers (as against 6 per cent in the population as a whole), and they also had appreciably higher-than-average proportions of mechanics and masons. Among European employers, the Babua had the general reputation of being good and efficient workers, and their services were much in demand.

The Babua's earliest settlement in the town had been in the older, in-lying part of Belge I, but over the years they had become relatively evenly dispersed throughout Belge I and in large areas of Brussels. As one of the oldest tribal colonies in the town, they enjoyed substantial advantages over the relatively recent immigrants. We shall see that a high proportion of Babua household heads were title-holders of compounds (Table 29), and that they frequently took in rent-paying tenants. We shall also see that only a small minority of Babua men had married in their tribal areas (Table 30). Both at home and in Stanleyville the tribe had a rate of fertility so low that it seems certain that as a population they were declining in numbers. The women of the tribe showed a strong spirit of independence from their menfolk, a fact which commonly drew comments of disapprobation from members of tribes like the Lokele who placed great store on large families and on virtuous women. Moreover, Babua men and women commonly married members of other tribes. Over a third of all Babua men in the sample were married to non-Babua women and, for marriages taking place in Stanleyville itself, the proportion was even higher (Table 33). As shown in Tables 20 and 21, nearly a half of all Babua men and women in the town were not married. In striking contrast to Lokele women, it was not uncommon for Babua women to live singly or with partners to whom they were not married.

Both the Lokele and the Babua were among the tribes most involved in the life of the town, though in very different ways. The contrast between them makes the point that in studying different colonies we may be studying differing processes of urban incorporation. The Lokele were, in their family, domestic, and neighbourhood relations, a relatively 'closed' group, maintaining and developing a distinctively Lokele urban way of life, and their urban situation calls for analysis in the context of a social and cultural system embracing both town and village. In contrast, the Babua colony in Stanleyville was made up of individuals many of whom were not in touch with their villages, and such relations as there were between town and tribal area were much less relevant to an analysis of their life in town than in the case of the Lokele. Moreover, the Babua's way of life in town had relatively little distinctive cultural content; there is a sense in which their way of urban life was 'the Stanleyville way of life', developed by persons with little continuing participation in rural-tribal life.

Our third case, the Topoke, had a social configuration markedly different to that of either Babua or Lokele. Though coming from a tribal area adjacent to that of the Lokele and, in some parts, no further than 100 kilometres from Stanleyville, the Topoke were in the early years of colonization little affected by the development of the wage-earning economy or by missionaries[9]; it was not till the 1930s that they entered wage-earning employment to any appreciable extent, and the growth of their colony in Stanleyville dates mainly from World War II and the immediate post-war period. By 1952 they had about 3,000 members settled in town and their rate of immigration far exceeded the rate for most of the principal ethnic colonies (Cf. Table 27). Though many Topoke men had been to mission schools in their tribal area for a few years, they came to town principally as ordinary labourers. As compared to the Babua and Lokele, who had nuclei of well-established fellow-tribesmen in the town, the Topoke had less possibility of being accommodated by kinsmen on first arrival or of getting assistance in finding job openings or of acquiring a modicum of occupational skills from established specialized manual workers. Only a third of all Topoke households had their own dwelling compounds as against two thirds of the Lokele and three quarters of the Babua (Table 29). And such dwelling compounds as were held by

TABLE 20

Marital status of a sample of 165 Babua women

STATUS	AGE CATEGORIES									
	16–25		26–35		36–45		46 and over		Total	
	No.	%	No.	%	No.	%	No.	%	No.	%
Married	28	63·6	32	52·5	19	47·5	11	55·0	90	54·5
Living with a man to whom not married	4	9·1	9	14·8	2	5·0	1	5·0	16	9·7
Widowed, living singly	0	0·0	0	0·0	5	12·5	3	15·0	8	4·8
Divorced, living singly	5	11·4	17	27·9	11	27·5	3	15·0	36	21·8
Never married, living singly	7	15·9	3	4·9	3	7·5	2	10·0	15	9·1
Total	44	100·0	61	100·1	40	100·0	20	100·0	165	99·9

Topoke title-holders were usually crowded with subsidiary households of kinsmen and fellow villagers. Moreover, the colony had an excessively disproportionate ratio of men to women (Table 26), many of the young men being unmarried or having left their wives at home. Such Topoke as could not find accommodation with kinsmen were commonly encountered as rent-paying tenants, sharing rooms in twos and threes on the compounds of members of other tribes.

As shown in Table 22, the women of the tribe were, with very few exceptions, married. Few Topoke families had been in town long enough to have urban-bred daughters of marriageable age, and the few women who found themselves widowed or divorced in the town seldom qualified to stay in the C.E.C. as residents in their own right. (They would probably seldom have done so anyway, given the Topoke's adherence to family and kinship obligations and sanctions.) Like the Lokele they had a high birth rate and large families. Except for youths, a high proportion of the men were married (Table 23), and the younger men who had come to town unmarried usually recruited brides from their home villages in preference to Stanleyville women.

Being predominantly recent unskilled immigrants, few Topoke men had diverse sets of social relations such as those which typically linked the Babua, and even to some extent the Lokele, to other members of the urban population. They were known in the town as an 'uncivilized' and 'backward' tribe. Their wide dispersal through all three of the

TABLE 21

Marital status of a sample of 178 Babua men

STATUS	AGE CATEGORIES									
	16–25		26–35		36–45		46 and over		Total	
	No.	%	No.	%	No.	%	No.	%	No.	%
Married	12	34·3	25	48·1	33	66·0	25	61·0	95	53·4
Living with a woman to whom not married	2	5·7	5	9·6	3	6·0	6	14·7	16	9·0
Widowed, living singly	0	0·0	0	0·0	0	0·0	2	4·9	2	1·1
Divorced, living singly	5	14·3	11	21·2	13	26·0	7	17·1	36	20·2
Never married, living singly	16	45·7	11	21·2	1	2·0	1	2·4	29	16·3
Total	35	100·0	52	100·1	50	100·0	41	100·1	178	100·0

townships of the C.E.C. was a direct consequence of their late arrival on the Stanleyville scene and of their high rate of influx at the time of the present study. As new immigrants in a generally disadvantageous position to compete with other tribes in town, the Topoke attached exceptional importance to their home villages as sources of security and as places to which to return in the event of unexpected difficulties in town. At the same time the pressure of an increasing population in their tribal area was an important factor keeping them in town.

The Lokele, Babua, and Topoke were all somewhat exceptional colonies. The Lokele were unique in being the only colony to enjoy the advantages of the particular combination of cheap and easy access to the town, and an agricultural surplus in their home areas, and of a growing population and a well-established position in the town's markets, offices, and workshops. The Babua and Topoke were not unique, but they were both exceptional in that each exhibited in high degree various characteristics which were common to many tribes but which were seldom found in such striking combinations. The Bamanga, for example, had a reputation similar to that of the Topoke for being

TABLE 22

Marital status of a sample of 91 Topoke women

STATUS	AGE CATEGORIES									
	16–25		26–35		36–45		46 and over		Total	
	No.	%	No.	%	No.	%	No.	%	No.	%
Married	39	97·5	33	84·6	7	87·5	1	25·0	80	87·9
Living with a man to whom not married	0	0·0	2	5·1	0	0·0	0	0·0	2	2·2
Widowed, living singly	0	0·0	1	2·6	0	0·0	2	50·0	3	3·3
Divorced, living singly	0	0·0	2	5·1	0	0·0	1	25·0	3	3·3
Never married, living singly	1	2·5	1	2·6	1	12·5	0	0·0	3	3·3
Total	40	100·0	39	100·0	8	100·0	4	100·0	91	100·0

Note: This table excludes two married women under 16 years of age.

TABLE 23

Marital status of a sample of 142 Topoke men

STATUS	AGE CATEGORIES									
	16–25		26–35		36–45		46 and over		Total	
	No.	%	No.	%	No.	%	No.	%	No.	%
Married	33	50·0	51	82·3	8	100·0	4	66·7	96	67·6
Living with a woman to whom not married	0	0·0	1	1·6	0	0·0	0	0·0	1	0·7
Widowed, living singly	0	0·0	2	3·2	0	0·0	1	16·7	3	2·1
Divorced, living singly	2	3·0	3	4·8	0	0·0	1	16·7	6	4·2
Never married, living singly	31	47·0	5	8·1	0	0·0	0	0·0	36	25·4
Total	66	100·0	62	100·0	8	100·0	6	100·1	142	100·0

'backward' and 'uncivilized', but their position in town was less difficult owing to a longer history of wage-earning, to a lower current rate of immigration, and to having a somewhat larger nucleus of well-established urban dwellers. (Cf. Table 27.) Or, to take another example, the Babali had many of the features of the Babua, but had been rather less successful in the field of employment. (Cf. Table 32.)

INTER-ETHNIC DIFFERENCES IN DEMOGRAPHIC COMPOSITION

The presence in one community of ethnic colonies differing as markedly as did the Lokele, Babua, and Topoke, holds important methodological implications for the study of urban social relations. Before referring to these implications, however, I present a series of data on the social and demographic composition of the nine largest ethnic colonies in the town. On the basis of the demographic data we are able to detect three main 'types' of age and sex structures, and it will be seen that the Lokele, Babua, and Topoke, are good examples of each of these three 'types'.

Figs. XV to XXIII depict the population pyramids of the nine principal ethnic colonies.[10] Inspection of the pyramids suggests that seven of the nine colonies fall into three 'types' and that the two remaining tribes can be seen as intermediate cases. Type 1 is represented by the Lokele (Fig. XV): it has a broad base tending to become steadily narrower with increasing age. Type 2 is best represented by the Topoke (Fig. XVII): it has a broad base like the pyramid for Type 1, but is pinched at the 'waist' (between the ages of 5 and 15 years) and then broadens between the ages of 15 and 35 years before again narrowing very rapidly above the age of 35 years. Type 3, which is best represented by the Babali (Fig. XXIII), is more in the shape of an onion than a pyramid: the base of children is narrow, the figure bulges in the middle, and the decline in the older age groups is more gradual than in Type 2, leaving a proportion of adults over 45 years approximately equal to the proportion of children below 16 years of age. Of the remaining principal tribes, the Babua (Fig. XXII) and the *Arabisés* (Fig. XXI) fit Type 3 fairly well, the Bambole (Fig. XVI) and Balengola (Fig. XVIII) tend to fit Type 2, while the Bamanga (Fig. XIX) and Bakumu (Fig. XX) are the two intermediate cases which can be viewed as approximating to either Type 2 or Type 3.

A partial explanation of these different 'types' of population emerges as we analyse further aspects of the nine populations and relate these to the three case studies of the Lokele, Babua, and Topoke. Table 24 shows a wide range of fertility ratios (number of live children aged 5 years or less as a ratio of women aged 16–45 years). For the entire population of Stanleyville, the ratio was 489 (i.e. 489 children under 5 years of age for every 1,000 women aged 16–45 years) and for the nine principal colonies taken together it was 465. But between the nine principal tribes, the ratio ran from the high levels of 983 for the Lokele and 863 for the Bambole, to the extremely low levels of 181 for the Babua and 159 for the Babali.[11]

Demographers have for long recognized that the ratio of children to women in any population is an exceedingly complex phenomenon. Firstly, this particular ratio is one which measures the effects not only of recent fertility but also of infant mortality. Secondly, reproduction is, we know, influenced by both biological and social factors. In examining any aspect of the problem we therefore need to distinguish between fecundity (the physical capacity for child-bearing) and fertility (the reproduction actually achieved). Bearing this in mind it is evident that the systematic study of the factors underlying the differential tribal rates revealed in Table 24 goes well beyond the scope of the present study. Yet it is of central importance for the analysis of different types of urban colony to note that differences in the fertility ratios of the nine tribes were perhaps partly a function of differential fecundity, and that, *whether this was so or not*, they were certainly to some extent a result of differences in actual fertility and not only, *if at all*, of differential infant mortality. This claim is based on two sets of information.

TABLE 24

Fertility ratios of the nine principal ethnic colonies

COLONY	'TYPE' OF POPULATION	EFFECTIVE SAMPLE OF WOMEN AGED 16–45 YEARS	EFFECTIVE SAMPLE OF CHILDREN AGED 0–5 YEARS	FERTILITY RATIO*
Lokele	Type 1	174	171	983
Bambole	Type 2	51	44	863
Topoke	Type 2	79	65	823
Balengola	Type 2	55	38	691
Bamanga	Intermediate	51	20	392
Bakumu	Intermediate	128	31	242
Arabisés	Type 3	208	41	197
Babua	Type 3	149	27	181
Babali	Type 3	69	11	159
Nine principal colonies	—	964	448	465
Total population in Stanleyville	—	1,352	661	489

$$* \text{ Fertility ratio} = \frac{\text{No. of live children aged 0–5 years} \times 1,000}{\text{No. of women aged 16–45 years}}$$

The first set refers to the fertility reported by women of the nine tribes in Stanleyville at the time of the study, and the second to available estimates of the demographic composition of some of the parent populations in the countryside.

POPULATION PYRAMIDS

FIG. XV   LOKELE

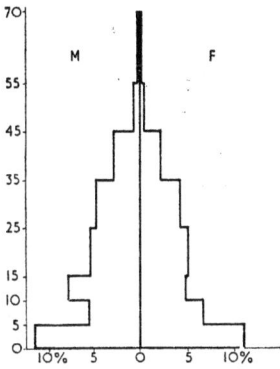

FIG. XVI   BAMBOLE

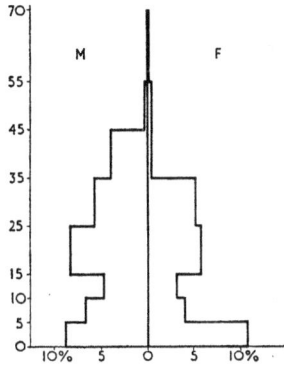

FIG. XVII   TOPOKE

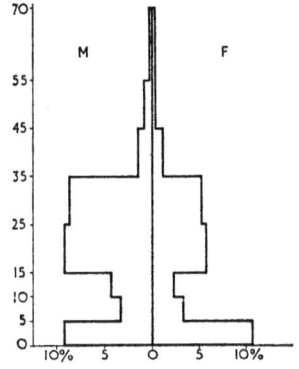

FIG. XVIII   BALENGOLA

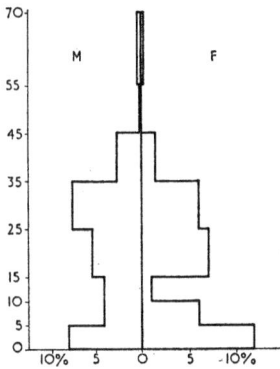

FIG. XIX   BAMANGA

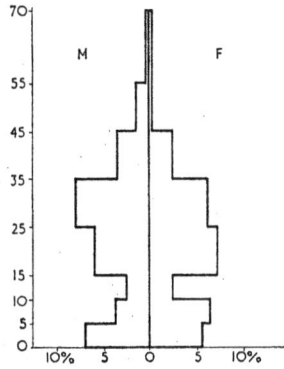

FIG. XX   BAKUMU

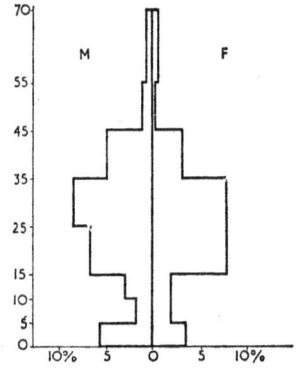

FIG. XXI   ARABISÉS

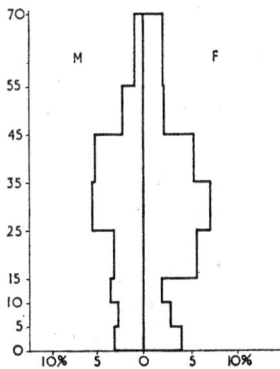

FIG. XXII   BABUA

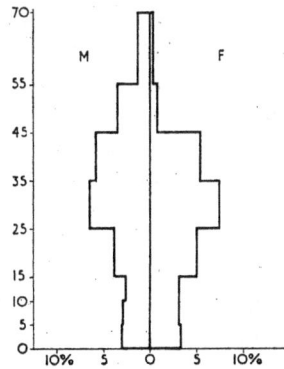

FIG. XXIII   BABALI

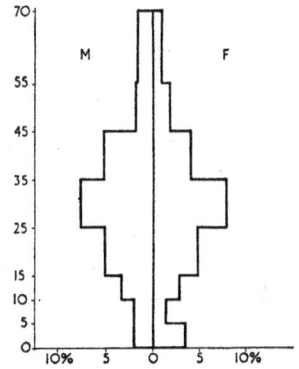

The achieved fertility (unadjusted for age) of the women of the nine tribes in 1952–53 was as follows:

A sample of 184 Lokele women had borne a mean of 2·82 children
,,   53 Bamanga   ,,   ,,   1·74   ,,
,,   84 Topoke   ,,   ,,   1·65   ,,
,,   56 Balengola   ,,   ,,   1·61   ,,
,,   274 *Arabisés*   ,,   ,,   1·57   ,,
,,   55 Bambole   ,,   ,,   1·55   ,,
,,   169 Babua   ,,   ,,   1·12   ,,
,,   137 Bakumu   ,,   ,,   1·20   ,,
,,   83 Babali   ,,   ,,   1·08   ,,

Apart from the wide range of variation between tribes, it is of interest to note that their rank order here approximates fairly closely to their rank order in Table 24. And when the above rates are adjusted for age, the tribes fall in the following order which is even closer to that of Table 24: Lokele (with 3·32 children per woman), Bamanga (2·23), Bambole (1·89), Topoke (1·87), Balengola (1·56), *Arabisés* (1·46), Bakumu (1·27), Babua (1·09), and Babali (1·03).[12] The above observations thus reveal a very close relation between differences in the fertility ratio and in achieved fertility.

The second set of information refers to the fertility of these tribes in their rural areas. It is well known that birth rates for different tribes in the north-eastern Congo varied markedly from one area to another, and often from one tribe to another in the same area. As early as 1930–31, Bertrand had classified various areas of the north-eastern Congo as having a '*mouvement démographique nettement défavorable*' or a '*mouvement nettement favorable*' or a '*mouvement incertain*'. A map he drew clearly classifies the rural areas of the Lokele and Topoke as having a 'mouvement favorable', the area of the Babua as having a 'mouvement défavorable' and the areas of the remaining principal tribes in Stanleyville of 1952–53 as having a '*mouvement incertain*'.[13] Since the time of Bertrand much evidence has accumulated to confirm his observation of marked differentials. For example, an investigation conducted in 1950 into the demographic composition of what were described by the author as 'specimen populations' from a number of rural areas in the Eastern Province yielded the following results for seven of the nine tribes with which we are here concerned: persons classified as 'children' constituted 21·0 per cent of the Babali, 22·7 per cent of the Babua, 27·8 per cent of the Balengola, 30·0 per cent of the Bakumu, 31·6 per cent of the Bambole, 39·7 per cent of the Bamanga, and 42·7 per cent of the Topoke.[14] Unfortunately, evidence of this kind is patently imprecise. But the frequency of similar reports by different observers at different times can reasonably be allowed to carry a good deal of weight.

Taking all such evidence into account and relating it to the data gathered in Stanleyville, it appears that differences in fertility in the rural areas persisted in town[15] and that the fertility ratios recorded in Table 24 may be regarded as demographic features carried over into the town from parent populations in the countryside. As such, these differences have to be taken as given; they are differences which certainly affected social relations in the town, but which do not necessarily call for explanation in terms of these relations, nor in terms of the process of urbanization.[16]

Table 25 gives the age composition of adult men in the nine colonies. In this respect too, there was not much difference between the popula-

TABLE 25

Inter-ethnic variations in the ages of adult men (16 years and over)

COLONY	'TYPE' OF POPULATION	EFFECTIVE SAMPLE OF ADULT MEN	APPROX. MEDIAN AGE IN YEARS	PERCENTAGE DISTRIBUTIONS				
				16–25	26–35	36–45	Over 45	Total
Bambole	Type 2	77	26	45·5	32·4	22·1	0·0	100·0
Topoke	Type 2	138	28	42·8	45·7	5·8	5·7	100·0
Lokele	Type 1	211	29	40·8	32·2	19·9	7·1	100·0
Balengola	Type 2	70	30	30·0	47·1	17·1	5·8	100·0
Bamanga	Intermediate	53	31	28·3	43·4	20·7	7·6	100·0
Bakumu	Intermediate	143	31	29·4	39·2	22·4	9·1	100·1
Babali	Type 3	97	33	24·7	34·0	22·7	18·5	99·9
Arabisés	Type 3	192	36	19·8	30·7	30·7	18·7	99·9
Babua	Type 3	180	37	16·1	32·2	26·7	25·0	100·0
Nine principal colonies	—	1,161	29	30·1	36·0	21·6	12·3	100·0
Total population of Stanleyville	—	1,895	29	28·2	35·7	21·4	14·7	100·0

tion of the town and the nine principal tribes taken together, but there were important variations among the nine largest tribes. Thus Bambole men had a median age of 26 years, and 45·6 per cent of them were between 16 and 25 years, whereas, at the other extreme, Babua men had a median age of 37 years, and only 16·1 per cent were 16 to 25 years of age.

The *adult* sex ratios of the nine colonies are given in Table 26. On this score, the nine populations taken together were clearly not representative of the population as a whole. As in other respects, however, there were marked differences between the nine samples, ranging from ratios of 164·3 for the Topoke, and 140 for the Bambole, to 100 for the Bamanga and to only 70·1 for the *Arabisés*. The *Arabisés* were in this regard a most exceptional case for they were permitted in their own village, though not in the C.E.C., to settle with more than one wife, and about 10 per cent of the men in the *Arabisé* village were in fact polygynist. Moreover, they had a large number of elderly women, most of them widows who had married and outlived polygynous men older than themselves. But even if we exclude the *Arabisés* from our comparison, the range of variation among the remaining eight colonies is still wide.

Table 27 gives percentage distributions for the adult men in each of the nine colonies according to their lengths of residence in Stanleyville. As in most previous tables the nine principal colonies taken together do not differ appreciably from the population of the town as a whole but there were again marked differences among the nine populations. Only 15·2 per cent of the Babali and 16·0 per cent of the *Arabisés* men

TABLE 26

Adult sex ratios of the nine principal colonies

COLONY	'TYPE' OF POPULATION	EFFECTIVE SAMPLE OF MEN AGED 16 YEARS AND OVER	EFFECTIVE SAMPLE OF WOMEN AGED 16 YEARS AND OVER	SEX RATIO: MEN PER 100 WOMEN
Topoke	Type 2	138	84	164·3
Bambole	Type 2	77	55	140·0
Balengola	Type 2	70	56	125·0
Babali	Type 3	97	83	116·9
Lokele	Type 1	211	184	114·6
Babua	Type 3	180	170	105·8
Bakumu	Intermediate	143	137	104·4
Bamanga	Intermediate	53	53	100·0
Arabisés	Type 3	192	274	70·1
Nine principal colonies	—	1,161	1,096	105·9
Total population of Stanleyville	—	1,895	1,612	117·5

had been in town for 3 years or less, but close on 40 per cent of the Topoke and Bambole were relative newcomers. Conversely, the proportions of men who had been in the town for more than 10 years ran from 5·9 per cent for the Topoke to over 40 per cent for the *Arabisés* and Babali.

To facilitate comparing the above characteristics for the three 'types' of populations identified on the basis of Figs. XV–XXIII, selected items of information drawn from Tables 24–27 are shown in Table 28. With the aid of this table we can discuss some of the general features of the social configurations of the three 'types' of population which emerge as three markedly different 'types' of ethnic colony.

The Lokele (Type 1) had a high fertility ratio, a high proportion of young adults, and a high proportion of recent immigrants. In these associated respects they had a similar configuration to the colonies of

TABLE 27

Percentage distributions of adult men in the nine principal colonies according to their lengths of residence in Stanleyville

COLONY	'TYPE' OF POPULATION	EFFECTIVE SAMPLE	PERCENTAGE DISTRIBUTIONS			
			Resident in the town 3 years or less	Resident 3–10 years	Resident 11 years and over	Total
Bambole	Type 2	84	39·3	41·7	19·0	100·0
Topoke	Type 2	135	37·8	56·3	5·9	100·0
Balengola	Type 2	77	33·8	50·7	15·6	100·1
Lokele	Type 1	206	30·6	34·5	35·1	100·2
Bakumu	Intermediate	151	24·5	43·7	31·8	100·0
Babua	Type 3	176	23·9	43·8	32·4	100·1
Bamanga	Intermediate	64	23·4	50·0	26·6	100·0
Arabisés	Type 3	188	16·0	37·2	46·8	100·0
Babali	Type 3	92	15·2	41·3	43·5	100·0
Nine principal tribes	—	1,173	26·5	43·0	30·5	100·0
Total population of Stanleyville	—	1,680	25·6	41·9	32·5	100·0

Type 2 and especially to the Topoke and Bambole. But in some other respects Types 1 and 2 differed appreciably. Thus the Lokele had a significantly lower sex ratio than the colonies of Type 2, as well as a significantly higher proportion of well-established urban residents. These observations suggest that the essential differences between the colonies of Types 1 and 2 were related to their differing histories of migration and urban incorporation and to associated differences in their patterns of rural-urban relations current at the time of the study. Both 'types' of colonies were drawn from tribes with high fertilities and increasing populations. Moreover, as it happens, they were tribes from contiguous areas of the town's hinterland and they had some general cultural affinities which, for all we know, may well have been related to their high rates of fertility. But, as we saw in the previous section, the Lokele and the Topoke had significantly different histories of urban incorporation. And the same was to a large extent true of the Lokele as compared to the Bambole and Balengola, both of which tribes were, like the Topoke, relatively recent arrivals on the Stanleyville scene. In particular, as is shown by their proportions of dwelling-compound title-holders (Table 29) and by data on occupations presented in the next section, the Bambole and Balengola were also colonies of poorly established immigrants though their members had clearly fared somewhat better in town than had the Topoke.

TABLE 28

Summary of some salient demographic features of the nine principal ethnic colonies

COLONY	'TYPE' OF AGE AND SEX STRUCTURE	FERTILITY RATIO	ADULT SEX RATIO	PER CENT OF ADULT MEN RESIDENT IN THE TOWN 3 YEARS OR LESS	PER CENT OF ADULT MEN RESIDENT IN THE TOWN 11 YEARS OR MORE	PER CENT OF ADULT MEN AGED 16–25 YEARS
Lokele	Type 1	983*	114·6†	30·6*	35·1*	40·8*
Topoke	Type 2	823*	164·3*	37·8*	5·9‡	42·8*
Bambole	Type 2	863*	140·0*	39·3*	19·0‡	45·5*
Balengola	Type 2	691*	125·0*	33·8*	15·6‡	30·0†
Bamanga	Intermediate	392‡	100·0†	23·4‡	26·6‡	28·3†
Bakumu	Intermediate	242‡	104·4‡	24·5†	31·8†	29·4†
Babua	Type 3	181‡	105·8‡	23·9†	32·4†	16·1‡
Arabisés	Type 3	197‡	70·1‡	16·0†	46·8*	19·8‡
Babali	Type 3	159‡	116·9†	15·2‡	43·5*	24·7‡
All tribes in Stanleyville	—	489	117·5	25·6	32·5	28·2

* above average for the town
† approximately average
‡ below average.

When we come to compare the configurations of Types 2 and 3 we find a wider range of differences deriving partly from differing histories of migration and urban incorporation and partly from differential fertility. The colonies of Type 3 had very low fertility ratios and appreciably lower-than-average proportions of recent immigrants from the countryside. Associated with these features, they had sex ratios ranging from very low in the case of the *Arabisés* to approximately average for the Babali, and they had low proportions of young adults and high proportions of longer-term residents. We have previously noted that in the case of the Babua some of these features were a function of their early settlement in the town, and the same was true of the *Arabisés* and Babali. All three were well-established tribes. This is reflected in Table 29 which shows that each had a high proportion of

TABLE 29

Percentages for the nine principal colonies of household heads who were title-holders of dwelling compounds in the C.E.C.

COLONY	'TYPE' OF POPULATION	EFFECTIVE SAMPLE OF HOUSEHOLD HEADS	NO. OF DWELLING COMPOUND TITLE-HOLDERS	PERCENTAGE OF HOUSEHOLD HEADS WHO WERE TITLE-HOLDERS OF COMPOUNDS
Arabisés	Type 3	77	64	83·1*
Babua	Type 3	125	94	75·2
Babali	Type 3	68	50	73·5
Bakumu	Intermediate	85	59	69·4
Lokele	Type 1	145	95	65·5
Bambole	Type 2	57	35	61·4
Balengola	Type 2	43	22	51·2
Bamanga	Intermediate	42	15	35·7
Topoke	Type 2	88	29	33·0
Nine principal colonies	—	730	463	63·4

* The figures for the *Arabisés* refer only to those living in the C.E.C. as there was no system of dwelling compounds in the *Arabisé* village.

title-holders of dwelling compounds and thus also of home-owners. In sharp contrast to the Lokele who also had a large nucleus of well-established members, however, each of the three tribes of Type 3 had low rates of reproduction and of immigration. Like the Babua, the *Arabisés* had fared well in town in achieving a disproportionate number of better-paid jobs, but the Babali, though relatively well established as title-holders of compounds, had failed to distinguish themselves occupationally. (Table 32.)

In general, then, the main differences between Types 1 and 2 were functions of differing histories of urban incorporation, whereas the differences between Types 2 and 3 were associated with differential fertility as well as with differing histories of urban incorporation. And differing histories of urban incorporation were in turn related to differing current patterns of rural-urban relations. For the purpose of the argument developed in Part III it is important to emphasize the direct links which many members of colonies of Type 2 had with their rural villages; the larger volume of current immigration in these tribes was associated with a lower level of involvement in town and, conversely, a greater dependence for some measure of security on a continuing rural involvement.

Another pointer to varying degrees of rural and urban involvement is found in the proportions of men who had married their wives in Stanleyville itself, in another centre of employment, and in tribal villages. This information is given in Table 30, from which it can be

TABLE 30

Extant marriages of men in the nine principal colonies classified according to the place of the marriages

COLONY	'TYPE' OF AGE AND SEX STRUCTURE	MARRIED IN STANLEY-VILLE		MARRIED IN AN EMPLOY-MENT CENTRE OTHER THAN STANLEY-VILLE		MARRIED IN A NATIVE VILLAGE		TOTAL	
		No.	%	No.	%	No.	%	No.	%
Arabisés	Type 3	99	75·0	16	12·1	17	12·9	132	100
Bakumu	Intermediate	46	53·5	9	10·5	31	36·0	86	100
Babali	Type 3	26	52·0	11	22·0	13	26·0	50	100
Babua	Type 3	43	50·0	36	41·9	7	8·1	86	100
Lokele	Type 1	64	43·0	23	15·4	62	41·6	149	100
Bamanga	Intermediate	14	41·2	8	23·5	12	35·3	34	100
Bambole	Type 2	15	30·0	8	16·0	27	54·0	50	100
Balengola	Type 2	14	26·4	17	32·1	22	41·5	53	100
Topoke	Type 2	15	19·0	20	25·3	44	55·7	79	100
Total	—	336	46·7	148	20·6	235	32·7	719	100

seen that whether we consider the positive indication of a high proportion of Stanleyville marriages or the negative indication of a low proportions of marriages in tribal villages, the populations of Type 3 again emerge as substantially different to those of Type 2. On this index, however, the Lokele (Type 1) lie between Types 2 and 3, which is what we would expect if we recall that their population contained appreciably large proportions of new immigrants as well as of longer-term residents.

DIFFERENCES IN EDUCATIONAL AND OCCUPATIONAL
ACHIEVEMENT

We have already referred to a few particular differences in the occupational achievements of men in various colonies. We may now examine differences in occupations in relation to the formal education of men in the nine colonies (Tables 31 and 32). We see that there were marked differences in both occupational and educational records. Differences in schooling ranged from the Lokele with only 32·7 per cent of men who had not been to school and nearly 20 per cent with secondary education, to the Balengola with 70 per cent unschooled and a large majority of those who had been to school having done so for 3 years or less. As regards occupations, the *Arabisés*, Babua and Lokele were the only colonies with minorities of ordinary labourers, and the Lokele were in turn distinguished from the *Arabisés* and Babua by having a substantially larger proportion of white collar workers. The slightly lower percentages of *Arabisés* and Lokele in employment reflect their small but significant nuclei of shopkeepers and other self-employed men.

When Tables 31 and 32 are compared, it appears that there was no consistent relation between tribes with good jobs and good records of formal education. The *Arabisés* and the Babua, for example, held higher-than-average proportions of good jobs but also had higher-than-

TABLE 31

Percentage distributions of adult men (16 years and over) in the nine principal colonies by level of education

COLONY	'TYPE' OF AGE AND SEX STRUCTURE	EFFECTIVE SAMPLE	PERCENTAGE WITH NO FORMAL SCHOOLING	NO. WHO ATTENDED SCHOOL	PER CENT WITH 1–3 YEARS SCHOOLING	PER CENT WITH 4–6 YEARS SCHOOLING	PER CENT WITH OVER 6 YEARS SCHOOLING	TOTAL
Lokele	Type 1	211	32·7	142	30·3	50·0	19.7	100·0
Bamanga	Intermediate	53	41·5	31	51·6	32·3	16·1	100·0
Topoke	Type 2	138	44·9	76	56·6	42·1	1·3	100·0
Bambole	Type 2	77	53·2	36	47·2	38·9	13·9	100·0
Babali	Type 3	97	58·8	40	40·0	60·0	0·0	100·0
Bakumu	Intermediate	143	61·5	55	63·6	32·7	3·6	99·9
Babua	Type 3	180	61·7	69	31·9	55·1	13·0	100·0
Arabisés	Type 3	192	62·5	72	40·2	54·2	5·6	100·0
Balengola	Type 2	70	70·0	21	71·4	19·0	9·5	99·9
Nine principal colonies	—	1,161	53·3	542	43·5	46·1	10·3	99·9
Total Stanleyville population	—	1,894	49·6	954	41·5	45·6	12·9	100·0

average proportions of men who had not been to school, and the Topoke and Bamanga had lower-than-average proportions of men with no schooling but they none the less held disproportionately small numbers of better jobs. This seems surprising at first sight, particularly

TABLE 32

*Occupational composition of adult men (16 years and over) in the
nine ethnic colonies*

COLONY	'TYPE' OF POPULATION	EFFEC-TIVE SAMPLE	WAGE EARNERS AS A PER-CENTAGE OF ALL MEN IN SAMPLE	PERCENTAGE DISTRIBUTIONS OF WAGE-EARNERS			
				White collar	Special-ized manual	Lab.	Total
Arabisés	Type 3	192	79·7	9·2	69·9	20·9	100·0
Babua	Type 3	180	91·2	6·0	65·7	28·3	100·0
Lokele	Type 1	211	83·5	18·8	43·8	37·5	100·1
Bambole	Type 2	77	94·9	8·2	38·3	53·4	99·9
Balengola	Type 2	70	92·9	1·5	40·0	58·5	100·0
Bakumu	Intermediate	143	97·9	4·3	35·7	60·0	100·0
Babali	Type 3	97	90·8	4·5	35·2	60·2	99·9
Bamanga	Intermediate	53	96·3	3·9	35·3	60·8	100·0
Topoke	Type 2	138	95·7	5·3	32·6	62·1	100·0
Nine principal colonies	—	1,161	89·8	8·0	46·8	45·2	100·0
Total popula-tion of Stanleyville	—	1,894	95·4	10·5	48·3	41·3	100·1

in view of the finding reported in Chapter III that there was in the
population at large a positive correlation between secondary education
and white collar jobs as well as between primary education and the
better specialized manual jobs. Part of the explanation of these seemingly contradictory findings is that some tribes (e.g. the Topoke) had
high proportions of men who had been to school but who had only done
so for very short periods, while others (e.g. the Babua) had higher
proportions who had not been to school but, of those who had, a good
proportion had stayed for longer periods. There were also two further
factors involved: one was that, as seen in Chapter III, opportunities of
acquiring the skills for specialized manual work were partly independent
of schooling; the other that the age composition of the colonies varied
and that young and old men had been differentially exposed to educational and occupational opportunities. Certain jobs which had in
earlier years gone to men without schooling were now less likely to do
so. Both these factors contributed to the marked occupational differences
between, for example, the *Arabisés* and the Topoke. The *Arabisés*
population contained a high proportion of older adult males; few of
these had been to school but many had been reared in town and had
enjoyed relatively good opportunities to acquire the often very elementary skills required for many of the specialized manual jobs. The

Topoke population, on the other hand, contained a high proportion of young adult males many of whom, though they had been to missionary schools in the countryside for a few years, had very little experience of town life. The *Arabisés* were a well-settled urban community despite their relative lack of formal education whereas the Topoke had all the features of a recent immigrant colony feeling its way in a strange world despite relatively good educational opportunities in their tribal areas. Formal education was associated with better jobs but a few years of elementary schooling were in themselves insufficient to compensate for the numerous disadvantages which recent immigrants had to face in town especially when they were not members of one of the well-established colonies. The limited correlation between formal schooling and general success in town is also apparent if we compare the rankings of tribes according to 'home ownership' (Table 29) and according to educational levels (Table 31); in contrast, their ranking according to occupational achievements (Table 32) is very similar to their ranking according to 'home ownership' (Table 29).

'Closed' and 'Open' Colonies

I implied in Chapter I that some tribal colonies in the town were relatively 'closed' (in the sense that members tended to restrict their personal relations to fellow members) as compared to others which were relatively 'open'. And in this chapter I have pointed to the Lokele and Topoke as examples of relatively 'closed' colonies and to the Babua as an example of a more 'open' colony. We may now usefully examine the index of 'mixed' or non-tribal marriages in the nine largest colonies. The information is given in Table 33, from which it can be seen that 17·5 per cent of all the extant marriages of men in the nine colonies were non-tribal, but that this proportion fell to 6·4 per cent for marriages contracted in native villages, and rose to 21·1 per cent for marriages contracted in Stanleyville and to the even higher proportion of 27·0 per cent for marriages contracted in labour centres other than Stanleyville. The proportion of non-tribal marriages for the various colonies ranged from 2·9 per cent for the Bamanga to 36·0 per cent for the Babali and the Babua, and we may note that the table tends to corroborate our view of the Topoke and Lokele as relatively 'closed' colonies and of the Babua as more 'open'. But there are several difficulties of interpretation that have to be considered.

Firstly, when the marriages for each tribe are classified according to the places where they were contracted the numbers in some cells are too small for us to attach much significance to them. Secondly, and more fundamentally, the figures in the table could be used only as precise indices of the extent to which colonies were 'open' or 'closed' if we were in a position to compare the actual proportions of tribal and non-tribal marriages with the proportions expected under the assumption that marriage partners were selected at random. Unfortunately, this is not possible because we have no means of establishing the tribal

TABLE 33

Extant tribal and non-tribal marriages of men in the nine principal colonies classified according to the place of the marriages

(1) Total number of marriages in sample
(2) Total number of non-tribal marriages
(3) Percentages of non-tribal marriages
(4) Number of marriages entered upon in Stanleyville
(5) Number of non-tribal marriages in Stanleyville
(6) Percentages of non-tribal marriages in Stanleyville
(7) Number of marriages entered upon elsewhere* in *Kizungu*
(8) Number of non-tribal marriages elsewhere* in *Kizungu*
(9) Percentage of non-tribal marriages elsewhere in *Kizungu*
(10) Number of marriages entered upon in native villages
(11) Number of non-tribal marriages in native villages
(12) Percentage of non-tribal marriages in native villages

TRIBE	(1)	(2)	(3)	(4)	(5)	(6)	(7)	(8)	(9)	(10)	(11)	(12)
Bamanga	34	1	2·9	14	1	7·1	8	0	0·0	12	0	0·0
Arabisés†	132	9	6·8	99	6	6·1	16	1	6·3	17	2	11·8
Topoke	79	8	10·1	15	3	20·0	20	4	20·0	44	1	2·3
Lokele	149	16	10·7	64	7	10·9	23	5	21·7	62	4	6·5
Bakumu	86	17	19·8	46	13	28·3	9	2	22·2	31	2	6·5
Balengola	53	12	22·6	14	4	28·6	17	8	47·1	22	0	0·0
Bambole	50	14	28·0	15	6	40·0	8	5	62·5	27	3	11·1
Babua	86	31	36·0	43	19	44·2	36	11	30·1	7	1	14·3
Babali	50	18	36·0	26	12	46·2	11	4	36·4	13	2	15·4
Total	719	126	17·5	336	71	21·1	148	40	27·0	235	15	6·4

* In employment centres other than Stanleyville itself.

† The *Arabisés* figures in this table are of limited significance for wives from other tribes *usually* became Islamized on marriage. A substantial proportion of *Arabisés* wives were in fact women drawn from a number of different tribes.

composition of the different universes of women to which men of the various tribes were exposed. Quite apart from variations in the age and sex composition of various tribes in town, there were large differences between the nine tribes in the proportions of men who had married in Stanleyville, in native villages, and elsewhere. (Table 30.) In principle we would therefore need to restrict our computations to marriages started in town. But we also know that many men in town commonly recruited brides from the countryside either out of preference or, in some cases, simply because of the scarcity of marriageable urban women. Thus, *even if we were to consider only marriages started in town* it would be extremely difficult to establish the size and composition of the relevant universe from which brides were chosen. Finally, there is a third factor which has important methodological implications. We have noted that the various colonies were unevenly distributed in different parts of the town, and in Part III of this study we shall see that social life tended to be strongly localized not only in the separate townships but also in smaller neighbourhoods within the townships of the C.E.C. Thus the effective universes of potential marriage partners to which the inhabitants of various neighbourhoods were exposed were liable to vary markedly in tribal composition. In principle tribal *preferences* in regard to marriage partners could therefore be assessed only by relating the varying incidences of tribal or non-tribal marriages in the several tribes to a series of universes which took account of the lay-out of the C.E.C. and of the neighbourhood composition of the townships. This is clearly impossible on the basis of the data we have.

In view of the above considerations we cannot take the figures given in Table 33 as *necessarily* reflecting higher or lower preferences for marriage within the various colonies. Yet the figures are valuable in contributing to a general definition of the social environments within which people of various tribes interacted in town. For example, it is clearly important for us to know that only one Lokele man in ten was married to a non-Lokele woman whereas nearly four out of ten Babua men were married to non-Babua women. Or, to take an example of wider relevance, it is very important to note that there was a high degree of correlation between colonies ranked according to the incidence of non-tribal marriage (Table 33) and according to residential dispersion and concentration (Table 17). Members of a tribe who tended to live close to each other were also more likely to be married to each other. This has importance irrespective of whether we are in a position to state that it reflects differential preferences; the observation contributes to our assessment of the situations under which people interacted in the town.

Apart from the Lokele, Topoke, and Babua, there were other tribes which were generally regarded as either distinctly more 'closed' or distinctly more 'open' than the average; the Bakumu and the Bamanga were certainly viewed as relatively 'closed', while the Babali were regarded as more 'open' and more willing to mix with members of other tribes. These impressions are clearly in keeping with the data on non-tribal marriages in Table 33.

I have drawn attention to the fact of 'closed' and 'open' colonies as a general contribution to the description of the population. The notions of 'closed' and 'open' are, however, too crude to be of much value in the analysis of 'tribalism'. The factors making for 'open' or 'closed' colonies were various and variable. Thus, for example, the 'closed' colonies of the Lokele and Topoke exhibited both important similarities and marked differences. There was some cultural affinity between the two tribes and they were from adjacent areas of the hinterland where they were traditionally well known to each other. As we have seen, however, their histories of urban incorporation and participation were very different. The Lokele had a highly successful record in town, and were regarded as 'clever', 'independent', and 'exclusive'; they made up a 'closed' group tending to reject association with other tribes partly on account of their success. In contrast, the Topoke were a colony of recent immigrants, clinging to the social security of their village homes, and regarded as 'backward' and 'uncivilized' by other tribes; they were a relatively 'closed' group partly because most other tribes tended to reject them, and partly because of their own tendency to resist branching out and becoming more involved in urban life.

METHODOLOGICAL IMPLICATIONS

At this juncture we may usefully draw attention to the main methodological implications of the data presented so far. Two sets of comments are called for. The first set concerns the implications of the similarities and differences between Stanleyville and some other African towns. Though it falls beyond the scope of this study to attempt a systematic comparative analysis, it is evident that Stanleyville was in some respects strikingly different to some other African towns that I referred to earlier. Its history of development, its distinctive kind of administrative regime, its setting in an ethnographic region largely characterized by small tribes, and its special relation to its vast and varied hinterland, were all factors tending to produce what we may well think of as a special case in any catalogue of African urban communities. Yet, on close scrutiny, many aspects of the community and its population turn out to be of a kind familiar to us from other studies. Thus, for example, we saw in Chapter III that despite the numerical imbalance between the sexes being less acute than in many other African towns the factors influencing the sex ratio were of a kind commonly noted elsewhere. Or, to take another example, the different categories of immigrants encountered in the town are familiar to us from the work of others despite the indications that the nature and degree of urban involvement and commitment in Stanleyville were somewhat unusual as compared to other parts of the continent. Similarly, to take an example from the present chapter, the population was to some extent exceptional in not having a dominant ethnic element, yet we know that tribal heterogeneity as such is a very common urban phenomenon and, equally, that differences between tribal colonies in features as varied as the fertility ratio and the occupational structure have commonly been reported from other towns. It is of course the existence of similarities that allows conceptual formulations derived from work in other regions to be applied to the Stanleyville materials, but the value of doing so depends largely on the existence of differences.

The second set of comments concerns the methodological implications of the wide range of variations noted between tribal colonies in Stanleyville itself. What do the inter-tribal variations noted in this chapter imply in relation to the three major sets of social relations postulated in Chapter I as comprising the overall urban system? The first point to emphasize is that the rural-urban relations of the various ethnic colonies varied enormously. Not having data on migration from the rural end, many of these variations cannot be spelt out, but our evidence from the urban end clearly points to far-reaching differences. We have specifically noted variations between tribes in their degrees of urban involvement and commitment; and, even though accepting Mayer's point that 'active involvement in within-town social systems is no index of non-involvement in extra-town systems',[17] there is no doubt that the nature and degree of rural involvement also varied widely. In saying this I do not imply that the degree of rural involvement necessarily ran in inverse proportion to degree of urban involvement. Indeed, the case of the Lokele demonstrates that this was not so; as a tribe and, in many cases, as individuals, the Lokele were highly involved in both town and country, and their high urban and high rural involvements tended to reinforce each other. In some other cases, however, high urban involvement went hand in hand with low rural involvement. This was certainly the case with the Babua and the *Arabisés* and, to a lesser extent, with the Babali. Conversely, the Topoke had limited urban involvement but a high degree of continuing rural involvement, and there was an important connexion between the two; their low urban involvement was partly a cause of their relative 'failure' in town, and this latter fact naturally tended to perpetuate their continuing high rural involvement.[18]

As a whole, the evidence shows, firstly, that different tribes had established markedly different forms of urban accommodation and, secondly, that these forms of accommodation were in some cases partly a function of the rural-urban relation. I contend that the set of urban-residential relations of tribes like the Babua, Babali, and *Arabisés* could be fairly adequately studied without a parallel rural study, but that in the case of tribes like the Lokele and the Topoke, any adequate analysis would require urban-residential relations to be assessed within the framework of a wider rural-urban study.

The second point to be made concerns the effect of the complex of African-European relations on the analysis of urban-residential relations. We have seen that some tribes tended to hold different jobs, and that in some cases the differences were between 'good' and 'bad' jobs. We have also noted that a section of the *Arabisés* lived under a different administrative system to that to which the greater part of the urban population was subjected in the C.E.C. Moreover, we know that the nature and degree of involvement in the African-European complex of relations was very appreciably different for *évolués* and non-*évolués*. Such differences were clearly important, and would undoubtedly have assumed much greater significance in the analysis if the study had been specifically focussed on the *évolués* or *Arabisés* or on tribes which, like the Lokele or the Babua, had wider-than-average ranges of involvement in African-European relations. But this is not the case, and we shall see that most of the analysis in Part III does not depend *directly* on the evaluation of differential involvements in the complex of African-European relations.

Finally, we have to refer to the implications of inter-tribal differences for the analysis of the set of urban-residential relations on which the study is focussed. Here there can be no doubt that the nature of social relations within any tribal colony, as well as between members of different tribal colonies, cannot proceed without taking account of a series of important differences. We have seen that there was wide variation between tribes in involvement in urban life, in the sex ratio, in age structure, in the fertility ratio, in the urban roles of women, in urban achievements, in patterns of residential distribution, and in a number of other related factors. All these constituted important differences closely related to the very nature of urban participation, but most of them partly coincided with differences between neighbourhoods. They are thus taken up in the next chapter.

FOOTNOTES TO CHAPTER IV

[1] Statistical description in this chapter is largely confined to the nine principal colonies in the town because the samples for separate tribes were in most other cases too small to warrant detailed analysis. It will however be seen that variations between the nine principal colonies were so wide that their analysis provides a useful framework for the assessment of inter-tribal differences in general.

[2] A breakdown of the population according to administrative areas of origin showed that 85·5 per cent came from the Eastern Province, 11·0 per cent from adjacent areas of Kivu Province and Equatorial Province, and under 5 per cent from all other areas of the Congo and beyond. See Pons (1956a).

[3] In the far north of the Eastern Province there were cases of larger politically coherent groupings (e.g. the Mangbetu and Azande) but these were only found on the periphery of the region from which the Stanleyville population was mainly recruited.

[4] Compare, for example, the far-reaching significance for urban society in Kampala of the dominance of the Baganda. See Southall (1956).

[5] The survey tracts used in this analysis are shown in Fig. V and are explained in Appendix A.

[6] In a previous analysis of tribal clusters in Tract B III, I showed that these clusters were spontaneous groupings maintaining themselves over time. See Pons (1956b).

[7] Pons (1956b).

[8] Detry's account of Stanleyville refers to the 'Lokele village' on the left bank as a well-established community of fishermen, basket-makers, and potters during the early years of this century. Detry (1912), p. 14.

9 Torday and Joyce, writing in 1922, referred to the Topoke 'town of Yakake' as being 'the only town belonging to the Tofoke (*sic*) tribe *that we have been able to reach at present, though we hear of others* . . .' (Italics mine). Quoted in Maes and Boone (1935), p. 321.

10 The percentage distributions on which Figs. XV to XXIII are based, are given in Appendix B, Tables 73–81.

11 It is of interest to note that Mitchell found a very similar range of fertility ratios for different tribal groups on the Zambian Copperbelt. Defining the fertility ratio in a slightly different way as the number of children *under five years of age* to every 1,000 women *aged 15 to 50 years*, and standardizing these ratios for age, he found a range in 12 tribal groups running from about 200 to nearly 1,000. Mitchell (1965), pp. 10–11.

12 Rates adjusted to the age structure of the total female population aged 16 years and over, i.e. 32 per cent aged 16–25 years, 35 per cent aged 26–35 years, 18 per cent aged 36–45 years, and 15 per cent over 45 years.

13 Bertrand (1931), p. 248.

14 *Démographie Congolaise*, (1950), an official unpublished document.

15 On the basis of a more thorough analysis, Mitchell came to similar conclusions in relation to women of different tribes on the Zambian Copperbelt. His final comment on the Copperbelt data is crucially pertinent for demographers and sociologists interested in the problem of fertility in African towns:

'The fact that differences in fertility in the same direction as those that occur in the tribal areas persist in women who have been in town for relatively long periods points to the operation of factors which came into being before the women came to town. These may be diseases from which the women suffered before they came to town, or an inherent low fertility, possibly due to genetic factors. So far not much evidence has been assembled to show that the morbidity patterns in tribal areas differ markedly from one area to another. On the other hand, there is, as far as I know, no proven connection between fertility and genetic factors.

'The sociologist working alone is in no position to explain differential fertility fully. Equally, the geneticist or the medical scientist cannot explain the pattern of fertility from the point of view of his specialism alone. I have been able to demonstrate that there are marked differences in fertility among the African peoples and suggest that some of the facile and common explanations of these variations are probably not valid. When we begin to examine in detail the problem of differential fertility we become embarrassingly conscious of our lack of knowledge of the subject and correspondingly acutely aware that this is a field in which we need desperately the close co-operation and pooling of research skills of both medical and social scientists.' Mitchell (1956), pp. 24–25.

16 We cannot assert that the process of urbanization did not affect fertility, but the evidence suggests little or no differential effect between tribes. It would in future studies be of interest to analyse fertility in terms of the births which took place in town and those which took place before the women reporting them had come to town. I have not attempted to do this as the women in the Stanleyville sample were not questioned specifically on this point. I do not consider the original field data on the migration histories of women to be sufficiently accurate in details to stand the weight of a retrospective attempt to match histories of migration and of child-bearing.

17 Mayer (1962), p. 581.

18 This kind of urban accommodation is clearly similar to the 'conservative dynamism' of the 'Red' Xhosa as described by Mayer (1961).

V

IMMIGRANTS AND DIFFERENTIATED
NEIGHBOURHOODS

We have seen that some inhabitants of Stanleyville were well-established urban residents but that a larger proportion were relatively new recruits of recent years. The absorption and settlement of these new-comers had become a constant feature of life in the town.[1] The very activities of finding accommodation, of seeking work for the first time, of struggling to acquire the often modest skills necessary for a better job, of arranging for wives and families to follow men to town, and simply of getting acquainted with the urban setting and its people, were major preoccupations for the steady stream of new arrivals.[2] For those who had already made their initial contact with the town, there remained the problems of acquiring their own compounds and of building their own houses, matters which commonly occupied them for years on end.[3] Conversely, welcoming new arrivals and helping them in various stages of the process of becoming established, were regular aspects of the day-to-day life of many of the inhabitants of longer standing.

In this chapter I examine aspects of the urban residential situation into which the new arrivals were being absorbed. We shall see that general processes of selection and differentiation had already created 'natural areas' within the three townships of the C.E.C., that social relations centred on the dwelling compound and the immediate locality were developing in an urban environment that was far from uniform, and that the existence of differing 'natural areas' had in itself become an important factor in the selection and distribution of new immigrants.[4] I first present some selected data on the population of the 13 survey tracts in the C.E.C. I then give a more detailed analysis of four selected neighbourhoods in the three townships in an attempt to elucidate the factors underlying the development and maintenance of 'natural areas'. After that, I compare the selection of newcomers to the four neighbourhoods and describe the practical accommodation arrangements of people who had been in town for varying periods of time. In the process of establishing themselves, most immigrants initially relied mainly on their pre-existing social relations with kinsmen and fellow-tribesmen. As they acquired their own compounds, they often found that their turn had come to offer free accommodation to kinsmen and fellow-tribesmen or to act as landlords to stranger tenants. There were, however, important differences in this process between neighbourhoods.

The Range of Variation between Neighbourhoods in the C.E.C.

We saw in Chapter II that the *Arabisé* village and the in-lying areas of the three main townships had all been settled in the early days of the town's growth and long before the establishment of the C.E.C. in 1932. Since then the *Arabisé* village had continued to exist as one distinctive 'natural area' but, as far as we know, had not altered very much in size and by 1952–53 there was little evidence of any internal differentiation *within* this area. On the other hand, the three townships of the C.E.C. had grown and changed very markedly; significant variations had developed within each township, and some parts of each were clearly undergoing marked change at the time of the study.

Belge I, which in 1932 was already the largest and most important settlement, had become more heterogeneous in tribal composition, had become very crowded, and had gathered the largest concentration of *évolués* and other higher-paid workers. Its in-lying areas had remained the busiest in the C.E.C. and had become the main areas of night life with numbers of modern bars and dance halls. Some aspects of this internal variation are reflected in Tables 34, 35, and 36. On moving from the in-lying areas of Tracts A I, A II, and A III to the out-lying areas of Tracts A IV and A V, there was an appreciable decline in the proportions of white collar workers and specialized manual workers and, correspondingly, in wages. At the same time there was a steady decline in the degree of variation in earnings within each tract. Thus the out-lying areas presented a picture of relative homogeneity in occupations and of uniformity in wages, whereas the in-lying areas exhibited much wider ranges in both respects (Table 34). In addition there were marked differences between in-lying and out-lying areas in the use of dwelling compounds. The mean number of households per compound decreased from 2·2 in Tract A I to 1·7 and 1·8 in Tracts A IV and A V, and this decrease was accompanied by an increase in the proportion of single-household compounds and a fall in the mean number of households per multiple-household compound; on the other hand, the mean number of persons per household increased from the inner to the outer areas (Table 35). These differences were in turn associated with variations in the proportions of rent-paying tenant households and of households accommodated free of charge. In the in-lying area of Tracts A I and A II about one household in three paid rent and smaller proportions were accommodated free of charge, whereas in the out-lying areas of Tracts A IV and A V the proportion of rent-paying households was low and the proportion of non-rent-paying households appreciably higher (Table 36).

In Brussels there was variation of a similar kind though it was not as marked. The in-lying area covered by Tract B I had a low proportion of labourers, a high mean income, and a fairly wide spread in incomes. The tract was, however, less crowded than any in Belge I; it had 1·6 households per compound as compared to the highest and lowest levels of 2·2 and 1·7 in Belge I, and it also had fewer persons per

TABLE 34

Distributions of wage-earners and wages in residential areas and survey tracts

AREAS AND SURVEY TRACTS	EFFECTIVE SAMPLE OF WAGE-EARNERS	PERCENTAGE DISTRIBUTIONS OF WAGE-EARNERS				MEAN SALARY* (FRANCS PER MONTH)	COEFF. OF VARIATION (%)	PERCENTAGE WITH INCOME OF 1,050 FRANCS AND OVER
		WHITE COLLAR WORKERS	SPECIALIZED MANUAL WORKERS	LABOURERS	TOTAL			
Belge I								
A I	69	10·1	63·8	26·1	100·0	1,215	117	29·2
A II	61	14·8	70·5	14·8	100·1	1,426	118	29·2
A III	100	13·0	52·0	35·0	100·0	1,023	87	26·4
A IV	106	9·4	43·4	47·2	100·0	904	80	18·8
A V	80	5·0	33·8	61·3	100·1	671	39	4·1
Total	416	10·3	51·0	38·7	100·0	1,015	107	20·9
Brussels								
B I	114	13·2	61·4	25·4	100·0	1,113	96	26·7
B II	81	9·9	51·9	38·3	100·1	946	83	22·1
B III	95	1·1	46·3	52·6	100·0	704	54	10·7
B IV	83	4·8	45·8	49·4	100·0	868	83	13·8
B V	66	0·0	59·1	40·9	100·0	770	37	10·3
Total	439	6·4	53·1	40·5	100·0	899	85	17·6
Belge II								
C I	78	12·8	41·0	46·2	100·0	1,016	113	20·3
C II	117	13·7	44·4	41·9	100·0	860	82	18·2
C III	41	9·8	34·1	56·1	100·0	693	30	4·5
Total	236	12·7	41·5	45·8	100·0	888	96	16·6
Railway camp	43	2·3	18·6	79·1	100·0	—	—	—
Arabisé village	79	11·4	70·9	17·7	100·0	1,213	106	40·2
All areas	1,213	10·2	48·0	41·8	100·0	959	100	20·2

* The incomes recorded included allowances in respect of housing, rations, etc. In the railway camp earnings were partly in kind and no attempt has been made to calculate the cash equivalent.

TABLE 35

Distribution of persons and households per dwelling compound in the survey tracts of the C.E.C.

AREAS AND SURVEY TRACTS	EFFECTIVE SAMPLE OF DWELLING COMPOUNDS	EFFECTIVE SAMPLE OF HOUSEHOLDS	EFFECTIVE SAMPLE OF PERSONS	MEAN NO. OF HOUSEHOLDS PER COMPOUND	MEAN NO. OF PERSONS PER COMPOUND	MEAN NO. OF PERSONS PER HOUSEHOLD	PER CENT DWELLING COMPOUNDS WITH ONE HOUSEHOLD ONLY	MEAN NO. OF HOUSEHOLDS PER COMPOUND *with more than one* HOUSEHOLD
Belge I								
A I	35	78	240	2·2	6·9	3·1	37·1	3·0
A II	39	74	257	1·9	6·6	3·5	48·7	2·8
A III	65	123	426	1·9	6·6	3·5	40·0	2·8
A IV	59	103	370	1·7	6·3	3·6	47·5	2·4
A V	45	83	301	1·8	6·7	3·6	51·1	2·7
Total	243	461	1,594	1·9	6·6	3·5	44·9	2·7
Brussels								
B I	81	128	401	1·6	5·0	3·1	66·7	2·7
B II	61	81	286	1·3	4·7	3·5	67·2	2·2
B III	63	87	277	1·4	4·4	3·2	68·3	2·2
B IV	62	84	268	1·4	4·3	3·2	72·6	2·3
B V	57	70	207	1·2	3·6	3·0	80·7	2·2
Total	324	450	1,439	1·4	4·4	3·2	70·7	2·4
Belge II								
C I	72	105	535	1·5	7·4	5·1	67·6	2·4
C II	93	148	539	1·6	5·8	3·6	55·9	2·3
C III	61	69	241	1·1	4·0	3·5	86·9	2·0
Total	226	319	1,315	1·4	5·8	4·1	68·0	2·3
All areas	793	1,233	4,348	1·6	5·5	3·5	62·0	2·4

TABLE 36

*Distribution of principal households and of rent-paying and non-rent-paying
subsidiary households in the survey tracts of the C.E.C.*

AREAS AND SURVEY TRACTS	PRINCIPAL HOUSEHOLDS		SUBSIDIARY NON-RENT-PAYING HOUSEHOLDS		SUBSIDIARY RENT-PAYING HOUSEHOLDS		TOTAL (EFFECTIVE SAMPLE)	
	No.	%	No.	%	No.	%	No.	%
Belge I								
A I	35	44·9	16	20·5	27	34·6	78	100·0
A II	39	52·7	9	12·2	26	35·1	74	100·0
A III	65	52·8	28	22·8	30	24·4	123	100·0
A IV	59	57·3	26	25·2	18	17·5	103	100·0
A V	45	54·2	30	36·2	8	9·6	83	100·0
Total	243	42·8	109	23·6	109	23·6	461	100·0
Brussels								
B I	81	63·3	23	18·0	24	18·7	128	100·0
B II	61	75·3	13	16·0	7	8·7	81	100·0
B III	63	72·4	21	24·1	3	3·5	87	100·0
B IV	62	73·8	18	21·4	4	4·8	84	100·0
B V	57	81·4	13	18·6	0	0·0	70	100·0
Total	324	72·0	88	19·6	38	8·4	450	100·0
Belge III								
C I	72	68·6	33	31·4	0	0·0	105	100·0
C II	93	62·8	36	24·3	19	12·9	148	100·0
C III	61	88·4	7	10·1	1	1·5	69	100·0
Total	226	70·2	76	23·6	20	6·2	322	100·0
All areas	793	64·3	273	22·1	167	13·6	1,233	100·0

compound and more single-household compounds than any part of
Belge I. The proportion of rent-paying tenants fell below the average
for Belge I but was higher than in its less crowded areas. The tract had
two modern bars and dance halls but these were seldom as busy and
crowded as the more numerous ones in the inner areas of Belge I, and
the general atmosphere of the neighbourhood was not as lively.
Beyond the area of Tract B I, the main features of Old Brussels changed
steadily. Thus Tract B II had a higher proportion of labourers, a
lower average income level, a lower number of households per compound and a lower proportion of rent-paying tenants, and Tract B III
was in turn correspondingly different to Tract B II. The decrease
between B II and B III in the incidence of rent-paying tenants was,
however, uneven. This is largely explained by the tendency for tenants
to gather along the Irumu Road which constituted the southern
boundary of the township. (See Fig. XXIV.) In New Brussels (Tracts

B IV and B V) which had only been established in recent years there
were very few tenants and high proportions of single-household
compounds.

In Belge II, Tract C I was inhabited mainly by Lokele and had a
combination of characteristics different to that of any other neighbourhood in the town. The income level and the occupational composition
were fairly high and, as in the in-lying areas of Belge I and Brussels,
there was a fairly wide spread in these. The composition of dwelling

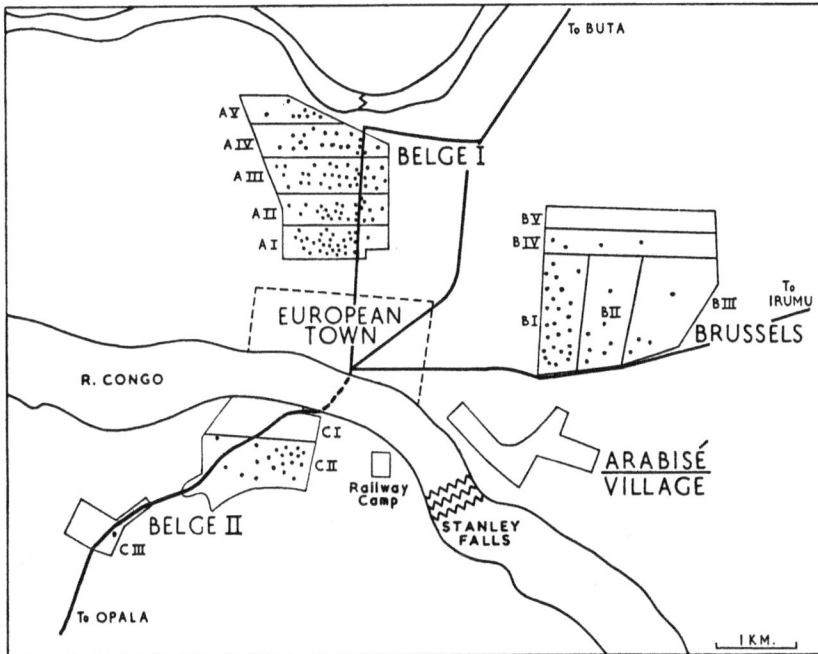

FIG. **XXIV** Sketch map of Stanleyville showing the location of a sample
of rent-paying households

compounds was, however, different. With the large families of the
Lokele, the mean numbers of persons per compound and per household
were higher than anywhere else. Moreover, there were no tenant
households, all the subsidiary households in the area being accommodated free of charge. But the adjacent area of Tract C II was strikingly
different. It was tribally heterogeneous and contained a small but
significant proportion of tenants. In these respects it bore a closer
resemblance to some areas of Belge I and Brussels than to Tract C I
of its own township. The number of persons per compound was also
lower than in C I, though the number of households per compound
was about the same. Like the in-lying area of Brussels, Tract C II had
its own bars and dance halls, and these were the central meeting places
on the Left Bank. Again, however, they were not as busy or fashionable
as the larger establishments in Belge I. The detached part of Belge II

(Tract C III) bore much the same relation to Tract C II in its own township as did the out-lying areas of Belge I and Brussels to their in-lying areas. There were few subsidiary households, there was a majority of unskilled labourers, and monthly wages tended to be uniformly low.

The spatial distribution of rent-paying households in the C.E.C. as a whole is of particular interest as an index of the rate and direction of changes in the community about the time of the study. Up to a few years previously, the in-lying areas of Belge I had been the only ones in the C.E.C. containing tenant households, but the increasing pressure of population in the post-war years had led to a spread of the practice of renting accommodation, first over large parts of Belge I itself and in the in-lying area of Brussels, and then, about the time of the study, in the far corners of Belge I, along the Irumu Road in Brussels, and in the central area of Belge II. (See Fig. XXIV.)

Four Selected Neighbourhoods

Having noted the range of variation between survey tracts in the three townships of the C.E.C., we may turn to a more detailed analysis of four selected neighbourhoods or 'natural areas'—Neighbourhoods I, II, III and IV.

Neighbourhood I was defined as the in-lying area of Belge I covered by Tract A I and A II. The total population of this area was estimated on the basis of the survey sample to be about 4,400. We have seen that this was an area with a relatively high proportion of *évolués*, with a high average income, and with a larger number of households per dwelling compound than anywhere else. It was thus both fashionable and crowded, and it was the area which best exhibited the distinctive social atmosphere associated with Belge I.

Neighbourhood II was defined as the out-lying area of Belge I covered by Tract A V, and *Neighbourhood III* as a stretch of Old Brussels lying along the Irumu Road and covering substantial parts of Tracts B II and B III. The population of Neighbourhood II was estimated at about 2,600 and that of Neighbourhood III at about 2,500. Both were chosen for analysis as examples of out-lying areas that were different from Neighbourhood I but which were being directly influenced by the changes attendant on the increasing pressure of population. There were some differences *between* Neighbourhoods II and III; thus, for example, Neighbourhood II was more crowded than Neighbourhood III and the average wage in Neighbourhood III was somewhat higher than in Neighbourhood II. But the similarities between them were more striking than the differences. Both were areas which had only recently begun to attract tenants. Neighbourhood III is of particular interest to us as the area within which Avenue 21, discussed in detail in the next chapter, was located.

Neighbourhood IV was taken as the area of Tract C I in Belge II. It lay on the bank of the river and covered the greater part of the

Lokele settlement which had been there since the early days of the town. The population of the neighbourhood was estimated at about 4,800.

The tribal composition of samples of compound title-holders and of two categories of subsidiary household heads from the four neighbourhoods is given for the four neighbourhoods in Tables 37, 39, 40 and 41, and a series of population indices for each is given in Table 42. These indices derive partly from data previously discussed, and partly from Tables 82–89 in Appendix B which show the marital status of men and women in the four neighbourhoods. With the aid of these tables we are able to supplement the general view we already have of the differences between the four neighbourhoods.

Apart from being an area of marked diversity in occupations and incomes, Neighbourhood I had several further striking characteristics. First, it was extremely heterogeneous in tribal composition and it contained the most diverse ethnic elements. As shown in Table 37, the sample of 152 households contained 53 whose heads were from three tribes—the Babua, Lokele, and Bakusu—and 99 from 33 further tribes. Secondly, the neighbourhood had a distinct 'class' of landlords whose incomes derived wholly or substantially from rents. Very few *évolués* or other better-paid workers ever took in tenants, and this 'class' of landlords consisted mainly of men with low wages and of women (Table 38). There were in the sample 27 title-holders who were landlords and they constituted over a third of all title-holders; six of these 27 were drawing between 500 and 750 francs per month in rents, and another seven were drawing between 250 and 500 francs. Most landlords in the area had more than one tenant each, and their relatively high incomes from rent were due to this as well as to higher rentals than were normally paid in other parts of the town. As shown in Table 37, tenants were only exceptionally members of the same tribe as their landlords, whereas the heads of subsidiary households accommodated free of charge were commonly members of the same tribe as the title-holders of the compounds on which they lived. The presence of numerous landlords and tenants was thus a part factor in the extreme ethnic heterogeneity of the area. Thirdly, there was a more distinct social cleavage between *évolués* and the mass of the population than in areas where there were fewer *évolués*. Indeed, the particular contrast between the 'class' of landlords and the 'class' of *évolués* was part of a wider general distinction in the area between the styles of life and patterns of social participation of white collar and manual workers. *Évolués* title-holders were younger, had very much higher salaries, moved in more exclusive social circles, and aspired to different standards of living, than did their immediate non-*évolués* neighbours. Beyond the limits of kinsmen and immediate neighbours, *évolués* seldom associated with non-*évolués* in the locality. Thus, for example, Clément found that 15 *évolués* in one avenue in this neighbourhood knew an average of 27 out of 39 *évolués* title-holders in

Stanleyville

TABLE 37

Tribal affiliations of heads of households in a sample of 75 dwelling compounds in Neighbourhood I

(Survey Tracts A I and A II)

TRIBES	HEADS OF PRINCIPAL HOUSEHOLDS	HEADS OF SUBSIDIARY NON-RENT-PAYING HOUSEHOLDS	HEADS OF SUBSIDIARY RENT-PAYING HOUSEHOLDS	TOTAL
Babua	22	4 (3)	3 (3)	29
Lokele	6	3 (3)	4 (2)	13
Bakusu	7	1	3	11
Babango	1	3 (3)	6	10
Azande	2	5 (3)	1	8
Babali	5	1 (1)	0	6
Budja	1	1 (1)	4	6
Bangelima	5	0	0	5
Basoko	2	0	3	5
Bambole	0	1	4	5
Babudu	3	1 (1)	0	4
Balengola	2	2 (1)	0	4
Baluba	3	0	1	4
Topoke	0	0	4	4
Bakumu	2	1	0	3
Ngombe	0	0	3	3
Turumbu	1	1	1	3
Malela	2	0	0	2
Bandande	0	1	1	2
Mongandu	0	0	2	2
Mongo	1	0	1	2
Mongola	0	0	2	2
Bangwandi	1	0	0	1
'Gold Coast'	1	0	0	1
Mago	1	0	0	1
Makere	1	0	0	1
Mangbetu	1	0	0	1
Mobuali	1	0	0	1
Mosonge	1	0	0	1
Auro	0	0	1	1
Bagendja	0	0	1	1
Balendu	0	0	1	1
Bangobango	0	0	1	1
Bapato	0	0	1	1
Mituku	0	0	1	1
Warega	0	0	1	1
No information	3	0	2	5
Total	75	25 (16)	52 (5)	152

Note: The figures in brackets indicate the numbers of subsidiary households living on dwelling compounds with title-holders of the same tribe as themselves. Thus, for example, there were 4 Babua non-rent-paying households of whom 3 were living on compounds held by Babua, and of the three Babua rent-paying households all were living on Babua dwelling compounds.

TABLE 38

Wages in Neighbourhood I of title-holders of dwelling compounds with and without tenants

MONTHLY WAGES (if any)	TITLE-HOLDERS WITHOUT TENANTS	TITLE-HOLDERS WITH RENT-PAYING TENANTS	TOTAL
Under 650 francs per month	13 (including 2 women)	18 (including 8 women)	31 (including 10 women)
650–1,749 francs	18	9 (including 2 women)	27 (including 2 women)
1,750 and over	14 (including 1 woman)	0	14 (including 1 woman)
Effective sample	45 (including 3 women)	27 (including 10 women)	72 (including 13 women)

the same avenue, but an average of only 4 to 5 out of 40 non-*évolués* title-holders.[5] This social division was an important factor contributing to a measure of anonymity encountered here but seldom found in other parts of the C.E.C. Finally, Neighbourhood I also differed markedly from other areas in having a large number of *femmes libres* who were attracted to the area on account of its lively and fashionable atmosphere and who lived mainly on illicit or semi-illicit means.[6] As shown in Table 42, 31·0 per cent of a sample of women aged 16–45 years in this neighbourhood were 'single' and most of these were either divorcees or widows without children in the town. (See Appendix B, Table 84.) Their presence in the neighbourhood in addition to wives was an important factor affecting the general social atmosphere and was clearly reflected in the sex ratio which was only 105 men to 100 women as compared to ratios ranging from 110 to 137 in Neighbourhoods II, III, and IV, and to a sex ratio of 117 in the adult population of the town as a whole. Equally, the local concentration of *femmes libres* was a factor affecting the proportion of children to women which was lower in this area than in the town as a whole and also lower than in any of the other neighbourhoods selected for detailed analysis (Table 42).

In general, then, Neighbourhood I was a crowded and lively area of great diversity. In contrast, Neighbourhoods II and III were much quieter; they lacked the main attractions, the bustling atmosphere, and the partial anonymity of Neighbourhood I. Both had higher proportions of ordinary labourers and very few *évolués*, and the wages of their inhabitants were much lower and more uniform than in Neighbourhood I. There were small proportions of tenants in each, but it was unusual

for a single landlord to have multiple tenants and the rentals charged
were lower; thus the highest incomes from rent reported by any landlords were 300 francs in Neighbourhood II and 250 francs in Neighbourhood III as against 750 francs in Neighbourhood I. Both neighbourhoods had a significant degree of ethnic heterogeneity (Tables 39
and 40) but, as explained in Chapter IV, there were marked tribal

TABLE 39

*Tribal affiliations of heads of households in a sample of 45 dwelling
compounds in Neighbourhood II*

(Survey Tract A V)

TRIBES	HEADS OF PRINCIPAL HOUSEHOLDS	HEADS OF SUBSIDIARY NON-RENT-PAYING HOUSEHOLDS	HEADS OF SUBSIDIARY RENT-PAYING HOUSEHOLDS	TOTAL
Bamanga	7	14 (10)	1 (1)	22
Lokele	5	2	2	9
Bangelima	3	3 (2)	1 (1)	7
Bakusu	6	0	0	6
Babua	5	0	0	5
Basoko	3	2 (2)	0	5
Babali	2	2 (2)	0	4
Bakumu	3	1	0	4
Bangobango	3	1 (1)	0	4
Topoke	1	1 (1)	1	3
Azande	2	0	0	2
Baluba	1	0	1	2
Turumbu	0	1	1	2
Babenjo	1	0	0	1
Budja	1	0	0	1
Malela	1	0	0	1
Bambole	0	1	0	1
Balengola	0	1	0	1
Banyaruanda	0	1	0	1
Bazimba	0	0	1	1
No information	1	0	0	1
Total	45	30 (18)	8 (3)	83

Note: As in Table 37, figures in brackets indicate the number of subsidiary household heads
of the same tribe as the title-holder of the compound.

clusters in each area. In Neighbourhood II there was a striking cluster
of Bamanga, and this is reflected in Table 39 which shows that 22 out
of the sample of 83 households had Bamanga heads. There was, however,
a lower proportion of Bamanga among title-holders than among heads
of subsidiary households, and this points to a different kind of clustering
to that encountered among the Babali, Bakumu, and Barumbi in
Neighbourhood III. As was the case among their fellow-tribesmen in
the town at large, the Bamanga in Neighbourhood II were largely

concentrated on the dwelling compounds of a small number of their members. (Cf. Chapter IV, Table 29.) In contrast to this, the clusters of Babali, Bakumu, and Barumbi in Neighbourhood III were to a greater extent clusters of title-holders who had over the years acquired dwelling compounds close to or in many cases adjacent to each other. As shown in Table 39, a number of Babali and Bakumu title-holders did have fellow-tribesmen living on their compounds, but this was not the main factor underlying their clustering. Moreover, in partial contrast to Neighbourhood II, the recent arrival of rent-paying tenants in Neighbourhood III was more directly associated with its current increase in ethnic heterogeneity.

Lastly, Neighbourhoods II and III had some common features in the demographic composition of their populations. In both areas the

TABLE 40

Tribal affiliations of heads of households in a sample of 63 dwelling compounds in Neighbourhood III

(Part of Survey Tracts B II and III)

TRIBES	HEADS OF PRINCIPAL HOUSEHOLDS	HEADS OF SUBSIDARY NON-RENT-PAYING HOUSEHOLDS	HEADS OF SUBSIDARY RENT-PAYING HOUSEHOLDS	TOTAL
Babali	15	8 (6)	2 (1)	25
Bakumu	13	9 (8)	2	24
Barumbi	10	1	0	11
Babua	5	2 (2)	0	7
Bakusu	5	1	0	6
Topoke	1	3 (3)	0	4
Mangbetu	3	0	0	3
Babira	1	0	1	2
Babudu	2	0	0	2
Balengola	2	0	0	2
Warega	1	0	1	2
Mituku	1	1 (1)	0	2
Bangobango	1	0	0	1
Budja	1	0	0	1
Logo	1	0	0	1
Mongandu	1	0	0	1
Balulu	0	1	0	1
Badongo	0	0	1	1
Balese	0	0	1	1
Bandande	0	0	1	1
Basoko	0	0	1	1
Lokele	0	0	1	1
Muyugu	0	0	1	1
Total	63	26 (20)	12 (1)	101

Note: As in Table 37, figures in brackets indicate the number of subsidiary household heads of the same tribe as the title-holder of the compound.

vast majority of women aged 16–45 years were wives (Table 42,
and Appendix B, Tables 85 and 87). Yet there were many men living
without domestic partners (Appendix B, Tables 84 and 86). Consequently, the sex ratio in each of the two neighbourhoods was very
much higher than in Neighbourhood I and higher than in the town as
a whole. The fertility ratios were about average for the town and thus
appreciably higher than in Neighbourhood I. These features of the
demographic composition of Neighbourhoods II and III were directly

TABLE 41

*Tribal affiliations of heads of households in a sample of 72 dwelling compounds
in Neighbourhood IV*

(*Survey Tract C I*)

TRIBES	HEADS OF PRINCIPAL HOUSEHOLDS	HEADS OF SUBSIDIARY NON-RENT-PAYING HOUSEHOLDS	TOTAL
Lokele	52	28 (28)	80
Bambole	6	1 (1)	7
Topoke	3	2 (2)	5
Turumbu	3	1	4
Mongandu	2	1 (1)	3
Balengola	2	0	2
Bakusu	2	0	2
Babali	1	0	1
Bangobango	1	0	1
Total	72	33 (32)	105

Notes:
(1) As in Table 37, figures in brackets indicate the number of subsidiary household heads
of the same tribe as the title-holder of the compound.
(2) There were no subsidiary rent-paying householders in the sample.

related to the essential contrast between the out-lying areas of all three
townships and the more fashionable parts of Belge I. In the out-lying
areas most households consisted of whole family units with the frequent
addition of single male immigrants; there were few *femmes libres* and
those that did settle in these areas were more likely to be older women
making their living as landladies and small shopkeepers than as
prostitutes or semi-prostitutes.

Neighbourhood IV in turn differed markedly both from Neighbourhood I and from Neighbourhoods II and III; we know that it was
predominantly a Lokele area, and it can be seen in Table 41 that most
of the few non-Lokele households were members of tribes with some
cultural affinity with the Lokele (i.e. the Bambole and the Topoke and,

to a lesser extent, the Balengola, Turumbu, and Mongandu). The neighbourhood thus had an even greater degree of cultural homogeneity than the high proportion of Lokele households would in itself suggest. Moreover, most of the non-Lokele in the area were related by kinship or marriage to one or more of the Lokele households, and most of the Lokele households were themselves interconnected with others either through marriage and descent *in town* or through kinship connexions in their home villages. These distinctive features of the neighbourhood were to a greater or lesser extent factors influencing all its salient characteristics. We have seen that there was considerable

TABLE 42

Selected population indices for Neighbourhoods I, II, III and IV

	I	II	III	IV
Adult sex ratio*	105	137	121	110
Per cent of women aged 16–45 years living singly	31·0	11·1	7·4	22·4
Per cent of men aged 16 years and over living singly	37·9	33·6	38·0	32·2
Fertility ratio†	354	457	482	912
Per cent men and women aged 16 years and over resident in Stanleyville under 2 years	19·4	22·5	22·7	22·4
Per cent of women 16 years and over regularly engaging in some form of trading or shopkeeping	14·0	14·4	15·0	61·5

* Men per 100 women.
† Children aged 5 years and under per 1,000 women aged 16–45 years.

variation in the occupations and wages of men in the area (Table 34) but in contrast to Neighbourhood I, there was, in this setting of cultural homogeneity and of multiple kinship interconnexions, no marked social cleavage between *évolués* and manual workers. Although there were occasional single lodgers paying for their accommodation, all subsidiary households in the area were accommodated free of charge (Table 36); and we shall see that most of the heads of these households were close kinsmen of the title-holders on whose compounds they lived. In addition, the position of women and the nature of family life were qualitatively different. Families were large and there was an extremely high ratio of small children to women (Table 42). Coupled with this, the adult sex ratio was lower than in the town as a whole and very much lower than in the out-lying areas of Neighbourhoods II and III (Table 42). The proportion of 'single' women aged 16–45 years was higher than in Neighbourhoods II and III, but, unlike the 'single' women from Neighbourhood I, a fair proportion of these were young

spinsters living with their parents or other kinsmen. Family supervision
of women was close. There were virtually no women living with men to
whom they were not married, and it was said that none of the *femmes
libres* in the neighbourhood was engaged in any form of prostitution.
(Cf. Tables 83 and 89 in Appendix B.) On the other hand, about 60 per
cent of all women in the area were regularly engaged in some form of
trade. In this respect, the neighbourhood stood in sharp contrast to the
fashionable areas of Belge I and the peripheral areas of the town like
Neighbourhoods II and III (Table 42).

The differences between Neighbourhood IV and other areas of the
town were thus very marked; it was known as 'the Lokele village', and
the very use of the term implied that it was a centre of trade, an area
of close kinship links, and a milieu where the virtue of women—as
wives and mothers and as hard-working traders—was extolled and
safe-guarded.

THE ABSORPTION OF IMMIGRANTS IN DIFFERING 'NATURAL AREAS'

Despite important variations between the 'natural areas' of the town,
the samples for Neighbourhoods I–IV failed to reveal any large differences in the *volume* of recent immigrants finding accommodation in
each. For example, the proportions of all adults who had been in town
for less than two years varied only between 19·4 per cent and 22·7 per
cent in the four samples (Table 42). There were, however, some important differences in the places of origin and in the characteristics of new
arrivals finding accommodation in the four neighbourhoods. Neighbourhood I attracted very few migrants from tribal areas in the countryside,
whereas substantial proportions of new arrivals in Neighbourhoods II,
III, and IV had come direct from native villages without any intervening period in smaller labour centres. Furthermore, Neighbourhood I
recruited a fair proportion of its newcomers from other *centres extra-
coutumiers*, whereas in Neighbourhoods II, III, and IV the majority of
migrants with previous experience of living in 'civilized' places came
from labour camps, plantations and other minor centres of employment. These inferences are drawn from information on the prior places
of residence of all adult men in the four neighbourhoods who had been
in town for less than two years. (See Appendix B, Table 90.) Similarly,
there were differences in the occupational composition of male immigrants coming to various 'natural areas' (Appendix B, Table 91). In
particular, the newcomers in the peripheral areas of Neighbourhoods
II and III were of distinctly lower occupational grades than those
settling in either Neighbourhood I or Neighbourhood IV. Finally, we
know that the tribal composition of the newcomers was in some cases
vastly different from one 'natural area' to another. We know, for
example, that the new immigrants coming to Neighbourhood IV were
almost exclusively Lokele, whereas in Neighbourhoods I and III—and
probably also in Neighbourhood II, though here the evidence is less

convincing—the presence of tenant households was currently contributing to increasing heterogeneity in tribal composition (Tables 37, 39,
40). In general, the tendency for 'natural areas' to recruit newcomers
resembling members of the established population was marked, though
in some neighbourhoods there were important trends of change.

To assess how new arrivals were absorbed in differing 'natural areas'
we may examine the accommodation arrangements of adult men at
different ages and after varying periods of residence in the town. In
the population as a whole, the proportion of men who were title-
holders rose from 12·4 per cent between the ages of 16 to 25 years to
34·2 per cent between the ages of 26 and 35 years, to 52·7 per cent
between 36 and 45 years, to 62·1 per cent between 46 and 55 years,
and to 73·0 per cent for men over 55 years of age. (Appendix B,
Table 97.) As we saw in Chapter II, the circumstances under which
title-holders had acquired their compounds varied considerably
according to the length of time an area had been settled. But, in all
areas, compounds had in most cases only been acquired after considerable periods of continuous residence in the town. (See, for example,
Appendix B, Tables 93–96). Table 43 shows that of all the title-holders

TABLE 43

*Lengths of residence in Stanleyville of heads of households in Neighbourhoods
I, II, III and IV taken as one sample*

LENGTH OF RESIDENCE IN TOWN	HEADS OF PRINCIPAL HOUSEHOLDS (I.E. TITLE-HOLDERS)		HEADS OF NON-RENT-PAYING HOUSEHOLDS		HEADS OF RENT-PAYING HOUSEHOLDS		TOTAL	
	No.	%	No.	%	No.	%	No.	%
Under 1 year	0	0·0	20	18·2	16	22·9	36	8·4
1–2	14	5·7	18	16·4	20	28·6	52	12·2
3–5	18	7·3	22	20·0	20	28·6	60	14·1
6–10	59	23·9	26	23·6	14	20·0	99	23·2
11–20	67	27·1	11	10·0	0	0·0	78	18·3
Over 20 years	89	36·0	13	11·8	0	0·0	102	23·9
Effective sample	247	100·0	110	100·0	70	100·1	427	100·1

The figures tabulated here are shown separately for Neighbourhoods I, II, III, and IV in
Appendix B, Tables 93 to 96.

in the combined sample for Neighbourhoods I, II, III and IV, only
13·0 per cent had been in town less than six years and over 60 per cent
had been there continuously for over ten years. In contrast much
higher proportions of heads of subsidiary households accommodated
free of charge had been in town for relatively short periods, and the

heads of tenant households were on average even more recent arrivals than the heads of households accommodated free of charge. The general practice was for newcomers to be accommodated either as tenants or guests for some years. A few became title-holders after a year or two but the majority did not succeed in doing so for considerable periods after their arrival.

Here again, however, there were important differences between the samples for Neighbourhood I, for Neighbourhoods II and III, and for Neighbourhood IV (Appendix B, Tables 92–95). Neighbourhood I stood out not only, as we have already seen, in having more tenants and higher rentals, but also in having more tenants who had been in town for relatively long periods; and some of these tenants were persons who could easily have acquired undeveloped compounds in the newly settled peripheral areas of New Brussels but who preferred to stay in Belge I even at the cost of paying high rents on an indefinite basis. In contrast, Neighbourhood IV, which had no tenant households, also had the lowest proportion of title-holders with long periods of residence in town. This was partly a consequence of the tendency for better-paid Lokele—especially *évolués*—to move from Neighbourhood IV after some years there to Neighbourhood I or to some other part of Belge I. Thus, for various reasons, the pressure of demand for dwelling compounds was highest in Neighbourhood I, lowest in Neighbourhood IV, and intermediate in Neighbourhoods II and III.

Some implications of this situation for immigrants in the four neighbourhoods are brought out in Table 44 in which the heads of households from each area are classified both according to their lengths of residence in town and to their status as householders. It can be seen that the samples revealed little or no difference between the four neighbourhoods in the status as householders of residents of over ten years' standing but that there were important differences for more recent arrivals. Thus in Neighbourhood I a half of the householders who had been in town between three and ten years were tenants and only a third were title-holders of their own compounds, whereas in Neighbourhood IV two thirds were title-holders and none was a tenant, and in Neighbourhoods II and III about half were title-holders and the majority of the remainder were heads of subsidiary households accommodated free of charge. Equally, there were significant differences between neighbourhoods in the positions of householders who had arrived in town during the three years immediately preceding the study: in Neighbourhood I a majority of these recent arrivals were tenants, whereas in Neighbourhood IV the majority were heads of households accommodated free of charge. Neighbourhoods II and III were intermediate to I and IV in this respect. (See also Appendix B, Tables 92–95[7].)

Further indices of the differences between the four neighbourhoods are found in the accommodation arrangements of *all* men who were not title-holders (i.e. including men who were not household heads but

TABLE 44

Male heads of households in Neighbourhoods I, II, III and IV classified according to length of residence in Stanleyville and to status as householders

(a) *Men with less than three years residence in town*

	NEIGHBOURHOODS						
CATEGORY OF HOUSEHOLD	I		II	III	II and III	IV	
	No.	%	No.	No.	%	No.	%
Principal	1	3·6	3	5	19·5	5	26·3
Subsidiary non-rent-paying	5	17·9	10	9	46·3	14	73·7
Tenant	22	78·6	5	9	34·1	0	0·0
Total	28	100·1	18	23	99·9	19	100·0

(b) *Men with three to ten years residence in town*

Principal	20	33·3	12	17	50·9	28	66·7
Subsidiary non-rent-paying	10	16·7	13	11	42·1	14	33·3
Tenant	30	50·0	2	2	7·0	0	0·0
Total	60	100·0	27	30	100·0	42	100·0

(c) *Men with over ten years residence in town*

Principal	51	85·0	28	41	86·3	36	90·0
Subsidiary non-rent-paying	9	15·0	6	5	13·8	4	10·0
Tenant	0	0·0	0	0	0·0	0	0·0
Total	60	100·0	34	46	100·1	40	100·0

additional members of existing households). Table 45 shows that in the four neighbourhoods taken as one sample, 53·2 per cent of men without their own compounds were staying with kinsmen with whom they had a known genealogical connexion. Another 15·2 per cent were dependent on the goodwill of persons whom they claimed as 'brothers' on the basis of a relationship other than a known genealogical connexion. (For convenience I refer to these two categories as 'real' and 'fictitious' kinsmen[8].) In addition there was a small number of men—representing 5·7 per cent of the sample—who were dependent on the goodwill of persons to whom they claimed no kinship connexion, 'real' or 'fictitious'. These are classified in the table as staying with 'urban friends'.[9] Finally, there were 26·0 per cent who paid for their accommodation as heads of tenant households or as single lodgers or as members of small groups of lodgers. When the proportions of men who fell in these four broad categories are classified according to their lengths of residence

TABLE 45

Accommodation in Neighbourhoods I, II, III and IV taken as one sample of all men other than title-holders classified according to their lengths of residence in town

TYPE OF ACCOMMODATION ARRANGEMENT	LENGTH OF RESIDENCE IN STANLEYVILLE											
	UNDER 1 YEAR		1–5 YEARS		3–5 YEARS		6–10 YEARS		11 YEARS AND OVER		TOTAL	
	No.	%	No.	%	No.	%	No.	%	No.	%	No.	%
Staying free of charge with 'real' kinsmen	42	53·8	37	45·1	44	47·3	40	54·1	44	71·0	207	53·2
Staying free of charge with 'fictitious' kinsmen	12	15·4	9	11·0	13	14·0	16	21·6	9	14·5	59	15·2
Staying free of charge with 'urban friends'	0	0·0	6	7·3	5	5·4	3	4·1	8	12·9	22	5·7
Paying for accommodation	24	30·8	30	36·6	31	33·3	15	20·3	1	1·6	101	26·0
Total	78	100·0	82	100·0	93	100·0	74	100·1	62	100·0	389	100·1

TABLE 46

Accommodation arrangements in Neighbourhoods I, II, III and IV of all men other than title-holders

ACCOMMODATION ARRANGEMENTS	NEIGHBOURHOODS								
	I		II	III	II and III	IV		ALL FOUR NEIGHBOURHOODS	
	No.	%	No.	No.	%	No.	%	No.	%
Staying free of charge with 'real' kinsmen	39	57·4	45	48	69·4	75	87·2	207	71·9
Staying free of charge with 'fictitious' kinsmen	21	42·6	15	13	30·6	10	12·8	59	28·1
Staying free of charge with 'urban' friends	8		9	4		1		22	
Total	68	100·0	69	65	100·0	86	100·0	288	100·0
Total with free accommodation	68	49·3	69	65	82·7	86	96·6	288	74·0
Total paying for accommodation	70	50·7	13	15	17·3	3	3·4	101	26·0
Total	138	100·0	82	80	100·0	89	100·0	389	100·0

in town, we find little variation among those who had been in town for periods of under six years. Among those with more than six years of town residence, however, the proportion of tenants fell appreciably, and an overwhelming majority of those with more than ten years of residence were accommodated free of charge, most of them as 'real' kinsmen.

In Table 46 all men other than title-holders are classified by neighbourhood according to their accommodation arrangements irrespective of length of residence in town. From this tabulation it can be seen that there were important differences between neighbourhoods not only in the proportions who paid or did not pay for accommodation, but also in the ratio of those staying with 'real' kinsmen to those staying with either 'fictitious' kinsmen or 'urban friends'. Thus in Neighbourhood I about a half of the sample paid for their accommodation and, of those who did not pay, only 57·4 per cent were staying with 'real' kinsmen, whereas in Neighbourhood IV nearly all the men in the sample had free accommodation and 87·2 per cent of these were staying with 'real' kinsmen. And Neighbourhoods II and III again occupied an intermediate position between Neighbourhoods I and IV.

THE NATURE OF 'NATURAL AREAS'

The existence of the differentiated neighbourhoods described in this chapter raises important problems of interpretation. Are we to attribute the observed differences between various neighbourhoods entirely to geographical and historical 'accidents'? We have seen that the tribal composition of the several townships was partly a function of their respective locations in relation to various regions of the hinterland. It is therefore at least conceivable that the tribal composition and some related features of the population in each township should have differed as a direct consequence of geographical 'accidents' and not necessarily as a function of urban interaction. Equally, we could conceivably argue that, since many migrants on coming to town first sought to settle with or near to kinsmen and fellow tribesmen, differences between neighbourhoods within the townships might be the consequence of historical 'accidents' which caused members of certain tribes to settle, or to be settled, in particular neighbourhoods within one or other township. And indeed it seems certain that both geographical and historical 'accidents' had played *some* part in determining the patterns discernible in the town at the time of the study.

But the data reviewed in this chapter contain overwhelming evidence that differences between neighbourhoods were also directly linked to the development of a complex internal pattern of specialization and differentiation. Hence my use of the term 'natural areas', but the term itself poses important questions: were the social features of various areas 'natural' in the sense of being expressions of forces and tendencies inherent in the urban situation, or were they 'natural' in the sense of reflecting the extension into the town of principles of association and differentiation stemming from tribal societies of the hinterland?

The evidence we have suggests that neighbourhoods were in varying degrees 'natural' *in both senses*. For example, family and neighbourhood relations in Neighbourhood IV were to a large extent governed by distinctively Lokele norms and customs, and ideally the area would have required investigation as an integral part of Lokele society as a whole. Neighbourhood IV was a 'natural area' of Lokele-land. Yet it was also an integral part of the urban social field. Social relations there were clearly affected by the neighbourhood's location in relation to the rest of the town, by its specialization over time as a focal point of trade within the urban area, and by various sets of social relations developed and maintained by its inhabitants with people in other neighbourhoods. It was thus equally a 'natural area' of the town, and it would be idle to argue for one view in preference to the other.

In contrast to Neighbourhood IV, Neighbourhood I was mainly a 'natural area' of or in the urban social field. The evidence we have is that there were here fewer families and people maintaining links with their rural areas of origin. It was typically an area which recruited its population either from other urban neighbourhoods in Stanleyville itself or from other towns and labour centres. Here kinship and 'tribalism' were, as compared to Neighbourhood IV, factors of less significance in relation to many social relations (e.g. accommodation arrangements) and relations between the sexes were markedly more 'contractual' than 'institutional'. The major social cleavages and alignments within the area were based on 'class' rather than on kinship or tribal affiliation. Moreover the main features distinguishing the neighbourhood from others in the town were related to urban-centred problems and activities. People from other areas of the town came to Neighbourhood I, whether as inhabitants or as daily visitors, to participate in a kind of social life that was distinctive and specialized. The services and the social opportunities of the area did not, for the most part, exist elsewhere. It was essentially the world of *évolués*, of fashionable independent *femmes libres*, of modern bars and dance halls, and of landlords and tenants. It was also the centre of organized voluntary associations stemming from the complex of European-African relations and it was in later days to become the centre of organized political activity in the town.[10]

Finally, as we have seen, Neighbourhoods II and III differed in their essential nature from both I and IV. The features which distinguished them were partly functions of their histories of development and partly of their location in relation to the rest of the town. As quiet peripheral areas they were not attractive to the more sophisticated urban inhabitants, nor were they areas exclusive to one particular tribal element. They offered no distinctive services and opportunities. Consequently, they were seldom visited by people from other parts of the town, yet their own inhabitants were to some extent dependent on the services and opportunities of the in-lying areas. Like Neighbourhood IV, they recruited numbers of their inhabitants from the countryside and from small labour centres of the hinterland, and their daily life was clearly affected both by relations extending to other parts of the town and by connexions maintained by many of the inhabitants with their tribal areas. Yet various aspects of their neighbourhood configurations were very different to those of Neighbourhood IV. Such differences were partly a function of their heterogeneous tribal compositions and associated variations, and partly a function of their 'dormitory' character.

FOOTNOTES TO CHAPTER V

[1] About 10 per cent of the *total* population had been in town for less than one year, and about 47 per cent for less than five years. The corresponding proportions were much higher for young adults: about 22 per cent of the population aged 16 to 25 years had been in town less than one year and approximately 67 per cent had been there for under five years. The basic data from which these figures are drawn are given in Pons (1956a), pp. 258–263.

[2] This range of preoccupations is fully illustrated in the case study of Patrice, given in Chapter VII, and in his letters and diary given in Appendices I and J.

[3] For example, the case study of Limela, given in Chapter VII, shows that he had only acquired a compound and begun to build his own house after nearly four years of continuous residence in the town. The importance of house-building as an activity in the daily lives of both new and old-established residents is illustrated in Chapter VI.

[4] The term 'natural areas' was originally used by Robert Park to refer to areas of extremely different natures in highly diversified cities. His general conception of 'natural areas' is well illustrated by the following quotation:

'The urban community turns out, upon closer scrutiny, to be a mosaic of minor communities, many of them strikingly different one from another, but all more or less typical. Every city has its central business district; the focal point of the whole urban complex. Every city, every great city, has its more or less exclusive residential areas or suburbs; its areas of light and heavy industry, satellite cities, and casual labour mart, where men are recruited for rough work on distant frontiers, in the mines and in the forests, in the building of railways or in the borings and excavations for the vast structures of our modern cities. Every American city has its slums; its ghettos; its immigrant colonies, regions which maintain more or less alien and exotic culture. Nearly every large city has its bohemias and hobohemias, where life is freer, more adventurous and lonely than it is elsewhere. These are the so-called natural areas of the city.' *Human Communities* quoted by Stein (1960), pp. 21–22.

In applying the term to differentiated neighbourhoods *within* the African residential areas of Stanleyville I do not imply differences of the kind and degree that existed in Chicago. The 'natural areas' to which I refer in Stanleyville were for the most part neighbourhoods within the relatively uniform townships of the C.E.C. which was itself a planned residential community under a system of close administrative control. But it could be said of different neighbourhoods within the C.E.C., as Park said of the 'natural areas' in large American cities, that they 'are the products of forces that are constantly at work to effect an orderly distribution of the population . . .,' that they 'are "natural" because they are not planned,' and that the differences between them were 'not the result of design, but rather a manifestation of tendencies inherent in the urban situation . . .' (Park quoted in Stein, p. 22). Thus, for example, the tendency for members of one tribe to reside in one or more particular neighbourhoods was not the product of a policy designed to re-group tribes. Such a policy had been attempted in the very early years of the C.E.C. but had later been abandoned and revised in favour of a determined policy to allocate dwelling compounds on a non-tribal basis.

[5] Clément (1956), p. 453.

[6] *Femmes libres* were women sometimes referred to in the records of the C.E.C. as *femmes vivants théoriquement seul*. They were spinsters, widows or divorcees who qualified for residence in the C.E.C. in their own right and who thus had their own identity books. Many of them were fashionable prostitutes or semi-prostitutes. For further explanation and discussion see Chapter VIII.

[7] As in Tables 90 and 91 of Appendix B, the absolute numbers involved are too small to allow precise estimates of the proportions in the various particular categories for different neighbourhoods. But the overall differences between neighbourhoods are statistically significant and, taken in conjuction with other features of the neighbourhoods, the weight of the evidence pointing to real differences is overwhelming.

[8] On being pressed for an explanation of kinship claims where they knew of no genealogical connexion interviewees typically said that they 'were from the same village or clan or tribe', or often simply that they 'spoke the same language', or were from 'the same country or territory'. For a fuller discussion of the principle of 'urban brotherhood', see Chapter VI.

[9] The category of 'urban friends' consisted of a variety of cases of friendship, convenience, and mutual aid: one householder lived on the compound of an elderly man and helped him to keep the premises clean; another had free accommodation in return for assistance given to the title-holder who was a cripple; some simply claimed to be 'friends' of the title-holder, explaining that they had worked for a long time for the same employer or that they had known each other in a small labour centre before coming to Stanleyville; there were two cases of householders who were kinsmen not of the title-holder, but of one of his more permanent tenants, and who had been given free accommodation by the title-holder for a short period as a favour to the tenant; there was one case of straight charity shown to a man who was old and isolated from his kin; and there was one case of free accommodation given to a man because, according to the title-holder of the compound on which he lived, 'we were both corporals in the army' (though not at the same time).

[10] It was in this part of the town that the more important non-tribal organizations such as *l'Association des Anciens Élèves des Pères de Scheut* (ADAPES), *l'Association des Évolués de Stanleyville* (AES), and *l'Association des Anciens Élèves de Mandombe* (CARITAS) normally met, and many of their members were recruited from this neighbourhood. There were also associations of *évolués* in Brussels and Belge II, but these were generally smaller and more local than those based in Belge I; some were in effect tribal associations with rather different aims to the broadly-based non-tribal associations of Belge I. See Clément (1956), pp. 479–480.

It is of interest to note that at least one of the associations based in Belge I (ADAPES) was later to develop into a mass political movement. It was first established as a markedly non-tribal association of *évolués* in January, 1952. At that time it had 28 members; by the end of 1952 the membership had risen to 68, but a few years later it was to change its character altogether and to enrol some 15,000 members. Van Reyn (1960), p. 18.

VI

NEIGHBOURHOOD RELATIONS

The central purpose of Part II was to define diverse features of the growing population and changing community of Stanleyville. In Part III the focus shifts to selected aspects of the system of urban relations within this changing community and, in particular, to certain sets of social relations in one avenue in a remote corner of the town. In the light of Part II we clearly cannot expect any single neighbourhood to be 'typical' of the town. On the contrary, we must constantly bear in mind that there were appreciable differences between 'natural areas', that there was considerable variation in the nature of rural-urban relations, and that there were important differences between ethnic colonies which were unevenly distributed in various parts of the town. The significance of a detailed study of social relations in one part of the town does not, however, depend on the relations observed being 'typical', and the aim of this and the following chapters is not confined to understanding the nature of social relations in one avenue. To the extent that we remain aware of differences between neighbourhoods and tribes, the analysis of social relations in one particular neighbourhood can be used to explore and illuminate the overall system of relations. This is what I attempt to do in the remainder of the study.

In the field I was led to start an intensive investigation in one corner of the town because I considered that my sphere of observation would in this way remain more manageable than if I tried to encompass a larger and more diversified area. At the beginning of the field study, I was only partially aware of the nature and extent of differences outlined in Part II between tribes, 'classes', and neighbourhoods. But I was soon to become increasingly aware of these differences; they impinged on me through my concurrent work on the census-type survey of the population as a whole, through continuous contact with my two colleagues who were conducting research in other social spheres in the town, and also, most importantly, through the individuals whom I came to know in the course of my intensive study. As was obviously to be expected, the social relations observed between neighbours, friends, kinsmen, fellow-tribesmen and others in one avenue were often found to be parts of broader sets of social relations extending outwards beyond the immediate environs to the wider neighbourhood of the township, to places of work, to the urban community as a whole, and even to the town's hinterland. I attempted, as far as possible, to follow the participation and connexions of avenue people into the wider society, and in this way I developed my own appreciation of the urban community. In presenting the reader with information on the total population before introducing him to the scene of my more intensive fieldwork I have thus to some extent reversed the order in which I myself became acquainted with the community. In this chapter, however, I largely revert to the order and the way in which my knowledge of the community was built up. Thus I describe some of my first experiences in the town, and it will be seen that I sometimes deliberately pose problems and queries about social relations in the manner in which they first struck me in the field. This method of reporting is also to some extent pursued in Chapter VII where I present detailed case studies of three men whom I came to know very well in the course of my fieldwork. In getting to know the personal histories of these and other individuals, I was able to attempt certain assessments of the development of social interactions in the avenue, and I was equally compelled to take account of various sets of social relations which were not confined either to the time or the locality of my direct observations.

The Social Landscape of Avenue 21

Avenue 21 is the name I have previously given to 23 dwelling compounds situated in one of the peripheral areas of Brussels.[1] The avenue led on to the Irumu Road which constituted the southern boundary of Brussels, and it was situated in the area referred to in the previous chapter as Neighbourhood III. The 23 compounds faced each other across one end of a long avenue which contained a total of 70 dwelling compounds. The avenue lay about four kilometres away from the central market, from the offices of the C.E.C., and from the centre of the 'European town'. A subsidiary market on the in-lying border of Brussels was just over a kilometre away. Across the Irumu Road, and within two minutes walk from the avenue, were a few European dwellings, a saw mill, and a general workshop. These establishments employed several men living in the avenue, though the majority worked in or near to the town centre.

Avenue 21 had first been settled in 1930, two years prior to the establishment of the C.E.C. It had thus been in existence over twenty years. It formed part of one of the quietest areas of the town, and few people from the busier areas ever had cause to visit it unless they had friends or kinsmen there. There was one brick house in the avenue occupied by the mistress of a European who had paid for its construction and who called there from time to time. A brick house was a rank exception in Avenue 21 and its environs and the occupant's lover was the only non-African I ever saw in the area. In addition to the brick house there were on the same compound two native-type houses of good quality, the unusual feature of a well with cement walls, and a latrine enclosed by a permanent structure instead of a rough barrier of sticks and leaves as on most other compounds. The total value of the property on this compound was over 15,000 francs. At the other end

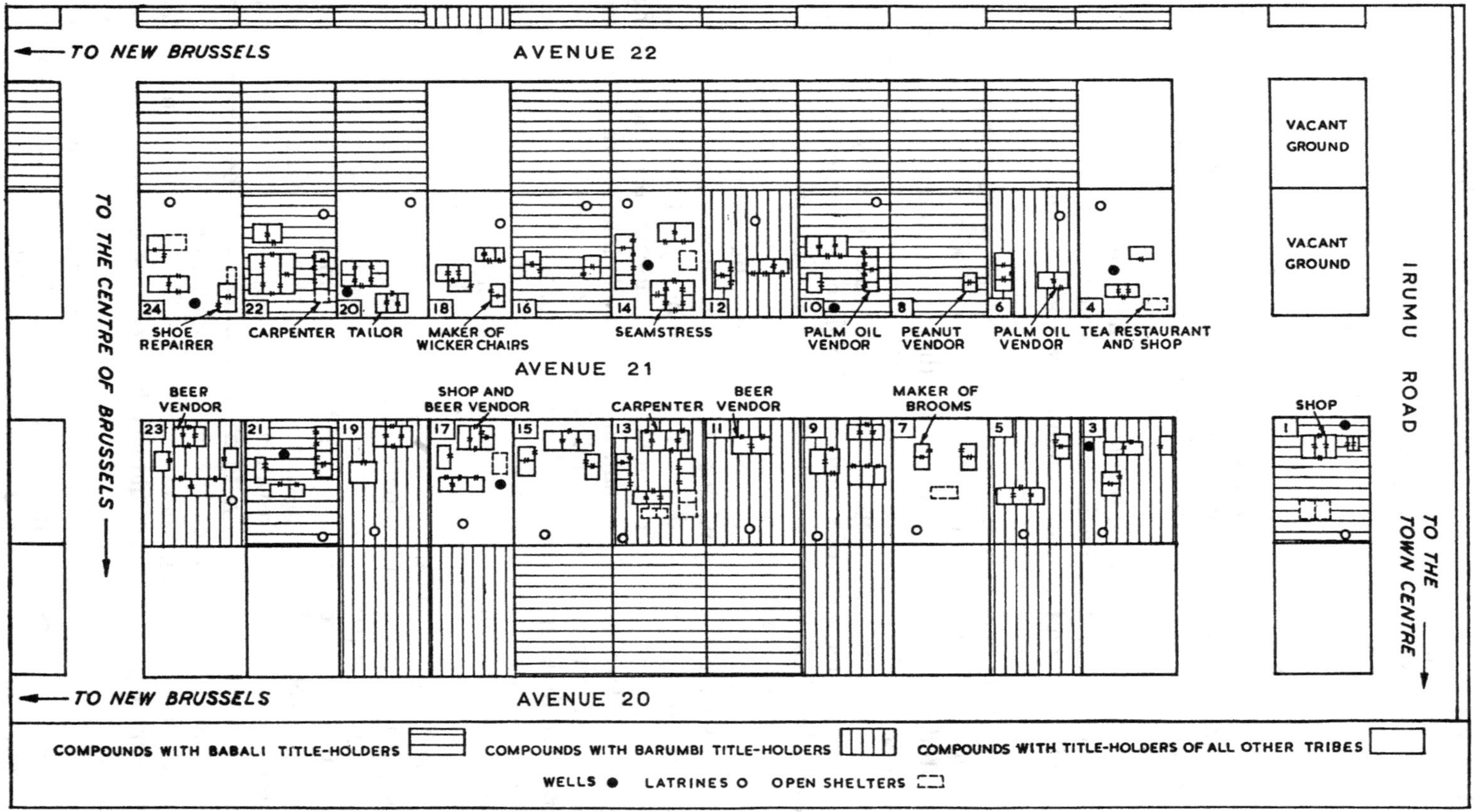

Fig XXV. Sketch map of Avenue 21

of the scale, there was a compound in the avenue with only one rough native-type house of two rooms worth no more than three to four hundred francs. Most compounds had at least two dwellings (See Fig. XXV) and were worth from 1,500 to 4,000 francs.[2] Ten of the 23 dwelling compounds had their own wells which cost two to three hundred francs to dig by hired labour. Most compounds had a few palm and other fruit trees, and several had small gardens of pineapples and sugar cane, and of cassava and other vegetables. There were three small shops in the avenue, and one of them was run in conjunction with a tea room. Up and down the avenue there were several irregular and illicit beer vendors but, somewhat exceptionally for the area, there was no regular bar selling native wines.

Conditions of daily life in Avenue 21 were such that most residents, even if of only a few weeks standing, were able to identify numbers of persons in the immediate locality. The compounds were open and a large part of the daily domestic routine of preparing food, cooking, eating, and washing was conducted out of doors. People could see what their neighbours were doing, they could watch comings and goings, and they could talk to each other from compound to compound. The inhabitants of compounds without wells normally drew their water from the wells of neighbours. Neighbours and near-neighbours were also often in contact with each other as customers and clients for various goods and services. People were thus continually thrown together, and privacy and anonymity were virtually impossible.

The seemingly ready mixing of people was a feature which attracted my attention very early during the course of my fieldwork. On one of my first visits to the avenue, for example, I made a note of the following incident. Two men, a woman, and her small child returned late one afternoon from a trip to a rural village. The lorry in which they had travelled drew up in front of Compound No. 15 where one of the men lived. As the four jumped out of the lorry a few fellow-passengers began to pass down bunches of bananas and other produce brought back from the countryside. Several avenue people immediately gathered round the lorry and helped to carry the goods to the main house on the compound, but at this point the owner discovered that he had lost the key to the padlock on his front door. The lorry drove away but a group of about ten people was left standing in front of the house. A woman strolled across from Compound No. 18 and, on seeing what the problem was, shouted to a woman from Compound No. 22 asking her to bring her bunch of keys to try on the padlock. The woman from Compound No. 22 joined the assembly and, as she did so, untied a bunch of keys hanging from her headscarf. She then herself tested her keys on the padlock. The child who had returned on the lorry began to cry and was picked up by his mother. Another woman who had been looking on from Compound No. 17 ran across and took the child from his mother's arms. Two men strolled down the avenue and paused to ask questions of the group. I recognized one of these men as a resident from Compound No. 13. As the struggle to open the door continued, yet another man walked across from Compound No. 22 accompanied by his small daughter. The owner of the house had by this time withdrawn to the periphery of the assembled group and was discussing his trip with yet another woman who had joined the group. After a few minutes the door was opened and nearly all the people who had gathered entered the house. The whole incident lasted only five to ten minutes but had involved some fifteen to twenty people. Not knowing most of the participants at the time, I gained the impression that they knew each other intimately. In the light of later fieldwork, however, I now very much doubt that they all knew each other well. I was later to come to see that fleeting incidents of the kind reported above were often the means whereby people new to the area identified older-established residents for the first time, and *vice versa*. As Clément has noted in a general description of social life in the town, every newcomer was very 'quickly spotted, observed, catalogued, located with reference to his tribe, the village he came from, the relations who were putting him up, etc'.[3] This was particularly true in the out-lying areas of the three townships of the C.E.C. where, in contrast to the in-lying areas, there was a lower population density and little traffic. Apart from specific incidents like the one reported above, people frequently lingered in the roadway to chat to passers-by or to converse with neighbours as they worked or relaxed outside their houses. Yet many were newcomers who knew few of the other residents at all well.

A second impression from my early period of field-work was that the neighbourhood was relatively self-contained and self-sufficient for a certain range of social activities. Most men went to work daily, most women went to market once or twice a week, and most children went to school; for all these purposes and for a wide range of others the inhabitants had to leave the immediate neighbourhood. Yet daily life still struck me as markedly localized and this impression was over time largely confirmed both by my regular observations and by certain more systematic analyses. For example, I scrutinized the addresses of all persons from the immediate environs of Avenue 21 who appeared before the urban courts in 1952 as parties to cases other than matrimonial suits (i.e. mainly cases of thefts, fights, and insults). Defining 'the immediate environs' of Avenue 21 as extending to two avenues on either side of it—an area roughly corresponding in its boundaries to Survey Tract B III—I found that about 50 per cent of the court cases involving one party from within this area also had their second party from the same area. In 30 per cent of the cases the second party was resident beyond 'the immediate environs' but in the township of Brussels, and only 20 per cent involved a party residing beyond the boundaries of the township. Moreover, over a half of all cases involving two parties from 'the immediate environs' were between persons resident in the same avenue. These figures suggest that my early impression of a relatively intense local life was substantially correct.

The avenue and its immediate environs were obviously not a discrete area, but they were an area of concentrated interpersonal contacts.

The People

We have previously seen that Neighbourhood III in which Avenue 21 was situated, had a tribally heterogeneous population. No single tribe outnumbered all others but the Bakumu and the Babali between them made up nearly 50 per cent of all household heads in the area (Table 40). There was also a smaller concentration of Barumbi making up about 10 per cent of the total. Each of these three tribes had marked clusters of residents in the neighbourhood, and two clusters—one of Babali and one of Barumbi—cut across Avenue 21. (See Fig. XXV.) We also have to recall that the mean monthly wage in this area was low, i.e. about 704 francs as against 959 francs in the town as a whole and well over 1,000 francs in some in-lying areas of the C.E.C. (Table 34.) There were few white collar workers in the area and none who was considered to be *évolué*. The male wage-earning population was approximately evenly divided between ordinary labourers and specialized manual workers (Table 34).

A complete enumeration of the inhabitants of the 23 dwelling compounds in Avenue 21 at one point in time yielded a *de facto* population of 128 men, women, and children, but there was a high rate of movement in and out of the avenue. An impression of the volume of movement is conveyed by Table 47. Over one eight-month period during which I attempted to keep a register the names of 164 persons were recorded as residents excluding persons who were obviously visitors. Of these 164, 50 per cent were recorded as being resident in the avenue over the whole period, but this figure is almost certainly

TABLE 47

Avenue 21: Population movement over an eight-month period in 1952–1953

	NUMBER	PER CENT
Residents throughout the period 29th July 1952–1st April 1953	82	50·0
Residents on 29th July 1952 who had left by 1st April 1953	32	19·5
Persons who came to the area after 29th July 1952 and were still there on 1st April 1953	29	17·7
Persons who came to reside in the area after 29th July 1952 and had left again before 1st April 1953	21	12·8
Total	164	100·0

too high as an estimate of the proportion of people who did *not* move
during the eight months under review. Keeping the register up to date
was a difficult task and it is highly probable that a few people with
short periods of residence were missed.[4] An attempt to record and
classify the places of origin and the destinations of persons coming to
and leaving the avenue proved more difficult. However, despite the
difficulties, the attempt served to show that the bulk of the movement
was between Avenue 21 and other parts of the town, and not between
town and country. Compound No. 17 had the highest turnover of
population. (See Table 48.) The title-holder, Christine, was a woman
who had for several years largely depended on her tenants and lodgers
for her livelihood.[5] Most other title-holders who took in tenants or
lodgers had fewer and chose them more discriminately. Christine's
compound was exceptional for this neighbourhood; as we saw in the
previous chapter, rent-paying tenants were for the most part new to
the area, and Christine must, for several years prior to 1952–53, have
been one of very few landlords or landladies in the neighbourhood.

At one point in time the 23 compounds in Avenue 21 accommodated
43 households, which was a slightly higher proportion than for the
neighbourhood as a whole. Nine of the compounds still had only one
household each and the remainder had two or more, one having four.
The growth in the number of people in the area and the rising ratio
of households per compound were accompanied by an increase in
tribal heterogeneity. As shown in Table 49, 15 out of 23 title-holders
were either Babali or Barumbi, and we know that both were old-
established tribes in the town, as were also the Bakumu and Bakusu
who together contributed three further title-holders to the avenue.
Moreover, most heads of non-rent-paying subsidiary households were
also of these tribes. In contrast, most of the new residents coming in as
tenants were members of tribes not previously represented in the
avenue. The newcomers, whether tenants or not, were also younger
than the old-established members (Table 50), and few had been in
town more than a few years (Table 51). There was, too, an appreciable
difference in the occupations of title-holders and all others. Only four
out of 16 male title-holders were ordinary labourers, the remainder
consisting of five masons, two shop-keepers, two carpenters, one
tailor, one labourer's foreman, and one domestic servant; but of 18
male heads of subsidiary households, ten were labourers and only
eight were specialized manual workers. Taking all this evidence into
account, it is evident that the newcomers constituted a relatively
distinct category of persons whose recent intrusion was affecting the
composition of the avenue's population to a marked extent.

The Beginnings of Field Work in Avenue 21

There is a sense in which the detailed field observations reported in
this chapter started in Avenue 21 by accident. During my first few
weeks in Stanleyville I frequently strolled through various parts of the

TABLE 48

The turn-over of population on dwelling compound No. 17, Avenue 21, between August 1952 and March 1953

PERSON	APPROXIMATE AGE	SEX	TRIBE	MARITAL STATUS	RELATION TO TITLE-HOLDER OR TO HOUSEHOLD HEAD	ARRIVAL	DEPARTURE
1. Christine	45	F	Mongandu	S	Title-holder	Resident since 1947	Left in November 1952 to become a tenant in a nearby avenue
2. Limela	34	M	Mongandu	M	'Fictitious' kinsman, not paying rent but helping No. 1 in various ways	Resident since 1950; came here from another part of Brussels	Left in September 1952 to stay with a friend next door following on a quarrel with No. 1
3. Resina	30	F	Mangbetu	M	Wife of No. 2	Resident since 1951; came here from a small outpost in the hinterland to rejoin her husband from whom she had been separated for a number of years	
4. Etienne	2	M	Mongandu	S	Child of Nos. 2 and 3	Resident since 1951; came with his mother	Left with mother in September 1952
5. Cornet	Under 1	M	Mongandu	S	Child of Nos. 2 and 3	Resident since 1951; came with his mother	Left with mother in September 1952
6.	30	M	Mongandu	M	Tenant	Resident since 1951	Left in September 1952 to stay with 'fictitious' kinsman nearby
7.	25	F	Mongandu	M	Wife of No. 6	Resident since 1951; came with her husband	Left in September 1952 to stay with 'fictitious' kinsman nearby
8. Patrice	22	M	Murega	M	Tenant	Resident since April 1952; came here a few days after arrival in town	Left in February 1953 for compound of a 'fictitious' kinsman in New Brussels where he had started to build his own house
9. Sangumasi	16	M	Murega	S	Brother of No. 8	Resident since April 1952; came with No. 8 a few days after arrival in town	Left February 1953 with No. 8
10.	30	M	Mumbole	S	Tenant	Resident since April 1952	Left in September 1952 when sent to gaol for theft of 500 francs from No. 1
11. Prosper	30	M	Murega	M	Tenant	Arrived in August 1952; came from a nearby avenue where he had been a tenant since his first arrival in town a few months earlier	Left in October 1952 to stay with 'fictitious' kinsman in New Brussels
12. Aluwa	30	F	Murega	M	Wife of No. 11	Arrived in August 1952; came with her husband	Left in October 1952 to stay with 'fictitious' kinsman in New Brussels
13.	3	M	Murega	S	Child of Nos. 11 and 12	Arrived in August 1952; came with his parents	Left in October 1952 to stay with 'fictitious' kinsman in New Brussels
14. Mangaza	20	F	Murega	M	Wife of No. 8	Arrived in September 1952; came here from her village to rejoin her husband	Left in February 1953 with No. 8
15. Kalanga	3	M	Murega	S	Child of Nos. 8 and 14	Arrived in September, 1952; came with his mother	Left in February 1953 with No. 8
16. Marguerite	Under 1	F	Murega	S	Child of Nos. 8 and 14	Arrived in September 1952; came with her mother	Left in February 1953 with No. 8
17.	35	M	Lokele	M	Tenant	Arrived in September 1952	Left in December 1952 but returned in February 1953 and was still there at the end of March 1953
18.	30	F	Lokele	M	Wife of No. 17	Arrived in September 1952; came with her husband	Left in December 1952 but returned in February 1953 and was still there at the end of March
19.	15	F	Lokele	S	Child of Nos. 17 and 18	Arrived in September 1952; came with her parents	Left in December 1952 but returned in February 1953 and was still there at the end of March 1953
20. Abeli	30	M	Mongandu	S	Tenant and later lover of No. 1	Arrived in November 1952	Left in March 1953 (destination unknown)
21.	25	M	Murega	S	'Fictitious' kinsman of No. 8	Arrived in November 1952	Still there at the end of March 1953
22. Mumbuli	20	M	Murega	S	Classificatory brother of No. 21	Arrived in November 1952	Left in January 1953 following a quarrel with No. 1 (destination unknown)
23.	25	F	Musoko	Div.	Friend of No. 1	Arrived in January 1953	Still there at the end of March 1953

Note: In Column 1 named persons are those referred to individually in Chapters VI and VII.

TABLE 49

Avenue 21: Tribal affiliation of heads of principal and subsidiary households

TRIBE	HEADS OF PRINCIPAL HOUSEHOLDS	HEADS OF NON-RENT-PAYING SUBSIDIARY HOUSEHOLDS	HEADS OF RENT-PAYING SUBSIDIARY HOUSEHOLDS	ALL HOUSEHOLD HEADS
Babali	6	4 (4)	I (I)	I I
Barumbi	9	o	o	9
Bakumu	I	2 (2)	2	5
Bakusu	2	I	o	3
Babira	I	I (I)	I	3
Bambole	I	o	o	I
Mongandu	I	o	o	I
Balengola	I	o	o	I
Mangbetu	I	o	o	I
Balese	o	o	I	I
Balulu	o	o	I	I
Bandaka	o	o	I	I
Bandande	o	o	I	I
Basoko	o	o	I	I
Lokele	o	o	I	I
Muyugu	o	o	I	I
Warega	o	o	I	I
Total	23	8	I 2	43

Note: The figures in brackets indicate the numbers of subsidiary households living on dwelling compounds with title-holders of the same tribe as themselves.

TABLE 50

Avenue 21: Ages of heads of principal and subsidiary households

AGE GROUP	HEADS OF PRINCIPAL HOUSEHOLDS		HEADS OF SUBSIDIARY HOUSEHOLDS		ALL HOUSEHOLD HEADS	
	No.	%	No.	%	No.	%
16–25 years	o	0·0	9	45·0	9	20·9
26–35	6	} 43·5	7	} 45·0	13	} 44·2
36–45	4		2		6	
46–55	5	} 56·5	I	} 10·0	6	} 34·9
Over 55 years	8		I		9	
Total	23	100·0	20	100·0	43	100·0

TABLE 51

Avenue 21: Lengths of residence in Stanleyville of heads of principal and subsidiary households

LENGTH OF RESIDENCE	HEADS OF PRINCIPAL HOUSEHOLDS		HEADS OF SUBSIDIARY HOUSEHOLDS		ALL HOUSEHOLD HEADS	
	No.	%	No.	%	No.	%
Under 1 year	0		8		8	
1	0	8·7	3	85·0	3	44·2
2	1		3		4	
3–5	1		3		4	
6–10	4		1		5	
11–20	5	91·3	0	15·0	5	55·8
Over 20 years	12*		2		14	
Total	23*	100·0	20	100·0	43	100·0

* Including two born in Stanleyville.

town to gain general impressions of the social scene. On one such occasion I passed through Avenue 21 and paused for a few moments at the entrance to Compound No. 24 where Libobi was repairing shoes. He greeted me and we exchanged a few words about shoes, about his customers, and about jobs and problems of accommodation. Libobi was a Mundande whose tribal home was in the mountain areas on the eastern borders of the province. I was subsequently to discover that he had left his home village five years earlier and that he had been in Stanleyville for two years. After working in several smaller labour centres he had come to Stanleyville with his employer for whom he had continued to work as a *boy de cuisine* for a few months after his arrival. He had then been unemployed for three months but had managed to stay in the town until he found employment as an ordinary labourer. He was now an *aide mécanicien* in a garage and a self-taught shoe-repairer after working hours. He had fellow-tribesmen in town to whom he referred as 'brothers' but no 'real' kinsmen with known genealogical connexions. He had lived on several compounds since his arrival, sometimes free of charge and sometimes as a tenant. He was now paying rent on Compound No. 24 and had been there a few months only. It was here that he had begun to repair shoes in an attempt to augment his income, but his work as a shoe-repairer was as irregular as it was unskilled, and he had few customers.

Some days later I again stopped to talk to Libobi. While I was there, Lusaka, the title-holder of No. 22, came out of his house to work at his carpentry bench. He greeted Libobi, and came across to No. 24.

TABLE 52

Key to main characters in Avenue 21

NAME	APPROX. AGE	TRIBE	COMPOUND NO. IF RESIDENT IN AVE. 21	BRIEF REFERENCE
Alphonse	35	Mubali	18	Accommodated free of charge on the compound of his 'brother', Amundala
Alufani	40	Murumbi	13	Title-holder of compound; friend and immediate neighbour of François; member of the 'club'
Amundala	30	Mubali	18	Title-holder of compound; 'fictitious' kinsman and close associate of Lusaka; friend of François and member of the 'club'
Antoine	65	Murumbi	9	Title-holder of compound; a much respected man whose advice was often sought by younger inhabitants in the avenue; initially nominated as 'president' of the 'club', though he never took 'office'
Antoinette	24	Mubali	—	Ex-wife of Lusaka, now living a few avenues away; mother of Safi. (See Chapter VII)
Asumani	30	Mubali	16	Title-holder of compound; friend of Amundala and François; member of the 'club'
Augustin	70	Mubali	1	Title-holder of compound; small shopkeeper; husband of Pauline
Baruti	60+	Mubali	—	One of the deceased whose funeral is referred to in the text
Bernadette	23	Mubua	22	Second 'wife' of Lusaka. (See Chapter VII)
Bernard	55	Mubali	10	Title-holder of compound; kinsman of Boniface and Kapitula; 'brother' of Henri
Boniface	35	Mubali	10	Kinsman of Bernard on whose compound he had settled and built his own house
Christine	45	Mongandu	17	Title-holder of compound; small shopkeeper and landlady; 'sister' of Limela
Daniel	20	Mukumu	15	'Village brother' of François on whose compound he lived free of charge
Dominique	30	Mukumu	9	Rent-paying tenant of Antoine
Elizabeth	25	Mubali	—	Mistress of Henri; for a short time lived with Henri on Bernard's compound
Felekini	70+	Mubali	—	The deceased whose funeral is reported in the text
François	50	Mukumu	13	Title-holder of compound; 'Founder' of the 'club' and host at meetings which took place in his house
Gabriel	60+	Mukusu	—	One of the deceased whose funeral is referred to in the text
Henri	25	Mubali	10	'Fictitious' kinsman of Bernard on whose compound he lived free of charge for short periods; lover of Elizabeth

TABLE 52 (*contd.*)—

NAME	APPROX. AGE	TRIBE	COMPOUND NO. IF RESIDENT IN AVE. 21	BRIEF REFERENCE
Jean	30	Mukusu	13	'Family friend' of long standing of Alufani on whose compound he had built his own house
Kapitula	40	Mubali	10	Kinsman of Bernard on whose compound he lived permanently and free of charge
Kisubi	30	Mubali	—	Half-brother of Lusaka (same mother); grew up in Avenue 21 but left it as an adult; in gaol at the time of the study. (See Chapter VII)
Libobi	30	Mundande	24	Rent-paying tenant; my first contact in Avenue 21; left the avenue shortly after I met him
Likuta	22	Murumbi	—	Former resident of compound No. 13; like Lusaka and Limela, made assessments for me of people in the avenue according to their degree of 'civilization'
Limela	30	Mongandu	17	'Brother' of Christine who lived on her compound, but left the avenue during the course of the study; personal friend of Lusaka. (See Chapter VII)
Lusaka	26	Mubali	22	Title-holder of compound; 'president' of the 'club'; friend of Limela; 'fictitious' kinsman and close associate of Amundala. (See Chapter VII)
Mariamu	60+	Mukusu	—	One of the deceased whose funeral is referred to in the text
Maua	20	Mubali	—	Occasionally resident for short periods on compound No. 21; normally stayed in Belge I; often in Christine's 'parlour' when staying in Avenue 21
Mayala	50	Mukusu	4	Title-holder of compound; owner of small tea restaurant and shop; brother of Pauline; '*Muzungu wa ine*'
Milambo	25	Mumbole	23	Lover of Zahabu on whose compound he lived
Mupanda	20	Mukumu	15	Kinsman of François' wife; lived free of charge on François' compound
Pauline	55	Mukusu	1	Wife of Augustin and sister of Mayala
Safi	5	Mubali	22	Daughter of Lusaka and Antoinette. (See Chapter VII)
Sakina	60+	Mukusu	—	One of the funeral cases reported in the text
Samenyao	65+	Mubali	22	Mother of Lusaka and member of his household; mother of Kisubi. (See Chapter VII)
Veronique	23	Mubali	—	Classificatory sister of Alphonse; a visitor to the avenue for 3 days during the period of the study
Zahabu	40	Murumbi	23	Title-holder of compound; mistress of Milambo

Lusaka spoke to me in French, and I later discovered that he was the only person in Avenue 21 who had been to a secondary school. He said he had previously seen me in Brussels, and asked me who I was and what I was doing there. He also said that other people had commented on my visits and had come to him to enquire whether he knew who I was. This was the first indication I had that Lusaka was a person to whom others in the avenue often turned for information and guidance. I was later to see that Lusaka was much respected in Avenue 21. He was regarded as reliable and trustworthy and as knowing the ways of the town. Lusaka was a Mubali, who had lived in Stanleyville all his life and in Avenue 21 since childhood. He was thus a true local in two senses: he had himself been in the avenue for a long time and he was a member of one of the best-established tribal colonies in the neighbourhood. He had been trained as a carpenter at school and was skilled at his job. He was now employed in the saw mill across the Irumu Road and a couple of minutes walk from his home. He also spent long hours at the work bench on his compound making doors, window frames, and small articles of furniture for private customers. He was never short of orders and in fact had an ever-increasing backlog of work which his customers were continually pressing him to complete. He had started working for private customers several years earlier, but the volume of his trade had only recently grown to its present proportions.

I returned to visit Libobi and Lusaka on several occasions during my first few months in Stanleyville. The contrast between their two situations was striking. Lusaka was a townsman by birth, he was well-established on his compound, skilled in his trade, and well-known in the neighbourhood. He had several 'real' kinsmen in town, and he was, in Avenue 21 and its immediate environs, surrounded by fellow Babali and *basaiba* (friends and acquaintances of long standing). In contrast, Libobi was a recent immigrant, he was unskilled, he was a tenant, and he knew, and was known by, few people in the neighbourhood. I was later to see Lusaka very frequently,[6] whereas Libobi was soon to leave Avenue 21, and I lost contact with him. But there were other men in the avenue in situations similar to Libobi's, and my field work inevitably became in part a study of the contrasts between old-established inhabitants of the avenue and the newcomers who were often transient residents.

An Afternoon on Lusaka's Compound

As I came to know Lusaka, I began to see that his compound was one of a series of nodal points of social contact in the avenue. I found that lingering on his compound as he worked at his bench was a sure way of getting to know people, of gathering news and gossip, and of assessing various norms of behaviour in the community. And many of the local inhabitants clearly found the same. This is well illustrated by the following record of the events and conversations which took place on his compound between 4.0 p.m. and 6.0 p.m. one Sunday afternoon. At the time of recording these observations I had been working in the avenue nearly nine months. I had already spent many hours on Lusaka's compound, and my presence in the avenue had largely ceased to attract the kind of attention which my initial visits had drawn. I had myself become part of the social landscape.

Lusaka was filing his saws after working at his bench most of the day. His mother, Samenyao, was sitting on the compound listening to his conversations with callers and passers-by. In between these conversations, Lusaka passed comments to his mother on people who happened to walk down the avenue. Sometimes he addressed her in Swahili, sometimes in Kibali. His tenants of two months' standing were not on the compound. His 'wife', Bernadette, was visiting her kin in Belge I.[7] She was a Mubua, and was also of Stanleyville birth. His daughter, Safi, was spending the day elsewhere in Brussels with her mother Antoinette, Lusaka's former wife.

Limela, a Mongandu who had previously been a near-neighbour and was a work-mate and a good friend of Lusaka, passed the compound.[8] He had until recently been a resident of Compound No. 17 and was a 'fictitious' kinsman of the title-holder, Christine. He was now on his way to visit his 'sister' but, seeing Lusaka, he stopped to greet him, came on to the compound, and began to chat. He first told Lusaka of the progress made with the new house which he was building in New Brussels, and for which he had already placed orders for doors and window frames with Lusaka. Limela spoke broken French, and the conversation was partly in French, partly in Swahili. They tended to start comments in French and to lapse into Swahili as they came closer to making a point. From time to time one or the other interrupted the conversation to exchange a few words with passers-by.

Limela explained to Lusaka that he was planning his new house in such a way that it would be necessary for the children to pass through his own bedroom to go outside. Lusaka expressed approval saying that it was particularly wise for growing girls who needed to be kept under strict supervision. The conversation went on until Asumani, the title-holder of No. 16, came on to the compound. He too was strolling down the avenue when he saw Lusaka chatting to Limela and decided to stop. Asumani was, like Lusaka, a Mubali. He had been in town 7 or 8 years, but had only recently acquired a compound in Avenue 21. He knew Lusaka fairly well as a fellow-Mubali and near-neighbour, but he and Limela knew each other by sight only. He was less 'civilized' than either Lusaka or Limela. (Lusaka once described him to me as a man who did not 'hold "civilization" well'.)

Asumani spoke no French, and after his arrival the conversation was almost entirely in Swahili, though at first he himself took little part in it. Lusaka and Limela continued to talk of house-building, and Lusaka explained that in the new house he was building there would be a room for visitors, but that when his elder half-brother, Kisubi, came out of gaol any visitors would have to go into an out-house. At this point in the conversation, Elizabeth, a Mubali woman from another avenue, walked past and greeted Lusaka who responded by chiding her with the fact that she had recently taken her lover to live on the compound of her kinsmen.

Neither Limela nor Asumani knew Elizabeth, and Limela enquired from Lusaka who she was. Lusaka explained that she was the *habara* (mistress) of Henri, who used to live on Compound No. 9 with his (Henri's) 'fictitious' kinsman, Bernard. Henri, Elizabeth, and Bernard were all three Babali whom Lusaka knew fairly well. Bernard was a title-holder of some years standing in the avenue. He and Lusaka were very cordial to each other if they met in the street or passed each other's compounds, but they were not intimate and did not visit each other. (Lusaka once described Bernard as 'a man of good influence'. But he was not 'civilized'. He was, as Lusaka put in, 'a man whose heart is still in the village'.)

In the course of conversation Lusaka explained to Limela and Asumani that Henri, whom neither of the two listeners knew, was not like Bernard whom they did know. Bernard was a stable man, but Henri was 'a vagabond, a man who never stayed still, and who was always wandering about the town'. Lusaka then went on to explain how Henri had recently left Bernard's compound to live on the compound of a kinsman of Elizabeth. Limela expressed surprise and disapproval that a man should leave his 'brother's' compound to live with a brother of his mistress. This led to a long discussion of the similar case of Milambo who had recently come to the avenue to live with his mistress, Zahabu, who was the title-holder of Compound No. 23, almost opposite Lusaka's house.

The case of Milambo and Zahabu was known to Limela but not to Asumani who now questioned Lusaka about Milambo. He asked what his tribe was, where he worked, what he did, how long he had been with Zahabu, and what kind of man he was. Lusaka gave the details while Limela, who did not know Milambo as well as Lusaka did, made one or two contributions to the effect that Milambo was 'a Topoke, a *musendji* straight from his village'. (Milambo was in fact a Mumbole, not a Topoke. I later discuss the significance of this mistake.)

Lusaka and Limela agreed that it was always reprehensible for a man to live on the compound of his mistress, and particularly so in this case because Zahabu was much older than Milambo, and also because, Lusaka said, 'everyone had advised Milambo over and over to leave the compound'. In the previous few days, Milambo had repeatedly quarrelled with Zahabu's mother who was also living on the compound. Lusaka conceded that the quarrels were largely the fault of Zahabu's mother, but from one point of view this only made Milambo's failure to leave the compound more difficult to understand. Milambo was, Lusaka said, like 'a man who had lost his memory'. In the end, however he simply laughed saying that it must be a matter of '*plaisir*' (meaning sexual pleasure).

Limela now left to visit Christine, and shortly afterwards Maua, a young Mubali woman, walked across from Compound No. 21. Maua was the classificatory sister of a man whom Lusaka knew well as a fellow tribesman and near-neighbour from another avenue. Maua herself was not a regular resident of the neighbourhood. She was an ordinary prostitute as distinct from a semi-prostitute.[9] She was not registered as a *femme libre* and was not officially entitled to reside in the C.E.C. She spent most of her time in Belge I, but would occasionally come to Avenue 21 for a few days or weeks on end to stay with 'fictitious' kin.

On walking across to Compound No. 22, Maua greeted Lusaka and then sat down next to Samenyao to whom she talked for a while. When a lapse occurred in the conversation between Lusaka and Asumani, Maua enquired whether she might borrow Lusaka's bicycle to go on an errand to the other end of Brussels. Lusaka lent her his bicycle and she left.

At this point Alphonse and Amundala, residents of Compound No. 18, passed down the avenue in a lorry belonging to Alphonse's employer. Alphonse and Amundala were both Babali whom Lusaka and Asumani knew very well. Amundala was the title-holder of No. 18 and had lived there for four years. He and Lusaka were close personal friends and 'fictitious' kinsmen in town (Amundala came from the same village as Lusaka's mother's kin, and Lusaka normally addressed Amundala as *muyomba* in Swahili or *oncle* in French). Lusaka often visited Amundala on his return from work and *vice versa*.

Lusaka greeted Alphonse and Amundala as they passed, but then immediately began to discuss with Asumani the illicit use of an employer's vehicle. He expressed strong disapproval of this, saying that it was foolish and that he was surprised that Amundala should be a party to this with Alphonse. (The implication here being that while Alphonse could not be expected to know better, Amundala should have known that it was a foolish thing to do.) If they had an accident, how would they explain themselves?

Lusaka and Asumani discussed at length instances of men who had used their employers' vehicles without permission. The conversation then developed into a general discussion about Europeans as employers. Lusaka drew contrasts between employers who were strict and those who were lenient and, later, between officials in the administration who had foresight, ability, and understanding, and those who, according to him, lacked all these abilities and simply relied on seniority for promotion.

The conversation was still in progress when Maua returned bringing Lusaka's bicycle back. She again sat down next to Samenyao, and gathered from her that Lusaka and Asumani had been discussing Alphonse and Amundala. Asumani soon left and Maua now began to discuss Alphonse with Lusaka and particularly the recent visit to the avenue of Alphonse's sister, Veronique. Veronique was a *femme libre* and a semi-prostitute. She was a striking woman who dressed fashionably. She was known in the avenue as a woman who had been to Leopoldville and who was said to associate either with European men or with African *évolués* in Belge I. Her brief visit to Avenue 21 had aroused considerable attention and comment. After two days she had quarrelled with Alphonse and had left on bad terms with him. Maua questioned Lusaka about Veronique's relation to her brother, and wanted to know whether it was true that on leaving Veronique had thrown a piece of burning wood on to the compound thus indicating that she was not prepared to be reconciled with Alphonse. Lusaka gave a brief account of the quarrel, and Maua then continued to discuss the incident in Kibali with Samenyao. At this point I myself left the compound.

I have given this detailed account of the events and conversations around Lusaka's work bench on one afternoon partly to illustrate the general atmosphere on one compound in the avenue, and partly because the account contains several incidents which I use in my analysis. Lusaka's compound was, of course, not the only one on which there was a continuous exchange of news and gossip—I refer to several others in this chapter—but it is one of particular interest on account of Lusaka's influential position in the avenue. Moreover, the early part of my field work was to an appreciable extent conducted from this base.

Getting to Know People

At the stage when, knowing only Libobi and Lusaka, I began to concentrate on the study of Avenue 21 and its neighbourhood, my first immediate concern was to identify and classify people. I soon found this relatively easy to do because many of the people I met were themselves constantly doing the same thing. The questions which Asumani asked Lusaka concerning Milambo, for example, were of much the same kind as I myself had repeatedly put to Lusaka when I first began to frequent his compound. In a situation where most persons were in the course of a day in contact with many others, and where there was a high turn-over of population over the weeks and months, people were of necessity constantly engaged in finding and checking their social bearings. In so doing, they naturally used any pre-existing social connexions which they may have had with kinsmen, fellow-tribesmen, workmates, and others.

My own position in attempting to get to know people in the avenue was different to that of the inhabitants. As a European, I was conspicuous and out of place in the area, and I had no pre-existing links there. Nor did I enjoy many of the advantages that actual residence in the avenue carried for establishing social contact. Yet my position turned out to be less disadvantageous and, in a few respects, more similar to that of *some* inhabitants than I had anticipated. I was an outsider but so were many of the inhabitants, and the common feature in their situation and my own helped me to see some of the important implications of the high rate of population turn-over and of the marked and increasing degree of social heterogeneity in the neighbourhood. A number of social networks were open and dispersed, and I was frequently able to enter *certain* social relationships as easily as many of the inhabitants did.[10] I was a customer at the local shops, and I bought beer, fruits and nuts from women vendors; I had occasion to use the services of Lusaka as a carpenter and of one of his neighbours as a tailor; and I was myself a 'photographer' taking (and sometimes selling) photographs in Brussels. Also, more importantly, I had time on my hands which made it possible for me to linger endlessly on the more 'public' compounds (such as Lusaka's) and to perform a series of practical services for members of the population. I sometimes wrote letters of introduction to European doctors in the town to whom direct access was often difficult for the inhabitants; I advised people on the procedures they were expected to follow in registering at the labour exchange and at the offices of the C.E.C.; I sometimes read and wrote letters for illiterates, and I occasionally helped schoolboys with their homework. In addition, as illustrated by my first encounters with Libobi and Lusaka, I had as a European *some* advantages for making social contacts which African inhabitants of the avenue did not have. I was a rank and conspicuous outsider, but in the situation my status as a European and my very conspicuousness carried marked advantages as well as disadvantages. I found that I came to know and identify people more rapidly than many a newcomer to the avenue, and the information which I accumulated over the course of a few months enabled me in some cases to follow conversations about local people better than *some* of the residents themselves. In the particular instance of the conversation about Milambo, for example, I already knew the answers to the questions which Asumani asked of Lusaka. Moreover, as my knowledge of people and situations in the avenue built up, I came to see that even a man like Lusaka was in conversations on his compound not solely a giver of news and information, but also often an inquirer. Though he had a large fund of knowledge built up since childhood about people who had lived in the neighbourhood á long time—and especially about Babali residents—he was himself partly dependent on persons outside his better-established networks for keeping up to date with information on the more recent arrivals, and even, in some cases, on non-Babali who had been in the neighbourhood for many years. There were in the avenue many people who knew each other very well, yet no one could live there without also interacting with newcomers and strangers.

I also came to see both from personal experience and from my observation of others that the process of adjusting to the avenue was much affected by the sheer multiplicity of tribal elements represented there. Though ethnic heterogeneity was less marked than in an area like that of Neighbourhood I, it was sufficient for even an urban-born resident like Lusaka to occasionally find himself interacting with members of tribes whose customs were unfamiliar to him. This had an important bearing on the actions and behaviour of all the inhabitants. The process of living in the avenue involved not only becoming acquainted with individual personalities, but also *learning* to differentiate between various tribal elements in the urban population. A first step towards determining one's relationship with a stranger was to ascertain his tribe, but this in itself could be a process conducted over time and sometimes requiring considerable knowledge. To appreciate this, we have to consider the wide variety of ways in which members of different tribes could be distinguished from each other. Some tribes or groups of tribes could be distinguished with varying degrees of precision on the basis of facial marks or other physical peculiarities (e.g. the elongated skulls of the Mangbetu and related tribes whose custom it was to strap heads in babyhood.) Often, too, ethnic identification could be established with a relatively high degree of accuracy on the basis of certain features of dress and ornamentation, or on the possession of distinctive articles of native manufacture such as stools, kitchen utensils, and musical instruments, which commonly varied in type and style from one tribe to another or, perhaps, from one region or culture cluster of the hinterland to another. Again, identification was usually possible for persons with the requisite knowledge on the basis of speech which might be in a vernacular tongue or which, even if in Swahili or Lingala, was liable to include a phrase in a vernacular tongue or particular expressions which betrayed one or other ethnic background. The very fact of whether a person tended to speak more spontaneously in Swahili or Lingala was an indicator of some reliability as to whether he or she came from the east or the west, and so on. Yet again, there were some gross behavioural indicators, such as style of native dancing, and there were more subtle ones in certain minor physical mannerisms. There were equally broad indirect indicators related to urban occupations and practices. Thus, for example, anyone who had lived in the town for some time would know that a white collar worker was more likely, other things being equal, to be a Lokele than, say, a Topoke, though on the basis of a number of other possible criteria the cultural affinity between these two tribes might well have led to a man from the north or the east to fail to distinguish between them. Similarly, an experienced Stanleyville dweller would always, other things being equal, be more likely to assume that a fashionable *femme libre* was a Mubua, and that a woman trading on the market was a Lokele, rather than the other way round.

With so many possible indicators, and with their varying degrees of reliability, it sometimes happened that people made errors in their assessments of each other's tribal affiliations. In this connexion, it is revealing to consider the particular reference in my account of an afternoon on Lusaka's compound to Milambo's tribal identity. We saw that Limela referred to Milambo as a Topoke whereas he was in fact a Mumbole. It would have been a gross error for Limela to mistake Milambo for, say, an Azande or a Mangbetu, but the Topoke and Bambole were peoples from the same region who were in many urban situations likely to be considered, and to consider themselves, as 'brothers'. Thus, in many situations, his slip might have been of little consequence even if he had been face to face with Milambo at the time; but the fact that the Topoke were generally considered to be less 'civilized' than the Bambole could in other situations have led Limela's slip to be construed as a deliberate insult. It is, however, of interest to note that had Limela been face to face with Milambo he would in all probability not have made the mistake in the first place; Limela was a Mongandu, and the Mongandu were themselves a tribe with some cultural affinity to the Topoke and the Bambole. That Limela did make the mistake thus illustrates a further implication of ethnic heterogeneity for interpersonal relations. To Lusaka—or to me after some months of field work in the town—Limela's error inevitably conveyed a good deal about his (Limela's) relationship with Milambo: it clearly indicated that he did not know Milambo at all well and that he had very probably never spoken to him. Had he known him better, it is highly probable that he would not have made the mistake and, indeed, that in the particular conversation on Lusaka's compound he would have referred to an aspect of Milambo's personal situation and character—as Lusaka had done—rather than to a general classificatory characteristic such as his tribal affiliation.

Assessing Situations and Norms of Behaviour

As my account of an afternoon on Lusaka's compound shows, the conversations around his work-bench were not confined to the identification of people and the straight exchange of news. During the course of two hours on the afternoon I have described, the character and behaviour of several people had been discussed and evaluated in terms of moral worth, wisdom, 'civilization', and the like. For example, although Asumani was, in the discussion about Milambo, primarily concerned to get factual information, Limela and Lusaka were, with different degrees of knowledge and insight, more interested in trying to find an explanation for Milambo's behaviour. In the event, their conclusions—Limela's that Milambo was a 'Topoke, a *musendji* from the village', and Lusaka's that Milambo's conduct could only be understood by taking into account the question of *plaisir*, and was therefore amusing—pointed to important factors affecting variation in the local norms of conduct between men and women.

Similarly, Lusaka's exchanges with Limela over the rearing of children in town, his comments to Asumani about Alphonse's use of his employer's vehicle, and Maua's questioning about the behaviour of Veronique, were in effect part of a process of consultation and discussion about one or other aspect of problems of personal behaviour. As such, they inevitably led Lusaka on to discuss the setting of these problems and to volunteer his views on more general subjects. On the afternoon in question, for example, he was led to discuss relations between European employers and their African employees and the promotions of different types of European administrators.

On many other occasions, Lusaka's comments on particular items of news and gossip drew him into general comparisons of the ways of life in town and in native villages. As a townsman born and bred, he had marked anti-village and pro-urban sentiments. He often maintained, for example, that 'village people are "jealous" of us in town', that 'a man is never free from difficulties in the village', whereas in town 'he is only troubled if he is a trouble-maker'. 'In town', he said, 'a man has liberty, and his eyes are opened to the world and to "civilization".'

In listening to the wide variety of discussions that took place on Lusaka's compound I found that these were quite as much a part of an on-going process of evaluating behaviour, of seeking solutions to problems, and of weighing up different norms (or sets of norms) as they were part of a process of incorporating newcomers to the avenue into a developing set of social relations. On his compound, as on many others, social norms were in effect constantly being examined, learnt, and taught at the same time as they were in the process of change, development, and elaboration.

This had important implications for field work, as it obviously has for any analysis of the data gathered. In the field, it often facilitated my participation in social life. In situations where people are in effect engaged in exploring modes of behaviour and discussing the relative advantages of different cultural solutions to common problems, relative lack of consensus can serve to lessen the embarrassment which an outsider may cause. Thus, on *some* occasions at least, my presence was undoubtedly seen by *some* people, Lusaka amongst them, as an advantage and a positive value. For example, discussions bearing on differences in the relations between men and women in *Kizungu* and *Kisendji* frequently caused participants to ask me to talk about relations between the sexes in European society. And this was also the case, in varying degrees, in discussions on a wide range of other subjects such as kinship obligations in town, the rearing of children, and relations between fellow-workers.

In the process of analysing social relations, on the other hand, the fact of relative fluidity and variety in the norms governing people's actions is, of course, a complicating factor which calls for detailed observational studies, for constant comparison between different groups and, wherever possible, for the assessment of change over time in one and the same group.

The Notions of 'Civilized' and 'Uncivilized'

Lusaka's conversations with other people frequently produced references to 'civilization', to 'civilized' behaviour, and to 'civilized' people. He himself was by common agreement in Avenue 21 'the most "civilized" man here'. Yet his concern with 'civilization' was no personal idiosyncrasy. Throughout the avenue some people were commonly considered, and referred to, as more 'civilized' than others, while some were thought of as rankly 'uncivilized'. At first I was inclined to think of 'civilized' and 'uncivilized' primarily as assessments of moral worth for people would at times use the term 'uncivilized' to refer very loosely to behaviour that was considered harsh, ill-mannered and objectionable. Thus if a man beat his wife or got boisterously drunk or was inhospitable to his friends and kinsmen, people might in effect say: 'What can you expect of him? He is not "civilized".' But individuals and their behaviour were also frequently assessed as 'civilized' and 'uncivilized' independently of moral worth. We have seen, for example, that Lusaka considered Bernard as a good and trustworthy man though he described him as 'not well civilized', explaining that 'his heart still lay in the village'.

The following selected examples help to convey the more general meaning and usage of 'civilized' and 'uncivilized':

(*a*) Mayala was a man of about 50 years of age who had travelled throughout the Congo as a domestic servant and who had been away from his native village for 30 or 40 years. He was the title-holder of Compound No. 4 where he ran a small tea-room and shop. He was not liked in the avenue, and was often referred to as miserly and self seeking. He lived alone and people said he was too miserly to keep a wife. The well on his compound had a wooden lid which was always padlocked to prevent others from drawing water there, and this too was often cited as an example of his selfishness. People also said that he never greeted those who passed his house, and he was sometimes referred to as '*Muzungu wa ine*'—'the European of No. 4'—an appella-tion which underlined his aloofness and unwillingness to share. He was, however, described to me as 'a well "civilized" man'. He was unpleasant and disliked, but he knew the ways of the town.

(*b*) Antoine, the title-holder of No. 9 was another elderly man who had spent the greater part of his life working for Europeans after having left his village as a child. He was highly respected in the avenue and was often called out to settle quarrels, especially between husbands and wives, and it was said that in days gone by the chief of the C.E.C. had 'appointed' him as 'counsellor' to the avenue. Of him, Lusaka said: 'He is a very "civilized" man; he has always been in *Kizungu* and has learnt 'civilized' ways even though he never went to school. He some-times says that he is a Mohammedan, but he does not know the ways of the *Arabisés*'. Another man assessed him somewhat similarly, saying: 'He is a good man; people listen to him and he understands their affairs. He is "civilized".'

(*c*) Dominique, a tenant on Antoine's compound, was a much younger man who had been in Stanleyville a few months only after working in several smaller labour centres. On the compound where he lived he was called *Bwana Muzuri* on account of his gentle manner, and he was described to me as a man who behaved in a quite exemplary way towards his family and neighbours. But, one man said, 'as far as "civilization" goes, he is only half way. He does not understand, he is not yet awake'.

These cases show that social approval and disapproval bore no constant relation to 'civilized' and 'uncivilized'. More generally, 'civilization' denoted familiarity with 'urban' norms, an attitude of mind responsive to non-traditional associations, and a way of life that could be, and was, practised by both good and bad men. The notions were closely related to those of *Kizungu*, the way of life with and of Europeans, and of *Kisendji*, a term which was occasionally used to refer very particularly to the African way of life in pre-European days but more commonly to the current tribal way of life in villages.

To test whether 'civilized' status was associated with educational and occupational achievements, I asked three men—Lusaka, Limela, and Likuta who, like Limela, was a former resident of Avenue 21— to classify as 'civilized', 'less civilized', or 'more civilized' all adult men in the avenue whom each knew personally. All three were men who considered themselves, and were considered by others, as being more, rather than less, 'civilized'. I gave the exercise separately to each man and discussed his classification at length with him. The results, cross-tabulated with the educational-occupational grades of the subjects, are shown in Tables 53, 54 and 55. The assessments of all three men show definite though limited degrees of correlation with the educational-occupational grades used in Chapter III (Table 9). Just as revealing as this degree of correlation, however, were two points which emerged from the way in which the three assessors carried out the exercise. First, there was the facility and confidence with which each did his grading once he had grasped what was required of him. To be asked to grade people according to degree of 'civilization' was a meaningful task and this in itself tended to confirm my impressions based on participation in the avenue of the importance of 'civilization'. Secondly, the assessments were clearly made on a relative basis. In the course of the exercise, each man came to his final assessment through a process of measuring various individuals against each other. Moreover, it can be

TABLE 53

Assessments by Lusaka of the degree of 'civilization' of 32 men in Avenue 21 classified according to educational-occupational grade

DEGREE OF 'CIVILIZATION'	EDUCATIONAL-OCCUPATIONAL GRADE						TOTAL
	1	2	3	4	5	6	
Less 'civilized'	—	—	1	5	9	3	18
'Civilized'	—	—	1	2	2	—	5
More 'civilized'	—	1	2	2	4	—	9
Total	—	1	4	9	15	3	32

TABLE 54

Assessments by Limela of the degree of 'civilization' of 26 men in Avenue 21 classified according to educational-occupational grade

DEGREE OF 'CIVILIZATION'	EDUCATIONAL-OCCUPATIONAL GRADE						TOTAL
	I	2	3	4	5	6	
Less 'civilized'	—	—	—	—	2	I	3
'Civilized'	—	—	I	5	3	I	10
More 'civilized'	—	I	2	4	6	—	13
Total	—	I	3	9	11	2	26

TABLE 55

Assessments by Likuta of the degree of 'civilization' of 30 men in Avenue 21 classified according to educational-occupational grade

DEGREE OF 'CIVILIZATION'	EDUCATIONAL-OCCUPATIONAL GRADE						TOTAL
	I	2	3	4	5	6	
Less 'civilized'	—	—	2	I	7	3	13
'Civilized'	—	—	I	3	4	I	9
More 'civilized'	—	I	I	3	3	—	8
Total	—	I	4	7	14	4	30

seen that Limela was less disposed to think of people as little 'civilized' than were either Lusaka or Likuta, and the discussion I had with him about his classification strongly suggested that his results differed from those of the other two because he was himself the least 'civilized' of the three. The notion of 'civilization' was important and certainly relevant in day-to-day life, but it was, in the exercises as in daily life, a relative and largely subjective concept.

The manner in which being 'civilized' or 'uncivilized' affected social relations in the avenue is discussed as we examine various small-group situations.

François's Compound and the 'Club'

The full range of Lusaka's friends and acquaintances was much wider than that represented in the account of one afternoon on his compound. (See Chapter VII.) Yet even on the afternoon described, there were in Limela and Asumani two men whose relations with Lusaka rested on quite different bases. Limela had first met Lusaka when they were both working for the same employer several years earlier. They had become friends at that time, and their friendship had continued to develop when Limela was living in Avenue 21 for some time. The two men used to visit each other, and each told me that the other was a man he would consult in times of serious difficulties. Each saw the other as relatively 'well civilized' and as understanding the problems of life in town, though the opinion in the avenue was definitely that Lusaka was much more 'civilized' than Limela. Asumani, on the other hand, was not a 'civilized' man and his relationship with Lusaka was essentially that of a fellow-tribesman who happened to live close to him. As a 'tribal brother' who knew Lusaka quite well, Asumani felt free to wander on to the compound and to join any group of people who happened to be there. Even though often partially or wholly excluded from the conversation, he clearly felt at home in the social environment of Lusaka's compound.

Limela and Asumani had no history of previous association and no tribal or other traditional affinities, and they had previously known each other by sight only. Encounters between people largely or entirely unknown to each other were common on Lusaka's compound, and his behaviour on these occasions clearly revealed his own evaluations of the status of the visitors. Thus, on the particular occasion of Asumani's arrival while Limela was already there, Lusaka continued to address himself mainly to Limela. While giving brief categorical answers to any questions put by Asumani, he would immediately return to his more general conversation with Limela. His conduct here was in keeping with his own status in the neighbourhood, and with the value which he clearly attached to friendships with 'civilized' or 'more civilized' persons. His workmates and other personal friends were always accorded preferential treatment over any less 'civilized' fellow tribesmen and neighbours who happened to arrive while he had other guests on the compound. In this respect Lusaka's position in relation to those who gathered on his compound was different to that occupied by François on his compound.

François was a Mukumu of about 50 years of age. He had left his village as a young man about 20 years before. He had come to live on Compound No. 15 seven years earlier and had later bought a house there and become the title-holder. His wife (a Mumbole) spent much of her time in Belge II where she co-operated with some of her kinswomen in trading bananas and other produce from the countryside. She was seldom in Avenue 21 for more than a few days at a time. François himself was also often away from his compound for periods of two or three days and his friends in the avenue teased him on account of his alleged wanderings from one mistress to another.

François' compound accommodated two households in addition to his own. Mupenda, the head of the first household was a kinsman of

François' wife, and Daniel the head of the second household, was a man from François' village to whom he referred as his brother though there was no known genealogical connexion between them. Mupenda and Daniel were young men who had recently come to town with their wives. Both were regarded by persons like Lusaka and Limela as 'uncivilized'; neither was well-known in the avenue, and their social connexions were mainly with other Bakumu. François himself, though a more 'civilized' man than the other two men on his compound, was also assessed as 'not well civilized'. The compound was frequently the centre of sociable gatherings of kinsmen and other 'brothers' of all three men. These gatherings were often exclusively Bakumu and on such occasions they seldom involved neighbours from the avenue where there were few Bakumu households. Most visitors to the compound were unknown to the immediate neighbours, and the conversation on the compound was normally in Kikumu which in itself tended to prevent non-Bakumu from joining in.

François himself had, however, built up some individual friendships with a few of his neighbours over the years. He was fond of company and was a jovial and likeable man. Often when he had no kinsmen or other Bakumu visitors he would go drinking in one of the palm wine bars in the neighbourhood, and at other times he gathered a few of his neighbours to drink with him on his compound. The most regular members of this drinking group were Amundala and Alphonse from No. 18, and Alufani who was François' immediate neighbour from No. 13. But others would occasionally join the group, especially on pay-days when drinking sessions were more prolonged than usual. Thus Amundala sometimes brought Lusaka with him, and Alufani (a Murumbi) would bring Jean (a Mukusu), who was a friend of long standing and who had built his own house on Alufani's compound.

I have previously described how, during the period of my field work, the six more regular members of this drinking group constituted themselves into a mock-formal association or 'club'.[11] They referred to their group as *l'association*, and they gave each other titles such as *président, gouverneur, commissaire de district, comptable,* and *avocat.* The formally constituted meetings of the 'club' were mainly celebrations as, for example, on Christmas Day. At such meetings, one man would act as 'chairman', another as 'secretary', and so on. The roles assumed by various members did not necessarily correspond to the formal titles they held, nor would one man necessarily keep the same role throughout the meeting.

During the meetings, which consisted mainly of drinking, joking, and gossiping, the group would fine members for 'offences' such as arriving late or 'allowing' a wife to call her husband away. After a fine had been imposed, the 'offender' would invariably 'lodge an appeal'. Similarly, there was much mock formality in the calling of meetings, and on one occasion during the period of my field-work a 'secretary' sent a written notice announcing a forthcoming meeting to each member despite the fact that all were neighbours who inevitably saw each other daily.

Although the 'club' had only six members, attendances at two pre-arranged meetings which I attended were 9 and 13. On the first of these occasions, the number was made up by Mupenda, Daniel, and a third kinsman of François who happened to be visiting him from another part of the town. At the second meeting which was on Christmas Day, Amundala, Lusaka and Alphonse brought their wives, and there

TABLE 56

Members of the 'Club'

NAME	TRIBE	APP. AGE	MARITAL STATUS	YEARS OF SCHOOL-ING	OCCUPATION	YEARS IN STANLEY-VILLE	YEARS IN AVE. 21	COM-POUND NO.	STATUS ON COMPOUND
François	Mukumu	50	M	Nil	Mason	7	7	15	Title holder
Amundala	Mubali	30	M	3	Mason	6	4	18	Title holder
Asumani	Mubali	30	M	3	Labourer's foreman	7	5	16	Title holder
Lusaka	Mubali	26	M	10	Carpenter	Since birth	21	22	Title holder
Alufani	Murumbi	40	Div.	Nil	Mason	21	21	13	Title holder
Jean	Mukusu	30	Div.	Nil	Carpenter	Since birth	18	13	Co-resident with his own house

were four additional men, all visiting kinsmen of one or other member of the group.

At the first pre-arranged meeting which took place on a public holiday a few days after the formation of the 'club', the members began to choose office-bearers and to allocate titles to each other. After some discussion, they decided to invite Antoine, who was not present, to be 'president'. We have already seen that Antoine was an elderly and much respected man. He was a Murumbi who had lived on Compound No. 9 since the avenue was first settled in 1930. Alufani, who was a fellow-tribesman and an old acquaintance of Antoine, was sent, there and then, to call him. As it happened, however, Antoine was not at home at the time. On hearing this the meeting unanimously chose Lusaka as their 'president'. Lusaka was thus a second choice, but the circumstances of his election emphasize his high standing in the group despite the fact that he was the youngest member of the 'club'. (The ages and other details of the six more regular members are shown in Table 56.) The attempt to bring in Antoine as president of the 'club' and the subsequent election of Lusaka, are in themselves further indications that the members of the 'club' saw themselves as a 'civilized' group acting in a 'civilized' way.

François' position in the club is of particular interest. He was to a large extent the founder of the 'club', but he was probably its least 'civilized' member. In the atmosphere of mock-formality in the 'club' he was the central target of criticism for contravening the 'club's' rules, for allegedly paying more attention to his personal and family affairs than to the 'club' and, more generally, for his frequent absences from his compound. These were all points for which he was in any case usually teased outside the club.

When François' position in the 'club' is viewed against the background of his other social connexions, it is clear that the 'club' served a very useful purpose for him. He used the 'club' to define, maintain, and develop a set of relations with friends and neighbours which differed markedly from his relations with kinsmen and other Bakumu 'brothers'. Lacking the security of status in the avenue enjoyed by Lusaka, François found it more difficult to deal with different sets of relations in the assured manner that Lusaka did, and the mock-formality of the 'club' clearly provided a partial solution to this problem by helping him either to keep his 'brothers' and his neighbours apart or to define the relationship between them when they did come into face-to-face contact. Moreover, in promoting the formation of the 'club' and in acting as host at its meetings, François achieved a higher status amongst his neighbours (and especially in relation to Lusaka) than had previously been accorded to him on the basis of his more casual day-to-day encounters in the avenue.

Bernard's Compound and his Brothers

In François' participation in the 'club', we have an example of a relatively 'uncivilized' man developing and re-defining his social relations with neighbours who were neither kinsmen nor fellow tribesmen. Bernard's case, which I now describe, differed from that of François in that Bernard was apparently little concerned to mix socially in the avenue or to participate in any social gatherings other than those of kinsmen and fellow-Babali. He was about 55 years of age. He had been in Stanleyville eight years, and had previously worked on a mission station near to his tribal area for about 30 years.[12] His attitude to town life was typically that of a migrant. Most of his kinsmen were in his tribal area. He had kept in close touch with them over the years, and had himself regularly visited his village for short periods. His expressed hope and intention were 'one day to return home, there to cultivate his fields, to marry a second wife, and have more children'.

A year or two after his arrival in Stanleyville, Bernard had bought a house on Compound No. 10 and had become the title-holder. Two years after settling in there, he was joined by one of his father's maternal kinsmen, Boniface, who later built his own house on the compound. A year after that, he was joined by Kapitula, a classificatory brother who lived in one of Bernard's houses though also on a permanent basis. In addition, Bernard commonly had one or more kinsmen or other Babali 'brothers' staying on his compound for short periods. Thus, for example, he had extended hospitality to Henri, a fellow-villager, for a few months when Henri had found himself without accommodation following on a quarrel with the title-holder of the compound where he had up to then been a tenant. After some time, Henri had brought his mistress, Elizabeth, to the compound until they both left together to live on the compound of one of Elizabeth's kinsmen. On later abandoning Elizabeth, however, Henri had once again returned to Bernard's compound. Similarly, both Boniface and Kapitula habitually extended hospitality and temporary shelter to kinsmen and other 'brothers' in need of accommodation.

Bernard had the reputation of being a stable man of moderate habits, and of treating his kinsmen well. It was said that he gave people good advice. Thus Antoine, who lived on Compound No. 9 opposite Bernard, described him to me as a 'giver of counsels', adding that 'he likes to talk, and people gather round him as they do round a teacher' and, as previously noted, Lusaka thought of him as 'a man of good influence'. But he was not a 'civilized' man, and the people who gathered on his compound were almost exclusively 'uncivilized' or less 'civilized' Babali. The general recognition of his compound as a place where Babali gathered was reflected in a greeting which Antoine (a Murumbi), who had on one occasion strolled across to have a word with Boniface, gave to another Mubali passing down the avenue: 'I am visiting "at yours" (in the sense of *chez vous*) today'. The passer-by had no particular kinship connexion with Bernard or members of his compound, and Antoine's reference to being 'at yours' was an expression of the tribal distinction between the two who were greeting each other.

Discussions on Bernard's compound were frequently about family and village matters, and were invariably conducted in Kibali. The day-to-day gossip was largely confined to people and events in the sub-community of Babali centred in the immediate neighbourhood of Avenue 21. Bernard's relations with Antoine and other non-Babali whom he had over the years come to know as neighbours were polite and correct but strictly limited.

Christine's Compound and her 'Guests'

I have described the social situations on the compounds of Lusaka, François, and Bernard as varying in the extent to which they drew in different categories of people. Lusaka's compound had the widest range of callers. These included kinsmen, 'uncivilized' tribal 'brothers' and immediate neighbours, but other categories, such as Lusaka's more 'civilized' personal friends, a number of whom came from other parts of the town, were also well represented and their presence had a marked influence on the subjects of discussion and on the tone of the conversations. The discussions ranged over a broader field than on most other compounds and were often specifically centred on the problems of 'civilized' life. François' compound attracted a narrower range of visitors and these fell into two very distinct categories: one consisted mainly of kinsmen and other Bakumu 'brothers', all of whom were relatively 'uncivilized', and the other consisted of a few personal friends drawn from nearby compounds. The persons falling in the second category were all non-Bakumu. They included men who were more 'civilized' than François himself, and they were largely drawn from the better-established section of the avenue's population. Bernard's compound differed from those of both Lusaka and François in that his callers were almost exclusively less 'civilized' Babali. Some of these happened to be from the avenue, which had a high proportion of Babali, but most of them were persons standing in some form of 'institutional' relationship to Bernard and his co-residents, i.e. as 'real' or 'fictitious' kinsmen, or simply as fellow tribesmen who might on occasion treat and claim each other as 'brothers'.

On Christine's compound (No. 17) I found social gatherings constituted on yet another basis.[13] Christine was a woman of about 45 years of age. She was a small shop-keeper and a landlady with a fluctuating number of tenants and lodgers. (See Table 57.) Also, like a number of women in the neighbourhood, she occasionally sold bottled beer illicitly at a slightly higher price than she had paid for it.

Christine had as far as I could ascertain never been married by tribal custom, but had for some years before coming to Stanleyville been the mistress of three successive Europeans. After her arrival in Stanleyville, some ten years before, she had entered into one temporary liaison after another in the C.E.C. She sometimes claimed that bridewealth had been paid for by the men whom she had divorced but on other occasions denied this. She had bought a house and settled in the avenue about five years before I met her. She was now living singly, depending on her 'guests' and customers for her livelihood. She had her own identity book and was thus a *femme libre* in the administration's records. Some people in the avenue said that she was mad, and she had the general reputation of being quarrelsome and unreliable. During my period of field-work there were two cases of tenants having to leave her compound following on bitter quarrels with her, and another resident was sent to goal for stealing 500 francs from her. This last incident in particular was the subject of much discussion in the avenue. People had no sympathy for the thief but at the same time they had little for Christine who, they said, was always involved in difficulties and quarrels of one kind or another.

On many week-day afternoons and evenings, the main room in Christine's house was empty, and on others there were only one or two people chatting to Christine as she waited for customers who might buy two or three cigarettes or a box of matches or half a bottle of paraffin. But on pay-days and usually on Saturdays and Sundays, the scene changed appreciably as some of Christine's clients, tenants, and lodgers lingered, chatted, drank, and sometimes played the gramophone and danced. I describe the scene as I saw it one Sunday between 7.0 and 8.0 p.m.

Christine was sitting in one corner of the room, next to the table on which she kept her small stock of goods for sale. There were ten people in the room, eight men and two women. Two of the men were drinking bottled beer at a table in another corner of the room. One or two others had bottles in their hands which they would occasionally pass to a companion. The gramophone was playing continuously, and a few of those present danced on and off. Of the two women, one was standing at the door watching, the other danced, usually by herself but occasionally with a partner. Similarly, the men who danced did so either with each other or on their own. During the hour that I was there, several passers-by stopped at the door for a short while, and a few came in to buy something. For example, François' wife from No. 15 bought one franc's worth of petrol which she poured straight into her lamp. She then lingered on, talking to Christine for about five minutes. Of the ten 'guests' present throughout the hour, three were Christine's tenants; one was a man who normally lived in another part of the town but was staying on Christine's compound for a few days; one was Maua, a prostitute temporarily resident on compound No. 21; one was Henri from Bernard's compound; another two were from a nearby avenue.

As the above details suggest, the catchment area of Christine's 'guests' scarcely extended beyond the immediate locality. Moreover, the participants were drawn from a fairly well-defined section of the avenue's population: they were young adults and they were largely

TABLE 57

Some of Christine's 'Guests'

GUESTS	TRIBE	APP. AGE	MARITAL STATUS	YEARS OF SCHOOL- ING	OCCUPATION	YEARS IN STANLEY- VILLE	COM- POUND NO.	STATUS ON COMPOUND WHERE RESIDENT
Man	Murega	30	Single	3	Labourer	Under 1	17	Tenant
Man	Murega	20	Single	3	Labourer	Under 1	17	Tenant
Man	Mubali	25	Married	5	Mason	3	21	Kinsman of title holder
Man	Mongandu	25	Single	2	Chauffeur	3	17	'Brother' of title holder
Man	Murega	22	Married	6	Labourer	Under 1	17	Tenant
Man	Mubali	25	Divorced	3	Houseboy	5	9	'Brother' of title holder
Woman	Lokele	15	Single	Nil	—	1	17	Daughter of tenant
Woman	Mubali	20	Single	Nil	—	2	21	'Sister' of title holder

people who had been in town for very short periods. (See Table 57.) It is equally interesting to note some of the conspicuous absentees from Christine's parlour. Limela, who was a 'brother' of Christine and who lived on her compound for a part of the period of the study, was seldom in Christine's 'parlour' unless he came in specifically to talk to me. Similarly, men like Lusaka or François might well come to Christine's to buy a bottle of beer, but only exceptionally would they linger there. This was not their milieu.

Amongst Christine's 'guests' there were sometimes one or two pairs of friends or kinsmen, but normally the company assembled in her house consisted of persons who scarcely knew each other. A few of the 'guests', and especially those who were also tenants on the compound, were fairly regular clients for periods of a few weeks or months, but even the tenants were usually short-term 'guests' for they were in most cases transient inhabitants, and their connexions with Christine were seldom maintained in any regular way after their departure from the compound.

The gatherings of the 'club' on Compound No. 15 and those of Christine's 'guests' on Compound No. 17 next door had some general features in common. Each was a leisure-time group operating at the level of the immediate locality and each was essentially 'urban' in the sense that it met needs and interests arising directly out of the 'urban' experiences and circumstances of the participants. But in other respects there were fundamental differences between them. The 'club' had a stable membership drawn from the better-established residents of the avenue; it was built on a set of 'egocentric' relationships between persons who knew each other well as individual personalities[14] but it had *some* formal structure imposing standards on its participants through its mock-formal 'trials' and through its very existence as a group sometimes meeting in a pre-arranged way at set times. While built on 'egocentric' relationships, there was thus a tendency for relations within the 'club' to become 'structural'. In addition, the high 'civilized' status in the avenue of the 'club's' president and of some other members set the group off from gatherings of less 'civilized' people. Amongst Christine's 'guests', on the other hand, there was no semblance of formal structure, and the participants were for the most part newcomers and strangers who reacted to each other on the basis of 'categorical' rather than either 'egocentric' or 'structural' criteria. Most of the 'guests' were relatively 'uncivilized' persons who were getting to know town ways and who were in the process of acquiring 'civilization'. In this process, Christine's own role was of far-reaching importance. She was quarrelsome and reputedly mad, but she was clearly a 'civilized' woman with considerable experience of town life, and in her outbursts of bad tempered abuse she frequently upbraided her clients and tenants as *basendji* who did not know how to behave in town.[15]

The Contrast Between Mayala's Tea Room and Augustin's Shop

The customers at Augustin's shop on Compound No. 1 and those at Mayala's tea room across the way on No. 4 exhibited differences somewhat similar to those between members of the 'club', on the one hand, and Christine's 'guests' on the other.

Augustin and his wife, Pauline, had been living in Avenue 21 for nearly 20 years. He was a Mubali and she a Mukusu, and both had extensive social connexions in the neighbourhood. Augustin was a frail and elderly man who seldom left his house. He usually sat in the front room where he kept his stock of goods for sale next to the window through which he served any customers who were strangers, though

I*a* An avenue in Brussels

I*b* The interior of a small palm-wine bar

II*a* European-style dancing on a compound at an end-of-mourning ceremony held by an *évolué* in Belge I

II*b* Neighbours and passers-by look on as the body of Felekini run over by a lorry is returned to his house (see Chapter VI)

friends and neighbours of longer standing normally came into the front room where they would linger to chat after making their purchases. As on Lusaka's compound, news and gossip from the avenue and from the immediate neighbourhood were constantly exchanged.

In contrast to Augustin's shop, Mayala's tea room was, like Christine's 'parlour', mainly a centre where new arrivals and other strangers to the neighbourhood gathered. Mayala was a Mukusu and a classifactory brother of Pauline who had helped him to start his tea room and shop when he first came to the avenue five years before. He was divorced, he lived singly, and had no dependants. Sometimes he cooked for himself, and sometimes Pauline sent a dish of food to him. We have already seen that he was regarded as miserly and selfish, and that people criticized and ridiculed him as a man with whom it was impossible to get on.

The well-established residents in the avenue tended to avoid Mayala's establishment, but passers-by on the Irumu Road and a few newcomers to the neighbourhood furnished him with a clientele which had a high turn-over but was seemingly stable in numbers. In the afternoons the tea room, which consisted of an open shelter with two benches and a table, often had a small number of men drinking tea and chatting, sometimes with each other but more often directly with Mayala. Many of these customers were men on their way home from work. They would tell of incidents they had witnessed during the course of the day: of accidents they had seen at work or on the roads, or of disputes with their European employers, or of fights and thefts. Occasionally their conversations would lapse into the telling of personal reminiscences from the past: about journeys, about experiences in gaol, about European employers or about fellow-workers and others. Or, again, as on most of the compounds described, the conversation sometimes turned to differences between tribes or to the problems of life in town, or to the characteristics and advantages of different residential areas of the town.

In this setting Mayala himself played a far more sociable role in relation to his customers than he did *vis-à-vis* his neighbours in the avenue. He often told of his experiences in Leopoldville and of travels with his former European employer in Katanga and beyond in Central and Southern Africa. Compared to most of his customers, he was an experienced and 'civilized' man. The customers usually addressed him as *Bwana*, and deferred to him in a way which most of his neighbours in the avenue did not.

In contrast to discussions such as those around Lusaka's work-bench, the talk in Mayala's tea room rarely dwelt on individuals known to several participants, and when individuals were discussed they were seldom identified. In this respect, social intercourse in the tea room was strikingly similar to that at Christine's. If anything, however, the atmosphere at Mayala's was even more anonymous and categorical.

Some of the participants, especially those drawn from passers-by in the Irumu Road, were persons who would perhaps never return to the tea room; and although a few newcomers to the area were relatively regular callers during the course of their usually short periods of residence in the environs, they seldom lingered as long in this setting as in the warmer and more convivial atmosphere of Christine's 'parlour'.

The Death of Felekini

The social situations of newcomers and of old-established residents in Avenue 21 differed significantly in that the newcomers had few social connexions in the neighbourhood and that a higher proportion of their face-to-face relations were based on categorical rather than egocentric criteria. These differences were, however, only two aspects of a broader and more general contrast. A third important difference was that many of the residents of longer standing were, to a much greater extent than the more heterogeneous newcomers, involved in social relations which were in varying degrees regulated by the institutions of 'real' and 'fictitious' kinship and of *basaiba* ('family friendship' as distinct from individual personal friendship[16]). They were in many cases members of relatively large local and tribal communities or subcommunities. The importance of the 'community' of 'brothers' and 'friends' was readily apparent even in many encounters of every-day life. There were several compounds, like that of Bernard's, where the overlapping principles of kinship, 'brotherhood', and 'tribalism', were the dominant influences pervading sociable gatherings, while on some others, like that of Augustin, 'friendship' of long standing also entered into the picture. But the full significance of these bases of association was most apparent at times of personal tragedy as the following account of Felekini's death shows.

Felekini was an elderly Mubali who had, I was told, first come to Stanleyville 'at the time of the Arabs'. He was too old to work, and he usually spent his day helping his wife who was almost totally disabled. From time to time he went to market for her, and it was on one such morning that he was run over on the Irumu Road by a car swerving to avoid an oncoming lorry. He was first taken to the dispensary of a nearby military camp, and from there to hospital by ambulance, but he died a few hours later and his corpse was returned to his house at about four o'clock in the afternoon.

A Belgian police officer visited the scene of the accident, but there was no further investigation and no charge was laid against the driver of the car who was a European. As the news of the accident spread in the neighbourhood of Avenue 21, I heard various versions of the way in which the accident was handled. Some people said it was not possible for the (European) police officer to take any action against the driver because all the (African) witnesses had run away when the officer arrived. Others complained that the officer had made no attempt to ascertain the facts of the accident, and others still took the more cynical view that no police officer would charge a European for killing an African. Similarly, there were several conflicting versions of the accident itself.[17]

The dramatic way in which Felekini met his death and the fact that his widow was unable to support herself and had no surviving children or close kinsmen to look after her combined to evoke a quick and strong response within the neighbourhood. By 7 o'clock in the evening over 200 persons had called at the deceased's house (see Plate IIb) and a further 100 or more called later during the course of the evening. In the customary way most of these brought contributions towards the cost of the funeral and of the mourning ceremonies. Three temporary shelters of sticks and palm leaves were rapidly erected outside the house for mourners who would be spending the night there. In the largest shelter facing the door of the deceased's house there was a table at which three men sat receiving the contributions brought by mourners. None of the three was a 'real' classificatory kinsman of the deceased, but all were considered to be 'brothers' in that they were sons of men from the same tribal village. Between them they assumed the responsibilities normally developing upon kinsmen of organizing the funeral and conducting the mourning ceremonies.

As gifts were brought to the table in the central shelter, the names of the mourners were recorded on six separate lists according to the relationship of each to the deceased man. Four of the lists represented broad categories based on criteria of kinship. There was one for *banduku* ('brothers'), one for *shemeki* or *beaux-frères* ('brothers' of the widow), one for *bayomba* or *oncles* ('brothers' of the deceased's mother or 'mothers') and one for *bayomba* or *neveus* (children of the 'sisters' of the deceased). In addition, there was a list headed *wajamaa ya mugini* (literally, 'families of the village' but, in the context, 'families of the neighbourhood'), and one headed, in a mixture of French and Swahili, *famille ya Bakusu* ('the family of the Bakusu'.) By the end of the evening 2,760 francs had been subscribed at an average rate of just over eight francs per head. The total donated was made up as follows. A sum of 1,535 francs was subscribed by *banduku*, 325 francs by *shemeki*, 300 francs by 'families of the village', 225 francs by *bayomba* (*neveus*), 190 francs by *bayomba* (*oncles*), and 185 francs by members of the 'family of the Bakusu'.

The *shemeki* and the two groups of *bayomba* totalled 25 persons who contributed an average of nearly 30 francs each. They were all persons with relatively well defined relationships to the deceased and their obligations to his family were seen as clear-cut and specific. The list of *banduku* contained 220 names, most of whom were 'brothers' only in a vague and ill-defined way. The list included some 'village brothers' and members of the same 'clan', as well as the names of many who had come to regard the deceased as a 'brother' though they had little or no conception of their traditional connexion with him. Some of these were his 'brothers' only in the sense that they were fellow-Babali in town. A few of the *banduku* contributed sums of 30, 40, or 50 francs each, but the majority gave much less, some only two or three francs each, and the mean donation from 'brothers' was just under seven francs. Contributors listed as members of 'the family of the Bakusu' numbered about 40, and they contributed small sums averaging between four and five francs each. Members of 'the families of the village' numbered about 50 and their mean donation also worked out at between four and five francs per head.

All the persons recorded on the first four lists—those of *shemeki*, *bayomba* (*oncles*), *bayomba* (*neveus*), and *banduku*—were Babali. They made up about two thirds of all the mourners and between them represented the vast majority of all Babali households in the immediate vicinity as well as a number from further away. The remaining third of the mourners were all non-Babali, and most of them were from the neighbourhood. The Bakusu were listed separately from other non-Babali tribes partly because there was a fair number of them, but principally because they were to some extent seen as a distinctive colony or group in the neighbourhood. They constituted one of the long-established tribes in the area and there were many connexions of kinship and friendship between them. Many of them were elderly and, like the Babali and like Felekini, a good proportion of them had come to Stanleyville in its earliest days. My impression was that in years gone by the Bakusu had been a group as prominent in the area as the Babali, Barumbi, or Bakumu were at the time of my study.

During the course of the ceremonies two 'village brothers' addressed the mourners assembled in the temporary shelters outside Felekini's house. They paid tribute to him as a wise and good man, and they commented on his death and on the general social situation in which they now found themselves. The first speaker began by suggesting that the death was the responsibility of the family of a man, himself dead, who had quarrelled with Felekini some years previously. 'But', the speaker said, 'this is a matter which we cannot "fight out" in town'. He then dwelt at length on the urban life and urban experiences of the deceased. He recalled that Felekini had first come to Stanleyville when he (the speaker) was still a child, and he explained that there were many people in the town to whom the deceased had acted as a father and to whom he had given good advice arising out of his own wisdom. He described the deceased as a man who had the *akili* (insight, intelligence, understanding) of the Babali as well as that of the Europeans and *Arabisés* with whom he had lived and worked.[18] The second speaker made similar points about the deceased and then dwelt on the differences between the ways and customs of *Kizungu* and *Kisendji*. In the course of his remarks he repeatedly asked the mourners to remember that they were living in 'the town of Europeans' where people did not 'fight and quarrel' as they did in *Kisendji*. He warned his listeners that 'in town if you accuse other people, you will be taken to the courts', and he ended by advising them to leave 'the death of Felekini to God'.

Both orations were delivered mainly in Swahili with occasional phrases in Kibali but both were clearly intended principally for an audience of Babali. Various aspects of the ceremony were unmistakably Babali and no member of another tribe could have failed to be aware of the distinctive 'tribal' tone of the occasion. Moreover, non-Babali mourners tended quite noticeably to remain on the fringes of the assembled group. At the same time, the more general features of the proceedings, such as the giving of donations, the practice of listing all contributions and of classifying them according to the relationship of each donor to the deceased, were standard procedures practised by virtually all tribes in the town. It was a tribal occasion, yet the contents of the speeches and other features stamped it as also being urban.

Further Cases of Mourning

Felekini's funeral which took place the following day, was, like the mourning ceremony at his house, the largest of a number that I witnessed in this neighbourhood during the course of my fieldwork. For comparison Table 58 sets out some details of attendances and contributions at four additional eve-of-funeral ceremonies for which I was able to gather full information of a comparable kind. The four deceased—Sakina, Mariamu, Gabriel and Baruti—were all well-established residents each of whom had been in town for the greater part of his or her adult life. On the occasion of the funerals of each of these the number of mourners was appreciably lower than at the time of Felekini's death but the mean donation per head was considerably

TABLE 58

Comparison between attendances and donations at the eve-of-funeral ceremonies for Felekini and four other old-established adults in the neighbourhood of Avenue 21

DECEASED	TRIBE	SEX	NO. OF MOURNERS SUBSCRIBING TO COST OF CEREMONIES	TOTAL SUM SUBSCRIBED	MEAN SUBSCRIPTION PER MOURNER (FRANCS)	APPROX. PERCENTAGE OF FELLOW TRIBESMEN	APPROXIMATE PERCENTAGE OF MOURNERS FROM IMMEDIATE NEIGHBOURHOOD
Felekini	Mubali	M	335	2,760	8	73	75
Sakina	Mukusu	F	197	2,403	12	80	60
Mariamu	Mukusu	F	118	1,529	13	80	75
Gabriel	Mukusu	M	79	2,116	27	40	90+
Baruti	Mubali	M	73	1,180	16	100	50

Notes:
(1) In calculating the total sums subscribed and the mean subscriptions I have excluded the few cases of mourners who made contributions in kind (usually tea or sugar).
(2) The percentages of persons from the 'immediate neighbourhood' are little more than informed estimates. I defined the immediate neighbourhood as an area of two avenues on either side of the address of the deceased. But usually I was unable to ascertain the addresses of more than some two-thirds of the mourners. The percentages of fellow-tribesmen are based on more adequate information and can be taken as fairly close approximations.

higher. These facts reflect the weaker response on each of these occasions from persons in the neighbourhood without *relatively* clear-cut and specific relationships to the deceased persons. As I did not know either Felekini or any of the other four deceased, it is difficult for me to assess accurately why the response of the general public was so much stronger in Felekini's case, but on the available evidence it seems that there were two general factors involved. The first was that Felekini's death had taken place in a dramatic way, the second that he was undoubtedly better known and of higher status than any of the others.

There were also differences between the several ceremonies in the categories of persons from whom mourners were recruited and in the manner in which these were classified. Baruti's death evoked a response from 73 persons. All were Babali and only about a half were from the immediate neighbourhood. Apart from 11 *bayomba* and *shemeki*, who contributed an average of 30 francs per head, all other mourners were on this occasion classified simply as 'female children' or 'male children' of the deceased, and they contributed a mean of 14 francs per person.

Gabriel had 79 mourners of whom 14 were classified as *shemeki*, *bayomba*, or *banduku* (in a restricted sense), and they contributed an average of 135 francs each. The balance of 65 mourners contributed an average of three to four francs each; they were all residents of the same avenue as Gabriel himself and were 'members' of a loosely organized 'burial association'. This 'organization' was referred to as *la réunion*. It had no officials and it kept no records. Its origins were difficult to ascertain, but it had certainly been in existence many years. Its only guiding principle was that each 'member' should make a donation on the occasion of the death of any one of their number. 'Members' brought their donations spontaneously, and there was no system of collection. Participation was confined to the residents of Avenue 22 in which the organization was referred to as '*la réunion* of our avenue'. About two-thirds of the old-established residents of the avenue were 'members', and these included persons of some ten different tribes, though the Bakusu, who were particularly well represented in this avenue, made up about a third of the total which was a much higher proportion than they constituted in the population. A few of the members, especially those who were Bakusu would doubtless have contributed to Gabriel's funeral expenses even if they had not been 'members' of *la réunion*, but the failure of any persons (even of Bakusu) in nearby avenues to contribute is clear evidence of the absence of a fully spontaneous response from the neighbourhood as such.

In partial contrast to the cases of Baruti and Gabriel, the deaths of Sakina and Mariamu produced quite appreciable measures of neighbourhood response on lines similar to those evoked by the death of Felekini. Of Sakina's 197 mourners, 24 were classified as *bayomba*, *shemeki*, *banduku* or *watoto* (in the more restricted senses of 'brothers' and 'children'), and they contributed an average of about 40 francs per head. The balance were listed in the four categories of *famille upande wa kabila* ('family on the side of the tribe'), *basaiba* (old or family friends), *watoto wa Brussels* ('children of Brussels'—mainly friends and 'brothers' of her son who had himself been brought up in the neighbourhood), and *banduku ya km 5, Route Ituri* ('brothers' from a peri-urban village 5 kilometres from the centre of the town and just beyond Brussels).

These four lists contained the names of 173 persons who contributed an average of 8 to 9 francs each ranging from an average of 5 francs per head of mourners from the 'village at kilometre 5' to an average of 19 francs from *basaiba*. About 20 per cent of the mourners were non-Bakusu, including all *basaiba* and a few from the village at kilometre 5. Excluding the persons from this village, where the deceased had once lived, about 65 per cent of the mourners were from the neighbourhood.

On the occasion of Mariamu's death there were, in addition to the better-defined categories of *shemeki* and *bayomba*, four lists: one for *banduku* (in an unrestricted sense), one for *watoto* ('children', male and female), one for *banduku ya mugini* ('brothers of the village', i.e. of the neighbourhood), and one headed *bayomba Baluba* for Baluba acquaintances, of whom there were only 11, who were classified as *bayomba* because the deceased's mother was a *Muluba*. In this case there were four *shemeki* who made up the only category of persons with relatively precise relationships to the deceased and they contributed just under 80 francs per head. The balance of 114 mourners contributed an average of nearly 11 francs per head, ranging from 7 francs for *banduku wa mugini* to 14 francs for *bayomba Baluba*. About 20 per cent of all mourners were from tribes other than that of the deceased, and about three-quarters were from the immediate neighbourhood.

The figures show that in each case there were a few people who contributed very substantially more than members of the general public. Equally, however, all the cases reviewed evoked *some* response from the neighbourhood or neighbourhoods where the deceased had lived. The extent to which mourners were recruited from the immediate neighbourhood where the deceased had lived prior to his or her death, the different categories in which they were placed, and the various ways in which their contributions were grouped and listed all contribute to an assessment of the nature of tribal 'sub-communities' in the area. They also illustrate the extent to which local residence gave rise to neighbourhood consciousness and the way in which neighbourhood solidarity tended to overlap or coincide with the lines of family and tribe. The principal social bonds given expression at times of mourning were between relatively close kinsmen and affines, but these were flexible and the principles of 'family' and of 'brotherhood' were liable to be extended to cover all persons of the same tribe, and even members of other tribes as in the case where Mariamu was reckoned to have a relationship of *muyomba* with *all* Baluba who came to mourn her.[19]

Eve-of-funeral ceremonies were not the only occasions on which the above groupings and classifications could be observed. The *kilio* or mourning (of which the eve-of-funeral ceremonies were only a part) lasted for periods ranging from a few days to a few weeks. The *kilio* was then followed by the *tanga* which was a ceremony marking the end of the period of full mourning and the beginning of the period of *musiba* or 'half mourning'. The *tanga* could take place a few days after the funeral, but was more usually held several weeks or months later. Finally, the *musiba* was in due course followed by the ceremony of *pili* or 'end-of-mourning'. This was normally about a year after a death, though again the length of time was variable and the minimum period considered appropriate was about six months. Some 'end-of-mourning' ceremonies were held two or three years after the *kilio*, and in rare cases up to five years later. Particular occasions for defining and re-defining relationships were thus fairly frequent, and the practice of keeping lists of contributors meant that all persons coming to the ceremonies had to be classified. Moreover, since the ceremonies were public they inevitably had the effect of notifying newcomers to the neighbourhood of such broad sets of 'institutional' or 'semi-institutional' relations as there were between the older-established inhabitants.

The Principles of 'Brotherhood' and of 'Neighbourhood'

As Clément has explained, the operation of the principle of 'brotherhood' varied greatly according to the numerical representation of a tribe in town: '. . . a Mumbole from Opala and a Mumbole from Isangi will automatically consider themselves "true" brothers if both live in Elizabethville'.[20] But the above analysis of responses to several deaths points to additional factors affecting the operation of 'brotherhood'. In dealing with the Babali cases, for example, we have to consider that there were many Babali in Stanleyville, that they constituted the largest single tribal group in the neighbourhood of Avenue 21, and that they did not necessarily consider themselves as 'brothers' in all situations. In the greater part of their day-to-day lives they related to each other as men and women who, far from being each other's 'brothers' and 'children', were often husbands and wives, or lovers and mistresses, or simply neighbours, friends, customers, clients, and the like. Though the fact of being fellow-Babali in town often affected these relationships in various ways, it did not automatically transform them into relationships of 'brotherhood'. As we have seen, there were cases of Babali giving free accommodation to fellow-tribesmen whereas they would not normally have done so for non-Babali. But there were also a *few* instances of Babali charging rent to other Babali, and there were *many* instances of Babali letting accommodation to non-Babali while some of their own fellow-tribesmen were paying rent for accommodation on nearby compounds. In this neighbourhood, where they were numerous as compared to other areas of the town, the Babali generally recognized obligations of 'fictitious' kinship to each other in mundane day-to-day relations only if they were also fellow-villagers, or if they had some other particular grounds for claiming a special connexion. Thus many of the Babali who came to mourn Felekini and who were on that occasion regarded as having 'fictitious' kinship connexions with him or his widow were persons who would not have been regarded in this way in other less extreme situations. And, of course, we know that many of Felekini's mourners simply stayed away from the funeral of

Baruti even though he was also a Mubali living in the same neighbourhood. The principle of 'brotherhood' was thus permissive and optative
rather than obligatory. It readily allowed 'brotherly' relations to
develop, and it predisposed fellow-tribesmen, fellow-villagers and the
like to claim privileges and accept favours from each other. But it did
not in itself confer obligations outside particular circumstances such as
when people with a certain connexion or affinity found themselves in
a small minority amongst others or when, even if not grossly outnumbered, they faced a situation of crisis or tragedy provoking a
mobilization of common bonds.

The principle of 'neighbourhood' was closely related to the principle
of 'brotherhood'. The significance of the large response of the Babali to
Felekini's death can only be fully appreciated if we remember the
extent to which mourners at his funeral—as on the occasions of the
other deaths reported—were recruited from the immediate vicinity.
Moreover, the existence of *la réunion* in the avenue where Gabriel
lived, and the recognition given at some of the eve-of-funeral ceremonies
to categories such as *banduku wa mugini*, *watoto wa Brussels* and *banduku
wa Km 5*, *Route Ituri*, clearly reflect the development over time of
loyalties between persons resident in the same neighbourhood despite
the absence of any other basis on which they could claim each other
as 'brothers'. We have seen how neighbours and near-neighbours
constantly interacted in a variety of small-group situations irrespective
of their tribal affiliations. Interaction in these situations led to the
development of 'egocentric' relationships which were often characterized by sentiments of familiarity and solidarity between individuals and
between families and groups of kinsmen. Where people in a neighbourhood were also fellow-villagers or fellow-tribesmen, or where they were
members of tribes from the same region or of tribes with some
marked cultural affinity, neighbourhood relations were of course
likely to be affected. But such favourable circumstances were not an
indispensable pre-requisite to development of neighbourhood bonds.
The process of living together in itself gave rise to interdependence and
to bonds of familiarity and solidarity. In the neighbourhood of Avenue
21 local groups with a semblance of formal structure (like *la réunion* and
the 'club') were few and rather exceptional, but extended networks of
personal relations were common and highly developed. The reactions
of the Babali to Felekini's death was thus partly the response of a group
of people sharing the same tribal sentiments and having an ill-defined
tribal loyalty, but also, very importantly, the response of people who
were involved in networks of friendship that spread right across the
locality. The 'local' and 'tribal' responses have to be seen as two
factors reinforcing each other.

Social Interaction and the Process of Social Relations

At this juncture we may usefully restate the main points made in this
chapter. We have seen that degree of 'civilization' was one important

13

principle on the basis of which *some* people in *certain* situations were drawn together and others were set apart, and we have noted various aspects of the widely different situations in which newcomers and old-established residents found themselves in the avenue. In this connexion, I pointed in particular to the contrast between groups which, like the 'club', were largely based on pre-existing 'egocentric' or personal relations, and those which, like the gatherings of Christine's 'guests', consisted of persons who were largely unknown to each other and who interacted mainly on the basis of various type categories. In this kind of interaction an individual's tribal affiliation was an important factor of identification. There was a wide range of characteristics that served to identify an individual's ethnic affiliation with a greater or lesser degree of accuracy. Some of these characteristics could be readily detected by any newcomer, others required skill, knowledge, and insight that could only be acquired over time. There was an important contrast between gatherings like that of Bernard's entourage and those which displayed such features as were common both to an assembly of Christine's 'guests' and a meeting of members of the 'club'. Members of groups like that of Bernard and his associates were mainly recruited on the basis of criteria of kinship and 'brotherhood' and were in effect 'tribal' groups but the degree of 'civilization' of their members was none the less liable to influence interaction between them. Christine's 'guests' and the members of the 'club' had it in common, despite other important differences between them, that they were principally selected through the very processes of urban interaction and were generally non-tribal groups of people brought together through common experiences and circumstances; criteria of 'civilization' affected the selection of members to a marked degree, but tribal affiliation remained an important factor liable to influence interaction in any situation of the moment.

Taken as a whole the evidence on the selection of group members and on the varying influence from one group to another of different principles of association is of very considerable interest in any attempt to assess the nature and process of social relations in the avenue. The data imply that people at times found themselves in positions where they had in effect to select their associates for any given activity from several possible categories of fellow residents. In doing this, they were often inevitably involved in making a choice between two or more patterns of behaviour and between two or more distinctively different sets of social norms. We may recall, for example, that Henri had in his recent urban experience lived on three different compounds: on the first he had been a tenant and had there associated mainly with relative strangers with whom he had no pre-existing relations either of an 'egocentric' or of an 'institutional' type; on the second compound he had been accommodated free of charge as a 'brother', and here his social relations had been mainly governed by the principle of 'fictitious' kinship; and on the third compound he had been accommodated as

the lover of a kinswoman of the title-holder with whom he had interacted on yet another basis. Or, to recall another example, we saw
how François sometimes drank with kinsmen and other 'brothers',
sometimes with a set of more 'civilized' friends and neighbours from the
avenue, and sometimes in a nearby palm-wine bar where he was
involved in a third kind of social situation. Somewhat similarly, *most*
of Mayala's customers and Christine's 'guests' were at *some* other times,
and in varying degrees, to be found participating in social activities
with kinsmen and 'brothers'; and, equally, *most* members of friendship
groups or cliques (like the 'club') and of kinship groups (like that on
Bernard's compound) would also at *some* other times, and in varying
degrees, participate in groups of different kinds to those in which the
reader was introduced to them.

In considering this range of opportunities and possibilities we have
to remember that the data being analysed were gathered in an urban
situation in a state of flux and change. Each of the 'small groups'
described was not only a developing cluster of face-to-face relations,
but a *developing cluster set in an immediate context of change*: of marked
population growth, of increasing social heterogeneity, and of high
population turn-over in a neighbourhood that was itself part of a
diversified town drawing its increasing population from a vast and
diversified hinterland. Even the 'club' with its semblance of formal
organization and its relatively clear-cut and easily definable membership had a fluid and changing form. It had come into existence as a
mock-formal association during the period of my fieldwork, and it
would be very surprising if it had continued to exist in anything like
the same form for any length of time. Indeed, it must in this connexion
be stressed that the form of the 'club', with its various titles and offices
and with its elected 'president' was a relatively new and unusual
phenomenon in this area of the town where there was as yet very little
development of formal voluntary associations. My account of the 'club'
thus has to be seen as a description at one point in time of a changing
clique set in a social scene that was itself changing. And this was true
of all the clusters of face to face relations described in this chapter. To
take another example, we know from Lusaka's evidence that the
gatherings around his work-bench were changing appreciably as the
demand for his services as a carpenter grew, as the ratio of 'customers'
to 'friends' visiting his compound increased, as more tenants came to
the area, and as these changes affected and were in turn affected by
other changes in the neighbourhood and the wider urban community.
But although individuals were constantly compelled to adjust their
social relations, and although many of them had perforce to interact
on the basis of little knowledge of each other, the avenue also had
many residents linked by enduring networks of more stable social
relations developed on the basis of continuous interaction over periods
of many years. These networks of personal relations were very
much affected by the institutional prescriptions of kinship, and the

semi-institutional behaviour loosely associated with the principles of
'brotherhood' and 'neighbourhood'. There was thus a wide variety of
clusters of different types of social relations, and the two broad
principles which we referred to in Chapter I as 'tribalism' and 'class'
mediated interaction in different ways within the various clusters.
In many situations people readily distinguished each other as having
different tribal affiliations and affinities, and they were quick to impute
qualities to each other on the basis of their varied ethnicities. In other
situations, and particularly when individuals knew each other well,
'tribalism' was not used as a basis for quick classification or for imputing
particular qualities to each other, yet consciousness of 'tribalism'
remained and was clearly an important factor underlying the principle
of urban 'brotherhood'. This principle was, however, flexible and
variable in its application. And the social bonds of 'brotherhood' tended
to merge and overlap with the bonds of 'neighbourhood' which were
in turn frequently inter-linked with the bonds of 'old family friends'.

To detect and classify the principles governing various face-to-face
relations, and to assess the range of opportunities open to an individual
in a given social setting, are important steps in the analysis of the urban
social system. But they are only first steps. Having detected, classified
and assessed in this way, we are inevitably led to pose a series of questions concerning the very processes by which different individuals were
led to differential participation in the system. How and why did some
people select particular patterns of behaviour which others rejected?
And, more crucially, how and why did one and the same individual
come to make different choices at different times? We saw in Chapter I
how, in his analysis of 'tribalism' and 'class' on the Copperbelt of
(former) Northern Rhodesia, Mitchell posed his central problem in
this way. After illustrating how "in certain situations Africans ignore
either class differences or tribal differences (or both), and in other
situations these differences become significant", he stresses the importance of trying to specify and define the kinds of situation in which
'tribal' differences override 'class' differences. In analysing social
relations such as those described in Avenue 21, we similarly need to
examine how and why different principles of association pervaded
some groups or clusters of social relations to a greater extent than
others, and why some persons tended to get involved in a wider
variety of social relations than others. Why, for example, was Bernard
so seldom involved in gatherings other than those made up almost
exclusively of his own kinsmen, 'brothers', and fellow-tribesmen, while
François regularly participated in a 'tribal' and kinship drinking
group on some occasions but enjoyed drinking with non-tribal friends
and neighbours on others?

In order to answer questions of this order, we need to look at the
social relations enacted within the several 'small groups' in the neighbourhood as integral parts of the overall system of social relations that
was changing and developing over time in the society as a whole. We

have to reiterate that none of the 'small groups' described had discrete limits, and that each was in fact not so much a small group as a cluster of face-to-face relations either developing, or simply being maintained, in a variety of particular social contexts. Nor, of course, was the avenue itself a corporate structure with any particular social boundaries. As stressed by Southall, the study of 'small groups' in this kind of social situation is a means to an end, rather than an end in itself. By focusing on various 'small groups' we are better able to define and assess different types of social relations, but the groups are not themselves our units of analysis.[21] Our aim in examining a number of 'small groups' was only to trace regularities in behaviour and to define and assess a few sets of social relations. Having done that, we have to see how different individuals qualified for participation in different 'groups'. The behaviour and the social relations observed within the 'small groups' are merely specimens drawn from larger universes. To proceed with the analysis we have to trace the extension of social relations into the immediate neighbourhood, into the urban community as a whole, and into the rural tribal world. And we would want to be able to assess the development over time of the system of urban relations. It is at this juncture that Epstein's analysis of changes in leadership on the Copperbelt is particularly pertinent for us. In Chapter I we saw how, faced with the problem of explaining the shift over a number of years from tribal to non-tribal leadership on the Copperbelt, Epstein was led to view the urban social system as made up of sets of social relations of different kinds and with possibly varying degrees of autonomy and uneven rates of change. This kind of formulation seems essential for any attempt to analyse the inter-relation between various clusters of social relations in Avenue 21. Here, however, the relative lack of time depth in my direct observations is a serious deficiency in the data. Ideally, we would want to be able to trace the way in which the application of different principles had developed within various sets of relations and in various spheres of action. I do not have such data and there is no way of fully compensating for the deficiency. Individual case histories can, however, be used to indicate how some people grew into and reacted to different situations over time. Case histories can also be used to illustrate different 'types' of people and to show how some were equipped with a greater variety of norms than others, and how social connexions beyond the immediate locality could affect social participation in the neighbourhood. The next chapter is therefore devoted to three case studies chosen for presentation on account of the very different positions which each subject occupied in the avenue. It will be seen that the three cases depict the differing patterns of participation in the neighbourhood of three men who had launched on urban life at different stages of their lives and in very different ways. The three subjects had over time found access to combinations of 'small group' situations that differed substantially from each other in type and in quality, and their social opportunities at the time of the study were far from equal. Taken together, the three cases thus afford examples of virtually the whole range of social relations in Avenue 21.

FOOTNOTES TO CHAPTER VI

[1] See Pons (1961).

[2] The detailed expenditure incurred by one man in building a house with five rooms is given in Appendix C.

[3] Clément (1956), p. 375.

[4] This evidence from Avenue 21 is in keeping with the opinion expressed in Chapter II that the estimate of a third of the population moving in the course of a year—an estimate based on official records—was substantially too low.

[5] A key to all persons mentioned by name in this chapter is given in Table 52.

[6] I later engaged Lusaka to help me with my work. He drew detailed diagrams of the dwelling compounds in Avenue 21, he helped me to keep my population register up to date, and he did some census-type interviewing for me. He was also one of half a dozen men who later kept diaries and detailed records of income and expenditure for me. A detailed case study of Lusaka is given with two others in Chapter VII; extracts from his autobiography are given in Appendix D; a transcription of the official record of his divorce is included in Appendix E; some letters written to him by his brother are given in Appendix F; his diary for a period of two months is given in Appendix G; and an extract from his monthly accounts is given in Appendix H.

[7] Lusaka and Bernadette were not married but were partners to a 'trial marriage'. See Chapter VII.

[8] Limela's case history is also given in Chapter VII; a transcription of the official record of his divorce is included in Appendix E; and some letters written by him and others received by him, are given in Appendix K.

[9] In Chapter VIII I use the term 'semi-prostitute' to refer to women who had one or more 'lovers' from whom they habitually received presents in return for sexual favours. Maua was an 'ordinary prostitute' in the sense that she normally received cash payments for her sexual services and her clients were not her regular 'lovers'.

[10] If my knowledge of Swahili was often less than adequate, so, quite commonly, was that of some of the participants. And when conversation was wholly or partly in French, it was I who had the advantage. On the other hand, of course, I was always at a complete disadvantage when conversations were in any one of the many tribal vernaculars or in Lingala. But as most residents in Brussels were from the North, East and South-East, Lingala was seldom used there.

[11] Pons (1961), pp. 205–216.

[12] It may be relevant to Bernard's conservative outlook that he first came to Stanleyville at a much later age than the average migrant.

[13] Like the 'club', Christine's 'guests' have previously been reported in Pons (1961), pp. 205–216.

[14] I am using the term 'egocentric' to refer to 'personal' or 'ego-centred' relationships and to distinguish these from 'structural' or 'institutional' relationships on the one hand, and from 'categorical' relationships on the other. This classification has been used and developed by several authors writing on African urban social structure. (See Mitchell, 1966, pp. 51–54.) Southall (1961a) distinguishes between the three types of relationships as follows:

'Face-to-face relationships of a structural type are aspects of roles defined within the structure of an institution. Thus, though people meet face to face either in the family or in the factory their relationship in these contexts is structural in this sense. Categorial relationships are those in which persons meet in an informal context yet without knowing one another very well, and consequently begin to act on the basis of intuitively assigning one another to various type categories as an empirical approach towards appropriate behaviour. Egocentric relations are those in which people know one another sufficiently intimately as persons to base their mutual expectations of one another's behaviour directly on this personal knowledge . . .', pp. 29–30.

[15] An example of such an outburst is recorded in Patrice's diary on Tuesday, 7.10.52 (Appendix I). In shouting at Patrice as a *musendji* who did 'not know the ways of Kisangani' and who could 'not tell the difference between the beginning and the end of anything', Christine was participating in the process of 'civilizing' him. As his diary entries show, he was

extremely hurt by such insults, and the more so when they came from a person like Christine whose own status in the avenue was marginal.

[16] The term *basaiba* was commonly used to refer to friends in general, but sometimes its use carried the special connotation of old and warm friendships between persons who knew each other as members of families rather than simply as individual acquaintances.

[17] For one account of the death of Felekini, see Lusaka's diary entry for 10/10/52 (Appendix G).

[18] In saying that Felekini had the *akili* of the Babali, the speaker clearly intended to convey that the deceased knew the ways and customs of his tribe. But he then went on to explain that he also knew the ways and customs of the *Arabisés* and of the Europeans which implied that he was not an 'uncivilized' man. Like many of the long-established residents of this area, Felekini was an old and illiterate man, yet his fellow-residents in the neighbourhood had clearly held him in high esteem as a relatively 'civilized' person.

[19] In this connexion it is pertinent to record that there were few Baluba in the area and that they tended to see themselves as 'brothers' of one 'family'.

[20] Clément (1956), p. 374.

[21] Southall (1961a), p. 25.

VII

THE SOCIAL RELATIONS OF THREE MEN FROM AVENUE 21

In the course of fieldwork in Avenue 21 I was constantly led to inquire into the individual life histories of the inhabitants. There were several reasons for this. First, the origins and backgrounds of the inhabitants were so varied that some classification of the population was necessary. Secondly, it was soon apparent that any analysis of particular 'small groups' in the avenue called for relatively detailed information on the antecedent activities and pre-existing social relations of the participants. Thirdly, neighbourhood participation was so obviously related to the differing pre-occupations of persons involved in urban life in different ways and degrees that it was clearly important to try to assess both the developing urban commitments and the continuing rural-tribal interests of the inhabitants. I thus adopted a 'case history' and 'case study' approach to all the inhabitants of the avenue. In some cases I obtained little more than outline histories of work and migration, but in others I was able to accumulate much more comprehensive information on the development of their whole lives. In this chapter I present three of these more detailed case studies.

Of the three subjects, two—Lusaka and Limela—are men we encountered in the previous chapter. The other, Patrice, was not referred to by name though he was one of Christine's 'guests', living on her compound and often frequenting her 'parlour'. Lusaka's personal history is of interest primarily as an illustration of the process of growing up in town. He was somewhat exceptional in several respects: he was recognized as the most 'civilized' person in the avenue where he was the 'president' of the 'club'; though only 26 years of age, he had for several years been the title-holder of his own compound; he was the only man in the avenue to have completed a full course of secondary education; and his total income—from employment and from his private trade as a carpenter—was over 1,500 francs a month, which was very high for this neighbourhood and appreciably above the average for the town as a whole.[1] As a Mubali, he was a member of one of the largest well-established colonies in the neighbourhood and of the tribe best represented in Avenue 21. In the town as a whole, the Babali numbered nearly 2,000 and about 60 per cent of these lived in Brussels. (Table 16.)

Patrice, the subject of the second case, was 22 years of age. He was a very recent immigrant and his social position stood in sharp contrast to Lusaka's in almost every way. As a Murega, he had some fellow tribesmen in the neighbourhood but he was a member of a small tribal colony with only 300 to 400 representatives in the town as a whole. Despite six years of primary education at a Protestant school close to his home village, Patrice was regarded as relatively 'uncivilized' as were the Warega in general. He had arrived in Stanleyville during the course of my fieldwork in Avenue 21 where he had found accommodation as a tenant within a few days of his arrival. When I first met him, his wife and children were not yet in Stanleyville. During the period of our acquaintance he had to face the practical problems of looking after himself and a younger brother who had come to town with him, of seeking rent-free accommodation, and of finding work after a short spell of unemployment. He also had pre-occupations concerning his rural kinsmen; his father had resented his departure from home and now expected him to continue carrying a share of the family's responsibility in his village. Yet, on a labourer's salary and with no other regular source of income, he was often out of pocket and experienced considerable material hardship in town. He saw urban life as dangerous, frightening, and insecure, and he was often homesick and disappointed in the failure of his 'brothers' in town to give him the succour he felt he was entitled to receive. Despite all his difficulties, however, he considered his prospects at home to be so poor that he saw no option but to stay in town indefinitely. Patrice is an example of a recent immigrant but he was scarcely a typical one; he undoubtedly had a larger-than-average number of kinsmen living in the hinterland and he took greater pains to keep in touch with them than did most immigrants I encountered in the avenue. On the other hand, he may well have been typical of Warega immigrants who constituted a colony with a social configuration somewhat similar to that of the Topoke described in Chapter IV.

Limela, the subject of the third case, was 34 years old. He was regarded as a 'civilized' man. He was a personal friend of Lusaka, but he occupied a strikingly different social position in the neighbourhood. First, he was a Mongandu and as such a person with even fewer fellow-tribesmen in the neighbourhood than Patrice, though the Mongandu in the town as a whole were more numerous than the Warega and probably totalled about 750. Secondly, while uprooted from his village of origin and seemingly disaffected from *Kisendji* as a way of life, he had failed to establish any effective network of stable social relations in the town. He knew many people in a casual way, but his more lasting relationships were mainly with people who were widely dispersed and unknown to each other. Thus, for example, though he had come to know a good deal about Lusaka's friends and kinsmen, Lusaka knew little about his (Limela's) connexions. He had first left his tribal area as a young boy, since when he had always been on the move. He had at different stages lived on mission stations, in military and labour camps, and in other small labour centres. He had been to Stanleyville before but his current period of residence there was under three years. I first encountered Limela when he was living rent-free on the compound of his 'fictitious' sister Christine where Patrice later came to live as a tenant. Three months after I met Limela he left Christine's compound to live as a tenant in a nearby avenue and, later still, he began to build a house on an undeveloped compound recently allocated to him in New Brussels. He is an example of men who had considerable experience of *Kizungu* but who had seemingly failed to settle down in town. He represents a fairly distinctive category, though his case was perhaps more dramatic than most.

The cases of these three men were expressly chosen for presentation as examples of three broad categories of inhabitants in Avenue 21. Yet, as I have stressed, none can be thought of as *typical* or *average*; on the contrary, each was to some extent an *exception* and they were selected for presentation in this chapter precisely because they exhibit certain features of social participation in a more pronounced form than the cases of more ordinary men. They are thus good 'clinical' cases. In each case I first give information on the subject's origins and childhood background. I then dwell on each man's social career, including his marital and domestic life, and I attempt to outline the range of his total social connexions at the time that I knew him. The marital histories of Lusaka and Limela are given in greater detail than is strictly necessary for the purposes of this chapter but are again used as case material in Chapter VIII.

THE CASE OF LUSAKA

Lusaka was born in Stanleyville in 1926. His father, Kilongozi, and his mother, Samenyao, were both Babali, but there was an important difference in their social orientations. Kilongozi had been brought up in his tribal area and had first come to town as a migrant labourer about the time of the first world war. Samenyao, on the other hand, was a permanent urban-dweller who had largely been reared in town and this partly under *Arabisé* influence. She had first come to Stanleyville in the 1890s when her own mother had been abducted from her village by the *Arabisés*. At the time of her mother's abduction she was still a young child and she was to spend the rest of her short girlhood in the *Arabisé* village in Stanleyville. Some years later, she was married at an early age to Yaleko, a Lokele from the Left Bank. She spent four or five years with Yaleko and bore two children before her marriage ended in divorce. Her first child died in infancy, but the second, Yalala, was reared to adulthood as a Lokele by her father and his family. (Yalala was later to be a significant factor in Lusaka's life, though she died before the present study when only 35 to 40 years of age.) After her divorce, Samenyao returned to the right bank and settled in Brussels, where in 1918 she married her second husband, Balindege, who was a Mubali immigrant. There were two sons to the marriage, Alamazani and Kisubi. Balindege died in town in 1922, but neither of his sons was sent back to his kinsmen in the countryside as they might well have been following tribal custom. About this time Samenyao encountered Kilongozi who, like Balindege, was a young unmarried Mubali labourer. She married Kilongozi in 1925, and Alamazani and Kisubi came to her new home. Lusaka was the only child born to Samenyao in her marriage to Kilongozi. Alamazani died soon after Lusaka's birth but Kisubi lived to adulthood, and he and Lusaka were thus brought up in the same house where they interacted as full brothers and came to share an exceptionally devoted attachment to their mother.

Kilongozi later married a second wife in his tribal area, but he never brought her to town and in 1944, after some 25 years of intermittent residence in town, he finally retired to his village leaving Samenyao in town with Lusaka who was then 18 years old. Kisubi, a few years older than Lusaka, was at this time already married and living in a small town in the interior where he was working as a *capita vendeur* (manager-salesman of a small European-owned shop).

With one important exception, all Kilongozi's 'real' kin were rural tribesmen with whom Lusaka had little direct contact over the years. The exception was Shani, one of Kilongozi's classificatory sisters. She had first come to Stanleyville with her husband some years before Lusaka's birth. Her husband had later returned to his village, but she had re-married in town and had lived there continuously since her arrival. As his *shangazi* (father's sister), Shani played an important part in Lusaka's upbringing. When he was a child, he often stayed with her for considerable periods; there had developed a strong attachment between them and this persisted into adulthood. While most of Kilongozi's 'real' kin remained relative strangers to Lusaka, he grew up surrounded by a number of his father's 'fictitious' kinsmen. Like Kilongozi himself, these were largely 'uncivilized' people.

Lusaka visited his father's village for a few weeks at the age of 13 years, and he returned for a second brief visit in adulthood, but village life remained unfamiliar to him. He often spoke of his father's kin as *basendji* from whom he was separated by lack of intimate personal knowledge as well as by the cultural barrier of his own upbringing in *Kizungu*. He did not know 'the work of the village', he distrusted the 'blindness' and 'jealousy' of village people, and he saw rural-tribal life as one of ignorance, hardship, and deprivation. He commonly said that whereas his father had never settled 'to the ways of the town', he himself felt ill at ease in the village and could never stay there.

Unlike Kilongozi, Samenyao had lost all direct contact with her rural kinsfolk, but she had for many years remained in touch with two classificatory kinsmen—a brother and a sister—who had come to Stanleyville at the same period as herself. By 1952 both were dead, but seven surviving children of one or the other were settled in or near the town. Together with their spouses and off-spring, the survivors made up a total of about 25 people who were to all intents and purposes Lusaka's only 'real' maternal kin. All were experienced urban-dwellers; several lived in Old Brussels and were members of the Babali sub-community there, but two of the women had married into *Arabisés* families and settled in the *Arabisé* village. One of the men also lived in the *Arabisé* village though he was not a Mohammedan and was not considered to be *Arabisé*.

The above details of Lusaka's parental connexions give some indication of the variety of cultural influences that bore on him as a child. In his own home, in the homes of Shani and of several of his maternal kinsmen and, more generally, in the sub-community of Babali where he had numerous 'fictitious' kinsmen and *basaiba* or 'family friends', he spoke Kibali, heard many accounts of traditional life in Babali villages, and was introduced to a number of distinctively Babali customs (e.g. the *mambela*; see Appendix D). He thus grew up conscious of his identity as a Mubali but with a keen awareness of the contrast between his father's 'uncivilized' rural-tribal outlook and his mother's more 'civilized' urban orientation. He was also exposed to several other distinctive influences. Firstly, through his mother, and especially through those of her kin living in the *Arabisé* village, he came into direct contact with the *Arabisés* and at the age of eleven was circumcised by the *Arabisés* 'according to their customs' (see Appendix D). Secondly, through his elder half-sister, Yalala, he was able to have the experience—very unusual for a Mubali—of some intimate contact with the Lokele. When he was still a boy, Yalala was a married woman living in Belge II. She befriended him and he often spent a day or two in her home. These visits gave him a working knowledge of the Lokele which he could not have acquired from a childhood confined to Old Brussels and the *Arabisé* village. His association with Yalala had waned before her death, but his early contact with her and her husband had given him considerable insight into the urban ways of a tribal group markedly different from his own. Finally, in addition to *Arabisés* and Lokele influences, he had in the course of daily life in Brussels come into frequent contact with members of several other ethnic colonies, particularly the Bakumu, Bakusu, and Barumbi, all of whom were well-established tribes in the neighbourhood of Avenue 21.

Lusaka's own neighbourhood and those of his kinsmen were, however, only part of the mixed cultural setting of his childhood and youth. In 1934, at the age of eight, he went to school for the first time and proved to be a good pupil. After six years of primary education, he entered the local secondary vocational school (*école professionelle*) where he was awarded a diploma in carpentry in 1944. During his school years he was naturally drawn into a series of social situations of quite a different order to those of his quiet residential neighbourhood. He was exposed to Roman Catholic missionaries, and he attended church, sang in the boys' choir, and participated in a variety of organized activities connected with school and church. Most importantly, too, he was thrust into the hustle and bustle of the town centre where the schools he attended were located. With his friends he lingered in the 'European town' and in the busy areas of Belge I, and he found ways of earning money for himself: as a ball-boy at a European tennis club, by working in the gardens of European homes and by selling old bottles and fruit (see Appendix D). In all these activities he encountered people drawn from a very much wider range of ethnic origins than in his home neighbourhood, and he began to see that his identity as a Mubali was often of comparatively little or no relevance. In these new settings he and his friends became more aware of their distinctiveness as town and school boys than as members of particular tribes. And, as they passed through secondary school and entered the labour market, they became aware of the further distinction between men who had achieved white-collar jobs and *évolué* status and those who continued associating primarily with other manual workers.

Lusaka's general education was good enough by local standards for him to have entered the ranks of white collar workers, and some of his school friends did so with qualifications no better, and in some cases poorer than his. But he entered employment as a carpenter immediately after leaving school and continued to work in this capacity till the time that I knew him. That he did not aspire to clerical work—and to its usual concomitant of an *évolué* way of life—can be attributed to several factors in his social background and in his particular situation at the end of his school career. First, his upbringing as a Mubali in the remoter parts of Old Brussels had contributed to giving him a relatively low level of occupational and status expectations. The Babali were a well-established tribe in the town but they had a high proportion of totally unskilled labourers, and their 'urban' achievements were very modest (cf. Chapter IV, esp. Table 32). And the same was true of the non-Babali population in the neighbourhood of Lusaka's home. Thus, by the standards of his most immediate reference groups, he was on leaving secondary school already a markedly successful person.

Secondly, he had at school responded to missionary teachings on the dignity of labour and to exhortations for Africans to guard against their allegedly 'inherent laziness' and their 'arrogant ambitions' to sit at desks giving orders and doing 'European work'. As a person of simple and modest disposition he had partly carried such views over into his personal philosophy,[2] and he tended to be critical of what he considered to be the pretentious emulation by some *évolués* of European standards in dress, manners, and public behaviour.

Finally, his conservatism in itself earned him considerable prestige and esteem in his immediate social milieu of the neighbourhood of Avenue 21. To appreciate his social attitudes at this stage in his life, we have to bear in mind that there were, in his particular situation at the time of leaving school, strong inducements for him to break away from the social circles in which he had been reared: his father was about to return permanently to his village leaving Lusaka his compound; his mother was in the absence of Kisubi being left in his charge; and, as explained below, he was wanting, and trying, to get permission to marry a girl who had already borne a child by him. Thus, though only 18 years old, he was on the threshold of becoming a responsible adult man at an age when very few men in the community could hope to achieve such status.[3] By choosing to stay in his neighbourhood of Old Brussels, and by refraining from competing for white-collar status and entry to the *évolués* circles of the town, he had in effect opted for an alternative which held its own very appreciable rewards in prestige and social recognition.

To appreciate the development of Lusaka's adult life, we have to return to his first encounters with his future wife, Antoinette. Like Lusaka himself, Antoinette was a Mubali born in Stanleyville. She was a year or two younger than Lusaka. She had never been to school, but she had relatively 'civilized' parents with origins similar to those of Samenyao. Her parents lived in Old Brussels, a few minutes walk from Avenue 21. Lusaka had known members of her family as fellow-Babali and near-neighbours since childhood.[4] He claimed that he had begun to take notice of Antoinette when he was 15 or 16 years of age, but it was not till he was 17 and in his last year of school that he approached one of his 'fictitious' kinswomen in the neighbourhood asking her to tell Antoinette that he would like to see her. The two became lovers, meeting clandestinely and without the knowledge of either his or her parents. A few months later Antoinette was pregnant. Lusaka sought to induce her father to accept bridewealth and to arrange for Antoinette to come to his house as his wife, but the father persistently refused and insisted that his daughter should discontinue the association. This she eventually did before giving birth to a boy, Adolphe, in May 1944. Her father then took her to the offices of the C.E.C. to have her registered as a *femme libre,* and in so doing in effect claimed the custody of the child. Some months later, however, Lusaka and Antoinette began to associate with each other again, and they now did so openly.

At this juncture Lusaka left school and began to work, and his father left Stanleyville permanently to return to his home village. In his new circumstances as a working man and title-holder of a compound, Lusaka once again tried to marry Antoinette. He discussed the matter with his father's sister, Shani, and her husband, Etienne, as well as with members of his mother's immediate circle of 'real' and 'fictitious' kin, but Antoinette's father remained implacable. According to Lusaka, this was partly because of the personal dislike which Antoinette's father had taken to him, and partly because the father had already accepted favours and presents in respect of Antoinette from another man. After months of discussion, however, Antoinette's father reluctantly agreed to negotiate bridewealth with members of Lusaka's family. Lusaka's principal intermediaries in the negotiations were Shani and Laini, the latter an elderly woman from Avenue 21 who had known Lusaka from childhood and who claimed a 'fictitious' kinship connexion with Samenyao on the grounds that their respective mothers had supposedly come from the same village. A sum of 900 francs was agreed upon as bridewealth. The initial payment (*kifunga mulango*: the closing of the door) of 400 francs was eventually paid in February 1945, and the final payment of 500 francs in April, 1945. Both payments were made out of Lusaka's own earnings. Even after accepting the payments, however, Antoinette's father persisted in expressing his disapproval, and it was only in December 1945 that he finally allowed Antoinette to 'enter Lusaka's house'.

Two months later Antoinette was pregnant for the second time. Apprehensive that her father might try to claim the custody of the child at birth, Lusaka now asked him to testify at the C.E.C. offices that bridewealth had been received so that Antoinette's name should be registered in his identity book.[5] As he had feared, however, the father refused to co-operate over the inscription; Lusaka thereupon laid a complaint against him and he (the father) was summoned to court where he took the opportunity of complaining publicly that Lusaka 'was not good to him'. In the face of the court proceedings, however, he had no option but to accept the inscription. The child, a daughter named Safi, was born in October 1946 and duly remained in Lusaka's custody though Adolphe continued to be brought up by Antoinette's parents.

Antoinette became pregnant again in 1947 and a second daughter was born in 1948 but died in 1950. According to Lusaka's account, which was on this point substantially corroborated by Antoinette's, the marriage was successful and satisfactory up to the time of the death of their second daughter. Antoinette had sided with her husband against her father, and over time her mother had adopted a conciliatory attitude which, Lusaka claimed, had been the crucial factor making the marriage possible in the face of the father's continued attempts to disrupt it. From the time of the death of their second daughter in 1950, however, Antoinette had, according to Lusaka, begun 'to turn against him' and to side with her father. He maintained that members of her father's family influenced her to take her father's side because they had become 'jealous' that she conceived so easily and seemed likely to give him a large family.[6] And they had, he claimed, persuaded Antoinette to have 'her stomach closed'. He first began to suspect this when, after the birth of the last child, she failed to conceive again. At this stage he consulted *Arabisés* diviners on several occasions, and claimed they had confirmed his suspicions. He had finally asked Antoinette to accompany him to a diviner, and he claimed that on hearing the diviner's verdict she admitted his charges of contraceptive intent. This severe disturbance of their marital relationship came to a head in the latter half of 1951, at which stage Antoinette began to be unfaithful to Lusaka. He claimed to have caught her in adultery on three occasions but said that he had taken no action against her because 'he felt sorry for her' and because he considered that he ought to be 'generous' to her as she had given him children.[7] Eventually, however, their respective families were brought into the dispute. Lusaka first approached Antoinette's father complaining of her adultery. At their first meeting the father rebuked Antoinette and told her 'to go back to her husband', but at subsequent meetings he made no attempt to conceal his animosity to Lusaka and took the attitude that, Antoinette being young, if Lusaka spent nights away from home, there was no reason why she should not do the same. This tacit admission by Antoinette's father of her adultery and, implicitly, of her general failure to be a good wife was later to lead to the reimbursement of part of the bridewealth. Lusaka considered the attitude taken by the father to be so outrageous and incomprehensible that for a time he ceased to seek any further redress from him. But he stopped entrusting Antoinette with money for the household and he made her sleep in an outhouse on the compound. He then called on his mother to run the household and, in particular, to take charge of Safi who was then about five years of age. He also began a series of consultations with kinsmen and other members of his immediate social circle. He first informed Kisubi, who was then in gaol serving a three-year sentence for embezzlement, that he was thinking of sending Antoinette away. Kisubi wrote three letters in reply pleading that Lusaka should await his return before taking any final action against Antoinette. Lusaka claimed that he would have followed this advice were it not that Antoinette had by then begun to provoke him into sending her away. He then spoke to Shani and her husband, and to Laini and her husband, Masudi. Apart from the fact that Laini was a 'fictitious' kinswoman who had acted as an intermediary in the original marriage negotiations, she and Masudi were respected neighbours who had close day-to-day contact with Lusaka and his family. Shani, Laini, and Masudi all advised Lusaka that, things having reached the stage they had, the only practical course left open to him was to send his wife away. Several other kinsmen, neighbours, and friends took a similar view. In the end Antoinette suggested that she and Lusaka should jointly approach Antoine, the title-holder of compound No. 9 in Avenue 21 as an impartial mediator. (Cf. Chapter VI.) As was expected of him, Antoine did not take sides in the matter. After listening to Lusaka and Antoinette in turn, he first gave them a general homily on marriage between 'civilized' people, and then suggested that instead of arguing further between themselves they should go to the urban court to settle their differences. Following on this interview they went to court in May, 1952. Antoinette accused Lusaka in court of wanting her to leave him. In particular, she complained that he no longer respected her or treated her as his wife. Lusaka admitted that he no longer wanted her to stay with him, saying that it was impossible for a man to be satisfied with a woman whose parents were dissatisfied with him. He added that he and Antoinette were agreed that they both wanted to end the marriage.[8]

Lusaka's marriage to Antoinette had lasted nearly seven years during which period his family and domestic responsibilities had altered appreciably in other ways. In 1948 he had taken into his home

Mambao, a boy of 12, who was the urban-born orphan of Samenyao's classificatory brother; since then he had helped Mambao through two years of schooling and had provided for him for another two years before Mambao began to work as an ordinary labourer. More importantly, too, Lusaka had in 1951 assumed a number of additional family responsibilities when Kisubi was sentenced to three years in gaol. He had become responsible for some of Kisubi's own family obligations and for looking after his interests in general, and he had taken over his role as Samenyao's senior son (see Kisubi's letters written to Lusaka from gaol, Appendix F). Kisubi's wife and children continued to live away from Stanleyville, but Lusaka found himself responsible for giving them financial assistance from time to time, for sending small sums of money to Kisubi himself, and for making occasional presents to Kisubi's *shemeki* (wife's parents and family). In addition, shortly after the imprisonment Lusaka had begun to plan and build a new and larger house so that he would be in a position to accommodate Kisubi on his release in 1954.

These developments had greatly amplified Lusaka's standing as a responsible adult man, and his approach to seeking a second wife was affected by his new role. After Antoinette's departure, his conversations with kinsmen and friends were often centred on the problems of marriage in town for a person with his standing and responsibilities. In the course of discussion he commonly referred with appreciation to the help his mother was then giving him in looking after Safi and in preparing food for the household. But there were many duties which she could not carry out, or which Lusaka felt he could not entrust to her; for example, she was too old to walk to the market or to keep the compound clean, and she could not be expected to look after his clothes or to handle more than very small sums of money. In this context, he continually dwelt on the difficulties of life in town without a wife, and he often added that it was particularly hard for a man like himself who received many friends and kinsmen on his compound. Finding a suitable replacement for his first wife was, however, a difficult problem. He could not entertain marrying an 'uncivilized' woman for she would be no companion to him and would not be able to welcome his guests or handle his money or give him messages from people calling at his compound when he was away. Nor could he easily contemplate marrying a *young* 'civilized' girl who had no previous experience of household responsibilities. Yet, he pointed out, there were very few women who, being both 'civilized' and experienced, were prepared to give up the independence enjoyed by *femmes libres*. Moreover, 'one needed to be very cautious' with those who were prepared 'to take on the duties of a wife' for, he said, 'the ways of Stanleyville women are often wayward'. He would thus often conclude that a man seeking a new wife needed 'to have great wisdom and foresight' if he wanted to avoid trouble, especially if he had children. In reviewing all these considerations, he would argue that the most prudent course for a man in his position was 'to take a *fiancée* (*sic*) into his home' so as to have the opportunity of 'watching her conduct and her ways very carefully'. And this is what he eventually did when he brought Bernadette to his house six weeks after Antoinette's departure.

Like Antoinette, Bernadette was a woman born and bred in Stanley-ville. Her father was a Mubua and her mother a Mukumu. Bernadette herself had during several years of her childhood been reared as a Mukumu by one of her mother's brothers, but most of her kin in the town at the time of the study were Babua. She had been to school for three years and was able to read and write. She was 23 years old when she came to Lusaka's home. She had not previously been married, but had been the regular mistress of two men in succession over a total period of three to four years. Throughout this period she had lived and worked either in the home of her parents or in the homes of urban kinsmen of one or the other of the two men. She had the reputation of being capable and hard-working and of being good to members of her family.

Lusaka first met Bernadette casually in 1947 when she was 17 years old. They were friendly, and he had, as he put it, 'played with her'. He visited her intermittently at her mother's sister's home for about a year until Antoinette heard of the relationship and put pressure on him to end it. From 1948 to 1951 he had seen Bernadette from time to time but it was not till the end of 1951, when his marriage was very strained, that he became Bernadette's regular lover. She was then living with her mother's brother in Brussels, and it was here that he visited her at this period. She now began 'to take care of him', i.e. she washed and ironed his clothes, and occasionally brought food for him to his house when his wife was away.

Shortly after Antoinette's departure from his house, Lusaka wrote to Bernadette's mother's brother, who had partly reared her, seeking permission for her 'to enter his house' and explaining that he was looking for a wife and not merely a mistress. Bernadette's mother's brother and his family were 'well disposed to him' and they readily granted per-mission. As he had expected, too, they themselves suggested that there should be no discussion about bridewealth until the two were satisfied that they were able to settle down together.

Bernadette's own father and mother were told of the arrangement and she 'entered Lusaka's house' in July, 1952. She immediately took over the household responsibilities including the care of Safi, the preparation of food for the household as a whole, and the role of receiving and welcoming guests and customers calling at the com-pound. On his side, Lusaka began to entrust money to her and to visit her kin who in turn began to visit him regularly. Several encounters between Lusaka and Bernadette's kin are recorded in the diary which he was keeping for me at this stage (see, for example, 20/9/52 in Appendix G). The nature and tone of the entries in themselves suggest that he and Bernadette's kin were very cordial to each other. From his conversations and conduct at this period it was clear that he was intent on behaving as correctly as possible towards his *'fiancée's'* family. (See, in particular, his punctilious behaviour towards Bernadette's kin over the period of the *kilio* for her father. Appendix G, 27/8/52 to 14/9/52.)

Bernadette was similarly anxious to demonstrate her good and capable behaviour; when guests visited the compound, for example, she would welcome them in a deliberate manner which unmistakably indicated her good will to Lusaka and his family. The relationship between Lusaka and Bernadette themselves was also marked by extreme cordiality and ready co-operation. Two months after her arrival Bernadette offered to undertake a trading trip in the countryside to help Lusaka meet expenses for his new house, and he willingly 'gave her permission to go' as her offer showed, he said, 'that she is interested in my family and my affairs'. (Appendix G, 2/10/52.)

Bernadette's stay with Lusaka was referred to in Swahili as a period of 'trying out' or 'weighing up' (*kupima*: to weigh, to test). At the time Lusaka frequently discussed his 'wife's' conduct and behaviour with friends and kinsmen. On a number of occasions, I heard him observing to Limela, for example, that 'she seemed to be satisfactory and that her conduct and behaviour interested him'. He would point out, in particular, that she looked after Safi well and that she was kind and good to his mother. He also frequently cited her trading as an example of her capability and worth.[9] Yet he remained unwilling to commit himself as a husband to his *'fiancée'*. He would say that he was not yet fully convinced about her, and that he wanted to 'watch her' a little longer. He was particularly troubled by her resentfulness whenever he gave Antoinette 'a helping hand' (financial assistance), and he complained that she was ill at ease with Antoinette whenever the latter came to visit Safi. He considered this unreasonable behaviour but, as the months passed, he was to observe with pleasure and relief that Bernadette was beginning to welcome Antoinette to the compound. He was also concerned about Bernadette's seeming inability to have children. Though she had never conceived before, he had hoped that she would become pregnant in his house; when she had not done so four months after her arrival, he asked her to consult a European doctor. She subsequently received treatment over a period of two months, and both she and Lusaka continued to hope that she would conceive.

I last saw Lusaka nine months after Bernadette had come to his house. The question of bridewealth had still not been settled. Nor had Bernadette become pregnant. The couple had, however, settled down to a harmonious domestic situation and relations between their families continued to be cordial. By now Lusaka discussed his 'wife' and her behaviour less frequently than he had done in the early months of their union. Had Bernadette become pregnant, Lusaka would undoubtedly have initiated negotiations for marriage. Or, had members of Bernadette's family had reason to be dissatisfied with Lusaka, they would in all probability have pressed either for Bernadette to leave him or for some other definition of the relationship. But none of these possible developments had yet taken place, and it may well be that the union endured unchanged for some considerable time after my departure. Given Lusaka's status in the neighbourhood, however, it is unlikely that the 'marriage' should have continued in this form indefinitely. Towards the end of the first nine months some of his friends had already begun to chide him about Bernadette. In private conversation with me, Limela was beginning to be critical of Lusaka, saying that he was 'one of the very best and most serious men in the neighbourhood and that he ought therefore to pay bridewealth for his wife.' 'If I were his brother', Limela would say, 'I would give him this counsel. As I am not his brother, however, I shall have to wait for the right opportunity to do so. He can surely see that the woman is good to his family and to his brothers and also to the child, Safi'.

Having traced Lusaka's childhood and the developments in his family and domestic situations up to the time of the study, we are now in a position to assess the significance for him of different sets of social relations in which he was personally involved. In describing an afternoon on his compound in Chapter VI, I pointed to the wide range of persons who commonly lingered around his work-bench and with whom he interacted very informally as he worked. The majority of people who called on him in this way were neighbours, near-neighbours and others from the immediate environs of Avenue 21. Many, though by no means all, were fellow-Babali, and a fair proportion were persons who in various particular situations would quite readily have claimed him as a 'fictitious' kinsman. These small informal gatherings on his compound sometimes included some of his personal friends (such as Limela who lived in the neighbourhood) or a few of his more intimate 'family friends' and 'fictitious' kinsmen (such as Amundala, his 'fictitious' *muyomba*, who lived one compound away). More commonly, however, his personal friends, his 'real' kin and his prospective affines would visit him formally. He would then set his work aside to receive them.

In an attempt to gauge the composition of Lusaka's visitors—as distinct from casual callers and others who lingered on his compound—I first listed, and then classified into four categories, all persons whose names appear in my notes, in his diary (Appendix G), and in his financial accounts (Appendix H), as having visited him on his compound during the period of the study. As shown in Table 59, I identified 53 such visitors. Of these 53, there were 27 with a 'real' connexion through kinship or marriage either to Lusaka or to his *fiancée*, and most of these were either Babali or Babua. Of the 15 visitors falling in the broad category of 'family friends', 'fictitious' kinsmen, and neighbours, seven were Babali and another five were Barumbi and thus also members of an old-established tribe in Avenue 21. The category of personal friends, however, was much more heterogeneous with only two Babali out of eleven, and the remainder representing eight different tribes. Moreover, of the total of 11 personal friends only three—Limela

TABLE 59

Lusaka's formal visitors classified by tribe and broad category of relationship

TRIBE	HIS OWN 'REAL' KIN AND THEIR SPOUSES AND CHILDREN	HIS 'WIFE'S' 'REAL' KIN AND THEIR SPOUSES AND CHILDREN	'FAMILY FRIENDS', 'FICTITIOUS' KINSMEN AND NEIGHBOURS	PERSONAL FRIENDS	TOTAL
Babali	11	0	7	2	20
Babua	0	11	0	1	12
Barumbi	0	0	5	2	7
Arabisés	3	0	0	1	4
Bakumu	0	2	1	0	3
Bakusu	0	0	1	1	2
Azande	0	0	0	1	1
Balengola	0	0	0	1	1
Lokele	0	0	0	1	1
Mangbetu	0	0	1	0	1
Mongandu	0	0	0	1	1
Total	14	13	15	11	53

and two others—were from the immediate neighbourhood of Lusaka's home, the others coming from various parts of the town including the *Arabisé* village, Belge I and Belge II. These personal friends constituted a distinctive category of persons of diverse tribal affiliations and often without common interests deriving from residence in the same neighbourhood. They were, as the following data on his six 'best friends' suggest, mainly men whom he had first met at work:[10]

1. Joseph, a Mubua, was a carpenter who worked at the same saw mill as Lusaka; he and Lusaka were *ikilemba* partners—each earned about 800 francs a month and their *ikilemba* arrangement was for 500 francs[11]; in French, Lusaka referred to Joseph as his *copain du travail*; they had known each other about two years, having first met when working for a previous employer and having moved to the saw mill together; they helped each other at work, and normally visited each other at home two or three times a week; Lusaka said that he and Joseph were friends 'who never argued, who never criticized each other, and who had great respect for each other and each other's families'.

2. Shindano, a Mubali, was a mechanic who was living in Bukavu at the time of the study; he had been there three years, but he and Lusaka had kept in touch by letter; they had known each other seven years, having first met as fellow-residents of the same neighbourhood; Lusaka described Shindano as a man who had always 'helped him with his difficulties and problems', and who was

at the same time 'not too "proud" to listen to any advice' that Lusaka gave him.

3. Bernard, a Lokele, was a carpenter whom Lusaka had known for three years; they had first met when Lusaka was the head carpenter of a previous employer and Bernard a new recruit to the workshop; Lusaka had helped Bernard 'to settle down to his work' and Bernard had 'remained grateful ever since'; they had last worked together two years before the time of the study, but they continued to visit each other at home from time to time.

4. Asani, a Murumbi, was a carpenter whom Lusaka had met at work five years before and with whom he had worked for about two years; Asani's wife had died at the time they were working together and Lusaka had 'helped him through his sorrow'; ever since then Asani had, Lusaka said, 'regarded him as a father'; they visited each other once or twice a month, usually on Sunday afternoons.

5. Limela, a Mongandu, was a labourer's foreman at the saw mill where Lusaka worked, but they had first met three years earlier when both working for the same employer as Bernard; about a year after their first encounter Limela had by chance come to live in Avenue 21; at the time of the study the two men were regular companions both at work and in the neighbourhood; though not as close and intimate a friend as either Joseph or Shindano, Limela was one of the first men to whom Lusaka tended to turn to discuss his marital and other personal problems.

6. Gerard, a Mulengola, was a carpenter whom Lusaka had first met three years before—about the same time, and at the same work-place, as he had met Bernard and Limela. At the time of their first encounter, Gerard had little experience as a carpenter and Lusaka had helped him with his work. Gerard now lived on the left bank, and only visited Lusaka on special occasions. They had a mutual friend in Asani who was at the time of the study working for the same employer as Gerard.

Though there was wide variation in the intimacy of the relations between Lusaka and his six 'best friends', there were some features common to all the cases cited as well as to several other friendships. Except for Shindano who was away, these were all friends who habitually visited him on his compound and whom he similarly visited at their respective homes. On such occasions they commonly offered each other beer to drink, and would at times be invited into each others houses (as distinct from being received on the compound). Also, they would from time to time give each other small presents *ya furaha* (lit. of joy or rejoicing). Thus, for example, it can be seen from Lusaka's accounts (Appendix H) that he received presents of 10 francs from Limela on 31/1/53, of five francs from Asani on 22/2/53, and of five francs by post on 4/3/53 from Mayaribu, another friend who was living in Elizabethville at the time. Equally, friends of this kind would

normally invite each other to mourning and end-of-mourning ceremonies for their kinsmen, and they would on these occasions pay much
personal attention to each other. (See, for example, the account in
Lusaka's diary of the *pili* he and Loboneka attended for the *tante* of a
mutual friend from work. Appendix G, 4/10/52.)

Through ordinary home visits as well as through attendances at
family ceremonies in response to formal invitations, Lusaka had over
time come to know a number of the friends of at least some of his own
personal friends, and *vice versa*. To some extent these friendships formed
part of a network of social relations among a number of working men
who were equals in occupational status and in degree of 'civilization'.
Being principally based on relations established at work, this network
tended to be separated from others invoking kinsmen and fellow-
tribesmen or 'family friends' and neighbourhood personalities. It was
also different to his neighbourhood and kinship networks in that it consisted almost entirely of men whom he had met in adult life. While
well-established as compared to the friendship networks of most other
men in the avenue, it was none the less relatively fluid and open to new
recruits.

Lusaka's personal friendships had important implications for his
other visitors, casual callers, and neighbours. The physical and social
situation in the avenue was such that visits from personal friends could
seldom be maintained as wholly private social encounters. Other
persons inevitably observed the visitors, came to identify them, and
not uncommonly had *some* direct contact with them when they came
to visit Lusaka. Thus news and views from the wider community were
to an appreciable extent handed down from personal friends to members of the neighbourhood who in turn passed them on to their own
associates. Conversely, too, some items of avenue gossip were constantly
fed back into discussions between members of Lusaka's friendship network. His personal friendships contributed to enhancing and confirming
his status as a 'civilized', knowledgeable, and reliable man. At the same
time, his key position as a member of both local and non-local networks
afforded him considerable influence over the semi-public discussions
that took place on his compound. He was almost invariably the participant with the greatest sum of factual knowledge about the people
gathered there, and he thus naturally 'presided' over the discussions,
providing explanatory comments and trying to reconcile the conflicting
views and values of persons with different social affiliations or different
cultural norms. In playing this role he was greatly aided by the diversity
of his own cultural background and the width of his urban experiences.

THE CASE OF PATRICE

Patrice was born in 1930 in a tribal village located in the (former)
Kivu Province and situated some 500 kilometres to the south-east of
Stanleyville. His father, Lupanzula, was a Murega tribesman who had
lived the greater part of his life as a cultivator in his tribal area. It was

not till 1944, when Patrice was 14 years of age and had already left home to go to school, that Lupanzula, who was then about 45 years old, first entered wage-earning employment. At this time he went to work for a few months as a labourer on a pontoon at a river crossing 25 kilometres from his home village. Between 1944 and 1952 he had undertaken several such trips, all of them to places close to his village and within his tribal area. Apart from these wage-earning trips undertaken comparatively late in life, Lupanzula had never 'entered *Kizungu*'. He was a polygynist, having married three wives of whom two were still alive. He had fathered eleven daughters and eight sons. Patrice was the fifth of nine children born to Lupanzula's second wife. Of the 19 children born to the three wives, four had died in infancy or childhood and four were children under 15 years of age; of the eleven surviving adult children, five were still living in tribal villages, four in small labour centres within the tribal area of the Warega, and only two were further afield. These last two were in Stanleyville. They were Patrice himself and one of his younger brothers, Sangumasi, who was 16 years old.

In addition to his siblings, Patrice had numerous classificatory brothers and sisters and other 'real' kinsmen. These were also well dispersed between their tribal villages and various labour centres, and he had at least three classificatory brothers in Stanleyville.

From the age of four or five Patrice had for a few years been reared by some of Lupanzula's kinsmen living in a village close to his own. During this period he lost an eye in an accident. Lupanzula had at the time received compensation from the kinsmen of one goat and three *vyuma* (ceremonial knives). Further compensation of ten *vyuma*, six cloths, and 20 francs, was paid when Patrice eventually returned to his father's home two years after the accident.

At the age of ten Patrice was circumcised according to traditional Warega custom. He then began to 'learn man's work' which consisted of cutting trees, clearing the forest for cultivation, and hunting. In 1942, at the age of 12 years, he left his village to attend school at a Protestant mission near Shabunda, an administrative centre within his tribal area. On the way to Shabunda he spent several weeks in the village of a *muyomba* (mother's brother), and from there he was sent to the home of one of the African teachers of the school near Shabunda. He stayed with this teacher for about a month before building his own hut and beginning to fare for himself. Two months later he was joined by Luzoka, a classificatory brother of about the same age as himself. For the next few years he and Luzoka attended school together and ran their own household, sometimes with other kinsmen who were either attending school or working locally. Among those who joined them were Patrice's brother, Sangumasi, and a classificatory brother, Pascal, who was two years younger than Patrice and Luzoka. In running their household, they depended partly on assistance from their families and partly on their own efforts in finding work at the mission station or the nearby administrative centre. Their school holidays were sometimes spent visiting their home villages and sometimes working in the immediate environs. Patrice attended school till 1949. Luzoka stayed at school five years, and Pascal and Sangumasi three years each. While at school Patrice had learnt to read and write Swahili, but he knew no French other than a few words picked up outside school. The religious influences to which he and his companions were exposed while at school seem to have made little impact on them. None of them kept in touch with the mission after their departure.

In 1948 Lupanzula arranged Patrice's marriage to Mangaza, a young Murega girl. Mangaza was a virgin, and Lupanzula paid a relatively high bridewealth of 80 *vyuma*, 3,000 francs and seven goats. Patrice had never seen the girl before the payment and, indeed, did not know of the marriage until he returned home on a school holiday in 1948 to find her already staying in his father's house. She continued to stay with his father until his final return from Shabunda in April 1949 when he began to live with her.

In August 1949 he again left his village, this time to follow Luzoka who was now working as a domestic servant in Kasese, another small labour centre in the same region. He found work there, settled with Luzoka, and sent for Mangaza. She arrived in Kasese in November 1949. But she was already pregnant on arrival and she soon returned to Lupanzula's village to give birth in April 1950 to her first child, a son named Kalanga. Some months after Kalanga's birth, she once again rejoined her husband in Kasese and stayed there with him until October 1951. Then, pregnant for the second time, she returned once more to Lupanzula's house where she gave birth in April 1952 to a daughter, Marguerite.

When Mangaza left Kasese the second time, Patrice had been there for about two years. In Kasese he had first lived with Luzoka and his wife whose household accommodated several young kinsmen and fellow-villagers. Later, Patrice had himself run a similar household to which more recent immigrants from his own village had come for accommodation. Among these newer arrivals whom he had welcomed were Sangumasi and Pascal, both of whom had been with him in Shabunda. Sangumasi had worked in Shabunda for about a year before coming to Kasese, and Pascal had ventured as far as Bukavu for about eighteen months.

When Mangaza returned to Lupanzula's village in October 1951 Patrice decided to leave Kasese and in November he set out with Sangumasi, Pascal, and two other Warega companions to walk to Stanleyville via Ponthierville. Their route to Ponthierville, about 250 kilometres from Kasese, took them through areas inhabited by Balengola and Bakumu. The journey, and the unfriendliness and hostility they encountered at the hands of the Bakumu in particular, made a deep impression on them. They were unable to buy food or to find lodgings at night and they were reduced to sleeping in the open and to living mainly off raw cassava. Considerably discouraged by these experiences, they decided to break their journey near Ponthierville where they were soon employed as labourers on a European plantation. They had no 'real' kinsmen there but they encountered several fellow-Warega with whom they lived and worked for nearly six months. At the end of this period Patrice, Sangumasi, and Pascal parted from their two other companions and paid lorry fares to Stanleyville which they finally reached in April 1952.

On arrival in Stanleyville, they found their way to the house of Edouard, a fellow-Murega who had lived in the town several years and whom they had first encountered in Ponthierville when he was there for a few weeks en route for Stanleyville after a visit to his home village. Edouard offered them temporary accommodation and they stayed with him for two days. During this period they were able to locate Prosper, a classificatory brother. Prosper had himself been in Stanleyville for only two months and his wife, Aluwa, for only two weeks; they were living as tenants in one room and could not offer any accommodation. But they knew of vacant rooms in the neighbourhood and directed Patrice and Sangumasi to Christine's compound in Avenue 21, and Pascal to another compound nearby. Patrice and Sangumasi rented a room from Christine for 100 francs a month and set about finding work.

I encountered Patrice when he came to Christine's compound and was able to follow the development of his life in town step by step. Before tracing the way in which he enlarged his social connexions in town, I refer briefly to two vivid impressions which Patrice made on me as I attempted to explore his social life during this early period. The first was of a man completely over-awed by the strange situation in which he found himself, frightened by daily life in town, and often shocked, insulted, and aggrieved by various incidents he witnessed. This early impression was substantially confirmed by his reactions to a variety of incidents in the neighbourhood and at work over the following twelve months, and is amply illustrated in the daily diary which he kept for me from mid-September 1952 to the end of January 1953. (An abridged and edited version of this diary is given in Appendix I.) There are in the diary numerous accounts of fights (see, e.g., 30/10/52, 6/11/52, 20/12/53, 7/1/53), accidents (see, e.g., 16/10/52, 28/10/52, 23/12/52, 29/1/53), thefts and burglaries (see, e.g., 19/12/52, 24/12/52, 30/1/53), arrests (see, e.g., 3/11/52, 7/11/52), insults and disputes (see, e.g., 24/10/52, 12/12/52), difficulties with European employers (see, e.g., 4/11/52, 8/12/52), spells of poverty and hunger (see, e.g., 15/9/52, 8/1/53 to 10/1/53) and of a variety of other difficulties, frustrations, and disappointments (see, e.g., 11/12/52, 27/12/52, 5/1/53, 7/1/53). Patrices's recording of these incidents often reflects astonishment and surprise of a kind which led more 'civilized' men like Lusaka and Limela to be tolerantly amused at his naive and innocent approach to town life. At the same time, his seeming fecklessness in the face of many simple demands made on him by urban life, such as the requirement of getting to work on time, often brought him face to face with intolerant abuse from people like his landlady, Christine, who on one occasion upbraided him as 'a *musendji* who had just come out of the forest, who did not know the ways of Kisangani, and who could not tell the difference between the beginning and the end of anything'. (Appendix I, 7/10/52.)

My second early impression of Patrice was of a man living from hand to mouth and often acting with unrealistic expectations and in a seemingly haphazard way. For example, at one time when working as a labourer at the saw mill he suddenly took a day off work and went to the town centre to apply for employment as a bank clerk. He took many impulsive decisions, and his attitude towards day-to-day matters often veered between the extremes of enthusiasm and determination and of despair and not caring. Some months after his arrival in Stanleyville, he began—against the advice of his kinsmen and fellow-tribesmen—to build his own house on Christine's compound where he was a tenant. As recorded in his diary over the period 15/9/52 to 21/9/52, he worked hard on his house for a short spell, but then abruptly abandoned the work when he discovered for himself how unreliable and offensive Christine could be. At this point he lost interest in house-building for some time only to start all over again on the compound of a 'fictitious' brother, Moke, a month or two later.

Within three days of arrival in Stanleyville, Patrice and Sangumasi had begun their search for work. Following the advice of Prosper, they simply walked from one firm to another. (A similar search for employment during a short period of unemployment some months later is described in Patrice's diary between 8/1/53 and 12/1/53. See Appendix I.) On the third day of their enquiries, Patrice found work as a low grade clerk (checker) in an Indian firm at a salary of 400 francs per month, and Sangumasi was later employed as a *boy-chauffeur* at 350 francs per month.

As Patrice settled down, he was rapidly integrated into a developing network of kinsmen and fellow-tribesmen. During their early weeks in town he, Sangumasi, and Pascal largely depended on Prosper and his wife, Aluwa. Up to the time of their first pay-day they visited Prosper almost daily to share with him food prepared by Aluwa. At the same time, they soon encountered several other Warega and, in particular, Kankamina and his wife Clementine. Kankamina was a close associate of Prosper, but also a maternal kinsman of Lwakama who was himself a classificatory brother of Patrice, and Patrice had in fact been told by Lwakama to try to contact Kankamina and Clementine on arrival in Stanleyville. (See letter No. 4, Appendix J.) Similarly, there were other Warega in the town whom Patrice had been told to contact. By following these contacts and either discovering or establishing other connexions, he was in the course of a few months to become an integral part of a network of Warega 'brothers' which had clearly existed before his arrival, and which continued to develop and to increase in membership throughout the period of my fieldwork. The members of the network with whom Patrice had regular contact from week to week numbered about 20. At least three-quarters were young men who, like Patrice, Sangumasi, and Pascal, had only recently arrived in town. (cf. Appendix B, Table 97.) Their mean age was 23 years; many of them were unmarried and were frequent visitors at the homes of the few who were married and who had their wives in town.

Just as Prosper had quickly found himself helping Patrice and his brothers, so Patrice was soon to find himself playing the role of host towards other yet more recent arrivals. To appreciate how he did this, we must first take note of the main developments in his employment and family situations during his early period in town. After receiving his first salary of 400 francs, he came to feel that he was, as he put it, being cheated by his Indian employer for whom he worked as a clerk for a wage lower than the average earned by labourers. This was also pointed out to him by several people and particularly by Limela, who was at that time living on the same compound and who was a labourer's foreman at the saw mill. Limela ridiculed Patrice's position as a 'so-called clerk earning 400 francs a month', and offered to find him employment as a labourer at the saw mill at a wage of 600 francs. Patrice thus abandoned his first employment after one month but continued to entertain quite unrealistic hopes of later finding work as a highly-paid white-collar worker. In the meanwhile, however, he became a labourer, and his joint income with Sangumasi, who handed him all his wages, now amounted to nearly 1,000 francs per month. This enabled him to begin reciprocating the hospitality of his kinsmen and fellow tribesmen.

A few months after his arrival, two rooms on Christine's compound fell vacant and were rented by Prosper and Aluwa. Their arrival on Christine's compound contributed to an important development in Patrice's situation. The compound began to be known as a meeting place for Warega and as clearing house for Warega news. When Prosper and Aluwa later left the compound, their rooms were immediately booked by Patrice for two new Warega immigrants. (Cf. Table 48.)

In addition, the arrival in Stanleyville of Mangaza and her children in September 1952 further contributed to the development of Patrice's network. With a wife to prepare food, he was in a better position to receive his 'brothers' who were already in town and to offer hospitality to newer immigrants. In addition, Mangaza's arrival increased the range of his social relations by bringing him into contact with some of her 'fictitious' kinsfolk and other Warega acquaintances.

To some extent Patrice's network comprised social relations developed *in town* in the course of a continuous process of mutual aid, shared activity, and sociable interactions. We have seen how new immigrants were readily given food and lodgings at the time of their first arrival in town. Recent and not so recent immigrants also constantly helped each other in a variety of ways, not least in the building of houses (cf. the references in Patrice's diary to help given and received in house building on, for example, 14/9/52 and 5/10/52, Appendix I). At some stages of building a house—for example when erecting the wooden frame and thatching the roof—help was given individually or in small groups, but the work of plastering the walls with mud was normally done in one day by a large working party consisting of both men and women. Working parties were particularly important for they led persons who were only distantly linked through the network to share an activity and in so doing to develop more intimate relations with each other. Despite such internal developments, however, Patrice's network was to a marked degree an extension from the tribal area and from smaller labour centres of numerous interlocking relationships. This is well illustrated by Patrice's letters given in Appendix J. A central topic in the letters is the movement of people to and from Stanleyville and other labour centres. In letter No. 1, for example, Luzoka, who had spent several years with Patrice in Shabunda and Kasese, gives news of current journeys of two of Patrice's brothers and suggests that he himself is thinking of leaving his employment in Kasese to follow Patrice; in letter No. 8, the same man enquires about pay and working conditions in Stanleyville, and he gives news of the departure from Kasese for Stanleyville of a classificatory brother and former associate of Patrice; in letter No. 4, Lwakama, a classificatory brother, tells of one of his own journeys and gives Patrice the address of a kinsman in Stanleyville; in letter No. 7, Joseph, another classificatory brother, recounts how he set out from Kasese for Stanleyville but was stranded in Yumbi where the driver of the lorry in which he was travelling was arrested and sent to gaol; and so on. If we further consider that letters were constantly supplemented by the verbal reports of new immigrants and of urban residents returning from visits to their home villages, it is easy to appreciate that members of this extensive rural-urban network were on the whole very well informed of each others' movements. At times there were lost letters and long delays in the course of journeys, but the multiple channels of communication between any two points in the network would seem to have very effectively ensured that news always came through in one way or another. (In this connexion it is interesting to note that the same particular items of news commonly appeared in more than one letter.)

In addition to information on movements from one place to another, the letters contained much family news especially on births, deaths and illnesses, and on marital and financial difficulties. One of the most interesting examples of a 'family letter' is No. 12, written to Patrice by Lupanzula, who clearly considered that his son continued to be partly responsible for members of his family in the village. Thus he gives an account of the family problems of the moment and asks for help. At the same time, he reports on the conduct of Patrice's wife who was still in the village, discusses the question of a wife for Sangumasi who was in Stanleyville, warns Patrice against enticing other 'children' from the village to follow him, and gives him advice and instructions on how to conduct himself in town. When the series of letters is read in its entirety, it is evident that Patrice was in touch with family news not only from his father's home and from his own village, but also from the homes of numerous kinsmen in nearby villages and in several small labour centres lying between his village and Stanleyville.

Patrice's widespread rural-urban network had a far-reaching influence on his behaviour in town. He was constantly aware that his actions were liable to be reported back to his kinsfolk at home. (Cf. Letter No. 10.) The wide rural-urban network of Warega also had important implications for social relations in another and more positive way. The constant flow of news from country to town commonly caused small groups of kinsmen and fellow-Warega to assemble either to celebrate and rejoice over good tidings or to mourn over sad news, and in these, as in all gatherings, inter-relations between members of the network were further developed and elaborated.

Patrice's kinsmen and fellow-tribesmen constituted the single most important source of succour available to him. There were, however, limits to the help which he could expect from this source, and these limits had clearly been reached between 5/1/53 and 12/1/53 after he had ill-advisedly resigned his job at the sawmill. During this period he pointedly refrained from asking his 'brothers' for help and, indeed, by the end of the week he was keeping away from them and visiting his 'urban' friends instead. (See Appendix I.)

Patrice's 'urban' friends were, however, few in number. At his first place of work he had met a young Mukumu, Ramazani, who had befriended him and with whom he sometimes exchanged visits (see, for example, his diary entries for 16/9/52 and 14/10/52). It was with Ramazani, too, that he occasionally went in search of women which he would not have dared to do with his 'brothers'. And he had similar, though not so close, relationships with Henri, a Mukongo, whom he had first met in Kasese, and with Fundi and Jerome, both Bakumu fellow-workers from the sawmill. From time to time he visited one or other of these friends, or went drinking with them, or simply hung about Christine's 'parlour' with them. But he could not expect much assistance from them. Nor did he have an *ikilemba* partner. Like Sangumasi and Pascal, he said he did not trust *ikilemba* arrangements which, he claimed, 'always led to trouble'.

In Avenue 21 he came over time to know a number of people by sight but there were few whom he knew really well enough to address by name. He had met Limela and a few others as co-residents on Christine's compound, and he had inevitably rubbed shoulders with his more immediate neighbours. He had also come to know one or two of the leading personalities in the avenue such as Lusaka. But there were none that he would have claimed as a friend or with whom he had anything approaching a self-sustaining relationship. For the rest, the inhabitants of the avenue remained strangers to him despite his nodding acquaintances with a substantial number. In February 1953, Patrice and his family finally left Avenue 21 to live in New Brussels. I continued to keep in touch with him, but I never again saw him in the avenue or its immediate environs.

THE CASE OF LIMELA

Limela was a Mongandu born in 1918 in a village some 300 kilo-metres west of Stanleyville. His father was a soldier who spent the greater part of his life in the *Force Publique*. For the first ten or more years of his life, Limela seldom saw his father and was almost entirely reared in a traditional village environment by his mother and several of his father's kinsmen. His mother died in 1928. At about this time he began to attend a Protestant missionary school and was baptized as a Protestant. He continued to attend classes here for three years, but he later claimed that he learnt virtually nothing at this school where such teaching as he received was in the vernacular. In 1931, when Limela was nearly 14 years of age, his father was stationed for a few months within the Mongandu tribal area. His father then sent for him, and from 1931 to 1935 he lived in military camps. Towards the end of 1931, however, his father was transferred from the Mongandu tribal area to a camp on the outskirts of Stanleyville. From here Limela attended a Roman Catholic school in the town until 1935 when he moved, again with his father, to Bafwasende, an administrative centre in Babali territory. The four years spent in Stanleyville made a deep impression on Limela. He had come there as a boy of fourteen with very little experience of *Kizungu*; by the time he left again at the age of 18 he had learnt to read and write Swahili, he had been re-baptized as a Roman Catholic, and he had become deeply involved in the life of his mission school where he was appreciably older than the average boy and was often used by the teachers as a messenger-boy and servant. During this period of his life he had acquired a smattering of French and become familiar with the town environment. He claimed that he had 'become a man' and had 'learnt about women'. As a pupil, however, he had not progressed beyond the level of the fifth or sixth year of primary education.

When his father left Stanleyville in 1935 Limela was referred by his teachers to the Roman Catholic mission in Bafwasende where he was employed as a *moniteur* in the local primary school. He was expected to supervise the children's physical exercises and to perform various practical tasks on the school premises. At this stage he left his father's military camp and lived on the mission station. In 1936 he left the mission station to look for other work, and during the following two years was employed as a *capita vendeur* by a series of Greek and Indian traders in the area. It was during this period that he married his first wife, Rosina, whom he had met when she was still a school girl at the mission.

Rosina was a Mangbetu, but she was born and brought up in Bafwasende where her father was a catechist at the mission. She had attended school for four years between the ages of 11 and 15. She had never lived in her tribal area, nor even visited it. Rosina and Limela were married in 1938 when she was a virgin of 16 and he an 'experienced man' of 21. The marriage was first arranged in a quasi-traditional way. Limela said that when he intimated to Rosina that he wanted to marry her she had told him to address himself to her father, Arumbengwe, and to her elder brother, Henri. Henri was a teacher at the mission school. Limela claimed that Henri had 'welcomed him as a husband for Rosina' and had said that Limela and his father should themselves decide what bridewealth to pay. Limela claimed that Henri had insisted that there should be no 'bargaining' over bridewealth, and he repeatedly quoted the following words attributed to Henri: "One can give presents to the family of one's wife, but one must marry through the love of God and one must never buy a wife". Living under missionary influence, Limela and Rosina were encouraged to celebrate their marriage in church. They both received preparatory instruction and attended mass and confession regularly. The church marriage ceremony was an important event on the mission station. It was attended by the whole school which was given a holiday, and the wedding was celebrated in European style.

Limela and Rosina lived together for about a year. Rosina soon became pregnant, but miscarried. In 1939 the marriage relationship was abruptly interrupted when Limela was sentenced to two years' imprisonment on charges of embezzlement. Rosina returned to her father's household and Limela was sent to serve his sentence in Stanleyville. On coming out of gaol in 1941, he found intermittent work in Stanleyville and lived there for nearly a year. Rosina joined him in Stanleyville for a few months before returning home on what was supposedly a short visit. In the event, however, Limela and Rosina did not see each other again till 1951.

After Rosina's departure, Limela was unemployed for a while and he left Stanleyville to look for work at railway camps along the line to Ponthierville. During the following eight or nine years he moved frequently from one place to another, most of his time being spent in railway and labour camps within a radius of 50 to 100 kilometres of Stanleyville which he occasionally visited. He held a series of different jobs, most of them as a labourer, until he was promoted to the post of labourer's foreman. In this capacity he was in 1949 sent back to Stanleyville by a firm which had first employed him in a smaller centre.

Limela claimed that between 1941 and 1945 he had on several occasions written to Arumbengwe and Henri asking for Rosina to join him. Henri had answered on at least one occasion, but only to say that Rosina was living with another man, Plangi, that he (Henri) disapproved of this, and that he would tell her to return to Limela. But she never arrived. In the years before he was to see her again he lived for varying periods with three women. The first was Marianna, a Mukumu, whom he met casually in 1942 at a small labour centre when visiting one of his classificatory brothers, Simon. Marianna accepted Limela as a lover when she was still married to another man, but she subsequently left her husband to live with Limela at the labour centre where he was then working. She stayed with him for six months only, but the relationship had a lasting effect on him. In talking to me about Marianna he consistently maintained that she was a good and competent woman who had helped him in many ways. It was she, he said, who first 'taught' him to build a house, to keep a garden, and to be a 'good husband'. At times he expressed regret that he had not stayed with her, but on other occasions he explained that this would have been impossible. First, he maintained that the Bakumu are very difficult people. 'The Bakumu never speak the truth; a Mukumu will often tell you that a woman is his sister when in fact she is his mistress; Bakumu women are always wanting to go back to their villages, and they think nothing of staying away from their husbands without permission'. Secondly, and specifically to Marianna, she and the family of his brother, Simon, had quarelled. No bridewealth had ever been paid though Simon had given Marianna and her family 'presents' totalling 500 francs, and he and Limela had treated Marianna's kinsmen as their *shemeki*. Marianna's kinsmen had, however, continued to make further demands on Simon until he and his wife put strong pressure on Limela to send her away. Limela eventually complied, but in retrospect he often regretted having done so. 'I still had the ways of a child', he said in explanation.

In 1943, a few months after Marianna's departure, Limela had, to use his own term, 'engaged' another Mukumu woman, Salima. She was an elder kinswoman of Marianna. According to custom Limela and Salima were thus *shemeki* or ex-*shemeki* and Salima should have treated Limela as her superior and to have addressed him as 'father'. Salima and Limela had known of each other at the time that Marianna was living with Limela, but they had never met. Their first encounter took place when, in the course of a journey from Stanleyville to her village, she spent a few days at a small labour centre where she knew Limela to be and enquired after him. Though Marianna had already left Limela, he had, he said, initially welcomed Salima as a *shemeki*. Later, however, he made sexual advances to her and they became lovers. Over the course of the next few months Salima came to live with him. The union lasted about eighteen months. He gave Salima presents totalling 600 francs, but said that these were never regarded as bridewealth. Nor did either he or Salima make any attempt to establish relations as *shemeki* with each other's kinsfolk. According to his account, he and Salima had a harmonious relationship for about a year. Then he began to quarrel with her and she became dissatisfied with him, especially after he had begun an association with another woman, named Nafisa. Salima finally left him in 1945.

Nafisa was a Mongandu and a kinswoman of Limela, being the daughter of a man who was a kinsman of Limela's father's mother.

Limela did not know the precise genealogical connexion between them, and further claimed that this was not known even by elderly people in their tribal area. Limela and Nafisa had known each other as children but their first encounter as adults took place in 1944 when he was visiting Simon in a nearby labour centre. Sometime after this encounter Limela asked Simon's wife to tell Nafisa that 'he wanted her'. Simon's wife protested at his incestuous intent and refused to act as a go-between, but he later approached Nafisa himself and they became lovers. The outcome over several months was that Nafisa left her husband to live with Limela. The bridewealth originally paid by Nafisa's husband was later repaid partly by Limela, and partly by Simon who found himself held responsible in the absence of other kinsmen. Limela also began to pay bridewealth for Nafisa to her rural kinsmen. Their kinship had been discussed at great length by both families before bridewealth was paid. There would seem to have been no clear decision to allow the union, but it was eventually accepted as a *fait accompli*. Eighteen months later the couple visited their tribal area and underwent a series of traditional purification ceremonies. In 1948 they settled in a small labour centre near Stanleyville, and in 1949 they moved to Stanleyville itself when Limela was transferred there by his employers. They then registered their marriage in the C.E.C. By this time Nafisa had been pregnant twice, but had miscarried on each occasion. Limela explained that 'by his Christian beliefs' he did not think these miscarriages were related to his kinship with Nafisa, but that, 'by his native beliefs' he thought they were due to 'the wrath of his father' who was not present when the purification ceremonies were performed.

In 1950, when living in Stanleyville, Limela and Nafisa had a series of arguments. He claimed that Nafisa had begun to deceive him in money matters and that she was committing adultery with several men. Equally, she began to accuse him of wasting his money on other women. They parted, and Limela came to live on the compound of Christine. Later still (in 1951) they were divorced in the urban courts,[12] and Nafisa returned to her tribal area.

In the meanwhile Limela had again begun to write to Arumbengwe and Henri and, at Nafisa's suggestion, had asked them to send Rosina back 'to look after him'. He had also written to the priest in charge of the Bafwasende mission station saying that he wished to be re-united with his 'religious wife'. Rosina was at this time still living with Plangi whom she had joined shortly after Limela's release from gaol in 1941. She had borne Plangi two children, Pauline in 1942 and Etienne in 1949. Her father was very much against her returning to Limela, but pressure was put on him by Henri and by the priests at the mission station on the grounds, quoted by Limela, 'that a religious marriage is the only real marriage a man and woman can make'. Limela claimed that the priests threatened to dismiss Arumbengwe from the mission station if he did not comply with their advice, and that the local administrator also put pressure on Rosina and her father. The final outcome was that Rosina rejoined Limela in Stanleyville in June 1951, bringing her two children with her. Bridewealth had never been paid by Plangi and the children thus came into Limela's custody.

Rosina stayed with Limela from June to October 1951 when she returned to her family in Bafwasende on the occasion of the death of one of her kinsmen. Limela had, he said, given her permission to stay away 45 days, but on arrival in Bafwasende she wrote to say that she was pregnant. She prolonged her stay at home, and in April 1952 gave birth in Bafwasende to her first child by Limela, a son named Cornet. She then again returned to Stanleyville in June 1952. It was about this time that I first encountered Limela, and I was soon to meet Rosina as well. I shall return to an account of their relationship at this stage, but first describe another development in Limela's life. Two or three months after Rosina's departure for Bafwasende, he had taken up with a Mubali woman, Maria, who was the wife of Bunduki, a Mubali who was a near-neighbour of Limela in Avenue 21. Maria and Bunduki came from neighbouring villages in their tribal area. They had married according to traditional custom before coming to Stanleyville. Their first child was born in their tribal area in 1947, but died in infancy. The couple had then migrated to town in 1948. Early in 1950 Maria had given birth in town to a second child who had also died under the age of one. Bunduki claimed that the death of the second child was due to Maria's bad conduct. He said that since coming to town she had begun to associate with other men and, in particular, that she had been having sexual relations before the child was weaned. In December 1951 Bunduki had sent Maria away from his home and in January 1952 she had taken him to court asking the judges to order him to pay her return fare to her home village. Bunduki had maintained that Maria was responsible for the breakdown of the marriage and had refused to pay whereupon the court had ruled that, since the marriage had been arranged in the couple's tribal area, they were to await an opportunity to return together to have the matter discussed by their families in their chief's court.[13]

It was against the background of these events that Maria first encountered Limela. Bunduki's assertion that Maria was living promiscuously at this period was accepted as true in Avenue 21, and Limela's account of his first sexual encounter with her is in keeping with this view; he had seen her passing down the street and had asked Christine to call her to his room. Subsequently, she became his regular mistress and began to look after him; she prepared his food which she brought to his house, and she looked after his clothes, and attended to him affectionately. Soon she became pregnant, and she gave birth to Limela's child in November 1952. Though she had been separated from Bunduki for about a year, she was not registered as a *femme libre*, and her child's name was therefore registered in Bunduki's book giving him the custody. Throughout 1952 Maria was living with 'fictitious' kinsmen who received Limela as her regular lover and treated him as their *shemeki*. Maria continued to attend devotedly to Limela, and during the period that his wife was in Bafwasende she came to his house daily to bring him food and to collect his washing.

When Rosina returned from Bafwasende in June 1952 she and Limela attempted to resume their domestic relationship, but the difficulties already inherent in it were much aggravated by constant quarrelling between Rosina and Christine. These quarrels occasionally attracted much attention up and down the avenue. Consensus of opinion gradually developed that Christine was so provocative that it was impossible for Rosina to continue living on the compound. Yet she had nowhere to go, neither she nor Limela having any 'real' kinsmen in the town. Limela discussed the problem with Lusaka who advised him to leave Christine's compound which he later did (in November). The immediate problem was temporarily solved when Laini—Christine's next-door neighbour and one of the old-established residents who was at about the same time helping Lusaka with his marital problems— offered to accommodate Rosina and her children. Rosina moved to Laini's compound in September 1952 and some weeks later went to *humwali* for a few days on Laini's advice.[14] In the meanwhile Limela and Rosina had both written to Rosina's brother, Henri, who was by this time living in Kindu, explaining their respective points of view about their marriage. The answers they received, and additional letters bearing on their marital problem at this particular stage, are given in Appendix K. The letters reveal that Limela was attempting to re-establish cordial relations with Rosina's family. Henri, was adopting a conciliatory attitude but Arumbengwe was still openly antagonistic to Limela.

In November 1952 Rosina once again returned to Bafwasende, this time to end the period of mourning she had begun to observe at the time of her last visit. As can be seen in letter No. 3, Limela gave Rosina "permission to stay away two months and not one week more", but by the time I left Stanleyville in April 1953 she still had not returned.

During Rosina's stay in Stanleyville between June and November 1952, Limela had continued to see Maria though she had ceased to call at his house. Her baby was born about the same time as Rosina returned to Bafwasende and as Limela left Christine's compound to live as a tenant in a nearby avenue. Maria now again began to call at Limela's house daily to bring him food and to show him the baby. His relationship with her was at this time of considerable importance in his day-to-day life. To appreciate this, we have to examine his overall social connexions in the town.

We have seen that Limela was a good friend of Lusaka, that he was a 'fictitious' kinsman of Christine, and a one-time co-resident of Patrice whom he tended at times to tease and at other times to cajole into keeping him company and performing minor tasks for him. His relationship with Lusaka and Christine were both of considerable value to him in the relative absence of other enduring relationships. He had no 'real' kinsmen in town, and he knew only four persons in Stanleyville whose own kinship connexions were in the same home village as his. He spoke of these four as his only 'family members' in town; they 'would bury him when he died' and they would tell his kinsfolk at home about 'his hardships and sufferings'. Apart from Christine herself, however, none of these 'fictitious' kinsmen played any significant part in his day-to-day life. And even his relationship with Christine had severe limitations. He kept in touch with her, but he was well aware that he could not rely on her. As can be seen in letter No. 7, Appendix K, he was on one occasion to write about her as "a truly strange person—[someone who] is like a cursed animal". Lusaka was his only trusted friend and mentor. Unlike other men in the avenue, he maintained two *ikilemba* arrangements independently of each other. Characteristically, however, neither of his *ikilemba* partners were special friends to him out of working hours. Most of his social connexions tended to be relatively dispersed and loosely-knit. To illustrate this I give the following detailed account of the way in which he celebrated the New Year of 1952–53.

After being paid at noon on New Year's Eve, he went to see the manager of the sawmill to ask for a New Year's present. He was given credit for a pair of new shoes. He also asked for beer but this was refused. He then returned to his house to find Maria waiting for him. She had come to invite him to spend New Year's Eve at the house of her 'brothers'. While Maria was still there Albert and Litua called to see him. Both were men with whom he had worked in the past, though he had not seen either of them over recent weeks and had not expected to see them over the New Year. He addressed both as 'brothers' because, he explained to me, 'one was a Topoke and the other a Mumbole and the Topoke and Bambole are brothers with the Mongandu in town'. Maria had never met either Albert or Litua, but she asked him to invite them to the house of her 'brothers'. They accepted, and at 2 o'clock the three men left with Maria. On arrival at Maria's, they found a gathering of about a dozen people. Mafuta, who was the owner of the house and whom Limela vaguely knew as Maria's 'brother', came forward to greet them and led them into a front room. Mitimiti, one of Mafuta's brothers, brought them a gramophone and sixteen bottles of beer. Greeting Limela, Mitimiti said that he was pleased to welcome him on New Year's Eve. He was also pleased that Limela 'had brought two of his brothers with him; even had he brought ten, they would have been welcome'. He then said that Maria's 'family' particularly wished Limela to spend New Year with them 'because your "wife" (i.e. Maria) has told us that it is not your *ikilemba* this month'. Mitimiti then left the room but later returned with eight bottles of wine. During the course of the evening other visitors to the house came to greet Limela. Most of them had not met Limela before, and Mitimiti, who kept coming in and out of the room, explained to each in turn who Limela was, saying that 'if Maria is well dressed it is due to him'. The gramophone was played continuously and two of Maria's 'sisters', Anna and Coletta, spent part of the night dancing with Limela, Litua and Albert. The celebrations continued into the small hours of the morning when Limela and his 'brothers' fell asleep on the floor.

Next morning Limela left the house saying that he had to return 'to see his brothers who would be coming to see him on this New Year's day'. Mitimiti invited him to return later as 'they had not yet finished welcoming him to their house'. Litua, Albert, Limela, and Coletta then left for Limela's house. On their way, they met a few Mongandu from the area and Limela invited them to his house. They settled down in front of the house to a session of drinking and singing. Limela explained to his fellow-tribesmen that Coletta was his *shemeki*. Litua served the drinks. As he did so, he passed comments on Coletta, who was the only woman present, as if he had known her a long time; he said she was a good woman and that they should all respect her. The celebration lasted several hours. When the group finally dispersed, Limela set out for Maria's house, still accompanied by Litua, Albert and Coletta. But he then decided to call at Christine's compound first. Here he was offered two bottles of beer by Abeli, a Murega, who was one of Christine's tenants. He drank the beer with Abeli and his brothers while Litua, Albert and Coletta waited for him. On arrival at Maria's, Mitimiti gave Maria a large basin of rice and a chicken for Limela and his friends, and later brought them more beer and wine. At about five o'clock in the afternoon Limela, Litua and Albert returned to Christine's compound where they met Patrice who offered Limela beer. They then returned to Limela's house where they found Coletta who had come from Maria's house to ask Limela to return. At this stage Litua and Albert fell asleep in Limela's house. Limela left them there and returned to Maria's with Coletta. At about 8 o'clock in the evening he returned to his house and fell asleep.

As this account shows, Limela did not lack acquaintances but they were poorly integrated and there was a strongly haphazard element in his social life. Maria was quite central to his life at this stage. He depended on her as a relatively stable element in a day-to-day existence in which most of his social relations were of a tenuous character. But, of course, his relationship with Maria was also lacking in commitment and depth. He used to say that Maria's devoted attention 'calmed him', and he was quite ready 'to help her' and to provide for her in return for her assistance and support. At the same time, he thought of her as a woman of little basic worth, and he had no intention of maintaining a permanent relationship with her. He was well aware of, and frequently referred to, his insecure social position with no effective network of kinsmen or close friends. Yet he consistently claimed that he could never return to his village of origin. He sometimes said that he hoped one day to settle down in marriage with Rosina. This

was what Henri hoped he would do, and he clearly attached considerable value to Henri's opinions and goodwill. When I last knew him he
was building a house in New Brussels and he hoped that this would be
for 'his' children—the two fathered by Plangi as well as his own son,
Cornet. He was also eager to have the custody of the child born to
Maria, and he thought he would one day be able to negotiate this with
Maria's kinsmen. He commonly discussed these problems with Lusaka,
whose opinions he greatly valued.

Unlike Lusaka, however, he was largely indifferent to the opinions
and pressures of other people in Avenue 21. It had been his immediate
social environment for about two years, but he had so far in his life
failed to settle permanently anywhere. Most of his relationships in
Avenue 21 took familiar outward forms: he had acquaintances whom
he addressed as brothers, friends, and kinsmen; he referred to Maria
as his wife, and assumed attitudes of authority, affection, gratitude,
and intimacy in relation to her; and he treated her 'family' as his
shemeki. But there was little commitment or permanence in his social
relations.

THE SIGNIFICANCE OF THE CASES

The cases of Lusaka, Patrice, and Limela may be seen as examples of
three broad categories of men in Avenue 21. Lusaka is an example of
the well-established residents who had been largely or wholly brought
up in Stanleyville and whose social connexions were almost entirely
centred in the town. Out of 38 men interviewed in the avenue at
one point in time, eight fell into this category which thus accounted
for about one in five of the adult male population. Patrice represents
the category of immigrants who had recently left their tribal areas,
and who had only arrived in town during the period of the study or in
the few years immediately preceding it. For an exact account of the
number of men in this category we would need to define criteria of
inclusion more precisely; even without doing so, however, it is certain
that it was the largest of the three categories. There were 11 men who
clearly qualified for inclusion and several others whose histories of
migration were broadly similar. They thus accounted for at least one
in four of the population. About a half of these were men who, like
Patrice, had begun 'to follow *Kizungu*' in childhood. The other half
consisted of men who were entirely reared in *Kisendji* and who had left
their villages for the first time as adults. Limela is an example of men
who had considerable experience of *Kizungu* and had largely shed
their rural-tribal connexions, but who had spent little time in Stanleyville itself and were not well established there. There were only three
or four clear cases of this kind and they thus accounted for about one
in ten of the men interviewed.

These categories made up nearly two thirds of the population of
Avenue 21. The remainder were either marginal cases or members of
another relatively distinct category: those who had completed the

process of settling down in town but who yet maintained close connexions with their tribal areas and continued to play a significant part in the affairs of their kinsmen at home. Some discussed in Chapter VI are good examples: Amundala is one, François another. Though I give no detailed case study of a man in this position, I refer to such cases in the discussion that follows.

The most important features of Lusaka's social situation were closely related to his local urban upbringing and to his membership of a tribal group that was well-established in the town. The circumstances of his birth and upbringing in Stanleyville had led him to identify with his mother's 'civilized' urban kinsfolk while separating him from his father's *basendji* connexions which had become a negative reference group for him. He thought of himself as a townsman, and his immediate domestic and kinship connexions in town included persons of all ages and of three generations—his mother's, his own, and his daughter's. He had throughout his adult life negotiated his personal and domestic situations with two women who both had urban connexions and orientations similar to his own. Neither had ever lived in a tribal village, and both shared his view of Stanleyville as their home community. He had grown up in an area where he had many 'family friends', 'fictitious' kin, and fellow-tribesmen, and many of these were equally committed to town life. (In this connexion, it is important to recall that the Babali were an ethnic colony with a high degree of urban involvement.) His personal friends were mainly skilled and semi-skilled workers most of whom had also turned their backs on village life. Yet he lived in a neighbourhood where he was constantly in touch with persons who were often much less 'civilized' than himself. Here he commonly participated in a comparatively wide range of different 'small group' situations. He was well equipped with the norms and the personal contacts to allow him to choose and select his associates and his activities. Thus, for example, he had easy access to François' 'club', where he was the member with the highest status, and he had contacts in the networks of all the principal tribes in the immediate neighbourhood. Yet he could also, if he so chose, very easily participate in gatherings of 'uncivilized' men in small palm-wine bars (which he sometimes did) or join the festivities at an end-of-mourning ceremony with 'uncivilized' neighbours and fellow-tribesmen (which he did partly in response to his particular connexions with the family of the deceased, and partly according to his inclinations of the moment).

Lusaka thus had access to a wider range of 'small groups', than either Patrice or Limela. In this sense he can be said to have had more freedom of choice in daily life. But his welter of local connexions also placed more constraints on his personal conduct. He was often in positions in which he had to weigh up the consequences of his actions and moral stands not only in relation to one network of associates, but in relation to several at a time. His personal friends, his own 'real' and 'fictitious' kinsmen, the members of his *'fiancée's'* family, his neighbours and near-neighbours, his 'family friends', and his fellow-tribesmen *tended* to form separate networks of personal relations, yet there was sufficient communication between these networks for his actions in relation to a member of any one to be notified to members of the others. In this sense he was effectively a member of a neighbourhood or sub-community rather than a person simply participating in a series of discrete groups or an actor in a series of separate networks.

Once we see Lusaka's social situation in these terms it is easy to appreciate why he had such a keen interest and near-obsession in discussing and evaluating social norms considered appropriate in different 'small group' situations and in different cultural settings. The status positions he occupied in his several networks were liable to affect each other, yet the social norms governing personal behaviour in these networks frequently differed to a greater or lesser extent. In order to maintain his social relations he therefore had to be constantly exploring the consistencies and inconsistencies between several sets of views and norms. And any explanations and evaluations which he gave to members of one network had to be reconcilable with those given to members of any other network.

In the discussions on his compound Lusaka was often in effect simultaneously engaged in explaining his own views and attitudes and in exploring their implications in a set of several contexts. Indeed, these discussions were also part of a continuous process of explaining the relative nature of different cultural norms and customs. He frequently commented on, and compared, minor or major differences between tribes. He would point out to me, that 'we, the Babali' arrange mourning ceremonies differently to the Bakumu or Babua, that the Lokele watch over their girls more strictly than the Bakusu, and so on. Similarly, he was frequently inclined to explain to me, as to other visitors, that different peoples have different ways of conducting themselves and that one should always respect the ways of others. And he was often led to weigh up the practical advantages and disadvantages of different cultural practices and solutions. His discussions on circumcision and initiation are a good example of this. The extracts of his autobiography show that, on recalling his youth, he was immediately inclined to compare the traditional *mambela* of the Babali—which he described as 'very, very painful'—and circumcision according to *Arabisé* custom with the less painful European expedient of surgery under anaesthetic. (See Appendix D.) This comparative approach was also marked in his discussions on the problems of finding a wife in town, and on whether it was a good or bad thing to send girls to school.

Lusaka's ready tendency to compare and evaluate was a product of his upbringing in a mixed cultural setting and of his access to a variety of social relations in the avenue and beyond. He had learnt various codes of conduct and was well qualified to adjust to diverse social settings. Yet his evaluations contained ample evidence of his primary commitment to a code of 'civilized' urban norms, and it was largely on the basis of his adherence to this code that he was accorded high status in the avenue and its environs. This is germane to any understanding of his attitude to his marital and domestic affairs. In a social and physical setting in which there was little privacy, and virtually no possibility of concealing the nature of relations between husbands and wives and between parents and children, public assessments of moral worth and 'civilized' standing were directly linked to a man's conduct in relation to members of his immediate family. Thus it was that Lusaka's divorce from Antoinette, and the preparations for his marriage to Bernadette, inevitably became the concern of his neighbours and friends and that he was so anxious to act within correct and proper norms. In this connexion it is particularly significant that, even after he and Antoinette had come to the conclusion that they were going to part, he refrained from sending her away from his house as a less 'civilized' man of lower social standing might well have done. Instead, he discussed his position at length with kinsmen, friends and neighbours, and it was only after a final joint consultation with Antoine, a leading figure in the avenue, that he and his wife took the formal step of going to court.

The neighbourhood exerted no comparable influence on Patrice. He came to live there by chance and left as soon as he found free accommodation elsewhere. Not having learnt 'civilized' urban norms, and lacking the varied contacts of the kind Lusaka had, Patrice's social participation was largely confined to gatherings of kinsmen and fellow tribesmen and to the mixed and transient company of Christine's 'guests'. The main constraints on him derived from his network of 'real' and 'fictitious' kinsmen and of fellow-tribesmen. And this network of Warega contained many who, like himself, were young immigrants with a marked rural-tribal orientation and limited experience of *Kizungu*. Some of these immigrants had wives and young children in town but many had not; and virtually all were first-generation migrants without parents or other older kinsmen in the community.[15] The differences between Lusaka and Patrice were more than differences between two individuals in the avenue; they were part of a wider and more general contrast between representatives of two tribes with markedly different histories of urban incorporation and participation.

I have stressed the importance of Patrice's membership of an immigrant group, but it is also of interest to note the extent of his emancipation from it. In a few months he had begun to develop a small set of urban friends, and they were clearly providing him with an alternative source of companionship. His diary shows that his relationship with Ramazani in particular was acquiring an appreciable significance in his life. Moreover, there is ample evidence of the way in which he had begun to acquire a 'civilized' urban outlook. He came to Stanleyville as a rank *musendji* but he was soon evaluating others as ignorant *basendji* (see, for example, Appendix I, 3/11/52).

Limela's social position in the neighbourhood was in turn markedly different from that of either Lusaka or Patrice. He had no appreciable network of kinsmen and fellow-tribesmen like Patrice; nor did he have a 'home neighbourhood' or a set of integrated networks comparable to Lusaka's. He was accustomed to regular and frequent moves from one place to another and, on coming to Avenue 21 for two years, he had continued to live without any important commitment or involvement. Unlike Patrice, he was well equipped to participate in the more 'civilized' social circles of the neighbourhood, but he had few pre-existing relations there either with 'civilized' or 'uncivilized' inhabitants. His personal friendship with Lusaka was isolated and seemingly self-sustaining.

Between the two extremes of Lusaka's diverse social connexions and multiple networks, on the one hand, and Patrice's relatively uniform connexions largely centred in a single network of immigrants on the other, there was a wide range of intermediate cases. Amundala and François, whom we discussed in the previous chapter, were both immigrants of much longer standing than Patrice and were both men with significant networks of urban relations; yet both maintained close connexions with fellow-tribesmen in their villages as well as in town. Amundala, for example, was a prominent member of the 'club', and he had numerous non-tribal friends. But he continued to correspond regularly with his own and his wife's rural-tribal kinsmen and to visit them every year or two. Though he did not envisage ever returning permanently to his tribal area, he considered it his home and felt that he had a stake there.

Relating the above cases to the analysis given in Chapter VI, we see that the increasingly heterogeneous composition and the high turnover of the avenue's population were accompanied by a considerable variety of individual patterns of participation. Lusaka was a 'civilized' man but his social relationships were by no means confined to 'civilized' people; his local involvement was strong and his participation varied. Patrice was an 'uncivilized' tribal man who was rapidly learning to associate with people other than fellow-tribesmen and, also, to distinguish between 'civilized' and 'uncivilized' standards, but he was a transient with little or no local involvement. If we had systematic data allowing us to trace developments over time in the 'small group' structure of the avenue they would probably reveal increasingly complex sets of social relations linking people to each other. But it seems unlikely that they would reveal any marked trend either towards, or away from, differentiation on the basis of either 'tribalism' or 'class'. There is nothing in our observations to indicate that either 'tribalism' or 'class' was becoming markedly more or less important. The principal development was towards the diversification of group structures without any appreciable change in the bases of differentiation.

Finally, it is at this point pertinent to refer to the general contrast between the processes of differentiation in Avenue 21 and those described by Mayer among the Xhosa of East London. Mayer shows how the Red and the School Xhosa can be analysed as two 'types' of migrants with two distinctive syndromes.

The Red syndrome, which has been termed incapsulation, has as one feature a 'tribal' type of moral conformism, stressing the superiority of the original undiversified institutions; such institutions make for multiplex relations and the close-knit type of network; and this again makes for consistent moral pressure and conservatism. The processes are two-way or circular ones. It is by refusing to branch out into new habits that Red migrants retain a basis for close-knit networks; while it is by keeping the networks close-knit that they inhibit cultural branching-out.

In the other syndrome, more characteristic of School migrants, we find a culture which has been more tolerant in principle of the engagement in diversified institutions; accordingly, a tendency towards the single-strand type of relation and the loose-knit type of network. Again this produces two-way or circular effects. Cultural specialization makes for looser-knit networks, while the looseness of the network allows for cultural specialization. The School culture, with its institutional diversification, thus carries within itself its own dynamic of change in the migrant situation.[16]

At first sight Patrice's case study seems to exhibit many features of the syndrome of Red Xhosa, and it is clear that the network of Warega in which he was deeply involved tended, up to a point, to incapsulate him in the way described by Mayer. Conversely, Lusaka's involvements over the course of his life in a more diversified set of institutions and his *tendency* to participate in some single-stranded relations and in some networks that were *relatively* loosely knit, are clearly reminiscent of Mayer's 'School' syndrome. Yet there was in Avenue 21 no striking evidence of the population dividing itself up into two cultural grooves; Mayer's two syndromes appear in Avenue 21 to be at most two extreme poles of a continuum. However, as will be stressed in Chapters VIII and IX, there is no reason to believe that Avenue 21 and its environs were typical of Stanleyville. The broad contrast traced in Chapter IV between the social configuration of the Babua and the Topoke (to take the cases of two extreme tribal colonies) suggests that an analysis in terms of Mayer's conceptualization may be rewarding.

FOOTNOTES TO CHAPTER VI

[1] Lusaka earned 800 francs from his employment as against a mean wage in this area of 704 francs per month (Table 34), and he made a profit of about the same order as a private carpenter. (See Appendix H.) Very few men in the area had a second source of income comparable to this.

[2] Like many others, however, Lusaka was highly antagonistic to missionaries and especially to Roman Catholics. He often explained that missionaries were 'the whites who really keep Africans down'. He maintained that government officials were in favour of increasing educational opportunities for Africans but that the Roman Catholic authorities always advised the administration to slow down the pace of African *évolution*. Such views were widespread in the town.

[3] Cf. Chapter V: only 12·4 per cent of men aged 16 to 25 years were title-holders of compounds. Most of these had, like Lusaka, 'inherited' or taken over compounds from their fathers or from other kinsmen.

⁴ The statistical chances of two urban-born Bababli marrying would probably have been low were it not that relatively high proportions of them were concentrated in particular areas of the town. Cf. my comments in Chapter IV on the proportions of tribal and non-tribal marriages shown in Table 33.

⁵ Residents of the C.E.C. were officially expected and urged to register their marriages but there was no legal obligation for them to do so. In practice the majority of marriages were registered. Wives who were not residents of the C.E.C. in their own right had to be registered in their husbands' books in order to qualify for residence in the town. Men marrying in town were normally eager to register their wives' names in order to ensure that their bridewealth payments and their rights to any issue from a marriage should be automatically recognized by the urban courts. In many cases, however, registration took place many weeks or months after the marriage.

⁶ To appreciate the full significance of this, we must recall that the Babali had a very low rate of fertility. (See Chapter V.) A Mubali woman with three live births by the age of 22 years was most exceptional.

⁷ I was often told by men in this neighbourhood that a reasonable husband ought not to take action against a wife caught in adultery once or twice only; but that even a reasonable husband ought not to tolerate repeated adultery. Three infringements were commonly cited as evidence of habitual infidelity. The Lokele and some other tribes were, however, much less tolerant.

⁸ A transcription of the official record of the divorce case is given in Appendix E. The court record tends to attach less blame to Antoinette for the break-up of the marriage than the account I have given. This may be partly because my account is mainly based on Lusaka's version. However, there may also have been another factor. Antoinette and Lusaka had agreed to part before going to court, and it would seem that they made little attempt to give the court their true respective viewpoints.

⁹ Whereas Lokele women were expected to trade, this was not the case among either the Babua or the Babali. Lusaka thus had good grounds in assessing Bernadette's offer to trade as evidence of personal merit and goodwill.

¹⁰ The six men are those whom Lusaka spontaneously named when I asked him who his best friends were. The names are given in his order of preference. All but one are included in Table 59.

¹¹ *Ikilemba* arrangements were common in Stanleyville as they were in Leopoldville (Baeck 1961, pp. 168–169) and Brazzaville (Balandier 1955, p. 148). Ardener (1964, pp. 206–207) implies that *ikilemba* in the Congo is similar to 'a very simple institution known as *chilemba* . . . in Northern Rhodesia'. Balandier does not describe the nature of the *ikilemba* arrangements in Brazzaville, and Baeck simply refers to *ikilemba* in Leopoldville as 'a procedure by which one receives the salary of two or more partners in order to live for some time ostentatiously or to meet a sudden and great expense. . .'

All *ikilemba* arrangements that I encountered in Stanleyville were confined to pairs. I was told that the arrangements were sometimes extended to cover three or more persons but that this was unusual. Lusaka's agreement with Joseph is a good example of a standard *ikilemba*. In principle the agreement was for Lusaka to pay Joseph 500 francs (out of his total monthly wage of 800 francs) at the end of one month and for Joseph to repay this sum the following month. As illustrated in Lusaka's accounts, however, it sometimes happened that a part of the sum was only paid mid-monthly. (See Appendix H.) Moreover, the two men commonly turned to each other for loans required to meet any unexpected financial demand at times when regular payments were not due. *Ikilemba* arrangements were often but not always between close friends. Lusaka's and Joseph's interpretation of their agreement was emphatically that it covered more than money. They saw each other as sources of help in any contingency arising at work, and they also extended mutual assistance beyond the work situation to helping each other's families. Their agreement was undoubtedly an important source of social and economic security for both men.

In Avenue 21 *ikilemba* agreements were common amongst men who had been in town some time but unusual amongst recent immigrants. For example, Patrice and his brothers tended to distrust *ikilemba*. Patrice himself had never had such an agreement and said that he would never entertain one. Instead, he tended to rely on his 'real' or 'fictitious' brothers.

Limela is an interesting case of a man who had more than one *ikilemba* agreement. In French he referred to his two agreements as his *grand tour* and his *petit tour*. In Swahili he referred to his *petit tour* as *ikilemba ya pembeni* (*ikilemba* 'in the corner' or 'on the side'). His *grand tour* was an arrangement for 300 francs, and his *petit tour* for 160 francs. The month that he paid his *grand tour* he received his *petit tour* and was therefore only 140 francs down on balance; when he received his *grand tour* he paid his *petit tour*, and was therefore 140 francs up. Unlike Lusaka and Joseph, Limela was not an intimate friend of either of his two *ikilemba* partners. The two were no more than casual work-mates and he did not visit them at home or know their families. Like Lusaka and Joseph, however, Limela definitely regarded *ikilemba* as a source of security. As the regular payments he made and received tended to cancel each other out, his monthly budget was not greatly affected, but having two agreements meant that he could turn to either of his partners in an emergency.

[12] A transcription of the official record of the court case is given in Appendix E.

[13] A transcription of the official record of the court case is given in Appendix E.

[14] Clément (1956, p. 408) has described *humwali* as an institution preparing 'those who pass through it for sexual and domestic life, and . . . (teaching) them how to behave as married women'. The institution was widespread in the town. It was commonly associated with the *Arabisés* and most *Arabisés* women had been to *humwali*, but it had also been widely adopted by many other groups, both pagan and Christian. Between a third and a half of all adult women in Avenue 21 had been to *humwali* at one or other stage of their lives. The nature of the practice varied quite considerably between different tribal groups. Most *Arabisés* girls were sent to *humwali* at puberty or in adolescence, either in preparation for marriage or, sometimes, as corrective treatment if they had begun to associate with men without their parents' consent. Many non-*Arabisés* women had first attended *humwali* when already married. Sometimes they were sent by their husbands in which case they usually stayed in *humwali* for two or three days only. In other cases, they were sent by members of their families or by friends who wished to help them at times of marital difficulties.

Various versions of the *humwali* legend were told me by inhabitants of Avenue 21. One version ran as follows: 'A man once came back to this house to find his wife, whom he loved very much, committing adultery. Instead of beating her in the usual way, he thought the matter over. He loved her and he wanted to keep her. So he sought out the seven oldest and wisest women in his village. He explained to them that he was troubled about his wife, but did not tell them that she had committed adultery. The seven old women suggested that he should bring his wife to them. This he did. On arrival, the wife was severely beaten by the old women till she confessed her adultery. They cut off her hair and kept her in seclusion for seven days to teach her to respect her husband. This was the beginning of *humwali*.'

[15] In terms of the criteria discussed in Chapter IV, the Warega were an ethnic colony of Type 2.

[16] Mayer (1961), p. 292.

VIII

RELATIONS BETWEEN THE SEXES

In the preceding chapters we have numerous references to particular relationships between men and women but no systematic attempt to examine any one aspect of the pattern of social relations between the sexes. That this is fundamental to a fuller discussion of social relations *between men* is evident from the cases of Lusaka, Patrice and Limela. For example, the case of Lusaka illustrates how the family, friends, and neighbours of a well-settled man were deeply involved in his negotiations for a divorce as well as in his preparations for another marriage; the case of Patrice shows how a migrant's wife could form an integral part of an extensive network of fellow-tribesmen and could in this way directly affect his social relations with his 'brothers' and his adjustment to town life; and Limela's case yields a clear illustration of how even a temporary liaison between a man and a woman could in day-to-day life involve a number of other people. In the present chapter I therefore set out to examine relations between the sexes especially as they reflected, and affected, the response of men to the urban situation. Although mainly based on data for the total population of Stanleyville, the analysis is specifically geared to allow us better to appreciate social relations *between men in Avenue* 21, and it is to this topic that I return at the end of the chapter.

I begin by referring to the major imbalances that have previously been shown to characterize relations between the sexes in many African towns. I then use the evidence on domestic and other sexual unions contained in the case studies of Lusaka, Patrice, and Limela to distinguish between marital and non-marital partnerships. After this I use the data from the social survey to establish the broad patterns of pairing between men and women in the community. In particular, I examine data on the age, number, and marital status of men and women, and I present measures of marriage duration in the community as a whole as well as within each of the nine largest ethnic colonies. At this juncture it becomes apparent that there were very substantial differences in relations between men and women in various sections of the population. I am thus led to consider relations between the sexes as a variable feature *within* Stanleyville, and this obviously has important implications for the further assessment of social relations studied in Avenue 21 and its neighbourhood. I briefly consider these implications before turning in the concluding chapter to a final assessment of the wider community in the light of our general analysis of Avenue 21.

Imbalances between the Sexes in African Urban Society

The first and perhaps the most obvious imbalance between the sexes
in African towns lies in their numerical inequality. In Chapter III we
saw that in Stanleyville the sexes were relatively well balanced as
compared to many other towns and that the available evidence pointed
to a marked trend *towards* parity over the period of twenty or more years
preceding this study. Despite this 'improving' and 'favourable' situation, however, many of the well-known consequences of an excess of
men were clearly present in the community to some degree. An important factor contributing to this was that the sex ratio varied appreciably
between tribes and between neighbourhoods, so that the imbalance
was much higher in some contexts than in others. In this chapter I
examine the imbalance within age categories, as well as within the
categories of persons 'living singly' and 'not living singly', and it will
be seen that the findings make a further important contribution to
assessing patterns of pairing in the community.

The second general imbalance frequently noted in African towns
derives from the relative lack of economic and occupational opportunities for women other than limited petty trading, the often illicit selling
of beer, and various forms of prostitution. In reviewing the evidence from
the different regions of the continent, Southall has stressed the broad
contrast between West Africa, where urban women of nearly all social
strata are great marketeers and petty traders, and those areas of East,
Central, and Southern Africa, where stricter administrative controls
and a series of associated factors have commonly divested the role of
women of much of its rural economic importance.[1] In this respect
Stanleyville had less in common with urban areas in West Africa than
in East, Central, and Southern Africa; most women had little or no
involvement in either wage-earning or trading and were largely confined to work in and around their houses. But, here too, there was
considerable variation. We noted in Chapter IV that some women,
especially the Lokele, were often full-time traders, whilst others seldom
were. We shall see that this variation was associated with important
differences in the composition of families and in behaviour between the
sexes, and that these differences in turn had far-reaching implications
for social relations between adult men.

Thirdly, and closely related to the imbalance in occupational and
economic involvement, there are in most African urban situations wide
differences between men and women in the extent of their direct
exposure to modern or Western organization and culture. This set of
imbalances was particularly acute in Stanleyville: only two or three
women in the town could conduct even the most ordinary conversation
in French; well under 5 per cent worked for wages; only about 15 per
cent had ever attended school as against 50 per cent of the men; and
only about 35 per cent of the relatively small number of girls under
16 years of age in the town were currently attending schools as against

nearly 80 per cent of the substantially larger number of boys. (See Chapter III.) The lives of women and girls were almost exclusively oriented to the few specific social settings of their immediate residential neighbourhoods, of the local markets (where all of them purchased, and some of them sold, foodstuffs for household consumption), and of a particular category of European and Asian-owned shops specializing in cloths and other items of specifically 'African' feminine apparel. Few women ever visited the centre of the 'European town', and there was virtually no attempt, even on the part of the wives of *évolués*, to emulate the styles and fashions of dress and public behaviour of European women.

The almost total exclusion of women from the main social fields through which men were involved with the European community had important consequences. It meant that the female elite had a qualitatively different frame of reference to that of the male elite. There was in fact no feminine status equivalent to that of the masculine *évolué*. There was a set of fashionable women setting modern or 'urban' standards for the masses but their fashions and their styles of feminine conduct were distinctively 'African' rather than 'European' or 'Western'. Most members of this fashionable set were formally registered as *femmes libres*, and many, though not all, led relatively independent lives as the mistresses of wealthier African men—and in a minority of cases of Europeans—or as semi-prostitutes of high status. The semi-prostitutes commonly had small changing sets of 'lovers' or clients who ordinarily gave then 'presents' in return for sexual favours granted regularly over a period of time rather than strictly contracted cash payments in return for intermittent sexual encounters. These fashionable semi-prostitutes were 'civilized', and most of them were urbanites who resided in the C.E.C. in their own right by virtue either of local birth or of continuous local residence for ten or more years. They were thus not liable to eviction from the C.E.C., but they were subjected to constant pressure from the administration which regarded their presence in town as undesirable and unfortunate. In contrast to the male *évolués*, members of the fashionable female elite were not usually involved in social relations of direct subordination to European men and women. They were in this respect largely independent of the European community and were, at the same time, relatively independent of *individual* African men for supply and demand were such that a *femme libre* was normally able to establish or break off relations with a 'lover' or client according to whim and fancy.[2]

The mass of women in town were, however, not *femmes libres* but ordinary wives. From Table 60 it can be seen that the few women who had some limited schooling were in high demand as wives by the more educated *évolués*. But the supply of women with a little formal education was so small that the overwhelming majority of men who had themselves been to school were of necessity married to women with no education. And even men with secondary school education were often married to illiterate women. The table also indirectly reflects the concern of educated men over the paucity of educated women: by comparing the extent to which certain categories of men were over- or under-represented as husbands of given categories of women, we can infer that the better educated men were more likely to seek out a spouse from amongst the few educated women available than uneducated men were likely to seek out uneducated women. Also uneducated men were less likely to be married to educated women than educated

TABLE 60

Extant marriages classified according to the number of years each spouse had spent at school

(Based on samples for the nine largest ethnic colonies in the town)

1. The figures at the centre of the cells are absolute numbers.
2. The figures in the top left-hand corners of cells are percentages run horizontally.
3. The figures in the bottom right-hand corners are percentages run vertically.
4. The figures in the top right-hand corners of cells are indices of under- or over-representation. An index of 1·0 indicates even or proportional representation. An index of more than 1·0 indicates 'over-representation' and an index of less than 1·0 indicates 'under-representation'. The indices of representation for cells in a row are established by dividing the percentage given in the bottom right-hand corner of the cell in the Total column into the percentages in the bottom right-hand corners of the remaining cells. For example, 5·5 per cent of *all husbands* in the table had over six years of schooling but 24·4 per cent of *husbands of women with over three years of schooling* had been to school for more than six years; men with over six years of schooling were thus 'over-represented' as husbands of women with over three years of schooling to the extent of 4·5. The indices were calculated in the same way as those in Table 17, Chapter IV.

YEARS SPENT AT SCHOOL BY HUSBANDS	YEARS SPENT AT SCHOOL BY WIVES			
	NONE	1–3 YEARS	OVER 3 YEARS	TOTAL
None	96·4　　1·1　370　　60·2	2·3　　0·3　9　　17·0	1·3　　0·2　5　　11·1	100　384　　53·9
1–3 years	83·9　　1·0　120　　19·5	9·8　　1·3　14　　26·4	6·3　　1·0　9　　20·0	100　143　　20·1
4–6 years	72·1　　0·8　106　　17·2	14·3　　1·9　21　　39·6	13·6　　2·2　20*　　44·4	100　147　　20·6
Over 6 years	48·7　　0·6　19　　3·1	23·1　　3·1　9　　17·0	28·2　　4·5　11†　　24·4	100　39　　5·5
Total	86·3　615　　100·0	7·4　53　　100·0	6·3　45　　99·9	100　713　　100·1

* Including one woman with more than six years schooling.

† Including two women with more than six years schooling.

men were likely to be married to uneducated women.[3] These findings
are of considerable interest; they reflect the difficult overall situation
in which women who had been to school found themselves. On the one
hand, *évolués* eagerly sought them out as wives but constantly complained
of the inadequacy of such education as they had. On the other hand,
uneducated men tended not to distinguish between women with and
without formal schooling but, if anything, usually regarded those with
some education as less trustworthy than others.

In any event a large majority of all wives—whether or not they had
been to school—continued to be directly dependent on their husbands.
Their dependence on the conjugal bond was partly a function of the
general economic and occupational inequality between the sexes, but
it was also in part a consequence of the administrative stipulation that
no women without legitimate family roles could reside in town unless
they were permanent residents of the C.E.C. in their own right. Since
adultery could well lead to divorce, and divorce could lead to repatria-
tion on the instruction of the urban courts, an unfaithful wife was in
many cases not only running the risk of losing her marital home but
also of losing her right to urban residence. This inevitably curbed such
economic independence as wives might otherwise have been able to
achieve in town by virtue of their sexual value.[4]

Finally, the social position of women in relation to men, and especially
of wives in relation to husbands, was to some extent both an outcome
and an expression of a fourth general imbalance encountered between
the sexes. As Southall has stressed, "polygyny (remains) the undoubted
goal of men in rural society . . . [and] is a built-in value for societies
based on patrilineal descent groups".[5] In the measure that modern
urban situations offer women freedom and personal emancipation we
must therefore expect a conflict of values to affect relationships between
men and women, and especially between husbands and wives. And,
indeed, there are many reports of men expressing resentment over the
relative loss of masculine privilege in towns, and, conversely, of women
according a high value to urban life as a way of gaining full or partial
release from the traditional feminine role of severe subordination.[6]
This range of attitudes was unmistakably present in Stanleyville. In the
region as a whole, the differences in the social positions of women in
town and village were so marked that the population held strongly
contrasting images of the urban and tribal feminine roles. And these
two sets of roles inevitably contained conflicting elements. Economic
development and general social change had of course undermined
polygyny and its associated values in the hinterland to *some* extent; yet
in most parts of the region the basic values of traditional polygynous
and patrilineal family life persisted in remarkable degree and remained
integral parts of an institutional complex which was still widely effective in governing daily life in the villages from which the urban population was drawn.[7] In labour centres, on the other hand, polygynous
family life was virtually impossible, and in *centres extra-coutumiers* it was

not only difficult and discouraged by practical considerations but also specifically forbidden to the extent that polygynous immigrants were normally refused entry by the administration even though accompanied by one wife only. In general, then, urban conditions had in various ways largely released women from some of the immediate constraints of traditional life, but their economic, occupational, and educational advancement still lagged far behind their personal emancipation. Most women continued to be directly dependent on their menfolk despite their new-found urban freedom, and urban feminine roles inevitably came to be defined and evaluated as more specifically sexual and domestic than the tribal roles to which most women had been reared in youth.

In summary, the community exhibited all the major imbalances and associated conflicts between the sexes common in many African urban societies. The inequality in the numbers of men and women was far less marked than in many of the larger urban areas of the continent, though we shall see that in some sections of the population it remained high. And the remaining imbalances and conflicts would seem to have been as acute, or more so, than in most African towns for which we have the relevant indications.

The Definition of Marriage

Before presenting evidence on the domestic pairing of men and women, we have to consider the distinctions commonly drawn in Stanleyville between several different kinds of marital and non-marital unions. Clarity on this point is of particular importance in view of the frequent suggestion that many cases of co-habitation in African towns are no more than marriage-like unions which lack the full intent and effect of marriage. The case histories of Lusaka, Limela, and Patrice given in the previous chapter contain some clear examples of several kinds of partnerships and I use these as illustrations.[8]

Lusaka's union with Antoinette is a good example of one common type of marriage. The union began in Stanleyville as a clandestine relationship between two young lovers. It later continued as an open association between a man and a woman who had by now been registered as a *femme libre* by her father, and it was finally sanctioned as a marriage by the negotiation and payment of bridewealth. The negotiations were initiated by Lusaka and he himself paid the bridewealth. Yet the arrangements were made over a considerable period of time and it is clear that they deeply involved members of the families of both bride and groom. Some time after the couple had begun to co-habit in Lusaka's house, the marriage was registered at the offices of the C.E.C. and thus gained the formal recognition and protection of the urban courts.[9]

Patrice's union with Mangaza followed a substantially different course, and is a good example of another type of marriage common in the town. The marriage was arranged in the countryside between

Patrice's father and members of Mangaza's family. The betrothal took place in Patrice's absence and without his knowledge or consent. The bridewealth was paid in full by Patrice's father and family, and was partly in cash and partly in kind. The marriage was registered in the couple's rural *chefferie*. Being registered in the countryside it did not fall under the jurisdiction of the urban courts, and Mangaza's status in town was solely that of the wife of a man who was himself living there *à titre précaire*. In the event of a divorce, Mangaza would not have been accorded the status of a *femme libre* and would not have been allowed to continue residence in the C.E.C.

Limela's marriage to Rosina had several features in common with that of Lusaka to Antoinette. The marriage was arranged in a quasi-traditional way in that it involved some measure of consultation and negotiation between members of the families of the prospective bride and groom. Though the couple were not lovers prior to the marriage, the initiative in arranging the union was entirely individual rather than familial. Limela's father provided the bridewealth but only after the marriage had been negotiated at Limela's instigation. The registration of the marriage took place at the offices of the administrative outpost near to the mission station where the couple had met and married. Finally, in addition to being contracted in keeping with customary law, the marriage was celebrated according to Roman Catholic rites. It was thus governed by ecclesiastical law and there were in the territory no provisions for its dissolution or for the legal recognition of any dissolution which the contracting parties might have arranged with their families according to custom.

The above were all marriages with clearly defined legal status. As it happens, too, they between them examplify three types of marriage that were common in the town. Patrice's marriage may be thought of as typically traditional in that it involved betrothal before marriage, the maximum involvement and the most explicit alliance of the families of bride and groom, and the minimum of individual initiative. By the same tokens, the marriages of Lusaka and Limela may be thought of as typically modern or 'urban' in that they were largely instigated and arranged by the individuals concerned; in both cases, however, family consent and involvement remained essential features of the process and fact of marriage. The differences between traditional and modern or 'urban' marriages conceived of in this way were largely differences of degree so that the two types represent the opposite poles of a continuum rather than discrete categories.

The second distinction to be noted is between Limela's marriage which was both Christian and customary and Patrice's and Lusaka's which were customary only. The incidence of Christian marriages in the town is given in Table 61, which shows that they accounted for about 15 per cent of all extant marriages, for about 8 per cent of the extant marriages of Protestant men, and for nearly 25 per cent of the extant marriages of Roman Catholic men. There was also a very small percentage of civil marriages[10]; some of these had been celebrated according to Christian rites and most of them had been negotiated as customary unions. There were also very occasional Christian marriages which were *not* arranged in keeping with customary law. I have no precise figures for these minor categories but in each case the numbers were extremely small. In effect, therefore, the main distinction to note is that between marriages based on customary law only and those based on customary law but also celebrated according to Christian rites.

We may now return to the case histories of Lusaka and Limela to examine the nature of the remainder of their partnerships with women. Limela's union with Nafisa is the only one of these that had *developed* into a customary marriage. We saw how the two partners were distant

TABLE 61

Extant marriages classified according to category of marriage contract and religion of husband

CATEGORY OF MARRIAGE	RELIGION OF HUSBAND									
	ROMAN CATHOLIC		PROTES- TANT		MOHAM- MEDAN		'PAGAN'		TOTAL	
	No.	%	No.	%	No.	%	No.	%	No.	%
Customary marriage only	484	74·5	127	92·0	132	100·0	233	99·1	976	84·5
Christian marriage (almost invariably also a customary marriage)	159	24·5	11	8·0	0	0·0	2	0·9	172	14·9
Civil marriage (sometimes also a Christian and/or a customary marriage)	7	1·1	0	0·0	0	0·0	0	0·0	7	0·6
Effective sample	650	100·1	138	100·0	132	100·0	235	100·0	1,155	100·0

kinsmen who had known each other in childhood. On meeting much later in life they became lovers and began to co-habit without the approval of their kinsfolk, without having negotiated a marriage, and without any initial arrangement or recognition that the union should be regarded as a 'trial marriage'. As things turned out, however, the union was in the course of time regularized as a customary marriage by the payment of bridewealth, and it was eventually registered as a marriage in the *centre extra-coutumier* when the couple later settled there.

On subsequently being divorced, Limela did not claim a refund of the bridewealth paid, but he could well have done so. According to ecclesiastical law, however, the marriage was null and void from the start for Limela's 'Christian wife', Rosina, was still alive at the time that he married Nafisa.[11]

Lusaka's union with Bernadette was different to Limela's with Nafisa in that it was explicitly recognized as a 'trial marriage' before the couple began to co-habit. The two partners had previously been lovers, but Bernadette only came formally to Lusaka's house under the terms of a specific agreement between Lusaka and members of her family that a period of co-habitation should take place with the assumption by the couple of marital roles in relation to each other and of affinal roles in relation to their respective families. When Bernadette came to live with Lusaka it was made clear to friends and neighbours and to members of the community at large that the period of co-habitation was undertaken with a view to marriage.

The remaining cases of Limela's unions with Marianna, Salima, and Maria were not considered as either marriages or 'trial marriages' by the parties concerned. In the case of Limela's co-habitation with Salima, no attempt was made to establish relations of *shemeki* between the two partners and each others' families. In the case of his union with Marianna, relations of *shemeki* had developed, but the account suggests that they were not fully sanctioned as in the case of a 'true' marriage; in the terms that I have earlier applied to kinship, these relationships of *shemeki* were 'fictitious' rather than 'real'. The same was true of the relations established between Limela and persons who were in any case 'fictitious' kinsmen to Maria. In the case of Maria it is interesting to note that there was an issue from the union, but that Limela did not consider that he had any right to the child. Indeed, in expressing the hope that he would one day acquire custody, he explicitly recognized that this would involve negotiating a payment with Maria's family in specific regard to the child but not necessarily to Maria.

In the tables that follow 'trial marriages' like that of Lusaka and Bernadette were not classified as marriages; nor of course were unions like those of Limela with Marianna, Salima and Maria. On the other hand, cases in which either 'trial marriage' or co-habitation for mutual convenience had later led to the payment of bridewealth were counted as marriages irrespective of whether they had ever been officially registered; and unions sanctioned by customary law were regarded as marriages even if, as in the case of Limela and Nafisa, they were null and void according to ecclesiastical law. In effect, therefore, my classification of unions as marriages is based primarily on the main feature which the vast majority of the inhabitants recognized as sanctioning marriage, namely, the payment of bridewealth. There was a very small minority of cases which could not readily be classified in this way. For example, it was not always clear whether payments made to the family of a woman were to be considered as bridewealth or simply as presents, and some cases were encountered where this was the subject of an on-going dispute between two families. In a few other cases it was evident that the man and his family had attached a different significance to a payment or payments than had the woman and her family, and that the two parties continued to differ in their interpretations. There were also occasional couples who convincingly argued that they were married in terms of customary law despite the fact that no bride-wealth had changed hands. But all these categories were so small that the decisions taken—either in classifying them or in altogether excluding them from the tables—cannot have affected the overall picture presented to any appreciable extent.

THE PAIRING OF MEN AND WOMEN IN MARITAL AND NON-MARITAL UNIONS

An inevitable corollary of an excess of men over women is that a certain proportion of men must live without female partners, and it will be recalled that the presence of men living singly was a prominent feature of the social situation in Avenue 21. Both in Avenue 21 and in the town as a whole, however, the numbers of men living singly were appreciably higher than could be accounted for solely by inequality of numbers between the sexes, and we know that the population also contained a substantial proportion of women living singly. In an attempt to establish patterns of pairing in the community I therefore distinguish between adults *living singly* and those *not living singly*, as well as between different categories of the 'single' and the 'not single'.

The precise marital status of the population in various age categories is shown for women in Table 62 and for men in Table 63, and the distribution and relative size of the categories of 'single' and 'not single' at different ages is shown in Table 64. Close inspection of these tables reveals several important features of the way in which men and women were paired and distributed amongst each other. Tables 62 and 63 show that 74·0 per cent of all women aged 16 years and over had a domestic partner (i.e. were either married or living with a man to whom not married) whereas only 67·8 per cent of adult men had a domestic partner. Conversely, the proportion of all men living singly was necessarily higher than the proportion of women living singly (32·2 per cent as against 26·0 per cent). But these proportions varied greatly at different ages for each sex, and any attempt to assess the supply and demand of domestic partners must take account both of the ages of men and women living singly and of the differing propensities of the two sexes to enter marital and other unions at different ages.

Comparing Tables 63 and 64, we see the extent to which the two sexes differed in marital status at various stages of life. Table 63 shows that 11·1 per cent of all girls aged 11–15 years had domestic partners, that this proportion rose very sharply to 82·6 per cent between the ages of 16 and 25 years, and that it stayed at a high level in the age category of 36–45 years. Between the ages of 46 and 55 years, however,

TABLE 62

Domestic status of different age categories of women in the total population

STATUS	AGE CATEGORIES						
	11–15	16–25	26–35	36–45	46–55	56 AND OVER	TOTAL FOR AGES OF 16 YEARS AND OVER
	%	%	%	%	%	%	%
Married	10·3	79·7	78·6	64·7	45·4	19·3	69·7
Living with a man to whom not married	0·8	2·9	4·2	8·2	6·4	0·0	4·3
(combined)	11·1	82·6	82·8	72·9	51·8	19·3	74·0
Widowed, living singly	0·0	0·5	2·2	7·1	27·8	65·3	9·1
Divorced, living singly	1·4	5·1	12·9	16·7	17·7	14·5	11·5
Never married, living singly	87·5	11·8	2·1	3·3	2·7	0·9	5·4
(combined)	88·9	17·4	17·2	27·1	48·2	80·7	26·0
Total	100·0	100·0	100·0	100·0	100·0	100·0	100·0
Effective sample	138	518	568	284	114	123	1,607

TABLE 63

Domestic status of different age categories of men in the total population

STATUS	AGE CATEGORIES					
	16–25	26–35	36–45	46–55	56 AND OVER	ALL AGES
	%	%	%	%	%	%
Married	42·4	74·7	73·7	66·5	62·9	64·0
Living with a woman to whom not married	2·2	2·9	5·8	7·9	3·0	3·8
(combined)	44·6	77·6	79·5	74·4	65·9	67·8
Widowed, living singly	0·0	1·6	1·2	3·5	15·8	2·2
Divorced, living singly	6·6	9·6	14·2	16·6	17·5	10·8
Never married, living singly	48·8	11·2	5·1	3·5	0·8	19·2
(combined)	55·4	22·4	20·5	25·6	34·1	32·2
Total	100·0	100·0	100·0	100·0	100·0	100·0
Effective sample	525	676	411	174	108	1,894

Note: About 8·0 per cent of the men classified as married in this table did not have their wives in town at the time of the enumeration. Most of these were men who had only recently come to town (see Chapter III, f.n. 5). Since most wives left behind in the first instance normally followed their husbands to town in due course, it seemed preferable to classify all men who had come to town without their wives as 'married' rather than 'living singly'.

the proportion declined markedly to 51·8 per cent, and it fell to 19·3 per cent for the category aged 56 years and over. In contrast, there was in the sample no boy under 16 years of age with a domestic partner, and only 44·6 per cent of men aged 16–25 years were living with partners as against nearly double that proportion for women in the same age category. But in the age categories 26–35 and 36–45 years, the proportions of men with domestic partners rose to 77·6 per cent and 79·5 per cent and were thus nearly as high as the corresponding percentages for women. Above 55 years of age the proportion fell to 65·9 per cent but was none the less markedly higher than the corresponding proportion of 19·3 per cent for old and elderly women.

TABLE 64

The percentage distribution of men and women of different ages according to whether they were classified as living singly or as married or living with a partner to whom not married

AGE CATEGORY	MEN		WOMEN		TOTAL
	MARRIED OR LIVING WITH A PARTNER TO WHOM NOT MARRIED	LIVING SINGLY	MARRIED OR LIVING WITH A PARTNER TO WHOM NOT MARRIED	LIVING SINGLY	
16–25 years	6·7	8·4	12·3	2·6	30·0
26–35	14·9	4·3	13·4	2·8	35·4
36–45	9·3	2·4	5·9	2·2	19·8
46–55	3·7	1·3	1·7	1·6	8·3
56 and above	2·0	1·0	0·7	2·8	6·5
Total	36·6	17·4	34·0	12·0	100·0

Effective sample: 3,501

Note: As in Table 63 all men who did not have their wives in town were classified as 'married or living with a partner to whom not married', and this partly accounts for the small excess of men *not* living singly over women *not* living singly. Another factor contributing to this excess was that a small proportion of men were married to, or living with, women under 16 years of age (cf. Table 62) whereas there was no case in the sample of a woman married to, or living with, a man under 16.

In general, then, women tended to enter into marital and other unions at much earlier ages than men; in the middle age categories there was not much difference in the proportions of men and women participating in domestic unions; and in later life women were much more likely to be living singly than men were.

Important implications of the above patterns, given the particular age and sex composition of the population, are revealed in Table 64 which shows the relative size of the categories of men and women who were either living singly or with a domestic partner at different ages. Between the ages of 16 and 25 years men living singly constituted 8·4 per cent of the *total* adult population and thus heavily outnumbered women living singly who only constituted 2·6 per cent of the total. As age increased, however, the number of men living singly fell sharply whereas the numbers of women living singly remained roughly constant from one adult age category to the next. Thus the *ratio* of men living singly to women living singly decreased very sharply as age increased, but precisely the reverse relationship obtained between men and women living with domestic partners, i.e. young women with partners heavily outnumbered young men with partners whereas elderly women with partners were heavily outnumbered by elderly men with partners. This contrast between the two sexes is brought out quite dramatically

TABLE 65

Sex ratios for adults of different ages living with and without domestic partners

AGE CATEGORY	NUMBER OF MEN OF A GIVEN AGE LIVING SINGLY PER 100 WOMEN OF THE SAME AGE LIVING SINGLY	NUMBER OF MEN OF A GIVEN AGE LIVING WITH PARTNERS PER 100 WOMEN OF THE SAME AGE LIVING WITH PARTNERS	UNDIFFERENTIATED SEX RATIO, I.E. NUMBER OF ALL MEN OF A GIVEN AGE PER 100 WOMEN (WITH OR WITHOUT PARTNERS) OF THE SAME AGE
16–25 years	323	54	102
26–35	154	111	119
36–45	109	158	143
46–55	81	217	150
56 and over	36	285	84

when the basic data presented in Table 64 are converted into the sex ratios shown in Table 65. Between the ages of 16 and 25 years there were as many as 323 men in the town living singly for every 100 women living singly. This ratio fell appreciably between the ages of 26 and 35 years and again between the ages of 36 and 45 years, but it was only in the two upper age categories that 'single women' outnumbered 'single men'.

The above analysis affords partial explanation for several features of day-to-life that might otherwise appear surprising in a community with a *relatively* well balanced sex ratio. In the light of the detailed figures we are no longer puzzled as to why, for example, so many young men were led to recruit brides from the countryside, or why single women in the town readily found roles as prostitutes, semi-prostitutes, and temporary mistresses, or why married women were also continually called upon to provide to *some extent*, and in *one way or another*, for the domestic, affectional, and sexual demands of the many men living without partners. The composition of the adult population—in terms of number, age, sex, and domestic status—in itself suggests why there was so much competition between men, and especially between younger men, for transient and temporary sexual partners as well as for permanent and semi-permanent domestic partners.

Moreover, if we also bear in mind the remaining general imbalances between the sexes (i.e. imbalances other than that of numerical inequality) we begin to see how and why the primary expectations attaching to various urban feminine roles were so largely—and almost exclusively—defined in some combination of domestic and sexual terms; in particular, we are led to appreciate why social relations between extra-marital sexual partners so often acquired marriage-like characteristics in a number of respects or, to state the problem in another way, why the community had developed such well-defined

norms governing both the behaviour of a man and his mistress in relation to each other and their behaviour in relation to each other's kinsmen and friends. Before discussing the implications of the analysis more
fully, however, we have to consider further aspects of the patterns of
pairing and distribution of the two sexes.

The Cumulative Marriage Experiences of Men and Women[12]

We have so far examined aspects of the pairing and distribution
of men and women amongst each other at one point in time. Yet we
know that few people remained with the same domestic partner
throughout their lives, and that even recognized marital unions were
commonly terminated through divorce before the death of one of the
partners. These were matters of everyday observation in the town
and they are partly corroborated by our figures on the marital status
of the population. For example, Tables 62 and 63 show that men and
women who were neither partners to a domestic union nor persons who,
though living singly at the time of the enumeration, had previously
been wedded, constituted very small proportions—under 5 per cent—
of the population in all the middle and upper adult age categories.
Moreover, with the exceptions of old women and young men, persons
living singly were in substantial majority divorcees rather than widows
and widowers or spinsters and bachelors. These observations in
themselves point to a high turn-over in marriage, but they lack precision
and clearly call for a more thorough assessment of the redistribution
of men and women amongst each other during the course of their lives.
As a first step in this direction, Tables 66 and 67 present various
measures of the extent to which the enumerated population of the town
had experienced marriage, divorce, and the termination of marriage
through the death of a spouse. In reading the tables we must remember
that the data do not refer exclusively to urban experiences; they are
based on entire marital histories and therefore include experiences
of migrants prior to coming to town. Our interest at the present stage
is, however, just as much in the characteristics of the population as on
the process of their distribution among each other.

From Table 66 we see that the proportion of ever-wedded men who
had been divorced *once or more* rose from 26·4 per cent in the age
category 16–25 years to over 60 per cent above 35 years of age. At
the same time, the proportion of men who had experienced widowhood
once or more rose from 1·6 per cent between 16 and 25 years of age to
nearly 40 per cent over 55 years of age, and the mean number of
marriages (including extant marriages) per ever-wedded man rose
from 1·15 between 16 and 25 years to 2·20 over 55 years of age.

Comparing the above with the corresponding figures for women
(Table 67), we note three main differences. First, though the mean
number of marriage experiences reported by women in the younger
age categories was of the same order as the mean number reported by
men of the same ages, the older women reported appreciably fewer

marriage experiences than older men. This difference is partly a consequence of some older men having married polygynously in their home villages in earlier life, but it also undoubtedly reflects the tendency for older men to re-marry more readily than older women. Secondly, the percentage of women who reported having lost a husband through death rose from 1·5 in the 16–25 year age category to 71·8 above 55 years of age, whereas the corresponding proportion of men who had lost a wife through death rose to only 39·7 per cent. An important factor contributing to this difference was, of course, that many wives were very much younger than their husbands. These wives commonly outlived their husbands in later years and in many cases did not re-marry. Thirdly, in the younger adult age categories the percentages of women who had been divorced at least once were of the same order as the corresponding percentages for men, but they were appreciably lower above 45 years of age. All these observations are in keeping with, and contribute to explaining, the more rapid decline with increasing age in the proportions of women than of men recorded as married at the time of the enumeration.

Marriage Termination and Marriage Duration

The above analysis provides useful indications of the age and sex categories that were differentially exposed to various contingencies in the course of their lives. More generally, too, it strongly reinforces the view that the distribution of men and women in marriage has to be assessed as part of a continuous and widespread process of shuffling and re-shuffling of domestic and sexual partners over time. We are thus logically led to examine the duration of marriages and the rates at which they terminated. Before developing this part of the analysis, however, we have to recall that a substantial proportion of the events in the marital histories of the enumerated population had taken place many years before the field study and that some had in fact occurred outside Stanleyville. We saw in Chapter IV, for example, that a sample of 719 extant marriages in the nine largest ethnic colonies consisted of 235 marriages (32·7 per cent) contracted in tribal villages, 336 (46·7 per cent) in Stanleyville itself, and 148 (20·6 per cent) in employment centres other than Stanleyville (Table 30). This has important implications for the handling of the data as we shift our focus of interest from the characteristics of the wedded population to the dynamics of marriage duration and marriage termination *in the urban community* as it was at *the time of the field study*. It means, of course, that we have to consider only selected parts of the marital histories reported by our sample. Some of the tables to follow are accordingly restricted to events that took place in the town over specified years immediately prior to the field enumeration. To illustrate the problem we may refer to Fig. XXVI which depicts selected parts of the marital histories of 27 men who were between 36 and 45 years of age at the time they were interviewed. The diagram depicts the marital history of each of the men from the

TABLE 66

Marital experiences of different age categories of the ever-wedded men in the total population

AGE CATEGORY	EFFECTIVE SAMPLE OF WEDDED MEN	PERCENTAGE OF WEDDED MEN DIVORCED ONCE OR MORE	MEAN NUMBER OF DIVORCES PER WEDDED MAN	PERCENTAGE OF WEDDED MEN HAVING EXPERIENCED WIDOWERHOOD ONCE OR MORE	MEAN NUMBER OF WIDOWERHOODS PER WEDDED MAN	MEAN NUMBER OF MARRIAGE EXPERIENCES PER WEDDED MEN
16–25 years	259	26·4	0·28	1·6	0.02	1·15
26–35	594	43·7	0·55	6·4	0·07	1·48
36–45	390	61·5	0·94	13·8	0·16	1·90
46–55	165	67·4	1·05	23·7	0·26	2·10
56 and over	106	65·6	1·08	39·7	0·51	2·20
Total	1,514	49·3	0·69	11·7	0·14	1·65

TABLE 67

Marital experiences of different age categories of the ever-wedded women in the total population

AGE CATEGORY	EFFECTIVE SAMPLE OF WEDDED WOMEN	PERCENTAGE OF WEDDED WOMEN DIVORCED ONCE OR MORE	MEAN NUMBER OF DIVORCES PER WEDDED WOMAN	PERCENTAGE OF WEDDED WOMEN HAVING EXPERIENCED WIDOWHOOD ONCE OR MORE	MEAN NO. OF WIDOWHOODS PER WEDDED WOMAN	MEAN NO. OF MARRIAGE EXPERIENCES PER WEDDED WOMAN
16–25 years	454	24·7	0·26	1·5	0·02	1·19
26–35	547	54·5	0·64	9·9	0·11	1·55
36–45	273	60·2	0·84	27·5	0·28	1·82
46–55	109	54·7	0·87	53·4	0·61	1·95
56 and over	120	46·3	0·56	71·8	0·83	1·63
Total	1,503	45·9	0·57	18·6	0·20	1·52

beginning of 1940 or from the year of arrival in Stanleyville—whichever was the shorter—to the end of 1952. On the basis of the information shown, we can make a variety of statements about these men
and their *urban* marital experiences: of the 27, sixteen had been in
Stanleyville since 1940 or earlier, whereas 11 had only come to town
at a date within the period under review; the 27 men had between them
reported 34 marriages lived wholly or partly in the town, and of these
34, thirteen had been established in Stanleyville between 1940 and
1952, 14 had been contracted elsewhere before the men had settled in
town, and 7 had been established in town before 1940; furthermore, of
the 34 marriages, 13 had ended in Stanleyville between 1940 and
1952—11 through divorce and two through the death of a wife; and so
on. It is evident that we can use such data to arrive at annual rates of
marriage termination specific to the town. Thus, for example, we can
see that in 1952 there were 22 extant marriages of which one or 4·5 per
cent ended in divorce during the course of that year, whereas in 1950
there were 21 extant marriages of which two or 9·5 per cent ended in
divorce. Annual divorce rates established in this way are of course liable
to be defective in that the original data necessarily exclude divorces
experienced by men who had either died or left the town before the
enumeration. Otherwise, however, they are in principle the same as
annual divorce rates calculated by taking the number of annual
divorces registered in a population as a percentage of the number of
marriages known to exist. There are two main advantages to termination rates calculated in this way. One is that they are *urban* rates based
only on events that took place in Stanleyville, and the other is that they
are specific to a particular year. Table 68 gives marriage termination
rates of this kind for the years 1946 to 1952. The table is based on
information drawn from the marital histories of all men in our sample
for the nine largest ethnic colonies in the town but, as in the case of
Fig. XXVI, the table includes only divorces and terminations through
death that took place when the men reporting them were either
living in Stanleyville or clearly based there.[13] Equally, of course,
the number of marriages in existence in each year refers to those either
in existence in the town or based there. The table shows that the proportion
of marriages reported as having ended in divorce in any one year
fluctuated between 2·2 per cent for 1948 and 5·2 per cent for 1946, while
the overall percentage of marriage terminations (through divorces *and*
through the deaths of wives) ranged from 2·7 per cent in 1948 to 6·5 per
cent in 1946. Considering the small absolute number of cases on which
some of these annual percentages are based, we have to be cautious in
interpreting the table. For example, it may well be that the relatively
large fluctuations between 1946 and 1948 are misleading. However, the
relative stability of the percentages over the remaining years, and the
larger numbers involved in the calculation of the mean percentages for
the entire seven-year period clearly allow us to attach considerable
weight to the evidence as a whole.

YEAR OF ARRIVAL IN STANLEYVILLE	* YEAR OF MARRIAGE	1940	1941	1942	1943	1944	1945	1946	1947	1948	1949	1950	1951	1952
1912	1930													
BORN IN STAN. 1915	—													
1927	1926													
1927	1933													
1928	1937													
1930	1937													
1932	—													
1935	—													
1935	1939													
1935	1938													
1936	—													
1937	1936													
1938	1934													
1938	1932													
1938	1939													
1940	1936													
1941	1940													
1944	1937													
1944	—													
1945	1931													
1945	1944													
1947	1943													
1948	1934													
1949	1938													
1951	—													
1951	1945													
1952	1931													

*YEAR OF MARRIAGE STILL EXTANT AT THE END OF 1939 OR AT TIME OF ARRIVAL IF LATER THAN 1940

START OF A MARRIAGE IN TOWN |
DIVORCE X
DEATH OF A WIFE O

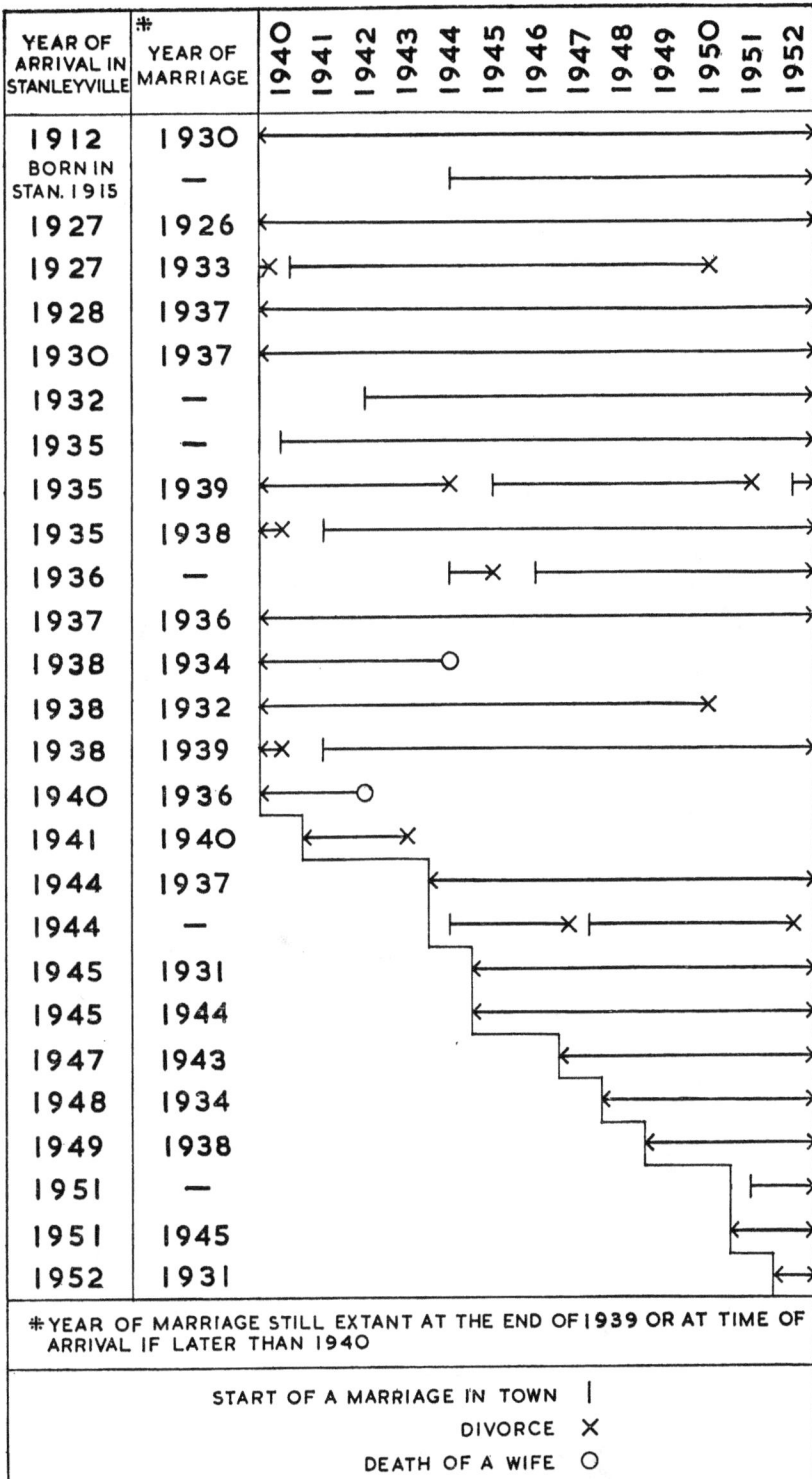

Fig. XXVI Diagram depicting marital histories in the town of a sample of 27 men aged 36–45 years

TABLE 68

The annual number of marriages in existence, divorces, and terminations of marriages through death of a wife: 1946–1952
(Based on marital histories of all men in the samples for the nine largest ethnic colonies in the town)

YEAR	MARRIAGES REPORTED AS HAVING BEEN IN EXISTENCE DURING EACH YEAR*	DIVORCES	PER CENT DIVORCES PER ANNUM	TERMINATIONS OF MARRIAGE THROUGH DEATH OF A WIFE	PER CENT TERMINATIONS THROUGH DEATH OF A WIFE PER ANNUM	TERMINATIONS THROUGH DEATH PLUS DIVORCES	PER CENT MARRIAGES ENDING THROUGH DEATH OF A WIFE OR DIVORCE PER ANNUM
1946	309	16	5·2	4	1·3	20	6·5
1947	348	12	3·5	2	0·6	14	4·0
1948	407	9	2·2	2	0·5	11	2·7
1949	465	21	4·5	4	0·9	25	5·4
1950	524	21	4·1	3	0·6	24	4·6
1951	594	23	3·9	3	0·5	26	4·4
1952	669	27	4·0	3	0·4	30	4·5
Effective sample	3316†	129	3·9‡	21	0·6‡	150	4·5‡

* Including marriages begun in the town during the course of each year and marriages migrating to town during the year.
† This figure represents the number of marriage years lived in the town by the men in the sample between 1946 and 1952 inclusive.
‡ These figures represent rates per cent per annum over the seven-year period.

The suggestion is, then, that there was a divorce rate of nearly 4 per cent per annum and a rate of marriage termination through the deaths of wives of about one half of 1 per cent. If we further allow for terminations of marriages through the deaths of husbands— cases not represented in this sample since the data were drawn from marital histories of men only—we can with reasonable confidence assume a total marriage termination rate of about 5 per cent per annum. If we apply this rate of termination through divorce and death to an imaginary cohort of marriages passing through time, we arrive at estimates of marriage duration of the following order: nearly 10 per cent of all marriages would have ended before the end of two years, about 19 per cent before the end of four years, about 46 per cent before the end of 12 years, and just over 70 per cent before the end of 25 years.

We would, however, not expect marriages of varying lengths to terminate at the same rates. If we wish to estimate marriage duration we should therefore base our calculations on termination rates specific to marriages of various durations. This is done in Tables 69–71 in which the marriages reported by the enumerated men are classified according to their duration and, in the case of terminated marriages, to the way in which each ended. Having first classified the marriages, the technique of analysis involves treating all marriages *as if* they had started at the same time. The original cohort of marriages is reduced by progressively applying the termination rates specific to the first, second, third, etc., years as we move from the top to the bottom of each table.[14]

We may consider Table 69 first. The central question posed in this table is: what proportions of all the marriages reported by the men enumerated in the town would have lasted given lengths of time *irrespective of where and when they were established and lived*? From column 5 we see that the calculations are based on 2,300 marriages of which 63 ended in divorce within a year of marriage (Column 2) and eight ended through the death of a wife within a year (Column 3). The proportion of the 2,300 marriages surviving divorce for one year was thus 0·9726 (Column 10), the proportion surviving death of a wife for a year was 0·9965 (Column 14), and the proportion surviving both divorce and death of a wife for one year was 0·9691 (Column 7). In a general way, then, we can say that just over 3 per cent of all marriages reported by men had failed to endure beyond one year and that divorce was by far the main factor contributing to termination in this year of marriage.

Turning to the table again, we see from Column 4 that 83 of the 2,300 marriages had been in existence for less than one year at the time of the enumeration; we cannot know how long they were to last and we therefore have to exclude them from our calculations of survival rates for the second year. Thus, as shown in Column 5, the rates for the second year of marriage are based on 2,146 marriages only (i.e. 2,300 *less* 63 that had ended in divorce during the first

TABLE 69

Marriage duration table for the effective sample of all marriages reported by all men enumerated by the social survey

1	2	3	4	5	6	7
DURATION OF MARRIAGE IN YEARS	MARRIAGES ENDING IN DIVORCE	MARRIAGES TERMINATED BY DEATH OF WIFE	MARRIAGES STILL EXTANT AFTER GIVEN NUMBER OF YEARS, BUT FULL DURATION UNKNOWN	MARRIAGES EXPOSED TO TERMINATION BY DIVORCE OR DEATH OF WIFE	MARRIAGES SURVIVING DIVORCE AND DEATH OF WIFE	PROPORTION OF MARRIAGES SURVIVING DIVORCE AND DEATH OF WIFE
Less than 1 year, say 6 months	63	8	83	2,300	2,229	0·9691
Less than 2 years, say 1½ years	110	13	98	2,146	2,023	0·9426
say 2½	130	16	88	1,925	1,779	0·9242
,, 3½	164	16	89	1,691	1,511	0·8936
,, 4½	84	10	80	1,422	1,328	0·9339
,, 5½	76	10	76	1,248	1,162	0·9311
,, 6½	56	14	70	1,086	1,016	0·9355
,, 7½	55	9	59	946	882	0·9323
,, 8½	39	10	57	823	774	0·9405
,, 9½	37	4	52	717	676	0·9428
,, 10½	29	7	49	624	588	0·9423
,, 11½	17	4	33	539	518	0·9610
,, 12½	17	6	38	485	462	0·9526
,, 13½	13	5	28	424	406	0·9575
,, 14½	8	2	41	378	368	0·9735
,, 15½	13	4	41	327	310	0·9480
,, 16½	5	2	24	269	262	0·9740
,, 17½	5	5	16	238	228	0·9580
,, 18½	5	0	23	212	207	0·9764
,, 19½	4	0	13	184	180	0·9783
,, 20½	11	3	32	167	153	0·9162
,, 21½	2	0	8	121	119	0·9835
,, 22½	3	2	11	111	106	0·9550
,, 23½	3	0	6	95	92	0·9684
,, 24½	2	0	4	86	84	0·9767
,, 25½	6	1	10	80	73	0·9125
,, 26½	0	1	6	63	62	0·9841
,, 27½	0	1	1	56	55	0·9821
,, 28½	1	1	5	54	52	0·9630
,, 29½	0	0	1	47	47	1·0000
,, 30½	3	3	8	46	40	0·8696
,, 31½	1	0	4	32	31	0·9688
,, 32½	0	0	3	27	27	1·0000
,, 33½	0	0	4	24	24	1·0000
,, 34½	0	2	3	20	18	0·9000
,, 35½	0	1	1	15	14	0·9333
,, 36½	0	1	2	13	12	0·9231
,, 37½	0	0	2	10	10	1·0000
,, 38½	0	1	3	8	7	0·8750
,, 39½	0	0	0	4	4	1·0000
,, 40½	0	1	0	4	3	0·7500
,, 41½	0	0	0	3	3	1·0000
,, 42½	0	0	0	3	3	1·0000
,, 43½	0	0	0	3	3	1·0000
,, 44½	0	0	0	3	3	1·0000
,, 45½	0	1	1	3	2	0·6667
,, 46½	0	0	0	1	1	1·0000
,, 47½	0	0	0	1	1	1·0000
,, 48½	0	1	0	0	0	0·0000
	962	165	1,173			

TABLE 69—(contd.)

8	9	10	11	12	13	14
CUMULATIVE PROPORTION SURVIVING DIVORCE AND DEATH OF WIFE	MARRIAGES SURVIVING DIVORCE	PROPORTION OF MARRIAGES SURVIVING DIVORCE	CUMULATIVE PROPORTION OF MARRIAGES SURVIVING DIVORCE	MARRIAGES SURVIVING DEATH OF WIFE	PROPORTION OF MARRIAGES SURVIVING DEATH OF WIFE	CUMULATIVE PROPORTION OF MARRIAGES SURVIVING DEATH OF WIFE
0·9691	2,237	0·9726	0·9726	2,292	0·9965	0·9965
0·9136	2,036	0·9487	0·9227	2,133	0·9939	0·9904
0·8443	1,795	0·9325	0·8604	1,909	0·9917	0·9822
0·7545	1,527	0·9030	0·7769	1,675	0·9905	0·9729
0·7046	1,338	0·9409	0·7310	1,412	0·9930	0·9661
0·6561	1,172	0·9391	0·6865	1,238	0·9920	0·9584
0·6138	1,030	0·9484	0·6511	1,072	0·9871	0·9460
0·5722	891	0·9419	0·6133	937	0·9905	0·9370
0·5382	784	0·9526	0·5842	813	0·9878	0·9256
0·5074	680	0·9484	0·5541	713	0·9944	0·9204
0·4781	595	0·9535	0·5283	617	0·9888	0·9101
0·4595	522	0·9685	0·5117	535	0·9926	0·9034
0·4377	468	0·9649	0·4937	479	0·9876	0·8922
0·4191	411	0·9693	0·4785	419	0·9882	0·8817
0·4080	370	0·8788	0·4684	376	0·9947	0·8770
0·3868	314	0·9602	0·4498	323	0·9878	0·8663
0·3767	264	0·9814	0·4414	267	0·9926	0·8599
0·3609	233	0·9790	0·4321	233	0·9790	0·8418
0·3524	207	0·9764	0·4219	212	1·0000	0·8418
0·3448	180	0·9783	0·4127	184	1·0000	0·8418
0·3159	156	0·9341	0·3855	164	0·9820	0·8266
0·3107	119	0·9835	0·3791	121	1·0000	0·8266
0·2967	108	0·9730	0·3689	109	0·9820	0·8117
0·2873	92	0·9684	0·3572	95	1·0000	0·8117
0·2806	84	0·9767	0·3489	86	1·0000	0·8117
0·2560	74	0·9250	0·3227	79	0·9875	0·8016
0·2519	63	1·0000	0·3227	62	0·9841	0·7889
0·2474	56	1·0000	0·3227	55	0·9821	0·7748
0·2382	53	0·9815	0·3167	53	0·9815	0·7605
0·2382	47	1·0000	0·3167	47	1·0000	0·7605
0·2071	43	0·9348	0·2961	43	0·9348	0·7109
0·2006	31	0·9688	0·2869	32	1·0000	0·7109
0·2006	27	1·0000	0·2869	27	1·0000	0·7109
0·2006	24	1·0000	0·2869	24	1·0000	0·7109
0·1805	20	1·0000	0·2869	18	0·9000	0·6398
0·1685	15	1·0000	0·2869	14	0·9333	0·5971
0·1555	13	1·0000	0·2869	12	0·9231	0·5512
0·1555	10	1·0000	0·2869	10	1·0000	0·5512
0·1361	8	1·0000	0·2869	7	0·8750	0·4823
0·1361	4	1·0000	0·2869	4	1·0000	0·4823
0·1021	4	1·0000	0·2869	3	0·7500	0·3617
0·1021	3	1·0000	0·2869	3	1·0000	0·3617
0·1021	3	1·0000	0·2869	3	1·0000	0·3617
0·1021	3	1·0000	0·2869	3	1·0000	0·3617
0·1021	3	1·0000	0·2869	3	1·0000	0·3617
0·0681	3	1·0000	0·2869	2	0·6667	0·2411
0·0681	1	1·0000	0·2869	1	1·0000	0·2411
0·0681	1	1·0000	0·2869	1	1·0000	0·2411
0·0000	0	0·0000	0·0000	0	0·0000	0·0000

year *less* eight that had ended in the death of the wife *less* 83 that had at the time of the enumeration not yet been exposed to a second year of risk.) Of the 2,146 exposed to a second year, 110 ended in divorce and 13 ended through the death of a wife before the end of that year. The rate of marriages surviving divorce in the second year of marriage was thus 0·9487 (Column 10), and the rate surviving termination through death of a wife was 0·9939 (Column 13). The general survival proportion was thus 0·9426 (Column 7) which, taken in conjunction with the corresponding rate for the first year, yields a cumulative survival proportion for the first and second years taken together of 0·9136 (Column 8). We can thus say, *inter alia*, that the divorce rate in the second year of marriage was appreciably higher than in the first, and that terminations through divorce and death of a wife amounted to nearly 9 per cent by the end of the second year of marriage.

Having explained the way in which Table 69 can be read, we may now examine its contents. Ignoring terminations through death of a wife for the time being, we see from Column 10 that the proportion of marriages surviving divorce did in fact vary appreciably at different periods of married life. The divorce rate in the first year was approximately 3 per cent; it rose to about 5 per cent in the second year, to about 7 per cent in the third year and to about 10 per cent in the fourth year. It then declined fairly rapidly to about 5 per cent in the tenth year and to a fairly stable rate of about 3 per cent between the fifteenth and twenty-fifth years. The cumulative effect of this divorce curve is shown in Column 11 which indicates that about 22 per cent of marriages would have ended in divorce in under four years, nearly 50 per cent in under 12 years and about 65 per cent in under 25 years. Above 25 years the rate of survival continued to increase and it seems that over a quarter of all marriages would have survived the risk of divorce for 40 years or more.

If we now ignore divorces and consider only the rate of terminations through the death of a wife, we see from Column 14 that there would have been a cumulative loss from this cause alone of under 3 per cent in the first four years, of about 9 per cent over 12 years, and of about 19 per cent over 25 years. After 25 years, however, the rate of termination through death rose fairly rapidly. Finally, if we consider the rate of loss through divorce combined with the rate of loss through the death of a wife, we find that about 25 per cent of all marriages would have ended within the first four years, about 55 per cent within 12 years, and about 72 per cent within 25 years (Column 7).

These estimates of marriage termination do not, of course, include losses through the deaths of husbands, and we would therefore expect the 'true' figures to be a little higher. Even without making an allowance for loss through the deaths of husbands, however, the figures in Table 69 suggest a general rate of termination higher than the average of approximately 5 per cent per annum suggested by the annual rates given in Table 68 for 1946–52. There is, however, no reason to expect close correspondence between the two tables. We have seen that the marriage samples used were differently constituted and, of course, the computations are specifically designed to assess different aspects of marriage termination. The two tables do not therefore cast any doubt on each other's validity. On the contrary, they can be seen as broadly concordant.

We may now compare Table 69 with Tables 70 and 71. Table 69 includes some marriages that had lasted up to nearly 50 years. It thus includes elements of marital experience from the early colonial days and it also undoubtedly includes some experiences from a wide variety of social settings of more recent times ranging from remote tribal villages, at the one extreme, to the large modern towns of Leopoldville and Elisabethville at the other. There are, however, some important advantages attached to treating all the data together. First, we have the benefit of large numbers in the table and, secondly, we are able to gain *some* working impression of marriage duration over a longer time span than when we take marriages from more recent years only. On the other hand, we are embarrassed by not having a clearly defined universe. Tables 70 and 71 are specifically designed to offset this disadvantage.[15] Both tables are constructed in the same way as Table 69, but Table 70 is based solely on marriages reported as having started in Stanleyville between 1940 and 1952, and Table 71 on marriages reported by persons living in Stanleyville at the time of the study as having started *outside* Stanleyville—whether in tribal villages or in various types of labour centres—over the same period. Comparing either the cumulative proportions of marriages surviving divorce and death (Column 8 in each table) or the cumulative proportions surviving divorce only (Column 11 in each table), we see that there are consistent differences between Table 69 on the one hand, and Tables 70 and 71 on the other. For example, the losses through divorce and death within four years amount to about 25 per cent in Table 69, but to about 22 per cent in Table 70 and to only about 14 per cent in Table 71; and losses within eight years amount to about 43 per cent, 36 per cent, and 26 per cent in the three tables taken in the same order.

The figures thus suggest that marriages established in the 1940s and up to 1952—whether inside or outside the town—were on the whole of longer duration than marriages reported as having taken place in earlier years. Here it is relevant to recall that there are many indications that the conditions under which migrants left their villages for centres of employment had improved enormously in the 1930s and 1940s, and especially that living conditions in C.E.C.'s in more recent years were undoubtedly far more conducive to relatively stable family life than they had been in the towns and labour camps of earlier years. We may thus be inclined to speculate that the above differences in marriage duration are simply a reflection of more settled times in the society as a whole. But this cannot be argued conclusively, and there are other possible explanations. It may well be that in earlier days

TABLE 70

Marriage duration table for the effective sample of marriages reported by men as having started in Stanleyville between the beginning of 1940 and the end of 1952

1	2	3	4	5	6	7	8	9	10	11
DURATION OF MARRIAGE IN YEARS	MARRIAGES ENDING IN DIVORCE	MARRIAGES TERMINATED BY DEATH OF WIFE	MARRIAGES STILL EXTANT AFTER GIVEN NUMBER OF YEARS BUT FULL DURATION UNKNOWN	MARRIAGES EXPOSED TO TERMINATION BY DIVORCE OR DEATH OF WIFE	MARRIAGES SURVIVING DIVORCE AND DEATH OF WIFE	PROPORTION OF MARRIAGES SURVIVING DIVORCE AND DEATH OF WIFE	CUMULATIVE PROPORTION SURVIVING DIVORCE AND DEATH OF WIFE	MARRIAGES SURVIVING DIVORCE	PROPORTION OF MARRIAGES SURVIVING DIVORCE	CUMULATIVE PROPORTION OF MARRIAGES SURVIVING DIVORCE
Less than 1 yr., say 6 months	4	2	40	375	369	0·9840	0·9840	371	0·9893	0·9893
Less than 2 yrs., say 1½ yrs	12	1	47	329	316	0·9605	0·9451	317	0·9635	0·9532
Say 2½	13	2	35	269	254	0·9442	0·8924	256	0·9517	0·9072
,, 3½	25	2	33	219	192	0·8767	0·7824	194	0·8858	0·8036
,, 4½	9	2	26	159	148	0·9308	0·7283	150	0·9434	0·7581
,, 5½	7	0	28	122	115	0·9426	0·6865	115	0·9426	0·7146
,, 6½	1	0	18	87	86	0·9885	0·6786	86	0·9885	0·7064
,, 7½	4	0	6	68	64	0·9412	0·6387	64	0·9412	0·6649
,, 8½	2	0	8	58	56	0·9655	0·6167	56	0·9655	0·6420
,, 9½	1	0	14	48	47	0·9792	0·6039	47	0·9792	0·6286
,, 10½	1	1	11	33	32	0·9394	0·5673	32	0·9697	0·6096
,, 11½	0	0	6	20	20	1·0000	0·5673	20	1·0000	0·6096
,, 12½	1	0	13	14	13	0·9286	0·5268	13	0·9826	0·5661
	80	10	285							

TABLE 71

Marriage duration table for the effective sample of marriages reported by men as having started outside Stanleyville between the beginning of 1940 and the end of 1952

1	2	3	4	5	6	7	8	9	10	11
DURATION OF MARRIAGE IN YEARS	MARRIAGES ENDING IN DIVORCE	MARRIAGES TERMINATED BY DEATH OF WIFE	MARRIAGES STILL EXTANT AFTER GIVEN NUMBER OF YEARS BUT FULL DURATION UNKNOWN	MARRIAGES EXPOSED TO TERMINATION BY DIVORCE OR DEATH OF WIFE	MARRIAGES SURVIVING DIVORCE AND DEATH OF WIFE	PROPORTION OF MARRIAGES SURVIVING DIVORCE AND DEATH OF WIFE	CUMULATIVE PROPORTION SURVIVING DIVORCE AND DEATH OF WIFE	MARRIAGES SURVIVING DIVORCE	PROPORTION OF MARRIAGES SURVIVING DIVORCE	CUMULATIVE PROPORTION OF MARRIAGES SURVIVING DIVORCE
Less than 1 yr., say 6 months	9	2	60	368	357	0·9701	0·9701	359	0·9755	0·9755
Less than 2 yrs., say 1½ yrs	12	2	43	297	283	0·9529	0·9244	285	0·9596	0·9361
Say 2½	8	0	40	240	232	0·9667	0·8936	232	0·9667	0·9049
„ 3½	6	1	34	192	185	0·9635	0·8610	186	0·9688	0·8767
„ 4½	7	0	30	151	144	0·9536	0·8210	144	0·9536	0·8360
„ 5½	3	0	15	114	111	0·9737	0·7994	111	0·9737	0·8140
„ 6½	6	0	20	96	90	0·9375	0·7494	90	0·9375	0·7631
„ 7½	0	0	18	70	70	1·0000	0·7494	70	1·0000	0·7631
„ 8½	3	1	13	52	48	0·9231	0·6918	49	0·9423	0·7191
„ 9½	0	0	18	35	35	1·0000	0·6918	35	1·0000	0·7191
„ 10½	0	0	6	17	17	1·0000	0·6918	17	1·0000	0·7191
„ 11½	0	1	4	11	10	0·9091	0·6289	11	1·0000	0·7191
„ 12½	1	0	5	6	5	0·8333	0·5241	5	0·8333	0·5992
	55	7	306							

disturbances in marital and family life constituted an important factor
in the selection of recruits for the town from the village populations
at large. Equally, it may be that disrupted marriages were in earlier
years a more important factor in the selection of permanent and longer-
term urban residents from amongst the mass of migrants who normally
came to town on a temporary basis. And if chequered marital histories
were indeed a factor influencing decisions either to migrate to town
or to stay there after arrival, we would expect a sample of marriages
obtained from personal histories taken in their entirety (and therefore
including many marriages from earlier years) to contain a disproportionate representation of marriages of short duration. Another distinct
possibility is that the observed differences were linked to changes over
time in the proportions of people coming to town from different areas
in the hinterland. This seems possible for we know that there were
changes in the areas of population recruitment and we shall presently
see that there were marked differences in marriage duration between
tribes. Or, yet again, it could be that the change—if indeed it was a
change and not simply a matter either of poor quality data or of built-in
selection in the samples—had come about as part of a general process of
change in the urban norms governing marriage rather than as a direct
function of one or more specific changes in patterns of recruitment or in
the social and economic environment. When we ponder this variety of
possibilities we must inevitably conclude that we have inadequate
systematic evidence for opting for one explanation rather than
another.

Somewhat similarly, it is impossible to argue conclusively on the
factors which may account for the differences shown between Tables
70 and 71, i.e. between the duration of marriages established in the
town from 1940 to 1952 and of those established outside the town over
the same period. Taken as they stand, the figures suggest that marriages
started *outside* Stanleyville were of longer duration than those embarked
upon *inside* the town, but we are again left to speculate as to the
reasons for this. Is it perhaps that, under the conditions in the C.E.C.
in the 1940s, immigrants with stable marriages were inclined to stay in
town longer than were those beset by marital difficulties? If so, this
factor in itself might have weighted the sample of *outside* marriages
reported by men living in town at the time of the study in favour of
longer duration. Men commonly complained of the difficulties of life in
town without a wife and it may be that migrants with broken marriages
were more inclined to return home than were those with stable marriages.
Equally, it could be that with the growth of urban conditions relatively
more suited to married and family life, the town was tending to
recruit from smaller labour centres disproportionate numbers of men
with more stable marriages. It may well be that the marriages of some
populations outside the town were no more stable than those contracted
in the town, but that *outside marriages coming to town* were a select category.
We have, however, no information on marriage duration in the town's

vast and varied hinterland. We cannot, therefore, argue for or against this possibility with any more confidence than we can about any of the others. Finally, of course, there is the straightforward possibility that married life in town in the 1940s was in fact less stable than it was at the same period in the villages and smaller labour centres from which most migrants came. It seems highly probable that this was so, but that outside marriages became less stable once they came to town and were then no more likely to endure than were marriages contracted locally. The longer duration of marriages shown in Table 71 would, according to this view, merely reflect the inevitable inclusion in this sample of some marital experiences in social settings other than that of the town itself.

We can speculate in these and other ways, but we have no satisfactory basis for advancing beyond speculation. Taking into account all the evidence we have, the most plausible general explanation of the three tables taken together would seem to be that marriage *in the town* was of longer duration in the 1940s than, say, in the 1920s, but that, despite this improvement over time, marriage in the town *in the 1940s* was of appreciably shorter duration than in the hinterland *at the same period*. This opinion was expressed in one form or another by a number of local inhabitants and it is clearly in keeping with two of our general assessments: the first that there had been a vast improvement in the conditions of domestic life in the town over the preceding twenty to thirty years; the second that, whatever may have been the case in the past, at the time of our study women in town had incomparably greater personal freedom than in villages and in most of the smaller labour centres of the hinterland, but that most women had established no legitimate economic roles in town to replace those they played in village life.

Whatever the differentials in marriage duration between town and village and between past and present, however, the statistical data of Tables 69–71 enable us to draw some general conclusions about marriage termination in town with a high degree of confidence. First, it is clear that many marriages failed to endure; not less than 14 per cent of all marriages reported by men—and very probably up to 20 per cent or more—failed to last four years, and somewhere between 26 and 43 per cent failed to last eight years. Secondly, all three tables suggest that the high rate of termination in the first ten years of marriage was largely accounted for by divorce rather than by death, and from the evidence of Table 69, it seems, as we would expect, that divorce continued to be the main cause of termination well beyond the tenth year. After 20 to 25 years of marriage, however, divorce became relatively infrequent as compared to the death of a wife. Thus, despite the high rate of divorce, the community had a small hard core of long-lived marital unions which normally ended through death.

If we now consider the data on marriage termination in conjunction with earlier observations on the marital status of the population at one point in time (Tables 62 and 63), we can arrive at a far more adequate assessment of the process of pairing than was previously possible.

We may first note that the high rates of marriage termination leave us in no doubt as to why there were such relatively large proportions of men and women living singly at the time of the study despite the very small proportions of persons in the middle and upper adult age categories who had never been married. We know from Table 63, for example, that 25·6 per cent of all men aged 46–55 years were living singly but that the largest sub-categories of 'single' men consisted of divorcees and widowers, and that those who had never been married constituted only 3·5 per cent of the total or about one seventh of all those without domestic partners. Similarly, although only 25·6 per cent of men aged 46–55 were 'single' we know from Table 66 that 67·4 per cent of the ever-wedded in this age category had experienced divorce at least once and that 23·7 per cent had been widowers at least once. The high rate of marriage termination clearly ties in with these observations. If we now relate the corresponding information for the remaining age categories of men, as well as for the various age categories of women, to our findings on marriage duration, the general inferences to be drawn are clear. Men married at an appreciably higher age than women but the vast majority of them did marry as did the vast majority of women; very substantial proportions of men and women were, however, again released into the community as 'single' persons during the course of their lives with the result that there was a constant pool of previously married persons living without domestic partners. This pool contained over 20 per cent of all men in the town aged 26 years or more and over 17 per cent of all women aged 26 years or more. Over time many of these men and women entered new domestic unions but their places in the pool of persons living singly were then largely taken by others coming out of marriage. We know from case histories, and from every-day observations, that in the intervals between marriages men and women commonly entered into non-marital unions, and we can infer from our tables that this was the practice of many men of all ages and of many women in the younger and middle age categories though not in the older age categories. But, since the average duration of non-marital partnerships was relatively short, the proportions of persons found at one point in time to be living with partners to whom they were not married was low: for men the proportion rose from 2·2 per cent between 16 and 25 years to a peak of 7·9 per cent between 46 and 55 years; for women it rose from 2·9 per cent between 16 and 25 years to a peak of 8·2 per cent between 36 and 45 years of age (Tables 63 and 64).[16]

VARIATIONS IN MARRIAGE DURATION BETWEEN THE NINE PRINCIPAL ETHNIC COLONIES

Having considered various aspects of the pattern of pairing in the town population as a whole, I now turn to variations *within* the community—first, between tribes and then, in the next section, between neighbourhoods. In Chapter IV we noted marked differences in the fertility ratios of different tribes and in the marital status of their members. We may recall, for example, that amongst the Lokele only 7·5 per cent of women and 2·8 per cent of men were recorded as divorced and living singly (Tables 18 and 19), whereas amongst the Babua the corresponding proportions were as high as 21·8 per cent for women and 20·2 per cent for men (Tables 20 and 21). Again, the fertility ratio for the Lokele rose to the high level of 983 (compared to an average of 489 for the total population of the town), whereas the corresponding figure for the Babua was only 181 (Table 24). Differences of this order of magnitude point to marked variations in the nature of the social situations confronting men and women within different tribal colonies, and we would obviously expect knowledge of marriage duration curves to contribute to a fuller assessment of these variations. Conversely, of course, an analysis of tribal differentials in marriage termination rates can be expected to contribute to a fuller appreciation of the patterns of pairing in the population as a whole.

Marriage duration curves were therefore calculated for the nine largest ethnic colonies in the town and selected items from these tables are given in a form convenient for inter-tribal comparison in Table 72. The figures show that the Lokele, who represent Type 1 of the classification established in Chapter IV, had marriages of appreciably longer duration than the colonies of Type 2 (the Bambole, Balengola, and Topoke), while these in turn had marriages of longer duration than

TABLE 72

Proportions of marriages reported by men in the nine largest ethnic colonies as having ended through divorce within specified periods

ETHNIC COLONY	TYPE OF COLONY ACCORDING TO CLASSIFICATION USED IN CHAPTER IV	PER CENT MARRIAGES TERMINATED WITHIN 4 YEARS	PER CENT MARRIAGES TERMINATED WITHIN 8 YEARS	PER CENT MARRIAGES TERMINATED WITHIN 12 YEARS	PER CENT MARRIAGES TERMINATED WITHIN 20 YEARS
Lokele	Type 1	13	21	30	37
Bambole	Type 2	18 ⎫	31 ⎫	35 ⎫	
Balengola	Type 2	21 ⎬20	27 ⎬31	41 ⎬36	53
Topoke	Type 2	22 ⎭	33 ⎭	38 ⎭	
Bamanga	Intermediate	21 ⎫	31 ⎫	47 ⎫	
Bakumu	Intermediate	24 ⎬23	43 ⎬39	51 ⎬49	56
Babali	Type 3	23 ⎫	44 ⎫	52 ⎫	
Babua	Type 3	23 ⎬24	46 ⎬45	55 ⎬55	63
Arabisés	Type 3	25 ⎭	39 ⎭	56 ⎭	
All colonies in the town	—	22	39	49	59

Note: The full tribal duration curves on which the table is based are not reproduced in this volume. They may be obtained on request from The Secretary, Department of Social Anthropology and Sociology, University of Manchester, Manchester 13.

colonies of Type 3 (the Babua, Babali, and *Arabisés*). And the Bamanga and Bakumu, who were classified as 'intermediate' cases (in Chapter IV), again fall between the colonies of Type 2 and those of Type 3.

The degree of correspondence between marriage duration and 'type' of colony thus appears to be remarkably high, and this leads us in the first instance to question the reliability of our samples for we know that the colonies of Types 1 and 2 contained higher proportions of recent immigrants than those of Type 3 (Chapter IV, Table 27). Could it be that the lower marriage durations shown for colonies of Type 3 are entirely a consequence of their samples containing disproportionate elements of urban marital experience? To test this possibility, two duration curves specific to marriages established *in town* between 1940 and 1952 were drawn up. The first of these duration curves was for marriages reported by men from the colonies of Types 1 and 2 taken together, and the second was based on the colonies of Type 3 taken as one sample. The curves revealed that the urban marriages of men from colonies of Types 1 and 2 terminated at the rate of approximately 16 per cent within four years and 24 per cent within eight years, whereas the corresponding figures for the colonies of Type 3 were about 21 per cent and 36 per cent. Taken in conjunction with the rest of the analysis these findings are convincing evidence of appreciable differences between the two sets of tribes and we may therefore proceed to consider the inter-tribal differences shown in Table 72.

The high degree of association between rates of marriage termination and 'types' of population suggests a strong positive correlation between longer marriage duration and high fertility, and a glance at the ranking of tribes according to their fertility ratios (Chapter IV, Table 24) clearly confirms this. But, as explained in Chapter IV, differential fertility was not the sole factor contributing to the distinctive social configurations of the three 'types' of population. Differing patterns of migration and differing modes of urban incorporation were also undoubtedly involved. Moreover, we have strong evidence to suggest that differential tribal fertility in the town was closely related to corresponding differences between the various parent populations in the hinterland. It therefore seems that the association of low divorce rates, longer marriage duration and high fertility must be viewed not only in relation to the urban situations of the tribes concerned, but also, very crucially, in relation to their rural social structures and to the way in which these were related to various patterns of migration.[18] We do not have the necessary information to pursue this analysis satisfactorily, but we can attempt some further assessment of the relation between the complex of high fertility and more stable marriage and differing types of urban social configurations.[19]

In the case of the Lokele we find a striking example of a particular combination of seemingly related factors. We know that their high fertility made for larger families and for extensive networks of immediate kin both in town and country. We also know that the tribe had close trading links with its rural area and that this was related to a high measure of female participation in the local urban markets. These features of their overall situation were in turn related to very much higher bridewealth payments than was usual in other tribes, and to a high degree of continued involvement of rural tribesmen in the affairs of their urban kinsmen and *vice versa*. We may also recall that the commercial success of Lokele women in town had been matched from the earliest days of urban settlement by considerable success on the part of their men in the competition for education and higher paid jobs. Finally, we know that, associated with all these factors, the tribe constituted an exceptionally exclusive colony with a marked tendency to stress familism and tribalism as group values and to expect their women to adhere to a strict code of sexual morality. It was said in the town that there were no Lokele prostitutes and very few Lokele *femmes libres*, and we have seen that our figures on the marital status of adult women seem to bear this out. (Chapter IV, Table 18.) The Lokele were thus a people who had succeeded in maintaining considerable continuity and harmony between their rural and urban values, and the relative stability of their marriages in town must be seen in the context of this group achievement and in relation to their distinctive social configuration.

The three colonies of Type 2 had several features in common with the Lokele: they all came from the same geographical area south of Stanleyville, they had a certain cultural affinity with them, and they all showed a similar complex of large families maintaining close links with rural kinsfolk. Like the Lokele, too, they kept a close watch over their wives and they had very few women leading independent lives in town.[20] But there were also some important differences between these tribes and the Lokele in histories of urban settlement and in the nature and content of their close relations with their home villages. As explained in Chapter IV, the Topoke in particular were very late arrivals on the urban scene, and the Balengola and Bambole also migrated to town in large numbers for the first time when the Lokele were already well established there. In addition, none of the tribes of Type 2 had the singular advantages which the Lokele enjoyed for maintaining a steady trade in agricultural produce between town and country. These differences had far-reaching consequences. Although the women of tribes of Type 2 normally traded as and when they found the opportunity, they were perforce much less involved in market life than were Lokele women and, like the Topoke, all colonies of Type 2 had thus far met with relatively little success in establishing themselves in town. (See the occupational distributions given in Chapter IV, Table 32, and the information given in Table 29 on dwelling compound 'ownership'.) Their relative failure to prosper as urban-dwellers led them to cling to their village connexions for security, and many of their men were young migrant labourers who stayed in town without abandoning their essentially rural-tribal orientations. Tribal morality thus continued to hold sway amongst these populations as an integral feature of a particular kind of rural-urban accommodation. The form of this accommodation, unlike that of the Lokele, was partly determined by their failure to break into better-paid jobs and was in itself an important factor militating against deeper involvement in other spheres of urban life. There was thus a tendency for adherence to tribal morality to perpetuate itself, and this was markedly reflected in relations between the sexes.

The particular histories of our three colonies of Type 3—the Babua, Babali, and *Arabisés*—differed very appreciably one from the other. In sharp contrast to the colonies of Type 2, however, they had all established themselves locally either during the early days of the town's growth or, in the case of the *Arabisés*, even earlier. All three were still receiving new immigrants from the countryside but these made up appreciably smaller proportions of their total populations than was the case in the colonies of Types 1 and 2. (Chapter IV, Table 27.) This in itself lessened the importance of rural connexions for them, as did also the very fact of their low fertility and small families. In addition, their relations with home villages were for reasons of history and geography largely devoid of economic content. This was especially true of the Babua and Babali. The case of the *Arabisés* was somewhat different in that an appreciable proportion of their men were full-time traders. Their trade was, however, not so much with agricultural villages in the hinterland as with other *Arabisés* settlements around small transport centres, and it did not involve the women of the colony as in the case of the Lokele. The womenfolk of all three colonies of Type 3 were thus almost totally excluded from the regular market life of the town. On the other hand, they were very much involved in intermittent petty trading on their compounds and in prostitution and semi-prostitution.[21] And there were a fair number who were small shopkeepers and land-ladies on the scale of Christine in Avenue 21. Bridewealth payments were lower than in the colonies of Type 2 and very much lower than among the Lokele. At the same time, the men tended to be much more involved in town life: high proportions of them were title-holders of dwelling compounds (Chapter IV, Table 29) and often these title-holders were landlords; in addition their occupational skills were, with the exception of the Babali, well above the average for the urban population as a whole (Chapter IV, Table 32).

The striking differences between the social configurations associated with higher and with lower marriage durations underline the diversity that existed in the community. Low fertility was associated with short marriage duration and the two existed in a social context vastly different from that of high fertility and longer marriage duration. Yet these markedly different contexts were found side by side in a single community. Within this community people were perforce engaged in a constant process of assessing each other's actions and of learning and appraising each other's norms and values; all inhabitants were in this way led to modify their own behaviour—and their expectations of other people's behaviour—to a greater or lesser extent. This prompts a variety of general questions as to whether the differing social contexts were tending to merge. Were the differences between the tribal colonies in fact being blurred over time? And, specifically to the particular question of relations between the sexes: was there over time any diminution in the ethnic differentials in marriage duration? Unfortunately, the field information I have on marriages does not allow me to answer these questions in a direct way. Nor does the nature and size of our sample even allow us to ascertain at all conclusively whether marriages between members of the same tribe were any more stable than marriages between members of different tribes.[22] On the other hand, we can at this stage profitably begin to relate our general findings in this chapter to earlier observations on the nature and composition of different neighbourhoods in the town, and in doing this we are able to move towards tentative answers to general questions of the kind posed above.

RELATIONS BETWEEN MEN AND WOMEN IN DIFFERING NEIGHBOURHOODS

In Chapter V we noted marked differences between neighbourhoods in various social and demographic characteristics that have a direct bearing on relations between the sexes. We may recall, for example, that between four selected neighbourhoods—Neighbourhoods I, II, III and IV—there were important variations in the sex ratio, in the fertility ratio, and in the proportions of women living singly (Chapter V, Table 41). Given such variations, it would be of singular interest to know whether marriage duration also varied between these neighbourhoods. The question has far-reaching implications for any attempt to assess our detailed observations on daily life in Avenue 21 in relation to the wider community. To what extent were there special factors affecting relations between the sexes in particular localities? And, by implication, to what extent can we assume that the general findings on the pairing of men and women and on their turn-over in marriage and in other sexual partnerships held good for the environs of Avenue 21 in Neighbourhood III? Here again the field data we have do not allow me to seek any direct answers,[23] but we can in the case of certain neighbourhoods arrive at useful working impressions by relating marriage duration rates for the tribes known to be well represented in particular areas to more general indicators of relations between the sexes in these localities. With this in mind, the situations of Neighbourhoods I, III, and IV are of particular interest.

We have seen that Neighbourhood I had developed partly as a fashionable area containing disproportionate numbers of *évolués* and of higher status *femmes libres*, and partly as a crowded and busy area in which there were numerous rent-paying tenants. The population was very mixed ethnically and the Babua—the only tribe to be appreciably 'over-represented' there—constituted less than a quarter of the total population. The sex ratio was low (105 men per 100 women), yet the proportions of adults who were married were only 53·9 per cent for men and 56·3 per cent for women (Appendix B, Tables 82 and 83) as against 64·0 per cent and 69·7 per cent in the total population of the town (Tables 62 and 63). These differences point to the fact that there were many women in the neighbourhood leading independent lives. The area tended to attract single, divorced, and widowed women who made a living there as prostitutes and semi-prostitutes in their young and middle years, and as small shopkeepers and landladies in later life. In keeping with these characteristics, the fertility ratio for the area was only 354 (Chapter V, Table 42), which was lower than for any other neighbourhood examined in detail and well below the average of 489 for the town (Chapter IV, Table 24). Taking all these facts into account it is virtually certain that marriages in the neighbourhood were of substantially lower duration than were those of the population at large. Even if we accept this conclusion, however, we cannot know the extent to which marriage duration in the neighbourhood was a consequence of selection rather than a function of social forces *in the area*, but on general grounds we would expect the two to go hand in hand.

Neighbourhood IV presented a striking contrast to Neighbourhood I. We may recall that some 80 per cent of its inhabitants were Lokele and that the neighbourhood was noted as a trading area. As we would expect of a predominantly Lokele population, high proportions of the adults were married—67·1 per cent of the men and 73·2 per cent of the women (Appendix B, Tables 88 and 89), as against the corresponding proportions of 53·9 per cent and 56·3 per cent in Neighbourhood I. Also in notable contrast to Neighbourhood I, the population of women 'living singly' consisted mainly of young spinsters staying with their families rather than of widows and divorcees leading independent lives. And the fertility ratio of over 912 was close to that of the Lokele population at large. Bearing these observations in mind, it seems highly likely that marriage duration in the neighbourhood was correspondingly high.

Neighbourhood III in turn differed appreciably from Neighbourhood IV, but in quite different ways. We know from Chapter IV, as well as from the description of Avenue 21 in Chapter VI, that the neighbourhood was a quiet area of the town where the level of wages was low, where the renting of accommodation had only recently begun, and where there were many recent immigrants living either with 'real' or 'fictitious' kin. The population was ethnically mixed though not as heterogeneous as in Neighbourhood I, and there were marked clusters of particular tribes. The most important of these were the Babali and Bakumu, both of whom were substantially 'over-represented' in the area. There was also a marked cluster of Barumbi, a small colony in the town, which had a social configuration very similar to that of the Babali. Between them these three tribes constituted about 60 per cent of the population. The quiet atmosphere and low average wages in the neighbourhood made it relatively unattractive for women living independently by providing men with illicit or semi-illicit services. As we saw in Avenue 21, however, the demand for such services was increasing, but few *femmes libres* had as yet come to the area and the adult sex ratio remained high—121 men to 100 women as compared to 105 in Neighbourhood 1. The proportion of women who were married was 67·6 per cent as against 56·3 per cent in Neighbourhood I (Appendix B, Tables 87 and 83), and the fertility ratio of 482 was appreciably higher than in Neighbourhood I, but no higher than the average for the town. Taking account of the tribal composition of the area in relation to these indicators, it seems certain that marriage duration in the area was no longer than the average for the town, and it may well have been shorter. In general, then, it is reasonable to conclude that specific instances of social relations between men and women in Avenue 21 reported in Chapters VI and VII were being enacted in a context of values far less conservative than that of some other areas in the town, such as Neighbourhood IV, yet markedly less libertine than in fashionable areas like Neighbourhood I.

IMPLICATIONS OF NEIGHBOURHOOD CONTRASTS FOR THE ASSESSMENT OF SOCIAL RELATIONS IN AVENUE 21

To emphasize the significance of the above contrasts, I now re-state them with more specific reference to the nature of social relations. Whereas Neighbourhood IV had large families, a relatively exclusive population of Lokele, stable marriages with high bridewealth payments and a high degree of family involvements, and dense networks of 'real' kinship ties, the neighbourhood of Avenue 21 had smaller families, less stable marriages and more 'individualization', far fewer interconnections between 'real' kinsmen and a population which was more heterogeneous tribally. These differences were in turn directly associated with a much higher incidence in Avenue 21 and its environs of 'fictitious' relations of kinship and with a weaker and more flexible system of social control over relations between men and women. Thus, although Lusaka's behaviour and conduct in regard to his wife Antoinette and to his '*fiancée*' Bernadette, were subject to a series of pressures from kinsmen, friends, and neighbours, they were not subject to any single overriding or insistent influence from any one source as was the case for the Lokele women whose marriages were to a much greater extent controlled by their immediate families and 'real' kinsmen. Equally, Limela's actions in relation to Maria and her 'fictitious' kinsmen represent a type of behaviour that was readily sanctioned and recognized as appropriate in the area, but which would have been totally out of place in the social context of 'the Lokele area' of Neighbourhood IV. Yet again, situations like that of Patrice, where the relations between a husband and wife were embedded within a network which, close-knit though it was, consisted mainly of 'fictitious' kin and fellow-Warega rather than 'real' kin, were more common in Avenue 21 and its environs than 'in the Lokele area'. In general, 'fictitious' kinship and 'semi-institutionalized' relationships between men and women, as well as *between men* and *between women*, constituted a far more important element in the texture of social relations in Avenue 21 and its environs than in Neighbourhood IV. Indeed, the high incidence of 'fictitious' and 'semi-institutionalized' relationships emerges from our analysis as an important factor of social integration in an area where the composition of the population and the situation of many individuals militated against the continued operation of traditional tribal controls. In this social context the permissive and flexible relations between the sexes fulfilled a positive function. As the case of Limela and Maria shows, a sexual liaison between a man and a woman could lead to the development of 'semi-institutionalized' social relations between men who would not otherwise have had direct and close contact outside working situations.

The second contrast of particular interest is between Avenue 21 and Neighbourhood I. The population in and around Avenue 21 was tribally heterogeneous, but it contained a more limited and less diverse range of tribal elements than that of Neighbourhood I; at the same time it was *relatively* uniform in occupational composition and in earning power. On the other hand, Neighbourhood I had a mixture of more diverse ethnic elements, a greater diversity of 'urban types' (which included *évolués* and *femmes libres*) and a much wider socio-economic range. In addition, we know that Neighbourhood I provided considerably more anonymity and impersonality than did the neighbourhood of Avenue 21 where people were unwittingly involved in each others' affairs and were continually led to identify and study each other. This is in keeping with our evidence on relations between the sexes in Neighbourhood I where it would seem that many sexual liaisons were considerably more 'individualistic' and did not normally carry the same implications for the kinsmen, friends, and 'brothers' of the partners as in Avenue 21 and its environs.

FOOTNOTES TO CHAPTER VIII

[1] Southall (1961), p. 50.

[2] The independence of *femmes libres* was the subject of constant comment on the part of men. The tone of the comment was often critical and sometimes resentful. The following free translation from Swahili of a song by a local guitarist illustrates a regular theme in discussions on the relationship between a *femme libre* and one of her 'lovers'.

    I. *Chérie*, you wander about the town; *chérie*, why do you roam around?
       You have a lover, why do you hang about?
       (The woman laughs) I am not a fool to wander about for nothing.
    II. Dear woman, you are always out and about;
       I come at mid-day and you are not there;
       I come in the evenings and you are not there;
       Surely you must have been with other men.
       (The woman laughs) I am not a fool to wander about for nothing.

III. *Madame*, you are always in the town;
   You ask me for a cloth of *mapomboli**, and for a headscarf, and a necklace too;
   Do you take me to be a supplier of goods for the benefit of other men?
   (The woman laughs) I am not a fool to wander about for nothing.
IV. Daughter of a father, ask other women who have seen the daylight;
   When you meet them, you will see that they have all they want;
   You will smoke, you will drink beer, and you will eat well;
   And you will see that they all have one lover only;
   To such a woman I would give everything, to give a *mapomboli* would be nothing;
   I would give whole-heartedly, and do nothing but give;
   What you have asked for is nothing as to what I would give.
   (The woman laughs) I am not a fool to wander about for nothing.

* *Mapomboli* is a cloth of a particular design.

[3] Similar results have been reported from the Copperbelt. See Mitchell (1961c), p. 9.

[4] Women sometimes maintained in a semi-jocular way that in town it was essential for a wife to have a lover to whom she could turn in times of hardship. While this view was certainly common, it is difficult to know how widespread the practice was. My general impression, based largely on cases in and around Avenue 21, is that many married women commonly entered into extra-marital associations from time to time, but that few found it possible to do so with any regularity or to keep one lover for a prolonged period.

[5] Southall (1961), p. 52.

[6] Such attitudes were marked in Brazzaville which was in several respects very similar to Stanleyville. See Balandier (1955), Chapter V.

[7] Official statistics on population and taxation returns allow us to gain some impression of the extent of polygyny in the Eastern Province in 1951. The total adult population of the province consisted of 747,130 men and 737,494 women. Of the 747,130 men, 110,107 had more than one wife, and these 110,107 men had 257,846 wives between them. There were thus 2·34 wives per polygynously married man. If, for working purposes, we assume that all adult women were married, the total number of 737,494 women would have consisted of 257,846 or 35·0 per cent who were married to men with more than one wife each and 479,648 or 65·0 per cent who were the sole wives of their respective husbands. On the same assumption, the total of 747,130 men would have fallen into the following categories: 110,107 or 14·7 per cent married to more than one wife, 479,648 or 64·2 per cent married to one wife only, and 157,375 or 21·1 per cent unmarried. It would seem that about a third of all women were married to polygynous men and a fifth of all married men were polygynous. The basic figures used here are from the *Rapport Annuel: Affaires Indigènes et Main-d'œuvre, Province Orientale*, 1951.

[8] The distinctions drawn in this section also derive from the account of 77 Stanleyville marriage histories analysed in Clément (1956), pp. 378–438.

[9] A registered marriage was referred to in everyday language as a marriage 'of the book', and a woman whose marriage was registered in this way was spoken of as 'a wife or woman of the book'. The act of registering a marriage had become an integral part of the process of getting married in town. Registration was not legally binding but there was a tendency to regard it as conferring special status on a marriage.

[10] Civil marriages were contracted according to the Belgian Civil Code. In the very early days of Belgian administration civil marriages were compulsory for soldiers and for officials of the State, but the number contracted in recent decades was negligible. For detailed references to the legal provisions governing marriage, see Clément (1956), p. 378.

[11] The urban courts had no jurisdiction over marriages contracted between partners according to Christian rites, and all cases of such marriages were automatically referred to a higher court presided over by a European official. As this case shows, however, the urban courts did not necessarily consider a customary marriage to be null and void because the man still had a pre-existing Christian marriage. According to customary law, second and subsequent marriages were legal, and in judging a divorce case the urban courts did not normally inquire into the husband's previous marital status.

[12] The approach to the measurement of marriage stability in this and the following sections derives from the work of Barnes (1951) and Mitchell (1961b).

[13] Since it was usual for the urban courts to refuse to judge the case of a man and a woman who had married in their tribal area, there were many cases of couples returning home to arrange a divorce, and often the man stayed at home for a period of two to three months or more. I have included all such cases in this and other tables to follow as divorces of men 'based in town'.

[14] The technique is fully explained in Mitchell (1961b).

[15] Tables 70 and 71 also tend to offset a further distinct disadvantage of Table 69. Basing our computation on marriages drawn from marital histories in their entirety inevitably means that we are partly basing our duration estimates on recollections and retrospective reconstructions of events that occurred early in the life histories of some elderly people. We would expect such data to be of somewhat doubtful accuracy, and Table 69 contains clear evidence that in many cases the durations of marriages of longer standing were in fact little more than informed guesses. For example, it can be seen that we recorded a total of 46 marriages either ending or still extant in their 20th year as against only 17 in their 19th year and 10 in their 21st year. A close inspection of the figures for other round-number years shows that bunching of this kind is more pronounced the further back we go in time.

[16] In compiling these figures an attempt was made to exclude non-marital unions arranged on an *ad hoc* basis for a specifically limited period. They thus exclude all cases of women engaged as 'substitute wives' by men whose regular wives were away from town for a pregnancy or simply to visit kinsmen in a tribal village. There were of course a number of marginal cases that could not easily be classified. In general, however, the practice of engaging a 'substitute wife' for a limited period was so well recognized in the community that most cases were easy to distinguish. The average duration of such arrangements was three to six months.

[17] Absolute numbers in the separate tribal colonies were much too small to allow for separate computations specific to recent urban marriages for each tribe. The tribal marriage duration curves were therefore drawn up on the same basis as Table 69.

[18] Apart from common sense and the evidence from Stanleyville there are very strong indications from work on the Copperbelt that we are not likely to arrive at an understanding of the general problem of marriage stability in towns without taking account of differing tribal structures. See the argument in Mitchell (1961c).

[19] In view of the suggestion originally made by Gluckman (1950) that duration of marriage can be expected to vary significantly between societies organized on the basis of corporate patrilineages and those organized on the basis of matrilineages, it is important to recall that all the tribes referred to here are essentially patrilineal. Whether predictions deriving from Gluckman's hypothesis can be expected to hold good under urban conditions is discussed in Mitchell (1961d). As far as I am aware, there are as yet no adequate studies of the nine principal tribes in Stanleyville to enable us to test the predictions made by Mitchell on the basis of derivations from Gluckman's original hypothesis.

[20] The relevant figures for the Topoke are given in Chapter IV, Table 22. The figures for the Bambole and Balengola were similar. The three tribes taken together yielded a sample of 202 women between the ages of 16 and 45 years and, of these, only 15 (7·4 per cent) were recorded as unmarried (i.e. either living singly or with a man to whom not married). This figure was even lower than the corresponding proportion of 14·9 per cent for the Lokele.

[21] This is reflected in the high proportions of Babua women found to be living singly. (Chapter IV, Table 20.) The corresponding figures for the *Arabisés* and Babali were not quite as high but still very much higher than the average for the town. Taken as one sample, the *Arabisés*, Babua, and Babali had a total of 395 women between the ages of 16 and 45 years. Of these, 129 or 43·7 per cent were unmarried as against 14·9 per cent among the Lokele and 7·4 per cent among the tribes of Type 2.

[22] In an attempt to broach this question I drew up duration curves specific to tribal and to non-tribal marriages. The curves suggested that tribal marriages were of slightly longer duration than non-tribal marriages. Knowing the extent to which marriage duration varied between tribes, however, we cannot attach much importance to this finding without supporting evidence from duration curves specific to marriages between members of particular tribes or of particular categories of tribes known to have longer or shorter marriage durations. Our sample did not warrant the breakdowns required for a more detailed analysis: it contained many more non-tribal marriages between members of tribes known to have short marriage durations than between members of tribes known to have long marriage durations; and it contained far fewer marriages between members of 'short-duration' and 'long-duration' tribes than between tribes with marriages of similar duration. The evidence is thus quite inconclusive, though *it would seem to point* to the shorter duration of non-tribal marriages.

[23] We know that the neighbourhoods were changing and developing over time and that, although they were *relatively* self-contained areas socially, they were by no means discrete units. Moreover, there was constant residential movement between them. Duration curves computed on the basis of marriages reported by men living in one neighbourhood

rather than another would therefore be impossibly difficult to interpret unless we also had detailed knowledge of the past movements within the town of all men falling in our samples. I do not have this information and, even if it were available, it seems very unlikely that we could have much confidence in duration curves hopefully designed to test for differences between neighbourhoods in this way.

PART FOUR

SUMMARY AND
CONCLUSIONS

IX

AVENUE 21 AND THE WIDER COMMUNITY

The study of Stanleyville was launched in an attempt to explore and delineate aspects of social relations in an African town about which very little was previously known in any systematic way; as written up in this book, however, it is also an attempt to test and validate a series of inter-related concepts which together constitute the most suggestive analytical framework so far developed in the study of African towns. There are thus two broad aspects that call for final comment and evaluation. In sections I and II of this final chapter I recall the nature of the original investigations reported and the way in which the analysis of the field observations was developed. At the same time I briefly re-assess the main inferences that can be drawn when the analysis of Avenue 21 is related to the African community as a whole. In section III, I then go on to consider the relevance of the study to the general task of constructing models suitable for the analysis of African towns.

I

We have seen that the two field investigations on which the book is based were essentially exploratory in nature. The social survey was launched primarily to assemble basic social and demographic data on the total population, and the 'community study' of Avenue 21 was a simple and straightforward attempt to obtain detailed first-hand information on day-to-day life and on the nature of social relations in what was thought to be an ordinary and unexceptional neighbourhood. As the two investigations were conducted concurrently, the study of the avenue was inevitably begun with little conception of any but the most readily discernible differences between its neighbourhood and other parts of the town. Casual observation had revealed that the avenue formed part of a quiet area in which there were very few évolués as compared to some other parts, and it was equally apparent that the ethnic heterogeneity of the people stood in striking contrast to the homogeneity of the population in areas like the *Arabisé* village and 'the Lokele quarter' in Belge II. But the nature and extent of a whole series of further differences were much less readily apparent and were for the most part only established as a result of systematic inquiry. Thus in launching the study of Avenue 21 I had no means of knowing that, for example, the sex ratio in the neighbourhood of the avenue was appreciably higher than in most parts of the town, or that the population of women who were married was well above the mean, or

that there was in the tribally heterogeneous population a clear dominance of a certain combination of tribes, or that the area had a rapidly
increasing number of tenant households and that these were mainly
members of tribes which were poorly represented among the title-
holders of dwelling compounds. Still less was I aware that neighbourhoods within the three townships of the C.E.C. exhibited any regular
ecological patterns, or that tribal representation in these neighbourhoods bore any particular relation to the routes of access to the town
from various tribal areas in the hinterland, or that some tribal colonies
had such markedly different social and demographic configurations.
These and associated features of the demographic and ecological structure of the community were all 'discoveries' which were to a limited
extent made through casual observation in the field but which only
emerged clearly from the later analysis of the survey data. Initially I
thus had little conception of the kind of questions to ask in Avenue
21 if my study was to yield information capable of interpretation as
part of an analysis of the system of social relations in the wider community, and I began my fieldwork with very modest aims of getting
to know the social atmosphere and of establishing a base from which
I could conduct systematic investigations. Knowing very little about
the way of life and basic values of the people, virtually all observations
were of some interest at this stage.

As explained in Chapter VI, however, several prominent features of
the avenue situation soon attracted my attention and these automatically led me to isolate certain broad aspects of social relations as particularly calling for systematic study in view of the community's ethnically
heterogeneous population and of its rapidly growing numbers. Thus
I soon became interested in the contrast between the insecure position
of newcomers and the secure position of the better-established residents;
I noticed the marked urban orientation of some inhabitants and the
persisting rural orientation of others; and I was forcibly struck by the
high rate of population turn-over and by the fleeting and transitory
nature of many inter-personal relations. Yet I also noticed that
despite the high turn-over of many inhabitants, anonymity was almost
impossible, and I came to see that many well-established residents
maintained social relations of an enduring nature. As I began to
distinguish between different types and categories of social relations, I
began to appreciate the significance in status ascription and status
evaluation of the distinction between 'civilized' and 'uncivilized'
persons, but I also found that tribal affiliation and kinship retained far-
reaching importance as principles according to which some people
were drawn together and others were set apart.

These early observations largely determined the kind of question
which dominated my subsequent fieldwork in the avenue: how were
diverse norms and differing principles of association applied and
operated in the same general situation and how were social relations
maintained in a situation containing so much fluidity and diversity?

As the field work developed, several partial answers began to emerge.

In the first place, I noticed that most inhabitants participated in only a few of the numerous types of 'small group' interactions described in Chapter VI. Some people were clearly equipped with a wider variety of norms than others and, indeed, very few had both the facility and the opportunity to participate in the *whole* range of relationships observed. In general, more diversified participation was only possible for those who enjoyed the combination of a long experience of urban life with a sound knowledge of the particular neighbourhood. In this connexion we may recall the important contrast drawn between Lusaka who was a 'civilized' urban-bred man with connexions in a considerable number of differing groups and networks, and Patrice who was a poorly 'civilized' newcomer with few pre-existing social connexions and access to relatively few groupings. Yet long urban residence did not of itself necessarily lead to diversified participation; there were in the avenue urbanites of long standing whose active involvement was confined to a range of relationships as narrow or narrower than that of Patrice. Such men were usually 'uncivilized' persons who seemed to exhibit a definite resistance to more 'civilized' norms. In many cases they were persons who were sometimes referred to by young 'civilized' men in terms which tended to imply that their lack of 'civilization' was related to their age; they were seen as men 'who had been left behind by "civilization".' They were commonly persons who remained in close contact with rural tribesmen and whose lives were in many cases still significantly linked to those of their kinsmen in tribal areas. In contrast, the majority of the more 'civilized' men with long urban experience were persons who saw themselves essentially as townsmen and who had in many cases openly rejected rural-tribal life. In spite of their more 'civilized' orientations, however, these townsmen often associated quite readily with kinsmen and fellow tribesmen who were less 'civilized' than themselves. Such a mixture of participation in 'civilized' and 'uncivilized' circles sometimes led a man like Lusaka to modify his conduct in various ways; on the whole, however, it was not a source of serious social embarrassment as it could be in areas with better established groupings of more 'civilized' men. Conversely, the fact of being 'uncivilized' was not, in this avenue, as decisive a factor in excluding a man from general participation as it could be in areas where the range between the more 'civilized' and the less 'civilized' was greater. Recent immigrants were on the whole relatively 'uncivilized', but they displayed varying inclinations and aptitudes for learning new ways with the result that some newcomers were distinctly less 'civilized' (or more 'uncivilized') than others. If we then further recall the high degree of ethnic heterogeneity in the population and the tendency for the members of any tribe to associate more readily with fellow tribesmen than with non-tribesmen, and also, quite commonly, with members of certain particular tribes rather than with others, it can be appreciated that there were numerous possible combinations of distinctions on the basis of which associates could be selected for various social occasions. In general, 'civilized' men with long records of urban residence clearly enjoyed much wider opportunities for selecting the persons with whom they wished to associate then did 'uncivilized' newcomers, but some limited degree of choice was usually possible even for those with little 'civilization' and with no pre-existing relationships in the area.

Secondly, the high turn-over of population, the fluidity of many social groupings, and the frequently blurred lines of social demarcation, combined with variations in degree of 'civilization' and with diversity of cultural background to create a situation in which people were often uncertain as what to expect from others. This led to a great deal of behaviour taking place on the basis of trial and error. Thus, by a seeming paradox, uncertainty of expectation was a factor indirectly inducing and promoting processes of adjustment. A newcomer who in the first instance failed to establish satisfactory 'ego-centred' relations found himself impelled either to move to another neighbourhood or, alternatively, to continue probing his existing environment for a set or sets of associates. Tentative, exploratory, and often semi-jocular inter-actions were commonly accepted as a normal part of daily life. Disturbing and provocative actions, or simply a general failure to adapt to the local situation, were on occasions partially excused on the grounds that 'he is not "civilized"' or 'that he is of such-and-such a tribe'. Instances of social mistakes and unsatisfactory encounters leading to quarrels and abuse were thus matched by others in which social relations were forged and developed by virtue of a sense of tolerance stemming from the recognition that one or other participant could not, given his background and circumstances, be expected to know any better. Here we may recall the experiences of Patrice who, in his early months in town, was alternately bullied and deceived by some people and tolerantly teased and helped by others. Both forms of experience were essential parts of the inter-related processes of learning new ways of behaviour and of establishing a viable set of social relations. It is also pertinent to re-call how even a 'civilized' and well-established inhabitant like Lusaka often found it necessary to explore other people's ways and habits.

Thirdly, a combination of certain further features—that the large majority of the inhabitants in the neighbourhood came from tribes without close rural-urban links, that most of these tribes had low rates of fertility and small families, and that, in consequence, few of the inhabitants had extensive sets of kinsmen—meant that a large volume of social interaction was perforce subject to *relatively* little pressure and control through networks of well-defined 'institutional' relations either in or beyond the town. On the other hand, much behaviour was affected by networks of personal relations with 'fictitious' kin, and with urban friends and neighbours, but these relations were largely governed by norms and principles which were to some extent flexible and liable to variable interpretation. The principle of urban 'brotherhood' was very notably of this kind. Not only were the norms of 'brotherhood' loosely defined but the principle itself was essentially optative and permissive rather than binding and obligatory. Men were 'brothers' in some situations but not in others, and an incident seen by one party as contravening the norms of 'brotherhood' was often as likely to provoke a discussion leading to an eventual re-definition of the encounter in question, or of the entire situation in which it occurred, as to cause an outright breech in social relations.

In brief summary, then, the population consisted of persons with varying degrees of ability and social equipment for diversified participation; both 'tribalism' and 'civilization' were important principles of association, and there was constant selection of norms and principles of behaviour according to different situations of the moment; there was continuous movement of people and, in the process, constant selection and rejection of inhabitants; there was a high incidence of tentative, exploratory behaviour, and the overall situation often induced considerable social tolerance, a willingness to compromise and an element of joking; partly as a consequence of small families and of comparatively loose ties with tribal kinsmen, there was a relative absence of strict 'institutional' control stemming either from within or from beyond the immediate urban community, and there was little evidence to suggest that social relations were to any marked extent integrated by virtue of pressures inherent in the rural-urban relations of the inhabitants; various sets of norms were constantly being discussed and elaborated in the very course of participating in day-to-day life, and the norms and principles operating in the neighbourhood were an integral part of a 'loose' or 'weak' system of social control that was progressively emerging within a changing situation.

These conclusions concerning the elements of variation, diversity, and fluidity in Avenue 21 go a long way towards answering the first part of the general question as to how differing norms and principles of association co-existed in the neighbourhood. To answer the second part of the question, we have to consider the sources of the stability and continuity within which variation, fluidity, and diversity were set. Here again there are three inter-related sets of factors to be recalled. The first set consists of factors stemming from the existence of the neighbourhood as an integral part of a subordinate community on which basic social order was imposed from 'outside' by authority deriving directly from the overwhelming political dominance of the colonial regime. Conflicts inherent in the neighbourhood, as in the African community at large, were automatically checked and limited by the very fact that, as one man put it at the time of Felekini's death (Chapter VI), 'we are in the "town of the Europeans" where people do not "fight and quarrel".' The authority of the administration and of the European community of employers and 'teachers' was a constant and invariable pressure. It affected all aspects of the daily routine and was not normally challenged in day-to-day life; it was part of the given situation within which life and death were set.

Secondly, quite apart from the important fact of the general political and economic subordination of all Africans, there were in the neighbourhood few ingredients of deep social antagonism or of particularly exclusive alignments. The rural-urban links of members of most tribes had little or no economic content and thus offered no particular inducement to tribal exclusiveness. Moreover, in the town as a whole, tribal colonies were small and numerous and, with the partial exception of the *Arabisés*, they were almost entirely lacking in any articulated administrative separation or political organization. These factors had over time combined with economic and political subordination to break down virtually all semblance of corporate tribal collectivities. Among the well-established section of Avenue 21, bonds of tribal 'brotherhood' were closely interwoven with bonds of 'neighbourhood' and of 'family friendship', and this plurality of ties tended to overlap and to cut across each other in a way which provided *some* stability and cohesion.

Finally, despite diversity and fluidity in social relations, there was a partially integrated set of *urban* norms and institutions which constituted an important common denominator to many of the interactions between most members of the population. In this study there is no attempt to trace the origin of any specific norms and institutions but a variety of incidents reported in the text show that there was a wide range of them and that some stemmed specifically from the very processes of social interaction within the heterogeneous wage-earning communities that had developed around diversified centres of economic activity. This set of norms and institutions was a legacy from half a century of 'civilized' life in the region. Whether developed *ab initio* in towns and labour centres of the area, or whether adapted from Western or *Arabisé* or tribal cultures, these norms and institutions constituted part of the prevailing 'urban culture'. The particular institutions of 'trial marriage', of *ikilemba*, of voluntary associations, and of prostitution and semi-prostitution are good examples of well-established practices that were clearly urban in the foregoing sense, as were many of the more specific norms governing diverse aspects of marriage and divorce, of child-rearing and mourning for the dead, of the inheritance of property, and the like. Equally, many less specific urban norms were constantly being invoked in more mundane interactions between 'brothers', between 'fictitious' affines, between men and women who were 'husbands' and 'wives' to each other in the temporary absence of spouses, and so on.

I have on occasion referred to social relations governed by some of these urban institutions as 'semi-institutional' rather than 'institutional'. This was intended to emphasize the frequently variable nature and imprecise definition of the norms involved. Despite variability and imprecision, however, the actors in these situations were patently behaving in ways supported by a considerable measure of agreed meaning in the community. Whatever terms we may wish to use to refer to these agreed meanings, it is evident that they were an integral part of the knowledge and social equipment which a newcomer had to learn and absorb before he could participate in the life of the neighbourhood with any measure of competence. To the extent that a man's behaviour was guided and influenced by these meanings rather than by the '*basendji* ways of the village', he was considered 'civilized'. By the same token, I suggest that the degree of 'civilization' of the inhabitants of Avenue 21 can be taken as some measure of the extent to which the life of the neighbourhood was governed by a common urban culture. The evidence is that most of the residents were markedly influenced by this urban culture, but that there was considerable variation in their knowledge of it and in their judgments as to the particular areas of their individual lives in which it was relevant and appropriate.

II

As my fieldwork in Avenue 21 developed, I was constantly led to assess features of social life there in relation to impressions gathered in other parts of the town and among members of tribes that were not well represented in the avenue and its immediate environs. The attempt to draw these comparisons led me to a progressive definition of the urban situation as a whole. In particular it pointed to a number of differences between various neighbourhoods and to the seeming individuality in a number of respects of the neighbourhood of Avenue 21. This raised important questions concerning the relation of the avenue to the wider community and concerning the principles of integration operating in the African community as a whole. Could the avenue be seen as a microcosm of the town or as representing any particular sector of it? Or, failing both of these improbable possibilities, to what extent was it a good example of a particular kind of locality standing in a certain functional relation to the town centre and to other kinds of locality? It had from the outset been evident that Avenue 21 and its environs were different to, say, the inner areas of Belge I and it seemed clear that a contrast of this kind was related to the differing locations of the two neighbourhoods in relation to the 'European town' as well as to their differing functions in relation to the urban area as a whole. But why should there be any significant differences between Avenue 21 and other peripheral areas? And, in keeping with this line of questioning, why were there such striking differences in a number of respects between two in-lying areas such as the 'fashionable' part of Belge I and 'the Lokele quarter' of Belge II? In more general terms, to what extent could differences between neighbourhoods be attributed to 'natural' forces of urban differentiation, and to what extent were there other important factors at work? It was evident that until these questions could be satisfactorily answered, it would be difficult to assess features of social organization in Avenue 21 in their correct context.

Comparisons between various neighbourhoods in the town were therefore accorded a high priority in the analysis of the survey data, and the findings were later evaluated in relation to the differences found between the larger tribal colonies. In the light of these comparisons, the seemingly unique combination of features in Avenue 21 and its environs was readily explicable. It became apparent that the nature of any locality in the town was a product of two broad sets of variables which were largely independent of each other. On the one hand, the composition of the population and certain aspects of social relations in a neighbourhood were partly functions of its location in relation to the town centre and of the position it occupied in the overall ecological structure of the town; on the other hand, neighbourhoods also varied appreciably according to their location in relation to routes of access to the town from the interior. Immigrants coming to town had in the past settled in areas close to their points of entry to the urban area and to a large extent they were still doing so. As a result various neighbourhoods contained markedly different combinations of tribal elements and, since different tribes commonly varied in their histories of urban incorporation, in their rural-urban relations, in their modes of accommodation to urban life, and in their fertilities and related social and demographic characteristics, the particular tribal compositions of some neighbourhoods were closely associated with social features and patterns of behaviour which had themselves become factors of internal differentiation in the community.

Taken in conjunction with the known influence of historical and geographical factors on migration to Stanleyville from various areas of the hinterland, the above observations showed that the processes of urban integration were taking place in an overall social context characterized by a series of variable factors. Moreover, it was clear that much of the variability derived from elements which were rooted in the past and which frequently stemmed from far beyond the town boundaries. First, there was appreciable diversity in the social, cultural, and demographic characteristics of peoples in various rural areas in the hinterland. Secondly, there was significant variation between 'natural areas' that had already developed in the town. Thirdly, the urban population was made up of tribal colonies which displayed marked variations in their general social configurations, and which had to varying extents established themselves within limited neighbourhoods in the town. Fourthly, the very processes of immigration and urban incorporation were taking place within social and economic contexts which varied appreciably for migrants from different parts of the region. Finally, as stressed at the very beginning of the study, the town and its region were developing within an overall context of unprecedented social and economic expansion, and this very expansion was uneven in its effects on different parts of the region as well as on different parts of the town.

In brief, then, new immigrants coming to Stanleyville were drawn from areas that often differed in nature as well as in the pace of current social and economic change; the histories of migration from village to town of these new arrivals were often appreciably different, some having come to Stanleyville direct and others having spent intervening periods of varying lengths in smaller labour centres; and, on arrival in Stanleyville, they were being dispersed in differentiated neighbourhoods according to processes which were clearly selective in regard to tribe and to geographical area of origin in some cases, and in regard to degree of 'civilization' and to previous experiences in wage-earning centres in others.

According to this view of the town, we would expect the pattern of social relations to vary appreciably in some respects from *one type of urban neighbourhood* to another, while also expecting it to vary in other respects from *one sector of the town* to another. And, indeed, as the analysis developed, it became increasingly clear that some of the differences encountered from one neighbourhood to another formed regular patterns of variation between 'natural areas' that had arisen out of the processes of urban differentiation, whereas others were related both to differences between parent populations and to differing patterns of urban incorporation and of rural-urban relations.

In the absence of intensive studies of other localities we have no basis for detailed comparative analyses of social relations either in different types of neighbourhoods or in different sectors of the town. We can, however, usefully re-assess the more striking differences that were noted between the neighbourhood of Avenue 21 and some other areas. First, we saw that the range between the more 'civilized' and the less 'civilized' (or most 'uncivilized') members of the avenue's population was much narrower than in the community as a whole, and also appreciably narrower than in most other neighbourhoods taken on their own. The range of 'civilized' people encountered in local areas could well have formed the basis of a three-fold classification of neighbourhoods in the town. In the *Arabisé* village, and in a number of areas in all three townships of the C.E.C., there were appreciable numbers of *évolués* and this introduced into the status system an element that was absent in Avenue 21; in another type of area there were fewer *évolués* than in the first type but higher proportions of skilled and semi-skilled workers than of unskilled labourers; and, in areas like that of Avenue 21, there were absolute majorities of ordinary labourers and virtually no *évolués*.

The second difference is related to the first. We have seen that there were in Avenue 21 and its environs some groupings which had a semblance of formal organization but which were in effect no more than either friendship groups or loose agglomerations of neighbours and near-neighbours. The two examples described in Chapter VI were the 'club', which amounted to little more than a clique of men who occasionally drank together, and *la réunion*, which was a very loose and amorphous burial association based on one avenue but having no committee,

no rules, and no meetings. The absence of more fully developed
voluntary associations was a striking fact which stood in sharp contrast
to the existence in the 'fashionable' areas of Belge I of the larger
associations of *évolués* and of many smaller ones of non-*évolués*, as well as
to the development even in many less 'fashionable' neighbourhoods of
both tribal and non-tribal associations. The difference can be partly
attributed to the low status of the inhabitants in Avenue 21 and its
environs; in the town as a whole participation in voluntary associations
was typically a feature of 'civilized' life, and it was unusual for persons
of low status to be members of formal associations whether of a tribal
or a non-tribal kind. But the difference was also undoubtedly related
to other aspects of neighbourhood relations in Avenue 21 and its
immediate environs. The relative absence of anonymity, the close-knit
texture of relations between well-established residents, the widespread
networks of personal relations established within the loose frameworks
of tribal 'brotherhood' and 'family friendship', and the measure of
neighbourhood solidarity that had developed over the years, were all
aspects of a situation in which formally constituted voluntary associations would have been rankly incongruous. There were in the area
some men—and also a few women—who were members of associations
meeting outside the neighbourhood, but they were rare and exceptional.
It is undoubtedly significant that, for example, I could find no Mubali
in the neighbourhood who was a member of the *Association des Babali*
located in Belge I. This general contrast between the prevalence of
voluntary associations in some areas and their absence in the environs
of Avenue 21 suggests that, despite the social diversity and the increasing
heterogeneity of the population, the fabric of social relations in the area
remained *relatively* uniform and undifferentiated; such social cohesion as
there was continued to be predominantly 'communal' rather than
'associational'. The number of inhabitants who did not readily find
their social niche through common affinities and pre-existing relations
was undoubtedly increasing, but this increase had not as yet led to any
fundamental change in the basis of neighbourhood relations.

Thirdly, as already recalled in the preceding section, the neighbourhood of Avenue 21 had few inhabitants with strong rural-urban links
and few with large families or with extensive networks of 'real' kinsmen.
In this respect it was similar to the inner areas of Belge I, as well as to a
number of other neighbourhoods in the town; but it was clearly very
different to all areas—whether in-lying or peripheral—where there was
a predominance of inhabitants from tribes like the Lokele, Topoke,
Bambole, and Balengola. Where these and similar tribes were well
represented, social control through kinship connexions was undoubtedly
much stronger. Avenue 21 and its environs were, however, a clear
example of a neighbourhood with a relatively 'weak' system of social
control, with a relatively high incidence of 'semi-institutional' relations,
and with a high ratio of 'fictitious' to 'real' kinship connexions. This
contributed to, and was in part a reflection of, a somewhat distinctive

pattern of relations between the sexes. We may recall that the neighbourhood had a high proportion of married women and that the incidence of prostitution and semi-prostitution was low. But it was an area with a high ratio of men to women, with small families, and with a relatively permissive code of sexual morality for women. Marriages were unstable and certain categories of non-marital and extra-marital liaisons were readily given 'semi-institutional' recognition as partnerships with limited rights and obligations. This resulted in the proliferation of 'fictitious' affinal relationships defined through partnerships ranging from explicitly negotiated 'trial marriages' and other well-recognized non-marital unions to much more ephemeral liaisons. And the high incidence of 'fictitious' affines, associated as it was with a high incidence of relations of 'fictitious' brothers, distinguished the neighbourhood not only from areas of the town like 'the Lokele quarter' with its appreciably more stable marriages, larger families, and higher ratios of 'real' to 'fictitious' kinship relations, but also from neighbourhoods like the inner areas of Belge I where social life was much affected by associational-type relations, on the one hand, and by the incidence of more specifically commercial and contractual relations on the other.

When these and associated differences between the neighbourhood of Avenue 21 and other areas in the town are considered in conjunction with the differences between the social configurations and patterns of urban incorporation of various tribal colonies, it is evident that an urban way of life was being developed and passed on to new immigrants in a variety of markedly different settings. Unfortunately, with little time-depth to our material, and in the absence of detailed comparative data for neighbourhoods and tribal colonies specifically selected on the basis of particular similarities and contrasts, we are not in a position to draw definite conclusions on some of the most crucial questions thrown up by the analysis. Thus, for example, there can from the present data be no conclusive answer to the question posed in Chapter VIII as to whether the common experience of town life was tending over time to blur differentials in marriage duration between different tribes or between 'types' of tribal colony. Nor can we draw any precise conclusions concerning the differences that clearly existed in the way in which various principles of association operated in settings as different to each other as Avenue 21, 'the Lokele quarter' in Belge II, the *Arabisé* village, and the inner areas of Belge I. Moreover, differences between localities and between tribal colonies make it foolhardy to try to draw close comparisons between Stanleyville as a whole and other African towns.

In this connexion, we may recall the general comparison drawn in Chapter VII between some of my findings in Avenue 21 and Mayer's in East London. I suggested that the process of 'incapsulation' of rural migrants as described by Mayer for the 'Red' Xhosa had no close parallel in Avenue 21. Indeed, in Avenue 21, and, I believe, in the town as a whole, the more usual and characteristic reaction of migrants

was not to 'incapsulate' themselves in close-knit networks and undiversified institutions but, on the contrary, to 'liberate' themselves through
the progressive acquisition of 'civilized' norms. And I have stressed that
the process of becoming 'civilized'—of 'seeing the light of day', of
'opening one's eyes', or of 'coming out of darkness'—was widespread.
Yet, in some sections of the population, a form of 'incapsulation' was
common, and I have suggested that this model of analysis may well be
particularly useful in comparing the reactions to town life of newcomers drawn from a tribe like the Topoke with those of recent immigrants drawn from a tribe like the Babua who were more open to
'civilization'.

In originally choosing Avenue 21 for intensive investigation, I had
unknowingly begun the study of a neighbourhood where certain processes of urban integration were more pronounced than others. I have
no doubt that the particular processes exhibited in Avenue 21 were also,
in varying degrees, encountered elsewhere in the town. At the same
time, I know that some of the processes common in other areas, and in
other sections of the population, were scarcely operating in the neighbourhood of Avenue 21. These included the 'incapsulation' of immigrants, the significant involvement in associational-type relations of
évolués and other more 'civilized' persons, and the seemingly successful
preservation by a tribe like the Lokele of a great deal of their tribal
morality while yet being deeply involved in 'civilization' and having a
striking record of urban achievement.

III

In view of the salience of diversity, variability and change in the
community, it is not surprising that our main conclusions concerning
the problem of 'tribalism' and 'class' with which we started in the
first chapter do not lend themselves to any concise summary. The
interplay of 'tribalism' and 'class' was no less variable than the multiple
factors which influenced the nature of each as a principle of association
and differentiation; neither of the two was a neat and easily definable
principle of association. Distinctions based on tribal affiliations and on
the persistence of tribal loyalties and values were closely interwoven
and associated with elements of 'fictitious' kinship and 'urban brotherhood', while hierarchical distinctions of status and prestige were based
partly on specific criteria of achievement such as income, occupation, and education, and partly on degree of 'civilization'. And we
know that assessments of degree of 'civilization' varied appreciably
in different social situations. The interplay between 'tribalism' and
'class' was thus not an interplay between two 'pure' factors but between
two sets of factors. In the town as a whole, the situations in which the
two sets operated were far from uniform, and the social significance
of their constituent factors was liable to vary according to the particular
sphere of life in which social relations were enacted. 'Tribalism' and
'brotherhood' were largely coterminous in some sets of relations, but

in others a man might well draw a distinction between 'brothers' and non-'brothers' even though they were all fellow-tribesmen; and, in others still, he might well draw distinctions between several categories of 'brothers'. In addition, the way in which such distinctions were drawn was liable to vary from one tribe to another and from one neighbourhood to another.

Somewhat similarly, distinctions based on 'class' and 'civilization' were also accorded variable recognition. The most obvious example here comes from the differences between the notions of *évolué* and of 'civilized'. A man readily recognized as an *évolué* might well in some respects be judged as less 'civilized' than another who was not normally regarded as an *évolué*. Equally, the degree of 'civilization' attributed to a man commonly varied from one social context to another. Thus A might be judged as more 'civilized' than B in his behaviour in relation to work-mates and friends but as less 'civilized' than B in regard to the way he treated his family and his 'brothers'.

Assessments of the relative significance of the several factors subsumed under the terms 'tribalism' and 'class' can therefore only be made in terms that implicitly or explicitly define particular factors, the nature of the interactions, and spheres of social life within which relations were set. Precise and definite assessments of social relations between particular categories of people are, however, not the aim and purpose of a community study. In keeping with the views expressed in Chapter I, I suggest that the main purposes to be served by community studies of African towns at the present time are to probe unknown types of urban situation, to try to isolate factors operating in these, and to test and develop the conceptual formulations so far developed for the progressive explanation of the inter-related social processes encountered in modern Africa. The principal findings of a community study may thus be expected to take the form of new questions formulated to supersede the ones initially posed on going into the field as well as those partly re-formulated in the course of the analysis, 'conclusions' may be expected to take the form of conceptual elaborations, or of new insights, or of revised definitions of the field and scope of the inquiry. What are the elaborations, insights, and revisions suggested by the present study?

In the first chapter I referred to Mayer's classification of three types of models for the analysis of the urban participation of immigrants in African towns; the model of 'one-way change', the model of 'alternation' between town and country, and the model of 'alternation' between 'tribal' and 'urban' frames of reference in towns. It is, I hope, abundantly clear that all three models are relevant to the analysis of various categories of people and of social relations encountered in Stanleyville but, for the sake of clarity, I refer to the relevance of each in turn. First, we have seen that although the terms 'civilized' and 'uncivilized' had a relative connotation in the town, they referred essentially to norms of behaviour and to types of conduct which had to be learnt and acquired by individuals. In discussing the process of becoming 'civilized' we are therefore dealing with an aspect of urban socialization, and here the model of 'one-way change' is relevant and appropriate. In using the model of 'one-way change', however, we have to be careful not to assume that on becoming 'civilized' a man *necessarily* 'forgets' or abandons his 'uncivilized' ways. In so far as the term 'one-way change' conveys this assumption, it is misleading. The evidence from Avenue 21 shows that in the process of becoming 'civilized' *some* individuals did 'forget' or grow out of some of their 'uncivilized' ways, but it equally shows that the majority did not abandon the will, or lose the ability, to enter into social relations governed by less 'civilized' norms whether in the town or in their tribal areas. Indeed, we have specifically noted that even a 'civilized', urban-born, and urban-bred man like Lusaka continued to switch back and forth between more 'civilized' and less 'civilized' sets of acquaintances and, in so doing, from more 'civilized' to less 'civilized' frames of references. Becoming 'civilized' involved an extension of social equipment but it did not necessarily imply a commensurate rejection or loss.

Secondly, despite the paucity in this study of detailed information on the alternate participation of individuals between town and country, it is clear that this kind of alternation had been widespread in the past and that it continued to be an important feature in the lives of many of the inhabitants. The model of alternation between 'two worlds' thus remains relevant and its value is in no way reduced by a simultaneous and parallel interest in 'cultural extension'.

Thirdly, following the lead given most specifically by Mitchell and Epstein, I have laid considerable emphasis on the significance in day-to-day life of the constant selection of differing sets of norms in different situations and, equally, of the choice by individuals of differing sets of associates on different occasions and in different spheres of social life. In effect, therefore, I have constantly invoked the principle of 'situational selection' and, in so doing, I have on occasion made implicit use of the model of alternation between 'tribal' and 'urban' frames of reference in town.

The analysis as a whole thus abundantly demonstrates the general validity of all three types of model, while at the same time directing us to re-formulate the model of 'one-way change' into a model of 'cultural extension'. It also strongly emphasizes that the model of alternation between 'tribal' and 'urban' frames of reference should be specifically recognized as applicable beyond the point where a 'tribal' frame of reference is necessarily seen as one of the major possible options. 'Situational selection' is the key principle in this model, and it is of secondary interest whether the selection operates between 'tribal' norms and 'urban' norms or between two or more sets of 'urban' norms. In essence this point has previously been recognized in the studies of Mitchell and Epstein. My concern is mainly to bring out its implications in the study of a town which had a wide spectrum of patterns of behaviour stemming from 'urban' as well as from 'rural' sources of differentiation. How can we best tackle the analysis of such variety?

In the study of Avenue 21 I dwelt mainly on differentiation encountered within a neighbourhood situation in which the principal tribal elements had *relatively* uniform backgrounds, but we know that in the town as a whole some of the most important social and cultural differences were closely associated with forms of urban incorporation and accommodation which were liable to vary from one tribe to another. I believe this underlines the need to study the development of urban social relations *within* tribal colonies as well as *within* various heterogeneous segments of the population. As long as tribal colonies continue to exhibit such marked differences as they did in Stanleyville, they clearly merit to be distinguished from each other in our analyses. If we fail to do this, we may be concealing the sources of important variations that do not stem from the processes of urban differentiation and we may thereby waste the opportunity to distinguish between essentially different phenomena. At the same time, however, we should not allow the systematic study of tribal differentials to divert our attention from the analysis of social distinctions generated *within* the town. I suggest that our safeguard must lie in the development and simultaneous application of inter-related models of analysis which will progressively allow us to take account of an increasing number of dimensions in urban behaviour.

This study illustrates how each of the three models of analysis had direct *relevance* and positive *value* in one and the same urban community. That this should emerge so strikingly is perhaps partly due to the very nature of Stanleyville, but I believe it is also due to the particular area of interest on which I happened to focus. It seems certain that, in deciding at the outset to concentrate on aspects of behaviour located mainly in the broad set of urban-residential relations rather than in the sets of rural-urban or of African-European relations, I was selecting an area of interest in which the relevance and value of all three types of model were liable to emerge most pointedly. In and around his home and neighbourhood the Stanleyville urban-dweller could be seen reacting to situations which, though essentially structured by the given opportunities and facilities for securing physical accommodation and the basic necessities of daily life, were also constantly affected partly by his social relations at work and partly by the social connexions which he and his neighbours maintained with their rural kinsmen and with their places of origin. There was in the urban resident's daily round of domestic and neighbourhood life more interconnexion with events and incidents in *both* the 'European world' and the 'tribal world' than in any other spheres of urban life. I suspect, for example, that social relations that were centred on the work-place would lend themselves more readily to analysis as relatively independent and autonomous sub-systems than those that were centred on neighbourhood and home. In Stanleyville at the time of this study, social relations of the work-place were by definition relations between Europeans and Africans, between African *men*, and between actors whose social roles were mainly defined in terms which took comparatively little account of the relations of individuals with their families, their fellow-tribesmen, and their village communities of origin. In partial contrast, domestic and neighbourhood relations were essentially relations between actors whose social roles could seldom be adequately defined in terms that excluded their connexions either with kinsmen and tribal areas on the one hand, or with fellow-workers and European employers on the other.

The implications may be discussed with particular reference to the set of rural-urban relations which have received more attention in this study than the set of African-European relations. The fact that a number of significant variations in neighbourhood relations within the urban community can be traced to the differing nature and varying degrees of contact which existed between town and country does *not* mean that we should deviate from Gluckman's injunction to concentrate on the analysis of 'an urban system of social relations, in which the tribal origins of the population may even be regarded as of secondary interest'. (Gluckman, 1961, p. 80.) Indeed, the presence of important differences between tribes serves, if anything, to reinforce the need to take an urban system of social relations as our starting point. But, it also serves to suggest, firstly, that we must as a matter of common sense devote considerable attention to comparisons between urban colonies in town and, secondly, that we should take particular care to define the urban situation broadly enough to allow us to include aspects of the rural-urban relation within our purview when the data suggest that they have a direct bearing on urban relations. Unless we are in a position to do this, it is difficult to see how we can satisfactorily distinguish between various processes attendant on the growth of domestic and neighbourhood life in town.

The general problem is readily apparent when we recall the findings of the present study on the stability of marriage. We saw that the duration of marriage varied significantly between different tribes and between 'types' of tribal colonies, but we were unable to answer conclusively the crucial question as to whether the social effects of urbanization on marriage were essentially different between, say, tribes with longer marriage duration in town and those with shorter marriage duration. This shortcoming stems to a considerable extent from the fact that at the beginning of the fieldwork we were not in a position to pose pertinent questions concerning marriage duration in relation to differences between tribes and their *modes* of urban participation. To answer this *kind* of question we would need data specifically gathered to test hypotheses deriving from both alternation models as well as from the model of 'cultural extension'. For a specific illustration we may recall the contrast between the Lokele and the Babua. We saw that the Lokele had relatively stable marriages, high fertility, large families, a strict code of sexual morality for their women, high bridewealth payments, and few unmarried women. In contrast to this, the Babua had unstable marriages, low fertility, small families, a permissive sexual code for women, low bridewealth payments, and a relatively large proportion of *femmes libres* living independently. We further saw that these two tribes had very different rural-urban relations and appreciably different histories of urban incorporation. Yet both were well-established tribes in town. In the light of these and related data, I have suggested that the difference between the duration of marriage in the two tribes was in part a function of their differing rural-urban relations and, also, at least in part, a function of important differences in their rates of fertility (and perhaps of associated cultural differences) in their respective parent populations in the hinterland. This interpretation is, however, not conclusive, and I doubt whether it would be possible to come to a definite conclusion without specifically setting out to study *the extent to which urban marriage norms were pervading marital relations in each of the two tribes*. It is this emphasis which is lacking in the analysis as it stands.

The need for comparative multi-dimensional analyses of two or more tribal colonies is also evident in relation to a whole range of further problems which had a direct bearing on the interplay of 'tribalism' and 'class'. For example, we saw that the Topoke appeared more prone than most tribes to 'incapsulate' themselves in the manner of the 'Red' Xhosa in East London, and I have suggested that this was to some extent a function of their late arrival in town, of their associated failure to achieve better jobs, and of their continued dependence on their rural-tribal connexions for security. Yet, unlike most other tribes, the Topoke were relatively well dispersed between the three townships of the C.E.C., and it might have been thought that their wide residential distribution, which was itself a function of their late arrival in town, would have promoted their 'liberation' rather than their 'incapsulation'. In the absence of a more comprehensive study of the Topoke, however, we are inevitably left with important queries concerning their distinctive reaction to life in town. We can say that they were refractory to 'civilization' because they had no need of it, but this is no explanation. Their relative failure to become more 'civilized' may well have been, and seems to have been, a crucial factor in perpetuating their situation. Ideally we would need to study the Topoke's process of 'civilization' within the structure of their particular rural-urban situation and to compare it with the corresponding process in tribal colonies in quite different situations.

The above examples refer to problems which were *not* central to the analysis of neighbourhood relations in Avenue 21. Though there were some inhabitants in the avenue whose urban social relations were, like those of Patrice, markedly influenced by their rural-urban connexions, there was no evidence of marked variation in the degrees of 'civilization' of the main tribes that were well represented in that area of the town. Yet the detailed analysis of social relations in Avenue 21 does, I believe, show conclusively how inter-personal relations and 'small group' interaction were related to the continuous processes of elaborating norms, of communicating 'civilization' to newcomers, and of assessing individuals in terms of their ability to establish varied sets of social relations within diverse situations. Thus our evidence from the avenue does not conflict with the arguments developed from interpretations of data gathered in the wider community. What we now need in order to advance the type of analysis attempted in this book is the opportunity to dove-tail intensive and extensive investigations in a more systematic and purposeful way than has hitherto been possible in research projects which were essentially exploratory in their aims.

APPENDIX A

Notes on the Social Survey and on the Survey Tracts

The random sample used for the social survey constituted between 12 and 14 per cent of the population in different parts of the African residential areas of the town. In the three townships of the *centre extra-coutumier* all dwelling compounds were officially recorded by number. A convenient sampling frame was thus readily available and the dwelling compound was used as the sampling unit. In the *Arabisé* village no suitable sampling frame existed and it was necessary to carry out a preliminary counting and marking of dwellings before a sample could be drawn. Here the dwelling was used as the sampling unit. In the railway camp the population was accommodated in houses carrying numbers and a sample was therefore drawn from these. The questionnaire used, and an account of the survey operation, can be found in Pons (1956a), pp. 244–249 and 272–273.

Usable questionnaires were filled in at 94·9 per cent of the addresses falling in the sample, but there were some cases in which certain items of information were for various reasons not available for one or more persons living at a given address. This accounts for the fact that the *effective sample* shown in different tables for any one category of persons is not always precisely the same. But the variations were slight, and I have dispensed with the usual convention of tabulating the number of persons falling in the sample for whom particular items of information were not available.

The determination of the survey tract boundaries was partly arbitrary though it was carried out with the following considerations in mind.

(*a*) It was considered essential that the tracts should be drawn up so as to throw into relief variations related to the distance of various areas from the town centre.

(*b*) It was considered desirable that no tract boundaries should cut across areas that were obviously relatively discrete unless such areas contained sufficiently large populations to warrant dividing them into two or more tracts.

(*c*) Tracts had to be large enough to yield appreciably large absolute numbers for the two principal categories of adult men and adult women.

The railway camp was taken as a single tract and the effective sample of all persons in the tract was only 147. The effective samples of other tracts ranged from 207 to 539, and estimates of the total population of these ranged from 1,511 to 4,797. A fuller explanation of the way in which the survey tracts were established is given in Pons (1956b), pp. 648–649.

APPENDIX B

Additional Tables

TABLE 73

Age and sex structure of the Lokele

AGE	MALES %	FEMALES %	TOTAL %
0–5	11·7	11·0	22·7
6–10	5·5	6·4	11·9
11–15	8·0	4·8	12·8
16–25	10·9	10·1	21·0
26–35	9·7	8·5	18·2
36–45	5·5	4·5	10·0
46–55	1·5	0·9	2·4
56 and over	0·7	0·4	1·1
Total	53·5	46·6	100·1

Sample size: 752

TABLE 74

Age and sex structure of the Topoke

AGE	MALES %	FEMALES %	TOTAL %
0–5	9·2	10·7	19·9
6–10	3·4	3·4	6·8
11–15	4·3	2·4	6·7
16–25	18·4	11·3	29·7
26–35	17·4	10·7	28·1
36–45	3·1	2·1	5·2
46–55	1·5	0·6	2·1
56 and over	0·6	0·9	1·5
Total	57·9	42·1	100·0

Sample size: 327

TABLE 75

Age and sex structure of the Bambole

AGE	MALES %	FEMALES %	TOTAL %
0–5	8·8	10·6	19·4
6–10	6·6	3·5	10·1
11–15	4·9	3·1	8·0
16–25	16·8	11·5	28·3
26–35	12·9	10·2	23·1
36–45	8·0	0·9	8·9
46–55	0·4	0·9	1·3
55 and over	0·0	0·9	0·9
Total	58·4	41·6	100·0

Sample size: 226

TABLE 76

Age and sex structure of the Balengola

AGE	MALES %	FEMALES %	TOTAL %
0–5	8·2	12·0	20·2
6–10	4·1	6·2	10·3
11–15	4·1	1·0	5·1
16–25	10·8	13·9	24·7
26–35	17·5	11·9	29·4
36–45	5·6	2·6	8·2
46–55	0·4	0·0	0·4
55 and over	1·4	0·4	1·8
Total	52·1	48·0	100·1

Sample size: 194

TABLE 77

Age and sex structure of the Bamanga

AGE	MALES %	FEMALES %	TOTAL %
0–5	7·0	5·7	12·7
6–10	3·8	6·4	10·2
11–15	2·5	2·5	5·0
16–25	12·1	14·6	26·7
26–35	15·9	12·7	28·6
36–45	7·0	5·1	12·1
46–55	2·5	0·7	3·2
56 and over	0·7	0·7	1·4
Total	51·5	48·4	99·9

Sample size: 157

TABLE 78

Age and sex structure of the Bakumu

AGE	MALES %	FEMALES %	TOTAL %
0–5	5·6	3·5	9·1
6–10	1·8	1·8	3·6
11–15	2·9	1·8	4·7
16–25	13·0	15·6	28·6
26–35	16·2	15·6	31·8
36–45	9·4	6·5	15·9
46–55	2·1	0·5	2·6
56 and over	1·7	2·1	3·8
Total	52·7	47·4	100·1

Sample size: 339

TABLE 79
Age and sex structure of the Babali

AGE	MALES %	FEMALES %	TOTAL %
0–5	2·0	3·4	5·4
6–10	2·0	1·5	3·5
11–15	3·4	2·9	6·3
16–25	10·2	9·8	20·0
26–35	15·6	15·6	31·2
36–45	10·2	8·3	18·5
46–55	3·4	3·9	7·3
56 and over	4·9	2·9	7·8
Total	51·7	48·3	100·0

Sample size: 205

TABLE 80
Age and sex structure of the Babua

AGE	MALES %	FEMALES %	TOTAL %
0–5	3·1	3·3	6·4
6–10	2·8	3·1	5·9
11–15	2·1	3·1	5·2
16–25	7·7	10·1	17·8
26–35	12·9	14·6	27·5
36–45	11·5	10·3	21·8
46–55	7·0	3·5	10·5
56 and over	3·9	1·2	5·1
	51·0	49·2	100·2

Sample size: 426

TABLE 81

Age and sex structure of the Arabisés

AGE	MALES %	FEMALES %	TOTAL %
0–5	3·1	4·0	7·1
6–10	2·6	2·8	5·4
11–15	3·5	1·7	5·2
16–25	6·5	11·2	17·7
26–35	10·8	14·3	25·1
36–45	10·1	10·8	20·9
46–55	4·7	4·4	9·1
56 and over	2·4	7·0	9·4
Total	43·7	56·2	99·9

Sample size: 573

TABLE 82

Marital status and age of a sample of 193 men living in Neighbourhood I

MARITAL STATUS	16–25 No.	%	26–35 No.	%	36–45 No.	%	46 AND OVER No.	%	TOTAL No.	%
Married	18	37·5	45	62·5	23	59·0	18	52·9	104	53·9
Living with a woman to whom not married	2	4·2	7	9·7	3	7·7	4	11·8	16	8·3
Widowed, living singly	0	0·0	1	1·4	0	0·0	4	11·8	5	2·6
Divorced, living singly	4	8·3	13	18·1	9	23·1	6	17·6	32	16·6
Never married, living singly	24	50·0	6	8·3	4	10·3	2	5·9	36	18·7
Effective sample	48	100·0	72	100·0	39	100·1	34	100·0	193	100·1

TABLE 83

Marital status and age of a sample of 183 women living in Neighbourhood I

MARITAL STATUS	AGE GROUP									
	16–25		26–35		36–45		46 AND OVER		TOTAL	
	No.	%	No.	%	No.	%	No.	%	No.	%
Married	34	63·0	46	64·8	15	45·5	8	32·0	103	56·3
Living with a man to whom not married	2	3·7	7	9·9	5	15·2	1	4·0	15	8·2
Widowed, living singly	0	0·0	0	0·0	2	6·1	12	48·0	14	7·7
Divorced, living singly	4	7·4	16	22·5	10	3·0	3	12·0	33	18·0
Never married, living singly	14	25·9	2	2·8	1	30·3	1	4·0	18	9·8
Effective sample	54	100·0	71	100·0	33	100·1	25	100·0	183	100·0

The table excludes three married women aged 11–15 years.

TABLE 84

Marital status and age of a sample of 128 men living in Neighbourhood II

MARITAL STATUS	AGE GROUP									
	16–25		26–35		36–45		46 AND OVER		TOTAL	
	No.	%	No.	%	No.	%	No.	%	No.	%
Married	19	43·2	35	79·5	19	82·6	10	58·8	83	64·8
Living with a woman to whom not married	1	2·3	0	0·0	1	4·3	0	0·0	2	1·6
Widowed, living singly	0	0·0	1	2·3	0	0·0	3	17·6	4	3·1
Divorced, living singly	5	11·4	5	11·4	2	8·7	3	17·6	15	11·7
Never married, living singly	19	43·2	3	6·8	1	4·3	1	5·9	24	18·8
Effective sample	44	100·1	44	100·0	23	99·9	17	100·0	128	100·0

TABLE 85
Marital status and age of a sample of 92 women living in Neighbourhood II

MARITAL STATUS	AGE GROUP								TOTAL	
	16–25		26–35		36–45		46 AND OVER			
	No.	%	No.	%	No.	%	No.	%	No.	%
Married	28	82·3	34	97·1	8	66·7	3	27·3	73	79·3
Living with a man to whom not married	2	5·9	0	0·0	0	0·0	0	0·0	2	2·2
Widowed, living singly	0	0·0	0	0·0	0	0·0	6	54·5	6	6·5
Divorced, living singly	1	2·9	1	2·9	3	25·0	2	18·2	7	7·6
Never married, living singly	3	8·8	0	0·0	1	8·3	0	0·0	4	4·3
Effective sample	34	99·9	35	100·0	12	100·0	11	100·0	92	99·9

The table excludes two married women aged 11–15 years.

TABLE 86
Marital status and age of a sample of 134 men living in Neighbourhood III

MARITAL STATUS	AGE GROUP								TOTAL	
	16–25		26–35		36–45		46 AND OVER			
	No.	%	No.	%	No.	%	No.	%	No.	%
Married	13	40·6	30	65·2	19	61·3	14	56·0	76	56·7
Living with a woman to whom not married	3	9·4	2	4·3	0	0·0	2	8·0	7	5·2
Widowed, living singly	1	3·1	1	2·2	1	3·2	1	4·0	4	3·0
Divorced, living singly	3	9·4	8	17·4	11	35·5	7	28·0	29	21·6
Never married, living singly	12	37·5	5	10·9	0	0·0	1	4·0	18	13·4
Effective sample	32	100·0	46	100·0	31	100·0	25	100·0	134	99·9

TABLE 87

Marital status and age of a sample of 111 women living in Neighbourhood III

MARITAL STATUS	AGE GROUP									
	16–25		26–35		36–45		46 AND OVER		TOTAL	
	No.	%	No.	%	No.	%	No.	%	No.	%
Married	28	73·7	27	90·0	12	70·6	8	30·8	75	67·6
Living with a man to whom not married	6	15·8	2	6·7	3	17·6	0	0·0	11	9·9
Widowed, living singly	0	0·0	0	0·0	1	5·9	13	50·0	14	12·6
Divorced, living singly	2	5·3	1	3·3	1	5·9	5	19·2	9	8·1
Never married, living singly	2	5·3	0	0·0	0	0·0	0	0·0	2	1·8
Effective sample	38	100·1	30	100·0	17	100·0	26	100·0	111	100·0

TABLE 88

Marital status and age of a sample of 152 men living in Neighbourhood IV

MARITAL STATUS	AGE GROUP									
	16–25		26–35		36–45		46 AND OVER		TOTAL	
	No.	%	No.	%	No.	%	No.	%	No.	%
Married	26	40·0	41	83·7	27	93·1	8	88·9	102	67·1
Living with a woman to whom not married	0	0·0	0	0·0	1	3·4	0	0·0	1	0·7
Widowed, living singly	0	0·0	1	2·0	0	0·0	1	11·1	2	1·3
Divorced, living singly	0	0·0	1	2·0	1	3·4	0	0·0	2	1·3
Never married, living singly	39	60·0	6	12·4	0	0·0	0	0·0	45	29·6
Effective sample	65	100·0	49	100·1	29	99·9	9	100·0	152	100·0

TABLE 89

Marital status and age of a sample of 138 women living in neighbourhood IV

MARITAL STATUS	AGE GROUP									
	16–25		26–35		36–45		46 AND OVER		TOTAL	
	No.	%	No.	%	No.	%	No.	%	No.	%
Married	42	77·8	36	78·3	19	76·0	4	30·8	101	73·2
Living with a man to whom not married	0	0·0	0	0·0	0	0·0	1	7·7	1	0·7
Widowed, living singly	1	1·9	2	4·3	3	12·0	7	53·8	13	9·4
Divorced, living singly	1	1·9	7	15·2	3	12·0	1	7·7	12	8·7
Never married, living singly	10	18·5	1	2·2	0	0·0	0	0·0	11	8·0
Effective sample	54	100·1	46	100·0	25	100·0	13	100·0	138	100·0

The table excludes five married women aged 11–15 years.

TABLE 90

Places of residence before Stanleyville of adult men with under two years' residence in the town

PREVIOUS PLACES OF RESIDENCE	NEIGHBOURHOOD						
	I		II	III	II and III	IV	
	No.	%	No.	No.	%	No.	%
Native village	3	9·1	13	7	35·7	11	30·6
Small labour centre	17	51·5	15	17	57·1	22	61·1
Another C.E.C.	13	39·4	2	2	7·1	3	8·3
Effective sample	33	100·0	30	26	99·9	36	100·0

TABLE 91

Occupations of men with less than two years' residence in town and living in different types of neighbourhood

OCCUPATION	NEIGHBOURHOODS							
	I		II	III	II and III	IV		TOTAL
	No.	%	No.	No.	%	No.	%	No.	%
White collar	3	9·4	1	1	3·5	4	11·1	9	7·2
Specialized manual	17	53·1	10	8	31·6	14	38·9	49	39·2
Labourer	11	34·3	19	18	64·9	18	50·0	66	52·8
Other	1	3·1	0	0	0·0	0	0·0	1	0·8
Effective sample	32	99·9	30	27	100·0	36	100·0	125	100·0

TABLE 92

Lengths of residence in Stanleyville of heads of households in Neighbourhood I

LENGTH OF RESIDENCE	HEADS OF PRINCIPAL HOUSEHOLDS (I.E. TITLE-HOLDERS)		HEADS OF NON-RENT-PAYING SUBSIDIARY HOUSEHOLDS		HEADS OF RENT-PAYING SUBSIDIARY HOUSEHOLDS		TOTAL	
	No.	%	No.	%	No.	%	No.	%
Under 1 year	—		2		6		8	
1–2	1	} 6·9	3	} 41·7	16	} 78·8	20	} 37·8
3–5	4		5		19		28	
6–10	16	22·2	5	20·8	11	21·2	32	21·6
11–20	24	} 70·8	5	} 37·5	0	} 0·0	29	} 40·5
Over 20 years	27		4		0		31	
Effective sample	72	99·9	24	100·0	52	100·0	148	99·9

TABLE 93

Lengths of residence in Stanleyville of heads of households in Neighbourhood II

LENGTH OF RESIDENCE	HEADS OF PRINCIPAL HOUSEHOLDS (I.E. TITLE-HOLDERS)		HEADS OF NON-RENT-PAYING SUBSIDIARY HOUSEHOLDS		HEADS OF RENT-PAYING SUBSIDIARY HOUSEHOLDS		TOTAL	
	No.	%	No.	%	No.	%	No.	%
Under 1 year	0	} 14·0	7	} 48·3	2	} 71·4	9	} 31·7
1–2	3		3		3		9	
3–5	3		4		0		7	
6–10	9	20·9	9	31·0	2	28·6	20	25·3
11–20	8	} 65·1	4	} 20·7	0	} 0·0	12	} 43·0
Over 20 years	20		2		0		22	
Effective sample	43	100·0	29	100·0	7	100·0	79	100·0

TABLE 94

Lengths of residence in Stanleyville of heads of households in Neighbourhood III

LENGTH OF RESIDENCE	HEADS OF PRINCIPAL HOUSEHOLDS (I.E. TITLE-HOLDERS)		HEADS OF NON-RENT-PAYING SUBSIDIARY HOUSEHOLDS		HEADS OF RENT-PAYING SUBSIDIARY HOUSEHOLDS		TOTAL	
	No.	%	No.	%	No.	%	No.	%
Under 1 year	0	} 15·9	2	} 56·0	8	} 90·9	10	} 34·3
1–2	5		7		1		13	
3–5	5		5		1		11	
6–10	12	19·0	6	24·0	1	9·1	19	19·2
11–20	15	} 65·1	0	} 20·0	0	} 0·0	15	} 46·5
Over 20 years	26		5		0		31	
Effective sample	63	100·0	25	100·0	11	100·0	99	100·0

TABLE 95

Lengths of residence in Stanleyville of heads of households in Neighbourhood IV

LENGTH OF RESIDENCE	HEADS OF PRINCIPAL HOUSEHOLDS (I.E. TITLE-HOLDERS)		HEADS OF NON-RENT-PAYING SUBSIDIARY HOUSEHOLDS		TOTAL	
	No.	%	No.	%	No.	%
Under 1 year	—	} 15·8	9	} 68·8	9	} 32·7
1–2	5		5		10	
3–5	6		8		14	
6–10	22	31·9	6	18·8	28	27·7
11–20	20	} 52·2	2	} 12·5	22	} 39·6
Over 20 years	16		2		18	
Effective sample	69	99·9	32	100·1	101	100·0

Note: There were no rent-paying tenants in the sample for this neighbourhood.

TABLE 96

Numbers and percentages of adult men of different ages who were title-holders of dwelling compounds in the C.E.C.

AGE CATEGORY	ADULT MALE TITLE-HOLDERS IN THE SAMPLE		TOTAL NO. OF MEN IN THE SAMPLE	PERCENTAGE OF MEN IN EACH AGE CATEGORY WHO WERE TITLE-HOLDERS
	No.	%		
16–25 years	65	9·4	525	12·4
26–35	219	31·5	641	34·2
36–45	222	31·9	421	52·7
46–55	108	15·5	174	62·1
55 and over	81	11·7	111	73·0
Total	695	100·0	1,872	36·7

TABLE 97

Some members of Patrice's network of Warega associates in Stanleyville

MEMBER	APPROX. AGE	SEX	MARITAL STATUS	APPROX. DATE OF ARRIVAL IN STANLEYVILLE	IDENTIFYING RELATIONSHIPS
1 Patrice	22	M	M	April, 1952	—
2 Sangumusi	16	M	S	April, 1952	Brother of No. 1
3 Pascal	20	M	S	April, 1952	Classificatory brother of No. 1
4 Prosper	30	M	M	February, 1952	Classificatory brother of No. 1
5 Aluwa	30	F	M	March, 1952	Wife of No. 4
6 Kankamina	30	M	M	1950	'Fictitious' brother of No. 1 and maternal kinsman of No. 21
7 Clementine	25	F	M	1950	Wife of No. 6
8 Mangaza	20	F	M	September, 1952	Wife of No. 1
9 André	25	M	M	1951	A fellow-villager of No. 8 and thus a 'fictitious' *shemeki* to No. 1
10 Adolphina	25	F	M	1951	Wife of No. 9
11 Clothilde	30	F	M	1950	Daughter of a classificatory sister of No. 1
12 Stanislas	30	M	M	1949	Husband of No. 11 and thus a *shemeki* to No. 1
13 Moke	35	M	M	1950	'Fictitious' kinsman of No. 1
14 Rose	30	F	M	Information not available	Wife of No. 13
15 Joseph	25	M	S	November, 1952	Classificatory brother of No. 1
16 Hamusini	20	M	S	1951	'Fictitious' brother and school friend of No. 1
17 Abeli	25	M	S	November, 1952	'Fictitious' kinsman and former associate of No. 1
18 Mumbuli	20	M	S	November, 1952	Classificatory brother of No. 17 and 'fictitious' brother of No. 1
19 Djopo	25	M	M (but wife still at home)	December, 1952	'Real' kinsman of No. 17
20 Asani	25	M	M (but wife still at home)	December, 1952	'Real' kinsman of No. 17
21 Lwakama	17	M	S	1949 (at a school near Stanleyville)	Classificatory brother and, in former years, a constant companion of No. 1

APPENDIX C

Building a House

The following is a detailed list of the expenditure incurred by one man in building an African-type house on an undeveloped compound in New Brussels.

	Francs
Payment to a woman to clear the compound	200
15 poles	20
Present to workers who carried sticks to the compound	30
First payment to the worker who constructed the greater part of the house	200
Fibre cord	145
First stock of leaves for the roof	340
Second payment to the worker who constructed the greater part of the house	200
Second stock of leaves for the roof	200
Doors and window frames	450
Third stock of leaves for the roof	200
Third and final payment to the worker who constructed the greater part of the house	300
Food and drink for the working party of kinsmen, friends, and neighbours who gathered to build and plaster the mud walls	420
Payment to a 'mason' for levelling the floor and finishing it in mud plaster	300
	3,005

This house had four rooms and was slightly larger than the average house in Avenue 21. The house was completed in about four months but most dwellings of this size were built in stages over periods of a year or more and often one part of the house was completed and occupied while the rest was still under construction.

A poor man building a small house normally did practically all the work himself and his expenditure was thus limited to poles for the framework and to leaves for thatching the roof. For a small one-room dwelling, poles and leaves might cost only 200 to 300 francs. But a larger house such as the one costed above could scarcely have been built single-handed in the free time of a man who was otherwise employed in a full-time job. It was thus quite usual for full or part-time labour to be employed and for family members, friends, and neighbours, to be drawn in to the tasks of house-building. Plastering was generally considered to be woman's work. The final stage in building, which included the plastering of the walls, was normally completed on a Sunday by a working-party of kinsmen, friends, and neighbours. On these occasions women built and plastered the walls while men prepared and transported the mud, and also attended to any uncompleted work on the roof, doors, and windows.

APPENDIX D

Extracts from Lusaka's Autobiography
(Translated from original French text)

(*a*) When I was very young, about five years of age, my father was struck down by a very serious illness. . . . I think it was a contagious chronic venereal disease, but at the time I still knew nothing. . . . I cried for him, I was always beside him, and I pitied his great agony. I was convinced that with such suffering he could not continue to live, and that he must die. I often prayed to God, asking him to heal the soul of my dear father. And the Good Lord, in his infinite compassion, listened to my prayers, and my father recovered. But he suffered in this way, with this terrible disease, for more than three years.

(*b*) *Ma tante*, Shani, and her husband, Étienne, were very good to me when I was a small boy. They looked after me very well . . ., they taught me many things, . . . they always gave me good advice, . . . they carefully protected me from all accidents.

(*c*) From the age of about seven years, I was beaten every morning before I had washed myself. This is part of our Babali custom—the custom of *mambela*. It is to prove that a boy is growing in strength and that his body is in good condition. Fortunately for us of this period, the *mambela* of olden days is now forbidden here, otherwise we would all have been through bad and painful times and suffered very much. Even though the Babali do not cut their foreskins, they have a very painful custom of cutting designs on the stomach. *Attention!* This is really very, very painful, but I do not know a great deal about it for it was never done to me.

(*d*) When I was old enough to go to school, I always arranged *un petit commerce* in order to earn some money to buy bread and other things which school children need. I used to sell empty bottles, pineapples and paw-paws to Indians and Europeans. I used to sell one bottle for 20 centimes, one pineapple for 50 centimes and one paw-paw for 30 centimes. We children used to do this with our friends. We would go together at night to a dwelling compound where we had found bottles left in front of the house. We would take the bottles away, clean them, and sell them the next day.

(*e*) There was a certain European who had pineapples in his garden, near to where the Indians live. . . . We would go there, even in the afternoons, to pick pineapples whether ripe or not . . . and we would eat them, if we did not sell them. The workers in the garden would chase us away, but we would throw pineapples in their faces. . . . In the mango season, we would get up very early in the morning to pick up the mangoes knocked down by bats during the night . . . [and] we would take them to town to sell them. Sometimes the policemen chased us, but we laughed and threw mangoes at them. . . . Sometimes they reported us to the *Frère Directeur* of the school, but he was never able to do anything for he could not discover which boys were responsible. We were still children then! We had no conscience, and no desire to be serious. . . .

(*f*) From my third year at primary school, I began to frequent a European tennis club to pick up the balls for the players. There were many of us who did this, so we arranged things as follows. Each boy had an arrangement with a club to work for a whole week, and at the end of the week he was paid six francs, being one franc per day. . . . In this way we earned money to buy food at the market. . . . I lived far from the school, and I needed money to keep hunger away. . . . We would buy palm nuts, guavas and other fruits. . . .

(*g*) When I was 11 years old, I was circumcised by the *Arabisés* according to their customs. One had to pay for this circumcision, as well as for the food and for a guardian who was there to give instruction and to enforce the rules. Many of the rules are difficult to follow and to bear, but I followed them all. . . . It is much more painful than going to the hospital. . . . I spent one month only for the circumcision as the *Frère Directeur* pressed for me to be allowed to return in time for the opening of school classes. . . . This was at the end of 1936.

(*h*) On a few days in the year, the *Frère Directeur* gave a school feast for the pupils of the primary and the secondary schools, . . . and on other occasions, the school bought bread, ground nuts, bananas, *chikwanges*, and other foods for feasts in the classrooms. . . . On Christmas days we [the choir boys] always slept at the school to sing midnight Mass. We were given presents of food and clothing, and after Mass we again had something to eat before returning home the next morning.

(*i*) I remember one day in 1940 when we were invited to play football at the Mission St. Gabriel. I was in my sixth year. We were well received. Soon after the match started, the mission scored two goals, but then they began to hit us in a way which we did not understand. As they were winning, it is our side which should have begun to hit them but, on the contrary, they hit us and even threw stones at us. This was real savagery . . . the boys at St. Gabriel were very foolish, and the teachers could do nothing.

APPENDIX E

Transcriptions of the Official Records of three Matrimonial Cases heard before the C.E.C. Court

1 *The Case between Antoinette and Lusaka, heard 27th May* 1952
(Translated from Swahili)

Chairman of the Judges: What is your complaint, Antoinette?

Antoinette: I have come to accuse my husband Lusaka because he no longer respects me. We were married here in the C.E.C. and we have two children, one deceased, the other still alive. Now my husband is no longer satisfied with me and does not want me any more. Every day he chases me out of the house, I can no longer sleep there and I and my daughter always have to sleep outside on the *baraza*. He no longer allows me to sleep in his house or to touch his bed. He regularly taunts me that I should come to the office to summon him before this court. He says that he wants to say in front of you, my judges, what it is that he wants to do.

Chairman of the Judges: Lusaka, is your wife speaking the truth?

Lusaka: Yes, it is true, my judges, I am refusing this woman because her parents refuse me. Her parents are no longer satisfied with me and it is for this reason that I no longer wish to be married to this woman. I was perfectly in agreement with this woman that she should come to you and that we should have the matter discussed before you so that you may pronounce the divorce for us.

Chairman of the Judges: Lusaka, how much bridewealth did you pay for this woman?

Lusaka: I paid 900 francs and my *shemeki* (wife's parents or family) have returned 400 francs to me so that 500 francs remain in the hands of her family.

Chairman of the Judges: Lusaka, do you want your *shemeki* to return these 500 francs to you?

Lusaka: Yes, I want my money back.

Chairman of the Judges: What marriage did you and your wife have. Was it a civil marriage? Or a religious marriage?

Lusaka: No, my judges, we only had the marriage of the C.E.C., the ordinary marriage.

Summing up: The judges of the court of the C.E.C. decide this matter as follows. As Lusaka no longer wants his wife Antoinette whose *shemeki* are dissatisfied with him and continually speak against him, the court 'rubs out' this marriage. The 500 francs which Lusaka paid will remain with his *shemeki*. That is to say that this money will remain as a present for the wife who remained in his house a long time and who gave birth to two children, that is to say one child who is now deceased and one who is still alive. That is all we have to say. We take the name of Antoinette out of Lusaka's book and the name of Lusaka out of Antoinette's book. We separate you and we cancel the names from your books.

2   *The Case between Limela and Nafisa, heard 8th June* 1951
(Translated from Swahili)

Chairman of the Judges: Limela, what news?

Limela: I have come before you with my wife to-day to ask you to separate us because she tires (annoys) me very much. Every day she leaves me to go to other men, and if I were to take action (in the court) about this she would go to gaol every day. Thus it is that we have come here before you to 'destroy' the marriage in my book.

Chairman of the Judges: Nafisa, is it, as your husband says, that you no longer want (each other)?

Nafisa: Yes, my judges, it is as my husband says. It is correct (the true position) that he is asking that my name be taken out of his book and that I want the same because he and I no longer listen to each other (understand each other) in our home.

Chairman of the Judges: Limela, how many francs did you give as bride-wealth?

Limela: I gave 4,363 francs, but I leave that wealth as a *matabishi* (present) for my wife.

Summing up: The court says as follows. This man, Limela, and his wife, Nafisa, no longer understand each other, and the woman 'has been to gaol every day' because she wants other men.* So to-day the two have come before us to ask us to separate them. Thus the court to-day 'destroys' their home (marriage), and the sum of 4,363 francs remains as a present for the woman for Limela himself says that he does not want this returned to him.

3   *The Case between Maria and Bunduki, heard 22nd January* 1952
(Translated from Lingala)

Chairman of the Judges: Maria, what are you asking?

Maria: I come before you with my husband to ask you to tell him to pay for the ticket for me to return to my home. We were married at Bomili in the country of our birth. After that we came here to Kisangani (Stanleyville). Now my husband 'refuses' me (in that) he does not give me money for food or for clothes.

Chairman of the Judges: Bunduki, what do you say? Is it true what your wife says?

Bunduki: My judges, the things my wife says are 'nonsense' and lies. It is true that we married in the country of our birth, and that we then came to Kisangani. But then, since our arrival here, my wife began to behave very badly and to run with other men. I have already caught her twice. And I have told her that as soon as my employer goes on leave (to Europe), we shall go to our country to discuss this affair, but when she heard me say this she began to argue and to make a lot of noise (difficulties), and she became very troublesome. Then she took some of the things from the house and went to stay with her brothers.

* It is not clear from the transcription whether Nafisa had in fact been before the court before as the judges' summing up suggests, or whether the judges simply accepted the suggestion made by Limela that 'she would go to gaol every day' if he were to take action against her for her frequent adulteries.

The Court's declaration: We decide as follows. As from this week Bunduki must pay to this court a weekly sum of 40 francs for food for his wife Maria. Then, when his employer goes on leave, Bunduki and his wife Maria will return to their country to have this affair settled there.

APPENDIX F

Some Letters written from Gaol by Kisubi
to his Brother, Lusaka

(Translated from Swahili. Explanations and comments in brackets)

The following letters should be read in conjunction with Lusaka's case history given in Chapter VII. They are selected from a collection of about a dozen letters written in gaol by Kisubi. The collection was clearly incomplete. During the first few months of his imprisonment, Kisubi had written frequently. Later the letters were less frequent though he still remained in regular contact with Lusaka. Among the main points of interest illustrated by the letters were Kisubi's strong affection for his mother and the nature of the close relationship between him and Lusaka.

1 *Letter written from Stanleyville gaol on 19/8/51, four months after Kisubi had begun his 3-year sentence*

Bwana Lusaka,

I want (from my clothes left with you) 1 pair of trousers, 1 shirt, 1 pair of shoes and 1 pair of short black socks. Put them all in the small suit-case and bring them to me on Sunday. Also let Bushiri [the son of a classificatory brother of Kisubi's and Lusaka's mother] come with you.

On the list of my things that are with father Matinda [the father of Kisubi's wife] add 1 large mirror of 120 francs. And I want to have 3 lists. One big list of all my things. Then one list of the things that are with Matinda, and one list of the things that are with you. Write all this down. Leave nothing out, not even one item. If I do not die, I want to see all these things.

The bridewealth I gave was one goat for 300 francs, things [articles] worth 534 francs, and 497 francs [in cash] = 1,321 francs. Write all this down.

That is all,

Kisubi.

2 *Letter written from Stanleyville gaol on 14/9/51*

Bwana Lusaka,

Arrange my clothes well, see that they are ironed. Put them away tidily and place them in the sun every day [regularly or often]. Choose a good place for them [when putting them out in the sun]. Look after mother as your own heart. Give her money for her own needs every month. Do not leave her with your wife [i.e. do not leave her in the care of your wife but look after her yourself]. Come to see me morning and evening [meaning that Lusaka could on certain days come either in the morning or the evening]. Avoid drink and tobacco, and attend to the affairs of your house. Look after your children and your wife. Do not beat your wife. Send me my little suit-case with all the things in it. Only take out a shirt and a pair of trousers. Write letters every day [often] that I may see someone bringing them 'every month'. Mother must never be without money so that she can always buy the things she needs. [Unintelligible passage omitted here.] Do everything possible concerning all the things I ask. I have permission to see you [for you to visit me] to-morrow, and I would like to see Safi [Lusaka's small daughter].

Greetings to all at your house,

Kisubi.

3   *Letter written from Stanleyville gaol on 15/10/51 on the eve of Kisubi's transfer to the Bengamisa gaol*

Monsieur Lusaka,

Goodbye Father [the term 'father' here used as a general term of respect]. Stay with the Good Lord till I see you again in two years and six months. Watch over Mother 'as if she were your eye'. Arrange to build a [new] house. Buy a bicycle and a sewing machine. Buy a gramophone. Stay close to your elder brother, Bushiri, and to the children of your *muyomba* [i.e. to the children of Bushiri, the son of a brother of Lusaka's mother; Bushiri was Lusaka's *muyomba* and not, strictly speaking, his elder brother]. He who loves you, is yours. [Meaning that as Bushiri loved Lusaka and was well disposed to him, Lusaka should value the relationship.] Each month that you get your pay, put aside savings of 50 francs. Leave the drink and the cigarettes alone. Do not tease [interfere with or trouble] others. Do not have disputes with your wife. Do not incur debts. For you are father of your children. [Meaning that Lusaka is now a man with responsibilities.]

We are being sent to Bengamisa to-morrow morning at 7 o'clock. Tell Mother and your wife to pack my clothes in green leaves like food [i.e. in banana leaves commonly used for wrapping food] or in the piece of paper that is with my clothes. There are seven francs in [the pocket of] my coat. I do not want my town clothes [i.e. best clothes]. Those will stay with you in Brussels. Give [my] news to *Bwana* Bushiri and also to Asumani [a 'fictitious' kinsman of Kisubi with whom he had a close personal relationship]. Send me at least 150 or 100 francs. Mother and your wife must meet me here in front of the door of the guard room of the prison. They must ask permission that I may see them for the last time. But they must not linger here. Greetings to your family. That is all. Arrange for letters to come to me. And let Mother and your wife bring my book of prayers with the clothes. That is all. *Bonjour*.

Kisubi.

4   *A brief note written from Bengamisa gaol on 31/3/52*

Bwana Lusaka,

Would you send me 100 francs for good extra food. Also a fountain pen to write letters. That is all. Greetings.

Kisubi.

APPENDIX G

Lusaka's Daily Diary between 27/8/52 and 12/10/52

This diary was kept by Lusaka on request and it is clear from the explanatory tone of some of the entries that it was in parts specifically addressed to me. In translating it from the original French text I have in some places added further explanations where these were available. All such additions are given in brackets.

Wednesday, 27/8/52

To-day I received the visit of a certain friend, Albert, who came to invite me to the *tanga* for his old father who died on 20/6/52. The *tanga* will be held on the Saturday after next at No. 49, Avenue 21, Brussels. [The deceased man for whom the *tanga* was being held was a Murumbi from the neighbourhood. Albert was one of the deceased's numerous kinsmen—'real' and 'fictitious'—in the area. He and Lusaka had known each other since childhood and they were just as much 'family friends' as personal friends.]

After leaving work I went to Avenue 10, Belge I, where I am currently spending the nights on account of the *kilio* for my *beau-père* Longondo [the father of Lusaka's 'wife', Bernadette] who died last week.

Thursday, 28/8/52

On my return from work I passed to see my *copain du travail*, Joseph, for I had not seen him since 8 o'clock this morning and we had no opportunity to chat during the day. [Joseph was Lusaka's *ikilemba* partner. He was a Mubua. Like Lusaka, he was a carpenter, and they had worked together for a previous employer before doing so again at the saw mill.] After that I again went to Belge I to spend the night there with my wife's family.

Friday, 29/8/52

After my day's work I moved all my belongings into my new house. [Lusaka had at this stage completed two rooms of the house, the rest still being under construction.] Soon after 1 o'clock my young brother, Mangala, came back from work. He moved into the room which I had been occupying up till now. [Mangala was a 'fictitious' brother, the son of a man from Lusaka's father's village. He had been in town 2 years, but had only recently come to live on Lusaka's compound; before that he lived with another 'fictitious' kinsman in the same avenue.]

This afternoon a friend, Raphael, came to tell me that he had recently left his previous work and was now engaged in the Finance Offices. He said he had a permanent appointment in the administration and was shortly to be sent to Costermansville. At first this news disturbed me and made me wonder why I do not myself look for work as a clerk in a firm or government office for my present occupation gives me little moral and intellectual satisfaction. Then I began to wonder whether Raphael was in fact so fortunate. I also began to think how unwise he had been to leave his former employer without giving notice. I thought to myself: will he not be pursued by his former employer? Well, as it happens, I have now heard that late this afternoon he was apprehended and is to be charged for leaving his job without permission. [Raphael was a Mukusu who lived in Belge I. Lusaka had known him since his school days; they did not normally visit each other unless they happened to be passing each other's homes.]

Saturday, 30/8/52

When I went to collect my money to-day, there was an incident between my employer and myself. My employer wanted to deduct a certain sum from my salary on account of what had happened on 8/8/52. On that day, when we had finished work and most of the men had already left, the supervisor came round to check the work that had been done. He found that it was not according to his satisfaction, though we had carried out all work during the day exactly as he had told us. We had worked very carefully. Despite this he criticized us and said that he would impose a fine on me at the end of the month. To-day the accountant wanted to impose this fine but I protested in front of him, the supervisor and a number of other workers. Eventually the manager arrived and I appealed to him. He listened to all the explanations, and then said that I was in the right. The matter was then shelved and I was not fined.

Sunday, 31/8/52, to Friday, 5/9/52
No entries.

Saturday, 6/9/52

This evening I went to the *tanga* to which my friend, Albert, had invited me (see 27/8/52). There was a large number of people. At 9 o'clock the guests were served with three *dame-jeannes* of palm wine and a case of beer. Later people danced, and this continued till 4 a.m. At the end the guests thanked Gabriel, the [classificatory] son of the deceased man for having offered them this celebration.

Sunday, 7/9/52

In the evening I went to Avenue 10, Belge I, where my wife is still staying following the death of her father. As I arrived I found my *belles-soeurs* and *belles-mères* looking troubled and angry. The reason for this was that on Friday a sister of my deceased *beau-père* had given 450 francs to a man who works at the hydro-electric plant asking him to buy her a goat. She trusted this man because he had known Longondo the deceased and had worked with him in Costermansville in years gone by. And this same man had on the eve of this affair spent the night with us at the *kilio*. But this man deceived her. He had said he could find a goat for sale but it was not true. He had also said that, as he worked at the hydro-electric plant, he would bring them a case of beer at a reduced price. But all these offers were lies. The man used the money, and on Thursday night my *belles-soeurs* and *belles-mères* reported him to the *Chef* of the C.E.C.

The *Chef* put the man in gaol for the night and yesterday phoned the manager in charge of the workers at the hydro-electric plant. They then agreed that the man should be set free to return to work, and that the manager should hold back the money from the man's salary at the end of the month.

Monday, 8/9/52, to Wednesday, 10/9/52
No entries.

Thursday, 11/9/52
To-day the wife of a [classificatory] father of my wife came to see me accompanied by a young half-caste girl who is the daughter of an elder sister [classificatory] of my wife. The woman had journeyed from Lowa. She came to see me on behalf of her husband for he was unable to come himself. He asked her to visit me in his place as he was expected to do. (i.e. following on Lusaka's 'marriage' to Bernadette in July). He had sent her to Stanleyville with his 'instructions' for the *kilio* of my *beau-père*. He had given her 2,000 francs to bring to the family. She also brought 1 goat and a large bottle of palm oil. After her arrival in Stanleyville it was decided that the *tanga* for my *beau-père* would be held on Saturday, 13/9/52, at 9 o'clock in Avenue 10, Belge I.

Last night a certain man named Sukali, a tenant on compound No. 17, stole 500 francs from Christine. He stole them from her shop. To-day, she suspected him and reported him. He was arrested and charged and has been sentenced to gaol for a year.

Friday, 12/9/52
No entry.

Saturday, 13/9/52, and Sunday, 14/9/52
I spent the night in Belge I for the *tanga* for my wife's father. All members of the family celebrated very happily. They danced the whole night until morning, and continued to do so until the evening of 14/9/52. The brothers and sisters of the family brought 6 cases of bottled beer. The guests arrived very late, but they were well received. Each table had some 30 bottles of beer. We, the *boaux-frères* of the family, were served more liberally than all the others. At the end of the celebrations it was decided that four persons would stay in mourning for eighteen months in remembrance of the deceased.

My *belles-soeurs* and *belles-mères* thanked me very much for the presents I gave them on the occasion of the death of their brother and father, Longondo.

Monday, 15/9/52
At 2 o'clock this afternoon my wife came back home. She came accompanied by her [classificatory] elder sister, Rose. They again expressed their gratitude to me for the help I gave them during their days of sadness. They brought me 50 francs, rice to the value of 20 francs, some goat meat, tomatoes and other things. I thanked them very warmly.

Tuesday, 16/9/52, to Friday, 19/9/52
No entries.

Saturday, 20/9/52
This afternoon I accompanied my wife to Belge I to visit a [classificatory] mother of my wife. My wife complained to her mother that she was hungry [thus asking her 'mother' to make a gift to Lusaka], and her mother gave me a fowl and 10 francs. My wife's family are very pleased with me.

Sunday, 21/9/52, and Monday, 22/9/52
No entries.

Tuesday, 23/9/52
During the night thieves stole some of the building materials—sticks and leaves for the roof—of the house which Limela is building in New Brussels. We all feel very sorry for poor Limela who thus loses a good part of the money he has invested in his house. [Though a close personal friend of Lusaka and a resident of Avenue 21 at this period, Limela seldom spent much time in the immediate neighbourhood and was not well known, but the theft of his building materials was the subject of much discussion in the avenue.]

When I went to work this morning it was raining so hard that nearly all the workers were late. The roll call was delayed for 30 minutes to allow the workers to arrive. Then, although they were all present, the *chef* sent back a number of them saying there was not much work to do on account of the rain. The men sent back were so annoyed that they went to the office to find the manager. He did not believe them and came himself to the saw mill to see what was happening. He found our *chef* and questioned him and, on finding that what the workers said was correct, he gave orders that they should all stay.

Wednesday, 24/9/52, to Sunday, 28/9/52
No entries.

Monday, 29/9/52
I felt very ill to-day, with blood and dysentery. I was so ill that I went to find a [European] doctor at the dispensary in Avenue 6. When my turn came to see the doctor, I explained to him the kind of pain which I had. He told me that I must go to the laboratory for an examination of specimens. But I did not understand properly what I had to do so I came back home, but later went back to the dispensary to ask the [African] *infirmier*. I then went to the laboratory and was examined but the result was negative, that is to say no 'insects'.

On returning home at half-past five in the afternoon I found Joseph, my intimate friend and *copain du travail*, waiting to see me. We discussed many things until 6.30 p.m.

Tuesday, 30/9/52
No entry.

Wednesday, 1/10/52
When I woke up this morning I heard the cries of a man saying that his house had been burnt down. It was Mamboina from compound No. 40 in the avenue [i.e. Avenue 21]. It appears that the house was burnt at 11 o'clock last night. A man wishing to do harm to Mamboina poured paraffin on the house and set a match to it. Mamboina was asleep and was woken by the cries of a woman who was also sleeping in the house. He thought that he was dreaming, but then woke up to find his house in flames. He does not know who it is who did this to him. All the people in the avenue

have been to see the house to-day. It is not altogether burnt, only one half of it. [Mamboina was an old-established resident.]

This morning my wife went to Belge I to see her *tante* [a classificatory sister of her father]. She arrived there to find that there was a gathering of the family and her *tante* gave them a case of beer so that they might rejoice together. They thought that I would perhaps join them there after work but as I had not received an invitation I did not go. It is unfortunate that I missed the opportunity. My wife stayed there till 5 o'clock, arriving back home at 7 o'clock. Her *tante* sent my mother a fowl, a bottle of oil, and some bananas. My mother has sent a message of warm thanks to my wife's *tante*. This certainly shows how well disposed my *belle-tante* is towards my family.

Thursday, 2/10/52

Towards 8 o'clock in the morning my wife and my sister, Shalufa, came to see me at work to bid me farewell as they were leaving on their journey. As it is evident that I cannot afford all the expenses for building my house, my wife has decided to help me. We discussed all this at length, and decided that my wife will do some trading. This shows that she is interested in my family and my affairs. She will buy meat and other foodstuffs in the country-side, and will bring these to Stanleyville for sale. She leaves to-day with Shalufa and I expect they will be away about two weeks. It will help us all, and that is why I have given my wife permission to go. [Shalufa was the daughter of Lusaka's mother's classificatory brother. She lived at a roadside village some distance away from the town and travelled back and forth with food for sale every few weeks; Lusaka's wife had never traded before, and he had asked Shalufa to help her.]

Friday, 3/10/52

No entry.

Saturday, 4/10/52

At 11.30 this morning I received an invitation from Jean, a friend who lives at the *Arabisé* village and who is a companion of mine at the saw mill. Some six months ago his *tante* died [a 'sister' of his father]. Now he has prepared a little feast for his friends as well as for members of his family. [This was the *pili* or end-of-mourning ceremony.] He bought two cases of beer and slaughtered a goat. I was invited together with another friend from work, Loboneka. Jean brought us a plate of rice, two dishes of meat, and two plates of soup. After an hour he brought us eight bottles of beer. The company began to dance to the gramophone. We danced the whole night till morning. Everyone was happy, and we were indeed very well served. We were most grateful to our friend for the pleasure and happiness which he afforded us on this day.

Sunday, 5/10/52

No entry.

Monday, 6/10/52

Towards evening I heard from 'my young Mambao' [son of Lusaka's mother's classificatory brother, and brother of Shalufa; member of Lusaka's own household], who had himself heard through the young sister of my wife, that my wife had been stopped on her journey by the District Commissioner. The news is that they have taken all her money away, and that she is now in distress not having sufficient to pay for her return to Stanleyville. I have tried to find some-one who would take money to her, but have not yet been successful for I an not well known to the lorry drivers along that road. Perhaps my wife will be helped by the husband of my sister Shalufa. I think this possible because my wife had left with my sister.

Tuesday, 7/10/52

This morning my intimate friend and *copain du travail* (Joseph) told me that he was going to the dispensary to have an injection following the blood test he had the previous week. At 2 o'clock in the afternoon I received a message from him that he would not be returning to the saw mill for the injection was hurting him. So I finished his work on his behalf. After leaving work I arrived home to find the clerk Ayali filling in questionnaires in the avenue. I stopped to talk to him but not for long as he had a lot of work to do. I then went to visit Joseph. [Ayali was employed on the social survey; he was a Murumbi who had lived in the immediate environs of Avenue 21 in his childhood.]

In the evening I received a visit from Ndalabu, a friend of my brother Kisubi who is in prison at Bengamisa. He came to see me because he had to-day received a letter from Kisubi asking for news from Stanleyville. We talked for a long time—I, my mother, Mambao, and Ndalabu.

Wednesday, 8/10/52

To-day at 5 o'clock my wife returned from her journey. She had left Kilometre 118 on the Ituri Road at 11 o'clock this morning, but unfortunately the lorry in which she was travelling had a puncture at Kilometre 32 so my wife continued to walk for a distance of three kilometres in order not to be found on the lorry for the driver did not have permission to transport her. After walking three kilometres she waited on the roadside for the driver to pick her up again after he had mended his puncture. When he arrived he stopped for her, but this time he asked her to lie under the hides he was transporting in order that she should not be found in the event of the lorry being stopped and searched by the District Commissioner. So she suffered very much on this journey, but came home with a good quantity of meat to sell. She arrived back just as I was cutting a bunch of palm nuts for making oil. My mother gave my wife a very warm welcome, especially on account of the bad news we had heard of her while she was away. After she had washed herself, my wife and I went to visit her *grand'mère*. We took her a good piece of meat as a present from my wife's journey. We then also went to visit her *oncle* who had himself just returned from a journey. He is a mechanic with a specialist position in his firm, and he travels to examine machines in various places where the firm has contracts.

Thursday, 9/10/52

No entry.

Friday, 10/10/52

Towards 9 o'clock this morning I heard from a young man at work that an elderly man had been run over by a motor car on the Irumu Road. The young man was not able to tell me who it was that had been run over. Later, when I was on my way home, I heard that it was Felekini, my *oncle maternelle*, and that he had died. He did not die at the moment that he was run over; it was four hours later that he gave up his soul. He first received attention at the dispensary of the Military Camp, then they phoned the hospital for an ambulance so that he might have immediate attention, but he died all the same. The Police Commissioner came to examine the place of the accident. He checked on the position of the motor car and he made all the enquiries that he could. Unfortunately, however, there was no witness to this bad accident so there will be no further investigation. Felekini was well known here, and was much respected by all of us. His corpse was brought back to the house by a lorry supplied by Bekieni of Avenue 9 (Brussels). At 6.30 in the evening I left to go to the house where the corpse was to be washed. There were many people, and all were paying their contributions. I stayed there till 8.30 p.m. [Felekini was a 'fictitious' *oncle maternelle* to Lusaka; he and Lusaka's mother, Samenyao, were both Babali who had come to Stanleyville 'at the time of the Arabs', and who thus saw themselves as 'brother' and 'sister' by virtue of their long common experience as members of the sub-community.]

Saturday, 11/10/52

No entry.

Sunday, 12/10/52

At about 10 o'clock this morning I received a visit from the [classificatory] elder sister of my wife. She came from Belge I accompanied by the widow of her [classificatory] father as well as by the young boy Jean-Pierre. Half and hour later they were joined by the *oncle paternelle du père de ma femme*. And a little later Nafisa, sister of Mambao, also came to visit. In the afternoon the young sister of my wife from Avenue 12, Brussels, came to visit with her daughter.

APPENDIX H

Lusaka's Receipts and Payments from 31/1/53 to 31/3/53

This balance sheet is based on information recorded by Lusaka on request. In translating the original, which was partly in French and partly in Swahili, I have wherever possible added explanations and details of identification concerning persons whom he recorded by name or by a particular relationship to himself. In order to preserve the general tenor of the original, however, I have refrained from adding any information concerning persons whom he referred simply as 'a certain man' or 'a certain woman'. Some of these persons were known to him by name, but his relationships with them were largely contractual; others were people whom he did not even know by name.

The 'daily balance' shown in the last column was calculated on the assumption that he had no cash in hand at the beginning of the period. The 'debit balance' shown for the end of March suggests that the assumption was incorrect, or that he forgot to record monies received at some stage during the period under review, or both. It seems very likely that he forgot some items as there is, for example, no record of any profit from his 'wife's' trading though he contributed 300 frs. towards it on 2/2/53.

Date	Sums received	Sums spent	Daily balance in hand
31/1/53	Monthly salary less advance of 200 frs. paid mid-month — 583 frs.	Gave to Bernadette, his 'wife', for the household — 50 frs.	
	Payment from Joseph, who was a fellow-carpenter at the saw mill where Lusaka worked, and who was his *ikilemba* partner — 500	Repaid a debt for three bottles of beer to 'a certain woman' in the avenue — 45	
	Present *ya furaha* (out of joy or rejoicing) from his friend Limela — 10	Repaid a debt to 'a certain man' for a piece of meat — 90	
		Gave to Samenyao, his mother, to enable her to repay a debt she had incurred for rice — 10	
		Bought two blades for his carpenters' plane from a shop in town — 60	
		Gave to 'a certain woman' — 5	
		Bought matches, paraffin, soap, a lantern glass and torch batteries — 62	771 frs.
1/2/53	Payment for doors and windows made for Limela's house — 150	Gave to his 'wife' for the household — 100	
	Payment for doors and windows made for the house of Yaososyo, an acquaintance from the neighbourhood — 1,000	Paid to 'a certain man' who brought him some building materials for his house — 25	
		Paid Christine, a small shopkeeper in Avenue 21, in respect of a debt from last month for tea and paraffin — 7	1,789

Date	Income	frs.	Expenditure	frs.	Total
2/2/53	Payment for a door which he sold to 'a certain man'	100	Bought poles and planks partly for his house, for his carpentry	500 frs.	
			Gave to his 'wife' for her trading	300	
			Gave a present to the wife of his elder brother, a respected 'fictitious' elder brother, when she came to visit him	20	
			Gave a present to his 'wife's' mother when she came to visit him	10	
			Bought at shops in the town centre: 2 prs. trousers (160 frs.), 1 shirt (70 frs.), 1 hat (45 frs.), and 1 pr. shoes (110 frs.)	385	
			Bought a bottle of lemonade for himself when he was shopping in town	3	
			Bought matches and cigarettes	5	666 frs.
3/2/53	'A certain man' came to settle a debt from last month for doors and windows which he had not paid in full	80	Gave to his 'wife' for food on a journey she was undertaking to buy meat in the countryside for sale in town	50	
	Received a present from Boniface, a 'real' maternal kinsman, on the occasion of the birth of his (Boniface's) first son	15	Gave to his mother for the household in the absence of his 'wife'	10	
	Sold a plank to 'a certain woman'	5	Bought a bottle of palm wine	5	
			Bought a packet of cigarettes	5	696
7/2/53	—		Bought planks for his carpentry	150	
			Paid for a lorry to deliver the planks to his compound	70	
			Paid a bottle of beer for the chauffeur who delivered the planks	15	
			Bought palm wine	5	456
8/2/53	—		Bought a packet of cigarettes	5	
			Bought a packet of powder	3	
			Gave to his daughter, Safi, for sweets	1	
			Paid a bottle of beer for Gabriel, a friend from his place of work, who came to visit him	15	432

Continued overleaf

Date	Sums received	Sums spent		Daily balance in hand
11/2/53	Payment for two frames made for 'a certain European'	60	Bought a bottle of bamboo wine	4 frs.	
			Bought cigarettes	3	
			Bought a bottle of lemonade and some bread at work	6	
			Gave to his mother for the household in the absence of his 'wife'	10	469 frs.
12/2/53	—		Bought one plate and four glasses	49	
			Bought soap from Christine, shopkeeper in Avenue 21, for the household	5	
			Bought bamboo and palm wine	10	405
13/2/53	Payment for a table made for 'a certain man'	50	Gave to his mother for her own needs	10	
			Gave to his mother for the household in the absence of his 'wife'	5	
			Gave to his daughter, Safi, for sweets	1	
			Bought a bottle of lemonade for himself	3	
			Paid Augustin, shopkeeper in Avenue 21, for cigarettes and soap bought the previous day	7	429
14/2/53	Mid-month advance on monthly salary	200	Paid an outstanding debt for three bottles of beer	45	
			Bought bamboo wine	5	
			Bought, at shop in town, one pair trousers (105 frs.) and two door hinges (10 frs.)	115	464
15/2/53	—		Gave to his mother for the household in the absence of his 'wife'	30	
			Bought palm wine	5	
			Paid 'a certain worker' who did a small job for him on his new house	10	419
17/2/53	Payment for work done for 'a certain man'	20	Gave to his 'wife' for the household	40	399

Date	Receipts	frs	Expenditure	frs	Balance
20/2/53	—		Gave to his 'wife' to buy rice for the household	32 frs.	367 frs.
22/2/53	Present *ya furaha* (out of joy or rejoicing) from his 'old friend', Asani, with whom he used to work years ago	5			372
24/2/53	—		Gave to his 'wife' for the household	15	357
28/2/53	Monthly salary less advance of 200 frs. paid mid-month	520 frs	Paid for small planks bought during the course of the month at the saw mill where he worked	50	827
1/3/53	Received from 'a certain man' at work to whom he had made a loan long ago	10	Gave to his 'wife' for the household	160	677
2/3/53	Payments for various pieces of carpentry done during the past month Drew monthly rent for the first time from the tenant he had recently accommodated on his compound	390 50	Paid to Joseph, his *ikilemba* partner, leaving 100 frs. to come	400	717
3/3/53	A present from his daughter, Safi	3			720
4/3/53	Present *ya furaha* (out of joy or rejoicing) received through the post from his friend, Mayaribu, a lorry driver from Elisabethville	5	Repaid a debt, owing since November 1952 to the young sister of his 'wife'	170	555
5/3/53	—		Bought cigarettes, matches and paraffin from Christine, shopkeeper in Avenue 21 Bought something to eat at work Gave his daughter, Safi, to buy her own rice	10 5 5	535
6/3/53	Payment for a small table made for 'a certain man'	35	Bought cigarettes and soap Gave to his daughter, Safi, for her to buy something to eat	10 5	555

Continued overleaf

Date	Sums received	Sums spent		Daily balance in hand
7/3/53	Payment for doing extra work after hours for his employer — 60	Gave to his 'wife' for the household	30 frs.	
		Gave a fowl and 10 frs. to his sister, Yohali, a 'real' maternal kinswoman, who came to visit him	10	
		Lent to 'a certain man' at work	20	555 frs.
8/3/53	—	Gave to his 'wife' for the household	35	
		Bought two bottles of beer when Limela visited him	30	490
14/3/53	Mid-month advance on monthly salary — 200	Gave to his 'wife' for the household	100	
	Payment for extra work done after hours for his employer — 40	Payment of the balance owing for this month to his ikilemba partner, Joseph	100	530
15/3/53	Payment for a door made for Yaososyo, an acquaintance from the neighbourhood — 100	Gave to his 'wife' for the household	50	580
18/3/53	—	Gave to his 'wife' for the household	40	540
19/3/53	—	Sent by post to Kisubi, his 'elder brother' (half-brother) in prison in Bengamisa	50	
		Bought leaves for part of the roof of his new house	355	135
22/3/53	—	Gave to his 'wife' for the household	100	35
23/3/53	—	Bought more leaves for the incomplete part of the roof of his new house	600	
		Transport for the leaves to his compound	50	— 615
31/3/53	Monthly salary less mid-month advance of 200 frs. — 693	Gave to his 'wife' for the household	150	
	Payments for several small pieces of work completed during the past month — 200	Bought cigarettes and other things for his own needs	80	
	Payment from his ikilemba partner, Joseph — 500			548

APPENDIX I

Patrice's Daily Diary between 14/9/52 and 31/1/53

Like Lusaka, Patrice kept his diary at my request. It was written in Swahili with occasional phrases in French. He commonly repeated himself in the entry for any single day, and he often had spells of a few days on end when he would repeat the same kind of information, e.g. on how he got up, washed himself, and went to work, or the times at which he went to work and came back home. In translating the diary, I have taken out many of these repetitions. It should be noted that he did not by any means write the diary daily, but on an average of once or twice a week and usually prior to bringing it to me. This partly accounts for variations in the amount of detail reported. The fact that he was in his own mind reporting to me clearly affected the nature of the entries. He sometimes tended to think that there was no point in mentioning by name 'real' and 'fictitious' kinsmen with whom he was in close association and whom he knew that I knew. Thus a number of his entries recorded in the first person plural in fact refer to activities with one or more members of his immediate circle. Where more precise information was available to me, I have added it. All such comments and explanations are given in brackets. Reference to Table 97, Appendix B, is helpful in reading the diary.

Sunday, 14/9/52

Yesterday my brother, Kankamina, had asked me to call on him early this morning. I went there in good time. He gave me four empty bottles of beer to take back to the Indian shops. I bought another four bottles for him and left these at his compound for him. [Kankamina was the maternal kinsman of a classificatory brother.] On returning to my house, Aluwa, gave me a bowl of broth. When I had finished this, I went walking in New Brussels. I then went home to rest. In the evening we had rice and cassava leaves prepared for us by Aluwa. After that we all went to sleep. [Aluwa was the wife of Patrice's classificatory brother, Prosper. At this stage Patrice and Prosper were both renting accommodation on Christine's compound. Patrice's wife had not yet arrived in Stanleyville and he and his brother, Sangumasi, often shared food prepared for Prosper by Aluwa.]

Monday, 15/9/52

I got up early and took my bucket to fetch water from the well. It was raining very hard but we worked in the rain as usual. After work I came home, but did not want to stay in my house so I went walking in Belge I. I met my brother, Hamusini, and he came back to Brussels with me [Hamusini was a 'fictitious' brother; he was a fellow-Murega whom Patrice had first met when they were both at school in Shabunda.] On arriving back in Avenue 21, I worked on my house. [The house he was currently building on Christine's compound but which he later abandoned.] I worked on my house till 10 o'clock at night, and then went to bed. I had nothing to eat this day. To spend the day without eating is bad and causes much suffering.

Tuesday, 16/9/52

. . . After washing I went straight to work. We start work at 6.30 a.m.
Towards eight o'clock we brought *chikwange* and ground nuts and after that
we worked till 2.30 p.m. when we all went home. On arriving at the compound I did not stop, but went straight to the forest to cut sticks for my
house, and on returning from the forest I continued to dig holes for the posts
(of the house). Thus I worked on the house from 3.00 p.m. to 10.00 p.m.
when I was very tired. Unexpectedly I received a visit from Fundi and
Ramazani. We chatted, [Fundi and Ramazani, two young Bakumu men,
were close associates of each other and they were both friends of Patrice
whom he had met at work.] After Fundi and Ramazani had left, we had a
meal of fish and stew. ['We' here refers to himself, Sangumasi, and Prosper.]

Wednesday, 17/9/52

. . . After work I went straight to the forest to cut sticks for my house.
On my return I heard with joy the good news that my wife, *Madame* Mangaza
(and his two children Kalanga and Marguerite) had arrived (in Stanleyville
from the village). She had in fact arrived at 11 o'clock in the morning. We
were all very happy. We did not sleep till 5 o'clock the next morning. We
talked and talked. We bought wine, we had food to eat [food brought by
his wife], we played the gramophone, and we talked. Christine, the mother
of the compound, was also very happy when Mangaza arrived. Well, that
was the news of to-day.

Thursday, 18/9/52

. . . I was very tired and hungry this day and at 7 o'clock (in the morning)
I stopped work to cook two bananas. The *chef* [European manager] found
me eating these bananas and said he would fine me 100 francs at the end of
the month. I was very angry. How can a man work when he is hungry?
I came away from work feeling great anger in my heart. I went back home
and worked on my house, and later that night had food with my brothers,
Sangumasi and Prosper. Only after that did we go to sleep.

Friday, 19/9/52

I awoke as usual and went to work earlier than the others. It rained very
hard that day from daybreak until 7 o'clock. After the rain had stopped we
worked very hard to remove a tree trunk from the saw. [He was at this time
working at the same saw-mill as Lusaka and Limela.] It was very difficult
work. After work I went to my house and worked all afternoon.

Saturday, 20/9/52

We worked from morning till mid-day. My friend, Ramazani, arrived to
see me. We chatted and then had food to eat. After we had eaten he went
back to his house about 6 o'clock in the evening. I stayed at my house.

Sunday, 21/9/52

I got up at 6.30 a.m. to work on my house. After working I had food prepared by my wife, and I went to rest and sleep at 10 a.m. Afterwards I
continued again with the building of my house. Then Hamusini arrived to
see me. When my wife saw that I had a brother to visit me she prepared

rice and beer for us. My friend enjoyed the food very much. [Patrice sometimes referred to Hamusini as a friend and sometimes as a brother.]

A woman was run over by a lorry near here. She was badly hurt.

Monday, 22/9/52

To-day it was raining very hard in the morning. We went to work in the
rain but could not start till 9 o'clock so we worked till 4.00 p.m. . . .

Tuesday, 23/9/52

. . . To-day a woman passed in the street and insulted me for no reason
whatsoever! I do not understand these ways.

The *chef* at work fined Fundi [Patrice's friend] 20 francs for taking a small
part from a lorry. When I came back from work I found that my wife,
Mangaza, had prepared rice for us, and that Aluwa, the wife of Prosper had
prepared stew and salted fish. We ate this with Limela [who was at this
time living on the same compound] whose wife had also prepared food—rice
and meat. When we had finished eating, we all went into our houses to sleep.

Wednesday, 24/9/52

. . . After four hours at work this morning I was so hungry that I came back
home to eat three bananas and cassava leaves which my wife, Mangaza, had
prepared. After this I walked back to work, and there was a woman walking
near me. People here [in the avenue] say that I was asking her if I could go
with her to her house. It is quite untrue that I was wanting to go with this
woman. I do not even know her name or where she lives. People were saying
this just to annoy me. [This refers to one of many incidents when Patrice
was teased by others on the compound and in the avenue. Limela, for example,
often laughed at him, saying that he 'knew nothing about town women.']

To-day my wife, Mangaza, went to visit her brother André, and his
wife in the 5th Battalion Camp. That is the news of to-day. [André was a
soldier who came from the same village as Mangaza. Patrice sometimes
addressed him as *shemeki* or *beau-frère*.]

Thursday, 25/9/52

I saw a man on a bicycle today and when we crossed in the road he asked
me: '*Bwana*, if you have 500 or 450 francs you can buy this bicycle from me.'
I said to him: '*Bwana*, is that bicycle yours?' Because a man does not sell a
new bicycle like that for so little. I said to him: 'I have 500 francs, but I
will not buy the bicycle because it is not yours and I think you are a thief.'
When he heard this he jumped on his bicycle and took flight. Two minutes
later this man was caught with the bicycle and accused of theft. He then
wanted to draw me into the affair. It is a bad thing to allow oneself to get
mixed up in other people's affairs. The police took this man to the Commissioner and he was sent to gaol for two years.

The same evening I was walking in the road when I saw a certain man
fighting with his wife. He was beating her because when he came back from
work he found no food at home, and his wife was not there. He went to
look for her, and then met her on the road and he beat her very hard.

Today we ate very good food and when we had eaten we played the
gramophone and drank palm wine, and after this we all went to sleep.
That is the news of to-day.

22

Friday, 26/9/52

Today my friend Fundi came to see me. We talked for a long time and he gave me a present of 10 francs. This gave me great joy. When my wife saw that he was here, she prepared food and we ate with my brother Sangumasi. After Fundi had left, my young brother Prosper received a letter containing the sad news that his mother had died. So we could no longer rejoice. We cried on receiving that news. And with this sadness we went into our houses to sleep.

Saturday, 27/9/52

This morning on my way to work I met a certain man who insulted me for nothing. I had given him no reason at all to insult me. I think he is mad, and I did not answer a single word to him. Later I arrived at work. I did not go anywhere else today, I just stayed at my house, and was struck by the matter of this man who insulted me without any cause. It is a very bad misfortune.

Sunday, 28/9/52

We went to Belge I today to a member of my family named Clothilde [a daughter of a classificatory sister]. She gave us a lot of food and a lot of drink. On our way home we saw a terrible accident at a cross-roads. A man was run over and must have died. On my return home I killed two fowls and a duck, I then invited my brothers to eat with me. During the evening we went on to drink beer and palm wine. When we had finished drinking we went to sleep with great joy.

Monday, 29/9/52

Today I went to work and on returning from there I stayed at home up till the time that I went to sleep. I do not wish to go out every day.

Tuesday, 30/9/52

Today I was very happy for I have reached the end of the month without being ill and without losing a single day at work. So I was paid 650 francs. I spent 400 francs on a cloth for *Bibi* Mangaza and 100 francs to pay my rent. Then my junior, Sangumasi, brought me his salary of 350 francs. I put it with mine in my box.

Wednesday, 1/10/52

Today I worked with joy. In the evening I heard the good news that my [classificatory] brother Lwakama, who is at school has passed his diploma. We were often together in our country.

Thursday, 2/10/52

. . . We went to the town centre today. Close to the market we came across a man who had died on the road after being run over by a lorry.

In the evening a certain *Bwana* struck his wife a hard blow in the eye and damaged it.

Friday, 3/10/52

This morning we went to work as usual. We finished our work without incident or injury.

Saturday, 4/10/52

When I came back from work I did not go anywhere. I only slept. And ate rice and beef. That was all today.

Sunday, 5/10/52

Today I helped father Kankamina to build his house. ['Father' is here used in relation to Kankamina as a term of respect.] We started in the morning and worked until 9 o'clock in the evening. His wife, Clementine, prepared a lot of food for us. When we had eaten this we were too tired to go walking and just went home to sleep.

Monday, 6/10/52

Early in the morning I took my two children, Kalanga and Marguerite, to the doctor, because both had illness and bad coughs. On account of this I did not go to work.

Tuesday, 7/10/52

I left for work at 9 o'clock this morning. When the owner of the compound, Christine, saw me she shouted at me and insulted me saying that I am a *musendji*. She said that I have just come out of the forest and do not know the ways of Kisangani [Stanleyville]. She said that I, Patrice, am a *musendji* who cannot tell the difference between the beginning and the end of anything. Things like this astonish me, but in matters of this kind there is nothing to do but to tell them to God.

Wednesday, 8/10/52

On leaving work I went to see my friend Ramazani. He gave me good food— rice, vegetables and beef. After that we had eight bottles of beer and a large flask of palm wine, and we then went to see two very beautiful women— those women who know how to play.

Thursday, 9/10/52

On leaving work I went straight back to my house and did not do anything else. I ate cassava and meat.

Friday, 10/10/52

Today I saw a very, very big quarrel. A certain man found his wife in his house with another man. He said nothing but waited outside and when the man came out he stabbed him with a knife.

Saturday, 11/10/52

We worked for the morning only, and I stayed at home this afternoon. I received very good food of rice and beef from my wife. When I had finished eating I stayed with my children, Kalanga and Marguerite, until evening. I did not go anywhere.

Sunday, 12/10/52

I spent the afternoon, at the hotel [small bar] drinking sugar cane wine. There was a quarrel. A certain man named Kawaya and his friend named Abeli began to fight all the others. Abeli was struck on the head and received several wounds. The police arrived and they were taken away.

Monday, 13/10/52

I did not go to work today. I went to the Post Office to collect 1,000 francs which my father has sent me to help on account of my children, Kalanga and Marguerite. This day I was full of joy when I received those 1,000 francs. In the evening my young brother, Sangumasi, returned from Buta with his chauffeur [Sangumasi was a *boy-chauffeur*.] He brought back meat from his journey and on this day we rejoiced very much. We ate, we drank, and we played the gramophone and danced until 4 a.m.

Tuesday, 14/10/52

When I came out of work I found my friend Ramazani at my house. He had brought me a present and I was very happy. My wife, *Bibi* Mangaza, cooked rice and a chicken, and my friend stayed and we ate together with great joy. Later he went back to his house.

Wednesday, 15/10/52

All the workers received [mid-month] advances on their salaries today. Some received 100 francs, others 200 francs. I received 200 francs. I did not buy anything. I gave it all to my wife to buy food for the children, Kalanga and Marguerite.

Thursday, 16/10/52

I am continually astonished at the things which go on here in Stanleyville. Everyday people are killed by lorries. Today a woman was killed. She died on the spot.

Friday, 17/10/52

I did not go to work to-day, that is I did not do *kazi ya Wazungu* [the work of the Europeans]. I went to the forest, and this single day I cut 250 sticks working from morning till 8.0 p.m. I then carried them all to (the compound of Moke), No. 169, Avenue 8, New Brussels. [By this time Patrice had abandoned the construction of the house he had begun on Christine's compound in Avenue 21, and he was now starting a larger house on the compound of Moke who had recently been allocated an undeveloped compound in New Brussels. Moke was a 'fictitious' kinsman from a village near to Patrice's. Moke had also given Kankamina permission to build on his compound and the three were helping each other to build their respective houses.]

Saturday, 18/10/52

We did not work today as it is a big holiday for the Belgians. I went to New Brussels to my friend, Fundi. We ate bananas and fish and when we had finished eating he bought six bottles of beer. We drank them all with joy. When I left there I did not go anywhere else. That was all today.

Sunday, 19/10/52

To-day we ate well and drank till we were very drunk. ['We' on this occasion consisted of Patrice, Sangumasi, Prosper, Pascal and Kankamina.] Late in the evening *Mama* Clementine [the wife of Kankamina] brought us chicken and rice.

Monday, 20/10/52

When I came out from work, I went to New Brussels to prepare the sticks that I had left there for my house.

Tuesday, 21/10/52

Today I had the great joy of meeting unexpectedly a friend of mine, Jean. He is from Shabunda, and I discussed with him the good fortune that we should meet here far away in Stanleyville. From our country to here is a very long way. In my imagination I think this would be a very long way to walk. We drank 12 bottles of beer and one flask of sugar cane wine.

Wednesday, 22/10/52

In a hotel in Avenue 19, some young men bought drink for joy. They were all drunk. One of them stabbed at another three times with a pen knife. It was a very grave affair that I saw on this day. After work I went to New Brussels where I am building my house. I went at 4 o'clock and returned at 6 o'clock in the afternoon. When I arrived home *Bibi* Mangaza gave me water to wash myself, and when I had finished that, she gave me a plate of food.

Friday, 24/10/52

I did not go to work today, I went to the Banque d'Afrique to look for work as a clerk. When I arrived there a senior clerk asked me to pay 500 francs. He asked me to give him those francs in order to find work for me in the bank, and said if I cannot pay there is no work for me. Those of us who come from afar are astonished. What shall we do? We know *barua* [letters or writing] but no bank will give us work. We shall only do other work, and other work is nothing [i.e. labourer's work is worth little].

Saturday, 25/10/52

We worked till mid-day only. When work was finished I went home. I did not go anywhere else so there is no news.

Sunday, 26/10/52

Father Kankamina invited me and my brothers to his house to-day. There he gave us vegetables, rice and beer. He had received money and had bought 22 bottles of beer. When I left there I did not go anywhere else.

Monday, 27/10/52

I went to work early and after the roll call the *chef* of the sawmill sent me with a message to his house and told me to go back to my house afterwards. So I stayed at home all day and was very happy.

Tuesday, 28/10/52

At work today a man who works there as a watchman had an accident. He got five cuts on his leg. I saw all this from close up. We risk danger for the love of money here. When I came out of work I went to sleep. I was mourning for my friend on account of this accident. I was given good food—rice and chicken—but was not able to eat well on account of the grief of that day.

Wednesday, 29/10/52

I went to roll call as usual. When the European had seen me, I returned to the house because I felt so much grief and compassion [for the man who was hurt yesterday]. On reaching the house *Mama* Clementine was there. She had brought me cooked bananas and vegetables.

Later today I heard, but did not see with my own eyes, that a lorry coming from Beni turned over on the road. No one was killed, only hurt.

Thursday, 30/10/52

In Avenue 19 today, two men fought with *pangas* on account of debt. One man, who lives in New Brussels, came with a *panga* in his hand and asked the other one for his money. The other man said: 'Friend, wait till to-morrow and you will receive your 50 francs.' But the man was furious and would not listen. He lifted his *panga* and hit the other one on the head. A brother of the wounded man took out his pen-knife and stabbed the man who had hit his brother six times.

Friday, 31/10/52

I did not work all the days of this month, but to-day I have 1,700 francs. [He had put aside 1,000 francs received from his father on 13/10/52, had received 350 francs from his brother, Sangumasi, who always handed over his salary to him, and had himself been paid 350 francs.] In the evening I bought four flasks of sugar cane wine for 60 francs [each] = 240 francs, and 20 bottles of beer for 9 francs [each] = 180 francs. We [he and a few of his 'brothers'] drank all this and we were very happy. But I did not sleep well because I had lost 420 francs all on drink.

Saturday, 1/11/52

In the morning I went to the shops [in town]. I bought two cloths for my wife: 350 francs + 380 francs = 730; two headscarves: 30 francs + 15 francs = 45 francs; one pair of sandals: 180 francs; and a bag for my wife: 50 francs. I also bought one pair of trousers for myself: 175 francs.

Total 420 + 730 + 45 + 180 + 175 + 50 = 1,600 francs.

Leaving me 100 francs for food [for the month].

Sunday, 2/11/52

This day I went to Belge I to see my *shemeki*, Stanislas. [Stanislas was the husband of Clothilde, a daughter of one of Patrice's classificatory sisters.] He and I went to the *Paris du Soir* [one of the larger bars in Belge I] and when we arrived there we felt of one heart. We had six bottles of beer and we ate rice and meat.

When I returned home I found two brothers, Abeli and Mumbuli, waiting for me. They had this day arrived from Shabunda. I bought ten bottles of beer and we rejoiced on account of the arrival of our brothers. [Abeli and Mumbuli were not 'real' kinsmen of Patrice; both were men from his home area and he had known them at home and in Shabunda; on arrival in Stanleyville they rented accommodation on the same compound as Patrice.]

Monday, 3/11/52

Today I saw men passing on the road in a lorry coming from Beni. They were real *basendji* for, in front of all the civilized people, they all six exposed their genitals. They did not know that the Police Commissioner was in a car behind them. He stopped them and all six were arrested on the spot.

Tuesday, 4/11/52

At work a man by the name of Fabien had a bitter quarrel with a *muzungu* [one of the European employees] on account of bad work. The *chef* of the saw mill dismissed him on the spot. It is the fault of a *capita* [African foreman]. His work is to quarrel with us and it is on account of him that Fabien was dismissed. The other workers say they will all leave at the end of the year. [In point of fact nothing more was heard of the incident.]

Wednesday, 5/11/52

When I came out of work, I went to the new compound where I began work weeding and clearing the ground. [The compound in New Brussels where he, Moke, and Kankamina were beginning to build houses.] I worked from 5 p.m. to 6 p.m. On returning home my wife greeted me. I washed and when I had finished washing I had two bottles of beer. After that I ate the food prepared by my wife.

Thursday, 6/11/52

Today a man named Tumba struck his own brother for the sake of a piece of *chikwange*. This astonishes me. He hit him four times.
  At work a man called Lutuba broke three fingers.

Friday, 7/11/52

A certain man, Henri, struck a woman on the road. He was passing this woman on the road when he said to her: '*Bibi*, I have five francs, I would like you to come with me to give me something.' The woman refused and became angry. Then the man hit her. The woman went to report him and he was sentenced for one month and fined 250 francs for beating and fighting with a woman who was not his. Friends, leave insults and interferences with other people aside. Slowly they turn into trouble.

Saturday, 8/11/52

I worked for the morning only and then came back from work. I did not go anywhere except home. I did not hear any news that day. In the evening I played with my two children, Kalanga and Marguerite. We played the gramophone and danced the *malinga ya kizungu* [European-style dancing].

Sunday, 9/11/52

In the morning I and *Bibi* Mangaza went to (the market in) town. We bought one plate for 20 francs and food and vegetables for 70 francs. As we were coming away from the market we met two of my sisters (two fellow-tribeswomen whom he did not know but to whom he stopped to talk).

Monday, 10/11/52 to Saturday, 29/11/52
Diary abandoned.

Sunday, 30/11/52

I went to Belge I to help my *shemeki*, Stanislas, with the work of his house. We worked there from 8 o'clock in the morning to 1 o'clock. When we finished the work, they [the women] gave us water to wash ourselves and after that Clothilde, the wife of Stanislas, gave us rice and vegetables and beef to eat. *Bibi* Mangaza was with me and the two children, Kalanga and Marguerite. Also Pascal. When we had finished eating we went to the hotel (bar) *Congo-Bale*. *Monsieur* Bernard [the owner of the bar] gave us [sold us] 18 bottles of beer. For three people—Pascal, Stanislas, and me, Patrice. After we had finished drinking *shemeki* Stanislas paid a taxi for us from Belge I to Brussels. He paid 150 francs for five people. We did not eat again that day. That is the happy news of that Sunday.

Monday, 1/12/52

I did not go to work today because I was ill. I did not go out from morning till night. I just stayed at home and was ill.

Tuesday, 2/12/52

Did not go to work because I was ill.

Wednesday, 3/12/52

Did not go to work because I was ill.

Thursday, 4/12/52

Did not go to work because I was ill.

Friday, 5/12/52

I started work again today but suffered a great deal because I am not well.
   The news of today: a *boy* [domestic servant] was coming back to his house from work at 3 o'clock in the morning when he crossed in front of a car with his bicycle. The car knocked him over. This was on the corner of Avenue 7, Brussels. He was badly hurt and died.

Saturday, 6/12/52

When I came out from work I went home and did not go anywhere else.

Sunday, 7/12/52

We went to New Brussels to my elder brother, Kankamina. There we had 3 bottles of beer, and rice and vegetables and chicken. Very well prepared. At 4 o'clock in the afternoon we began *chezo ya malinga* [European-style dancing]. There were many of us. *Bon!* At 8 o'clock we bought 16 bottles of beer.

Monday, 8/12/52

A certain man, Louis, hit the *muzungu*, our *chef* at the saw mill. He hit him four times because the *chef* called him *nyama* [an animal, meat], and this *chef* never does any work, not even a little, only looks at us working.

Tuesday, 9/12/52

After work I did not go to the house, I went straight to the forest to cut sticks for my house in New Brussels. From morning till 7 o'clock in the evening I did not eat anything. I only ate at 8 o'clock after I got home. I had two plates of rice and cassava leaves.

Wednesday, 10/12/52

I did my work well and with joy today. I did not interfere with anyone and no one interfered with me. In the evening I did not go anywhere, only stayed at home to play with my two little children, Kalanga and Marguerite. We ate bananas and pig meat.

Thursday, 11/12/52

This morning they told us at work at 10 o'clock the sad news of the death of our governor of Stanleyville, *Monsieur* Bock! [The Provincial Governor who had the widespread reputation amongst Africans of being pro-African and of being hated by Europeans. His death was widely discussed in the neighbourhood as a set-back for Africans.]

When I came home before even washing myself or eating I heard very bad news. Behind my back, Christine, the owner of the compound, gave permission to her child, Aziza, and a man to go to my bed to do *mauvaise conduite* ['child' here is simply used to mean a younger friend or acquaintance]. And that woman has already done her *mauvaise conduite* with that man in my bed. And they took my bucket of drinking water and used it for their dirt and urine and that dirt they did not take away. When I heard all this I broke the bucket because it is filthy to use a bucket of drinking water for such things. I was very cross with Christine. No one must use my bed. It is a very bad thing. It is not *kizungu*, nor is it *kisendji*. This is just the way of *nyama* [animals]. Nothing else but animals.

Friday, 12/12/52

This morning I saw a woman by the name of Alima insulting her husband as if he were any other man. I do not know the reasons for her insults, she was calling him *musendji*. This woman does not know polite behaviour.

Today Clementine the wife of my elder brother Kankamina struck a certain woman because this woman came on to her [Clementine's] compound and insulted her without any reason. Clementine, on hearing these insults, became very cross and beat the woman in the manner of *kisendji*.

Sunday, 14/12/52

This morning I went with Prosper and Sangumasi to cut trees for the house of Prosper. [Prosper was at this time also beginning to build his own house.] After we had finished this work, we went to Belge I and on arriving there went to the hotel (bar) of *Monsieur* Bernard. We bought 17 bottles of beer at 15 francs = 255 francs lost. On arriving back in Brussels *Madame* Mangaza gave us well prepared food. In the evening I did not go anywhere.

Monday, 15/12/52

At work each man received 1,500 francs. This is because it is the 15th of the month and *Noël* [usual mid-month advance plus a Christmas bonus].

Tuesday, 16/12/52

We went to Stanleyville [to the town centre]. I bought two shirts for 120 francs = 240 and a hat for 175 francs and good black trousers for 180 francs = 595 francs.

Wednesday, 17/12/52

Where we live at No. 17, Avenue 21, Brussels there is a child named Nabuluki who is a thorough-going thief. He stole 485 francs from his mother, Christine. She beat him with a stick over his whole body. [Nabuluki was a boy of about ten years of age. He was spending a few days with Christine though she was not his mother or even a classificatory kinswoman.]

Thursday, 18/12/52

I saw two men fighting so badly that blood and flesh were streaming from their mouths and noses. Both had to be taken to hospital.

Friday, 19/12/52

Bwana Pascal caught a man entering his house very late at night. He hit him six times for a whole minute until the man escaped in the dark.

Saturday, 20/12/52

I was happy today for two Warega from our country arrived in Stanleyville from Shabunda. [The two new arrivals were Djopo and Asani; they were kinsmen and associates of Abeli who had himself arrived in Stanleyville on 2/11/52.] As I walked up and down Avenue 21 this evening I saw two young men fighting over one woman. It was a fight in earnest, and later they were both taken to the police. How the matter ended I do not know.

Sunday, 21/12/52

Today my *shemeki*, Stanislas, and his younger brother arrived at my house at an early hour. *Bibi* Mangaza prepared rice and beef for them. They ate so well that they left some food. [It is customary etiquette for *shemeki* not to finish food offered to them.] After eating, I bought six bottles of beer for 54 francs and a flask of wine for 60 francs. They drank well but again did not finish the drink. They left here at mid-day and I accompanied them as far as Avenue 1, Brussels, when they were on their way to Belge I.

Monday, 22/12/52

Today I was not well and I went to work feeling that my body was not right, but I do not want to stay at home without working for a single day. I want to go to work even if only to do a little. Why? Because I have a large family, myself, my wife, my two children and my younger brother, Sangu-masi. All their problems and sufferings are my responsibility. It is I who have to find food for them. When I came out of work, I went straight home, did not go out at all.

Tuesday, 23/12/52

. . . A certain young girl was returning home from school and passing near the market when a lorry suddenly came upon her. She got a fright and tried to run away, but the lorry knocked her down and killed her. There is a saying: do not leave till tomorrow what you can do today. But this poor virgin had not had time to live.

Wednesday, 24/12/52

Two white men had a fierce argument on the corner of Avenue 21. They quarrelled in front of very many black people. But they only shouted and did not hit each other.

A certain man heard, on coming back from work, that his wife had stolen 600 francs from the house of another man next door. When he found his wife he gave her a beating. She denied that she had stolen the money, but the more she denied it the more he beat her.

Thursday, 25/12/52

Noël. This day we began to drink early in the morning. There were many of us gathered on the compound, and the women were there also. We bought six flasks of sugar cane wine and 60 bottles of beer. [The group of men gathered on the compound for most of the day consisted of six Warega: Patrice himself, Sangumasi, Pascal, Abeli, and Djopo and Asani both of whom had only arrived in Stanleyville the previous Saturday. This group was joined at one stage by Limela, who had by then left the compound, and by Camille, a Mubali living on the next compound.] When we had finished all that drink we went to the house of Kankamina at No. 169, Avenue 8, New Brussels. We were very well received with six plates of rice and vegetables. After eating we drank beer, a whole case of bottles. We left there late in the afternoon to return to our houses, and I did not go out again.

Friday, 26/12/52

A certain man had asked the wife of his brother to lend him some money. When she went to his house to give him the money this man bought six bottles of beer and asked the woman to drink with him. They finished the beer, and then the man said to the woman: '*Bibi*, now I want to be with you.' The woman was astonished and refused, and she was so astonished at this that she tried to run away, but the man held her back and prevented her from leaving. He said to her: 'Woman, do you think that you have drunk my beer for nothing? No, when a man and a woman drink beer, it is for them to go together.' The woman then ran away and went to tell her husband who is a corporal in the army. Her husband came to the house, but the man had run away and they did not see him again.

Saturday, 27/12/52

When I came out of work, I did not go anywhere. And I did not do anything or hear anything—only hunger, for today we were very hungry.

Sunday, 28/12/52

I and Pascal went early this morning to Belge I to a *muchezo wa wazungu* [game of the Europeans] called Tombola. Many people received prizes, but we did not receive so much as a match. That is bad fortune. One man received a bicycle, another a gramophone, another a camera. And other things too.

Monday, 29/12/52

It rained very hard during the night until 7 o'clock this morning. At one time when the rain stopped a little about 3 o'clock in the night I went out to clear my bowels. Everyone was asleep and no voices could be heard.

Tuesday, 30/12/52
No entry.

Wednesday, 31/12/52
No entry.

Thursday, 1/1/53 (Nouvelle année)
This morning I went to No. 35, Avenue 8, New Brussels, to see my friend
Henri who is a clerk at the clinic. [Henri was a man whom Patrice had known
in Kasese.] We drank 10 bottles of beer. He had bought five and I bought
five. When we had finished drinking, his woman [mistress] arrived at
his house so I left him with her to come back to my house. When I was
nearly back home I met *Monsieur* Pons who bought me four bottles of beer
which I drank with my friends at home. This European asked me to come to
his house at 7 o'clock this evening. When the time had come I started out
with my family to celebrate the New Year in the European's house. We
arrived there as follows: I, my brother Sangumasi, Asani, my wife *Bibi*
Mangaza, and my children Kalanga and Marguerite. We drank beer till
midnight. Then we ate in the manner of Europeans. And we smoked.
After the feast we went back home. There is nothing else to say, we slept
like corpses.

Friday, 2/1/53
In the morning we went to roll call as usual. When we arrived there, the
muzungu told us that we would all return home today. No work, a holiday.
A holiday to drink and to dance and to walk about. So we went back to
Brussels each disappearing into his own house. I did not go walking very
much, only for a little while with my friend Jerome [a Mukumu companion
from his workplace]. Then I returned home. In the afternoon we played
the gramophone and danced [in Christine's house]. Then we went to sleep.

Saturday, 3/1/53
I went to work and returned home at mid-day. At work the European
told me that I would be dismissed from work next Monday. [In a spell of
annoyance, Patrice had himself said that he no longer wished to continue
working there.] Then I went straight to New Brussels to my friend Henri
to chat with him for a while, and from there to the house of my brother,
Prosper, who gave me rice and fish to eat. Then I came back to my house.
On that day no one quarrelled with me and I quarrelled with no one.

Sunday, 4/1/53
In the morning I did not go anywhere. At 1 o'clock I left home to visit Moke.
We talked for a long time, up to 3 o'clock in the afternoon. I then went to see
Prosper at his house. We ate rice and after eating he accompanied me back
on the road to my house. Then I met Limela who asked me to walk back
with him to New Brussels. I went with him, and on our return as we passed
the house of Lusaka we stopped to talk to him. We did not drink or eat there
but we discussed many things with great joy, and we laughed a great deal.

Monday, 5/1/53
The *chef* of the sawmill dismissed me from work at 11 o'clock. For this month
I have worked two days and I asked for that money till I was tired of arguing.

He said that he refused to give me the money. He said that I was refusing the work because I had asked to leave. How could I then expect to be paid for those two days?

Tuesday, 6/1/53

In the morning I went back to the office at the saw mill to ask again for my money. I was there from early morning till mid-day, but they refused again so I came back home at 3 o'clock in the afternoon. My brother Pascal came to my house to find me and I went with him for a walk. We then went to the house of Prosper. We talked for a long time and then Pascal stayed there, and I went on to visit my friend Henri. I left Henri at 7 o'clock in the evening and returned home.

Wednesday, 7/1/53

When I woke up in the morning I climbed a palm tree to cut nuts for *Bibi* Mangaza. My young brother Sangumasi had difficulties during the night. Three women tried to enter his house and to beat him for no reason. They are witches. Sangumasi screamed in the night so that we all woke up. When we went to his room we did not find anyone there. He was on his own, but we asked him why he had shouted. He said that three women had come to try to break in. They had a Coleman lamp and were trying the doors and the windows. These three women must be from Avenue 19. They often come to Christine's to drink and they want Sangumasi to have sexual relations with them. But he refuses so they are seeking their revenge.

Later in the morning I went to visit my brother Joseph. On that compound I found a certain man beating his wife. He stripped her clothes off and wanted to plunge a knife into her vagina. At that very moment my brother Prosper came out of Joseph's room and stopped the man. But that man was in a ferocious mood and he turned against Prosper who said to him: 'If you want to kill, then kill me instead of your wife.' Then a certain woman passed by and went to call the police. When the man saw the woman going to report him, he took his bicycle and fled.

Since I was dismissed from work not one person has given me so much as a piece of cassava to eat. I reflect that a man is not liked when he has no work. Your brothers like you when you have work but not when you have no work.

I went to see my friend Henri and talked to him for a long time. Then I went as far as the house of Maria, the woman [mistress] of my friend Limela. The woman greeted me when she saw me and gave me a chair to sit down. I stayed there a short while.

Thursday, 8/1/53

To-day I went in search of work in the town from 7 o'clock to mid-day, but I did not find a place. I asked for work at 15 places. On my return I found Mangaza ill with fever. This is because she has not eaten food. Who will give me food? But even if I had food I would not be able to eat on account of the illness of my wife, and because I have not found work.

Friday, 9/1/53

I got up at the first cock and went to town to look for work again. I asked at 9 places, but as yesterday there is nothing to be found. On returning to Brussels I went directly to my friend Henri to tell him my unfortunate news.

In the evening I had two pieces of banana to eat and then went to sleep with great sadness in my heart for I do not know where I shall find work.

Saturday, 10/1/53

In the morning I went to town to look for work. I asked as usual on the previous days. Eventually I went back to my house and stayed there, without going anywhere, till night. At 7 o'clock *Bibi* Mangaza brought me a little food. I ate this and went to sleep.

Sunday, 11/1/53

At 8 o'clock my friend Ramazani arrived at my house and found me in my sadness. He talked to me for 25 minutes and then left to visit his brothers.

Monday, 12/1/53

In the morning I went to town to look for work again. I came to the oil mill where my brother Mumbuli works. They gave me work as a labourer. From there I went to the employment office to register my work, but I had to go back home without getting the signature.

Tuesday, 13/1/53

Early in the morning I went again to the employment office to register my work but I waited for long and came away at 10 o'clock without the signature. In the afternoon I did not go anywhere because my feet were so tired. I ate a little food but only a little.

Wednesday, 14/1/53

I again went to the employment office and waited for six hours to have the inscription made. I then came home and from there went to visit my brother, Kankamina, who said that his employer had also dismissed him saying that he was not regular at work. Kankamina was very unhappy.

Thursday, 15/1/53 to Thursday, 22/1/53
No entries.

Friday, 23/1/53

I started work this morning at 7 o'clock and worked till mid-day. When I came home I did not go walking.

Saturday, 24/1/53

In the morning I went to work from 7 o'clock to mid-day. I did not go home but started work again from 1 o'clock to 6 o'clock in the evening.

Sunday, 25/1/53

This afternoon I went to work on my house in New Brussels. On coming back from there I found on the compound a woman named Safi, a junior of Christine. This woman is *demi-fou*. She arrived today and pretends to know us all. This astonishes us.

In the evening we played the gramophone [in Christine's house] and drank palm wine, and after that we went to sleep.

Monday, 26/1/53

Went to the oil mill. At mid-day I had *chikwange* and ground nuts to eat. This morning a certain European in a lorry knocked over a man on his bicycle in Avenue 5. The man was hurt but did not die. He escaped death by the love of God.

In the afternoon the police stopped Mumbuli and wanted to take him away to the Army camp, but he told them that he works at the oil mill and was going to work there tonight. They let him go and he went to work at 8 o'clock this evening. [Mumbuli was apprehended by a police patrol checking on men without work or without permission to be in the C.E.C.]

Tuesday, 27/1/53

I did not go to work to-day, and at 10 o'clock I received a letter with very bad news. News that the sister of Sabina is dead! Secondly, the news that an old man Kimbikwa from our village is dead! Then the third news that our headman Kisumba has been dismissed. Kisumba is also one of ours. Those three sad things made me unable to go to work. And I did not eat today for I cannot eat on account of the sadness which closes my heart.

Wednesday, 28/1/53

The father of my friend Jerome died in hospital today. He leaves a girl who is still a baby. This afternoon they are going to bury him.

Thursday, 29/1/53

Early this morning I met in Avenue 7, a woman from our country.

At work a certain young man caught his fingers in the machine for crushing ground nuts. He stopped the machine himself and then tried to get his hand out, but he put the machine on again and suddenly he caught the other hand and all his fingers were cut off. There does not remain one, not one!

Friday, 30/1/53

A man stole a bicycle from his own friend, but they caught him near the Army camp. The police came and took him to the Commissioner. Then a certain woman stole a cloth from her friend. She was walking behind her friend. The cloth fell, she picked it up and hid it in her headscarf. She thought that she had not been seen by other people, but people on the roadside shouted at her. The cloth fell out of her headscarf, and her friend hit her three times until she gave the cloth back.

Saturday, 31/1/53

At work two men fought each other with knives. Both were taken to the Police Commissioner—it is their affair. Today I met my young brother, Gilbert, and I gave him 30 francs. [Gilbert, a boy of 14, was a classificatory kinsman who attended a school near Stanleyville and occasionally came to visit his kinsmen in the town.] When I came back from work I did not go anywhere except to borrow a flask of wine from *Baba* Asumani in Avenue 18. [Asumani ran a small palm wine bar; he was not related to Patrice and the term *Baba* was used out of general respect.]

APPENDIX J

Some Letters by and to Patrice between 18/1/52 and 31/9/52

The following letters should be read in conjunction with Patrice's case history given in Chapter VII. The letters are a selection out of about 60 either written or received by Patrice over a period of nine months covering a part of his stay in Ponthierville and his first five months in Stanleyville. The main interest of the letters for our analysis lies in their clear demonstration that Patrice's network of social relations with kinsmen and fellow tribesmen in town was an extension of a much wider network covering both town and country. The letters are also of general interest in illustrating conditions and attitudes surrounding migration and letter-writing. Most letters to and from Patrice's tribal area were despatched through lorry drivers, and some were undoubtedly mislaid or never delivered. The letters are translations from Swahili. All explanations and comments are given in brackets.

1 *Letter from Luzoka, a classificatory brother of Patrice. Dated 18/1/52, the letter was written from Kasese, where Patrice and Luzoka had been close associates. It was sent to Patrice in Ponthierville about two months after his departure from Kasese with his brother Sangumasi*

Monsieur Patrice,

My brother, I received your letter of 17/12/51. The news from here is that I have received no letters from home [from their families in the village], but I will have news on the return of our young Christophe [Christophe was a boy of 13 years attending school in Kasese and living with Luzoka; he was one of Patrice's brothers] who is now at home [in the village]. When he returns here I will let you know if your wife has given birth. Brother, have you yet found work in (Ponthierville)? The child, Fazil, [an adult brother of Patrice but younger than himself] was attacked by some Walendu [members of the Walendu tribe]. They wanted to kill him. He was on the road travelling back from Usumbura [where he had been working]. Fazil has now gone to see Elizabeth [his wife] who has given birth to a boy by the name of Mubam-yara. Here I have already learnt the sewing machine, but it is difficult to earn money. I have only 1,300 francs per month [presumably from his wages—earned as a cook in a European household—and from some part-time tailoring]. As I now have the sewing machine which I wanted so much, I shall leave my employer. I have been with him for four years but I receive no consideration from him. I asked him for a loan for my sewing machine, but he refused. Now I am tired of working for him. I will let you know later what I do. *Monsieur* Patrice, you will have news as soon as Christophe returns from our home. All the children are here with me and are well. Your brother Munyololo [the writer of letter No. 2], and Egeri, and Sadiki and his three children send you their greetings. [Munyololo, Egeri, and

Sadiki were all living in Kasese at the time.] Let me have news of Ponthier-ville, whether it is a good place to work, for I may follow you. Has the child Sangumasi found work yet? Let me have news of him.

Goodbye. We shall see each other when God allows. That is all. This is the end of my letter.

Meilleure bonjour,

Luzoka

Cuisinier de M. ——,

Kasese

2   *Letter from Munyololo, a Murega from the same village as Patrice. Dated 20/2/52, the letter was written from Kasese, where Munyololo had been one of Patrice's immediate associates. Like letter No. 1 in which there is mention of Munyololo, it was sent to Patrice in Ponthierville after his departure from Kasese*

From Munyololo Bernard, *Tailleur Personnel au Poste de Kasese.*

Monsieur Patrice,

I received your letter with great joy, but the parcel you ask me to send, it is impossible for it would all be eaten on the way by the carriers. I ask you to send me your address. [The present letter, like many others, was despatched through a lorry driver. Muyololo is asking for Patrice's employer's postal address so that he might write by post.] I am well and all the children are well, and my wife is well. News from our home [tribal area] is that Saki-midi died in the village of Kiamusoke. The daughter of Salehe, tailor, also died. Matunda died here in Kasese of a snake bite. [The three deceased were all persons whom might well in town have been claimed by Patrice as 'fictitious' kinsmen.] Greetings to you and to the child Sangumasi [another case of the term 'child' being used because Sangumasi was one of Patrice's younger brothers]. My young brother Patrice, I am well and I send greetings to you and your child [i.e. Sangumasi].

I am your,

Munyololo

3   *Letter from Gaston, a fellow-tribesman and close associate of Patrice. Dated 20/2/52, the letter was written from Kasese and, like letters Nos. 1 and 2, was sent to Patrice in Ponthierville*

Monsieur Patrice,

Many greetings to you in the love of God. I received your first letter sent long ago with much joy. I would again like to receive letters from you. Other news. My two wives have arrived here and send greetings to you ten times. *Bwana* Patrice, do not ever forget to write letters to us.

I am your,

Gaston

4 *Letter from Lwakama, one of Patrice's classificatory brothers,*
who was attending a secondary school at a Protestant mission
station close to Stanleyville. The letter, dated 13/4/52, was
written from the mission station to Patrice in Ponthierville a few
days before he moved to Stanleyville. The letter was in answer to
one from Patrice explaining how he and Lwakama missed seeing
each other when Lwakama passed through Ponthierville on his
recent journey from their tribal area to his school

Bwana Patrice,

I received your letter with great joy. I am truly glad to have your explanations, dear friend! For I had looked for you everywhere when I passed through Ponthierville, but the boat [on which he had travelled to Ponthierville] only arrived late in the evening. Until I received your letter to-day I thought you had returned home [to the village], and that you were now already there. Your father and your wife gave me letters to pass on to you, but they are lost. But they are well, your father and your wife. Your wife asks me to tell you that if you find work in Stanleyville you must send her some money for clothes for herself and the child. She spoke to me of very many things which I no longer remember. Now, *Bwana*, I know very well where Kankamina lives. [Kankamina was a classifictory kinsman of Lwakama living in Stanleyville; Patrice did not know him personally but had been told to contact him on arrival.] Perhaps he has changed his work place, but he lives in Brussels, Avenue 17, No. 14. When you arrive in Stanleyville go to No. 14, Avenue 17, and you will find him there. The name of his wife is Clementine Mayumu. When you arrive, you must tell me and come to visit me at the end of the month or at the beginning. (For then) I will be able to receive you well.

That is all. Greetings,   Lwakama

5 *Another letter from Munyololo, the writer of letter No. 2.*
Dated 24/5/52, the letter was written from Kasese in answer to
news of Patrice's arrival in Stanleyville

Monsieur Patrice,

I received your letter with great joy. I was very pleased to receive this first letter (from Stanleyville) and I ask you to write always.

I give you news from home that Lubala is dead and the child of Salehe is dead. Moliso is also dead, and also Sakimidi. [Two of these deaths had already been announced to Patrice in Munyololo's letter of 20/2/52.] The news from here is that I am still in Kasese with my family and we are well. Since your wife returned to your father's house I have not had news or greetings from them. [Patrice's wife, Mangaza, had left Kasese to return home in October 1951, shortly before Patrice himself left for Ponthierville]. Greetings to you and to the child, Sangumasi, and to my namesake Prosper, and to Moke. [Prosper and Moke were both men who had worked in Kasese before moving to Stanleyville. Munyololo was himself also called Prosper hence the reference to his namesake.]

That is all, I am your,   Munyololo

P.S. The children and the woman, Anzelina, greet you and they greet the child Sangumasi (Anzelina was Munyololo's wife).

6　*Letter from Mangaza, Patrice's wife. Dated 19/6/52 it was written from Patrice's village where Mangaza was at this time still staying with Patrice's father after the birth of her second child in April*

Monsieur Patrice,

I tell you that you do not know how to be a father and how to be married to a woman. You are a simple man [i.e. a man of little worth]. Did you leave others here to feed me and to buy me clothes? Your father has money but he never gives me as much as five francs, not a match to light the fire, nor even one franc to buy soap. I have given birth to a child, her name is Marguerite, and your son Kalanga is growing into a child. [Patrice had previously heard from others of the birth of his daughter.] If you do not want to send me clothes, then send for the children because it is you who gave them life. Since I came back here I have little food. Every day I suffer, and I think of you because we go to sleep hungry every night. I often write to you but no reply. [Cf. Letter No. 4 in which Lwakama reported having lost letters from Patrice's wife and father.] I tell you again that I am hungry, and that I am getting thin on account of the absence of food and clothes. I am looking for a way to follow you to Stanleyville but it is not possible. You will accuse me of refusing to join you, but it is not like that. It is you, my husband, who are refusing me [i.e. by not sending her money for the trip]. Your father asks you to send him a leather belt. We are all well, but I ask you to send me clothes. Greetings,

I am,

Mangaza

7　*Letter from Joseph, a classificatory brother of Patrice and associate with whom he had worked in Kasese. Dated 23/6/52, the letter was written from Yumbi, a small labour centre on the road from Kasese to Stanleyville*

Monsieur Patrice,

My sincere greetings to you. Your child, Joseph, [i.e. the writer] finds himself in Yumbi. I left Kasese with the chauffeur, Alimete, who was going to bring me to you in Stanleyville. [Alimete was also a Murega based in Stanleyville but known to Patrice by name only.] Now, on the way here he was arrested and sent to gaol. So I find myself here and have no means of joining you. I have already started to work here in Yumbi, but the work in question does not interest me, and my brothers [associates] here are not happy with me. As my brothers are not satisfied with me, I will not continue to work here. I await the end of the month to have my wages, and I will pay a ticket on a lorry to come to Stanleyville. [In fact Joseph did not arrive in Stanleyville till November, 1952. See also letter No. 17.]

Greet the child, Sangumasi. Greetings from me, Joseph. On receiving this letter, reply by next week.

Yours,

Joseph

8   *Another letter from Luzoka, the writer of letter No.* 1.
    Dated 27/6/52, *the letter was written from Kasese*

Monsieur Patrice,

Greetings. Receive my sincerest greetings. I, your elder brother, Luzoka, let you know that I received your letter of 21/6/52. Our junior, Christophe, has now finished his schooling here in Kasese. The child Fazil is now working here with *Monsieur* —— and is at present with him on safari. [Christophe and Fazil were both brothers of Patrice and were referred to in letter No. 1.] Other news. I intend to come to Stanleyville. Tell me how much you earn per day and how much for rations per week. When I come to Stanleyville I will no longer work as a *boy* [domestic servant]. I will look for another job to earn more money. What is your work in Stanleyville? Where do you work? And what is the wage of Pascal? [Pascal was the classificatory brother with whom Patrice and Sangumasi had travelled first from Kasese to Ponthierville and then from Ponthierville to Stanleyville.] The news of Joseph is that he left (Kasese) on 30/5/52 to come to you (in Stanleyville). But I heard from others that he stayed for a while in Yumbi with our brother Alimete who is a lorry driver for Houdmont Co. in Stanleyville. But I also heard that Alimete is in prison. [Cf. Letter No. 7.] As soon as Alimete is free we shall all have the possibility of coming to Stanleyville without difficulty. Other news is that I and my wife, Fatuma, are having some difficulties, that is to say that she went to see her family and stayed for three months instead of two as I had given her permission. On her return she found me with another woman. She made trouble, but not very much, and I sent the other woman back to her family in Shabunda. Even so, my wife is still annoyed and she has told my employer about this matter.

That is my news. Our father and our children are well, and also our mothers.

I am your,

Luzoka

9   *Another letter from Munyololo, the writer of letters Nos.* 2
    and 5. *Dated* 8/7/52, *the letter was written from Kasese*

Monsieur Patrice,

Greetings to you and the love of God.

Now my news is that I am here [i.e. in Kasese as before] but I am now a *capita vendeur* [salesman] for *Monsieur* —— [i.e. since his last letter to Patrice, Munyololo had given up work as a private tailor]. Other news is that my wife has given birth to a boy. Please acknowledge the receipt of my letter as soon as possible. I had no answer to my last letter. Greetings to the child Sangumasi. My wife and the children greet you.

Your,

Munyololo
Capita vendeur for M. ——

10   *Note from Clothilde, a Murega woman in Stanleyville who was a daughter of one of Patrice's classificatory sisters. Clothilde was living in Belge I and the note was addressed to Patrice and his classificatory brother, Prosper, on 5/8/52*

For *Muyomba* [mother's brother] Patrice and *Monsieur* Prosper,

Oh! my brothers, I wish to die without anyone to bury me. Why do you refuse to help me with money? You make me feel ashamed in front of my husband, especially you Patrice. When I go back to our country I shall tell my mother about this. I no longer count myself as your brother [in the broad sense of 'one of you']. Do not bother to come and see me any more.

Clothilde

[This breach in relations between Patrice and Clothilde was soon made up.]

11   *Another letter from Luzoka, the writer of letters Nos. 1 and 8. Dated 14/8/52 the letter was written from Kasese where he was still working as a cook for the same employer as before*

Monsieur Patrice,

My brother, thank you very much for your letter, I received it with joy. You have not received a reply from me before now because *Monsieur* ——— [his employer] told me there were no stamps in his office. This is why your letter has not been answered. My brother, I let you know that I and my wife, Fatuma, have a very big argument. We argue every day and that is why I have now given her permission to go *en congé* for 25 days. As soon as I leave the service of *Monsieur* ———, I shall no longer work in the forest. I am still working here because I do not want to insist on leaving, otherwise I would be put in prison. At the moment I am here, but I wish to come to Stanleyville so I have sold my bicycle to another man for 2,000 francs.

Monsieur Patrice, Joseph is at Yumbi with *Monsieur* ———. He ended his contract here for three years as a tailor. [See letter No. 7.] Fazil is at the moment in Kindu (see letters Nos. 1 and 8) and his employer is *Monsieur* ——— who is the administrator there. Here is the address. Fazil, *Boy de Monsieur* ———, *Le Ministre Principal à Kindu.* Write to him.

I am your,

Luzoka

I no longer remember the address of Malasi [a classificatory sister of both men].

12   *Letter from Patrice's father, Lupanzula. Dated 14/8/52, it was written from Lupanzula's village*

Dear *Monsieur* Patrice,

I regret that I told you of the marriage of Sangumasi for I see that I have neither money nor goats to pay. This grieves me for since your birth I have never beaten [been hard on] any of you, nor has your mother. And you have left me with the matter of Mwanini whose husband gave 2,000 francs and the matter is not yet settled. [Lupanzula was wanting to pay bridewealth for a wife for Sangumasi as he had earlier done for Patrice. Mwanini, one of Lupanzula's daughters, had left her husband and Lupanzula was expected to repay the bridewealth he had received for her.] Also, your wife needs clothes. I have given her 85 francs to buy a cloth and 35 francs for a head-scarf. Since you left I have bought no clothes for myself. It is all this question of Mwanini that weighs heavily on me. Since you left one letter only from you, the letter to your wife. If you see lorries from Kima, give your letters to these drivers for then we will have them without difficulty. If you find work, do not tell any of our children here for they are of bad heart and will want to follow you. Tell me what work you do there, and send me money to help me to arrange for a wife for Sangumasi. The matter of Mwanini was too much for me. That is why your wife was dissatisfied [annoyed] with me, saying that I do not look after her. [Cf. letter No. 6.] Your wife will soon follow you; you must be good to her, you must not beat her. You, Patrice, must be careful, you are a fool because you always associate with people who do not know how to be careful, who do not behave well and who do not know how to use money. I give you this advice that you may buy things of value such as a sewing machine, a bicycle, a gramophone and other things like that.

Greetings to Sangumasi and to you,

Your father,

Lupanzula

Your mother greets you, and especially do I, your father, Lupanzula, greet you. I want to know what work you do. Up till now I have no criticisms on the conduct of your wife. She is always here with us. She does not ask permission to go anywhere.

I am your father,

Lupanzula

13 *Another letter from Patrice's wife, Mangaza. Dated 15/8/52, it was written from Patrice's home village where Mangaza was still staying with Patrice's father and his family*

Cher Monsieur Patrice,

I have given birth to a daughter, her name is Marguerite. And your son is growing into a child. [A repetition of news given in letter No. 6 written two months earlier]. Your father says that you must pay me a ticket so that I may come to Stanleyville in September. Your mother and other members of the family greet you. I will go by the Kima road and I am first going to Kima to Veronique [Veronique was the sister of Mangaza's father]. Her husband [Kikuni, a lorry driver and writer of letter No. 14] will help me to get to Stanleyville. My husband, Patrice, you must look after your money. Do not waste it on drink and women. That is all I have to say. Greetings to you and to *Bwana* Sangumasi.

I am your *Madame* Mangaza

14 *Letter from Kikuni, husband of Veronique the sister of Mangaza's father. Dated 30/8/52, it was written from Kima, another small labour centre in Warega territory*

A letter for our child Patrice,

I send you news of your wife who is at my house. She has been here seven days and that is why I, Kikuni, am now writing to you to ask you to send money for your wife to buy a ticket for Stanleyville. You must send this because our lorry [that of which he was the driver] is not on the Stanley-ville road any more. We are now working on the Shabunda road. That is why you must send 300 francs for your wife immediately. They say that I will not again work on the Stanleyville road. Thus you must send 300 francs, that is the price of the ticket. I, your father, have difficulties. They have promised me 1,000 francs but I do not know when I will see those 1,000 francs. [Kikuni is explaining why he cannot help Mangaza himself. Kikuni refers to Patrice as 'our child', and to himself as Patrice's 'father', in a general sense. He and Patrice were not kinsmen but were both married to women of the same family. Kikuni was, however, senior to Patrice in years and experience, and also by virtue of his marriage to the *shangazi*—father's sister—of Patrice's wife.] I want you to send me a letter quickly. Do not allow many days to pass before sending the money for your wife's ticket. I, your father Kikuni, weep that I do not see you, my son Patrice. If we do not help each other, who will help us? Your wife is downcast and weeps very much. She does not want to eat, nor to chat, nor to sleep, she just cries. But she sends her greetings to you. Your children are well. I want one child, your son, Kalanga, to stay here with us. Send your letter quickly. quickly. I am your father, Kikuni. We do not live eternally.

That is all,

Kikuni

15   *Letter written by Patrice to his wife, Mangaza, in answer partly to her letter No. 13 and partly to Kikuni's letter No. 14. Dated 14/9/52, this letter was sent to Mangaza in Kima where she was staying with Kikuni*

Chère Madame Mangaza,

Bon! my dear, receive this letter with great joy from the one who loves you without any doubt. I write to tell you that I am sending 350 francs [by postal order], 300 francs for your journey by lorry and 50 francs for food on the way. Before you set out on the journey, you must send me a letter by post from Kima.

Now I must tell you that father Kikuni asks me permission for the child, Kalanga, to stay there with him, but I do not want this for I have spent many days without seeing my son. Not to see my children causes me grief.

That is all,

With *besi* [baisers]
Patrice

16   *Letter written by Patrice to Kikuni in answer to Kikuni's letter No. 14. The letter was dated 14/9/52 and written at the same time as letter No. 15*

Monsieur Kikuni,

Thank you very much for your letter written 30/8/52 and received by me 10/9/52. I receive the news of the arrival of my wife at your house. Now I am sending her 350 francs, 300 francs for the ticket and 50 francs for food on the journey. But I ask you, what kind of big difficulties have you had? [A reference to Kikuni's complaint that he was unable to help Mangaza on her way.] Difficulties with thieves or difficulties with women?

Then as regards the permission you seek to keep the child, Kalanga, with you: Father, forgive me a thousand times, but so many days have passed since I saw him. This grieves me and so I cannot leave him with you. *Pardon. Pardonnez moi s.v.p., père.* That is all. Greetings to you,

Patrice

17   *Another letter from Joseph, writer of letter No. 7. Dated*
14/9/52, the letter was written from Yumbi where Joseph had
found himself stranded in June

Monsieur Patrice, *Cher Monsieur,*
   Receive my greetings. I am well. I would like to receive a reply to my first letter. I want to leave here and to join you in Stanleyville. Please look for a house for me to buy. Let me know the price of the house.

Greetings to you,

Joseph

18   *A letter written by Patrice to Luzoka, the writer of letters*
Nos. 1, 8, and 11. Dated 16/9/52, it was sent from Stanleyville
to Kasese

Monsieur Luzoka,
   Receive the news that for many days I have not had news from you. I do not know how you are and how you have been all this time. Then, I have to tell you that my wife has left home [the village] and is now in Kima, and I have sent her 350 francs for a ticket to come here.
   That is all,

Greetings to the house,

I am your younger brother,   Patrice

19   *Another letter from Gaston, writer of letter No. 3. Dated*
18/9/52, it was written from Kasese

Monsieur Patrice,
   Greetings to you. Thank you very much for your letter which gave me great joy. I have nothing else to tell you, but I hope that I will hear from you again. The women [i.e. specifically Gaston's two wives] were overjoyed to receive news from you. I am waiting for work. In the meanwhile I am here with *Bwana* Homari. He is the younger brother of *Bwana* Swafuri [Homari and Swafuri were Warega living in Kasese. Only Swafuri was known to Patrice]. Now he [Homari] says he and I should work together in commerce. So this is my news.
   Other news. I heard that your wife is well, and that she gave birth to a daughter, and that the daughter is well too, and that they are all well at your home.

I am your

Gaston

20   *Letter from Damiano, a classificatory brother living in a village close to Patrice's home village. The letter was dated* 31/9/52

Cher Monsieur Patrice,

   I give you news that I am well up to this day. I ask whether the letter I sent you arrived. Because it is two months since I wrote and no reply. Did it arrive or did it not arrive? Then I ask you about your wife, Mangaza. Did she arrive or did she not arrive? Because we have had no letters from you. [Unintelligible sentence omitted here.] If your wife is with you, greetings to the two children. You will send a reply quickly because from the time she left there are no letters. So I ask you now. Then I also ask something else. Tell me if you have great difficulties because I want you to send me 200 francs in an envelope through the post. Now also there is the question of the child, Jacques [a brother of the writer]. I have asked about him many times. Why does he not write to me? I have heard that he is a *boy-chauffeur*, but I do not know where. Perhaps he is in Stanleyville, but perhaps he does not know what work you do, or where you are. Greetings to Sangumasi and to you.

                                                                    Damiano

Some Letters by Limela and Henri, the Brother of Limela's Wife Rosina

The following nine letters were written between 2/10/52 and 2/1/53. They all refer to difficulties at this time in Limela's marriage to Rosina and to his relationship with her family. They should be read in conjunction with the account of the marriage given in Chapter VII. They are the only letters bearing on the subject to which I had access and are clearly only some of a longer series. They were translated from Swahili. Explanations and comments are given in brackets.

1 *Letter from Henri to his sister, Rosina, in answer to a letter in which she had told him of her marital difficulties with Limela and of her quarrels with Christine. Dated 2/10/52, it was written in Kindu where Henri worked, and was received by Rosina in Stanleyville shortly before her second departure for Bafwasende*

Bibi Rosina,

Thank you for your letter and for what you have explained to me. I understand but there is little I can say. I am well and so are my wife and children.

I understand all the difficulties you write of, but what shall I say? What shall I say about all these affairs? I ask you to wait and to be patient for you have children. If your husband Limela does not love you any more, let him say so in one word and let him return you to your home. If there is very grave difficulty and you do not receive food or money at the end of the month you must ask him quietly. Ask him every day but always be polite. In this way you will be in the right in the eyes of God and of people.

As for the matter that his sister Christine asks you to bring her a goat from us, that makes me laugh. It is nonsense. Ask her whether she is not the sister of your husband? Let her bring me presents! How many goats did we receive from his family? We received 700 francs! [i.e. as bridewealth. The statement is made with the clear implication that it was a small payment, and that none of Limela's kinsmen can possibly have any claims on Rosina's family, rather the reverse]. Then she adds that she is going to kill you. She may well do so, but she herself and her whole family would then die on account of the death of one person. Tell her!

You wish to come here. Yes, but wait till 1st January 1953. I will write to you and send you a ticket, but I have other urgent matters to attend to first. And when you go to Bafwasende, you must let me know, and you must put an end to your mourning. You have mourned enough, and you must now wash your body [i.e. come out of mourning].

I am sending you a photo. Greetings to the children, and greetings to you.

Henri

2   *Letter from Henri to Limela in answer to a letter in which
Limela had written of his marital difficulties with Rosina. It was
written in Kindu, and dated 7/10/52*

Monsieur Limela,

Bwana, thank you very much for your letter which I received with pleasure. All the news you give I understand very well and I have not much to
say except to advise you to change your ways and your character. That
is what I have to say. One can tell people and teach them in earnest, but
if they do not wish to listen and follow the advice then that is their own
responsibility and misfortune. Rosina has also written to me, telling me that
there are difficulties. And she writes that your sister continually quarrels
with her and annoys her by saying that you are poor and that Rosina
should give your family a goat. All this is just trouble-making, and I advise
you not to follow your sister's ways and bad behaviour. Your sister must
know that she is in the wrong. I advise you to be good to your wife, to look
after her well, and to stay with her lovingly. But if you wish to send her back
to Bafwasende, that is for you to decide. That is your affair. I simply ask
you both to stay well together, and to have children. God helps us to bring
children into the world, and allows us to increase the Earth. To have children
is the custom of the world and it profits the world.

I am well and so is my wife, and the children are also well. They greet
you. If you should send Rosina to Bafwasende write to me before her journey
to let me know the date. My work here will be finished in April 1953,
when I shall come to Stanleyville.

Best greetings to your family, my greetings to you.

Yours,   Henri

3   *Letter from Limela to Rosina's brother, Mambele. Dated
11/11/52, the letter was addressed to Mambele in Bafwasende
at the time of Rosina's second visit to her family there*

Mon cher supérieur et cher beau-frère Mambele,
Monsieur,

Here is your daughter [in fact sister] accompanied by my children. I
have given her permission to stay away two months and not one week more.
At the end of November, *Monsieur* Arumbengwe [Rosina's father] will
receive a postal order from me. I wanted to send him this money but you
know that a head cannot wear two hats and your sister has to end her mourning and so this past month I gave her all I had, a sum of 1,500 francs for her
needs.

Now, *Monsieur* Mambele, I wish to see my wife and all my children back
here in 60 days for I have neither brother nor sister to give me food here.
You must please listen to me, and I assure you that at the end of November
there will be a present for you without any doubt.

My wife is a little quieter [happier] with me now. It was all a matter that a
sister of mine troubled her, and all these difficulties were over nothing and
for no reason. Now, I have already left the compound of this sister. That is
all, *Monsieur.* You will have another letter from me. I thank you for looking
after Rosina when she was pregnant [i.e. on her previous visit home].

Greetings to you all,

Limela

4 Letter from Limela to Rosina's father, Arumbengwe. Dated 12/11/52 it was also written at the time of Rosina's second visit to Bafwasende

Monsieur et cher beau-père Arumbengwe,

Greetings to you and to Mother and to all the children. I am to-day sending Rosina to you for her to wash herself with water [i.e. to end her period of mourning] and to show you the children. Also, Father, you know that we have a difficulty here on account of the children not being registered in my book. The children are not inscribed in my book and so cannot stay here. [This was not a problem of any urgency *vis-à-vis* the administration at the time, but Limela was eager to have the children's names inscribed in his identity book as he feared that he might one day find it difficult to claim their custody.] I ask you to go with Rosina to the mission to get a letter or certificate to show that they are her children. [If Rosina returned with such evidence he would then show it at the C.E.C. offices together with the certificate of his 'religious marriage' and he would thus have no difficulty in entering the children's names in his book.]

On the 5th or 10th December you will receive a postal order from me. I do not know how much I will send. I will see at the time I receive my money from the white people.

I am your child,

Limela

5 Another letter from Henri. Dated 18/11/52, it was written from Kindu in answer to one from Limela telling him that Rosina had returned to Bafwasende

Monsieur Limela,

Thank you very much for your letter which I received. All that you say I understand very very well. Thank you very much for the news of the children and of their mother. I want to have news like this every day. The matter of money does not trouble me. For me, money is nothing; it is only worldly—money you receive here and money you will leave here on earth.

Rosina will not, I think, stay long at Bafwasende. I want her very much to come here in January for a month or three weeks. I very much need to see her. And if you have given her 1,500 francs as you say that will suffice for her to come here from Bafwasende.

I and my wife and children are well except that the little Suzannah had a fever, but she is now better. She was in hospital for one week, but is now with us. My wife and the children greet you very much.

Yours,

Henri

6 Another letter from Henri, written from Kindu on 20/11/52

Monsieur Limela,

I have received news that Rosina has arrived in Bafwasende and that she is well and the children too. You had written that you would let me know the date of her departure but I received nothing. In my last letter I asked you to let me know the date of their departure but you did not.

Greetings to you,

Your wife's sister, Albertina, gave birth to a child on 15/11/52, but I do not know whether it was a boy or a girl.

Greetings to you,

Your *shemeki*,

Henri

7 *Another letter from Limela to Rosina's father, Arumbengwe. Dated 23/12/52, it was written after Arumbengwe had refused to accept 1,000 francs which Limela had sent him early in December*

Monsieur et Baba Arumbengwe,

Father, greetings to you and to Mother Agnes [Arumbengwe's wife]. I see that my postal order for 1,000 francs has been returned and that you are refusing me. Oh! My Father! Oh! My Mother! The Germans and the Belgians fought each other, but are they not now in agreement? Are they not? I do not hide my face because, even if I did, God would still see me.

Why is this? It is true that my sister, Christine, quarrelled with my wife every day. But we cannot take notice of her. She is truly a strange person. She eats and she works, but she has no heart, and she has no mind and she cannot think. She is like a cursed animal.

Father, since I saw those 1,000 francs returned, I no longer have the courage to live. My whole body feels ill. I would like you please to write to me. And if you refuse me, tell me why you refuse me.

Greetings to all,

I am your,

Limela

8 *Letter from Limela to Henri. Dated 29/12/52 it was in answer to letters Nos. 5 and 6*

Monsieur et Beau-frère Henri,

Dear brother,

I received your two envelopes on one day. Do not think that I did not take note of the birth of a child to my wife's sister. This letter is late but I have so many affairs here. I received a letter from my country and the news is that my *muyomba*, Kalongi, is dead. At work I have to prepare an inventory for the end of the year, and that is not yet finished. I still have a few days to finish.

Brother, Father, *Bwana* Henri, I sent 1,000 francs to Father Arumbengwe as a present but he refused it. Oh! Brother! What shall I do? What is there between my father and myself? Since you wrote to me, *Monsieur* Henri, to advise me to look after Rosina we have had no more difficulties. But perhaps father does not want Rosina to return to me. He returned the money but sent me no word with it. Brother, he ought to tell me why. Do you not think so? Oh! *Bwana* Henri, one must not fight. *Bwana* Henri, I think it is that my father [wife's father] does not want me any more, and so he is taking my wife back and also the children. Henri, what shall I do? Advise me what to do.

I did not send presents to my wife's father before because I did not feel love and respect for my wife. But since you advised me to look after her, I have done so.

It is true that when my wife was not here, my behaviour was not good. But does my wife's father wish me to continue falling into difficulties and misery? You know that I have no brothers. For me my real brother is my wife. Where shall I be without her? On Christmas Day I was without her. Now on New Year's day it will again be the same. Who shall I have to calm me? These are my sufferings, my elder brother.

To-day there is no news except for two things: (1) the death of my *oncle* [*muyomba*] (2) the refusal by my wife's father of the money.

Greetings to you and the children

Your,

Limela

9   *Letter from Henri, written in Kindu on* 21/1/53, *in answer to letter No. 8*

Monsieur Limela,
My dear *Bwana*,

I received your letter, and I understand all the things that you explained. Firstly, I send you my sympathy over the death of which you tell me. Secondly, I thank the Good Lord for the New Year 1953. I and my family are well and we send greetings to yours. As regards the 1,000 francs which you sent to your wife's father and which he refused. I have not yet received a letter from there. No doubt I shall receive one later. I think that it would have been better for you to have sent the money here. You know that your wife's father is an old man and that his intelligence is diminishing and that he is becoming like a little child again. You should not worry about the refusal. . . . Do you think that your wife and children are going to be taken away from you? I am not a stupid man. I know that every man has his children here on earth. The Good Lord knows this too, and if someone takes away a man's property it can only be because he is stupid or ignorant. You say my father has refused the 1,000 francs. Well, send them here. Send me a postal order. I have urgent matters to attend to. Do not cry on account of your children, for the good Lord sees everything. I am not one to try to deceive you in front of the eyes of God. If God gives to a man, I am not going to try to take away from him. A child is born for his father and his mother and not in order to be alone.

Greetings to your family. My wife also greets you.
Goodbye,

Your affectionate,

Henri

If I receive a letter from Bafwasende, I shall let you know what is happening.

REFERENCES

ARDENER, S. (1954). 'The comparative study of rotating credit associations', *Journal of the Royal Anthropological Institute*, Vol. 94, Part 2.

BAECK, L. (1961). 'An expenditure study of the Congolese *évolués* of Leopoldville, Belgian Congo', in Southall, A. (Ed.), *Social Change in Modern Africa*. London: Oxford University Press for International African Institute.

BALANDIER, G. (1955). *Sociologie des Brazzaville Noires*. Paris: Armand Colin.

BALANDIER, G. (1956). 'Urbanism in West and Central Africa', in Forde, D. (Ed.), *Social Implications of Industrialization and Urbanization in Africa South of the Sahara*, Unesco, Tensions and Technology Series.

BARNES, J. A. (1951). 'Measures of divorce frequency in simple societies', *Journal of the Royal Anthropological Institute*, Vol. 79.

BARNES, J. A. (1954). 'Class and committees in a Norwegian island parish', *Human Relations*, Vol. 7, No. 1.

BAUMER, G. (1939). *Les Centres indigènes extra-coutumiers au Congo Belge*. Institut de Droit Comparé, Paris.

BERTRAND, MONSIEUR LE COLONEL (1931). *Le Problème de la main-d'œuvre au Congo Belge: Rapport de la commission de la main-d'œuvre indigène*, 1930–31, Province Orientale, Bruxelles.

BOTT, E. (1957). *Family and Social Network*. London: Tavistock Publications.

CLÉMENT, P. (1956). 'Social patterns of urban life', in Forde, D. (Ed.), *Social Implications of Industrialization and Urbanization in Africa South of the Sahara*, Unesco, Tensions and Technology Series.

DAVIS, K. and GOLDEN, H. H. (1954). 'Urbanization and the development of pre-industrial areas' in *Economic Development and Cultural Change*, Vol. III, No. 1. Re-printed in Hatt, P. K., Reiss, A. J. (Eds.), *Cities and Society*. New York: The Free Press (1963).

DENIS, J. (1958). *Le Phénomène urbain en Afrique Centrale*. Académie Royale des Sciences Coloniales, Brussels.

DETRY, A. (1912). *à Stanleyville*. Bruxelles.

DOUCY, A. and FELDHEIM, P. (1956). 'Some effects of industrialization in two Districts of Equatoria Province (Belgian Congo)', in Forde, D. (Ed.), *Social Implications of Industrialization and Urbanization in Africa South of the Sahara*. Unesco, Tensions and Technology Series.

ELKAN, W. (1960). *Migrants and Proletarians: Urban Labour in the Economic Development of Uganda*. London: Oxford University Press.

EPSTEIN, A. L. (1958). *Politics in an Urban African Community*. Manchester University Press.

EPSTEIN, A. L. (1961). 'The network and urban social organization', *The Rhodes–Livingstone Institute Journal*, No. 29.

EPSTEIN, A. L. (1965). 'Gossip, norms and social network', in Mitchell, J. C. (Ed.), *Social Networks in Urban Situations*. Manchester University Press (forthcoming).

EPSTEIN, A. L. (1966). 'Urbanization and social change in Africa', *Current Anthropology*, Vol. 8, No. 4.

FORDE, D. (1956). 'Some aspects of urbanization and industrialization in Africa: A general review', in Forde, D. (Ed.), *Social Implications of Industrialization and Urbanization in Africa South of the Sahara*, Unesco, Tensions and Technology Series.

GLUCKMAN, M. (1950). 'Kinship and marriage among the Lozi of Northern Rhodesia and the Zulu of Natal', in Radcliffe-Brown, R. A. and Forde, D. (Eds.), *African Systems of Kinship and Marriage*. London: Oxford University Press for International African Institute.

GLUCKMAN, M. (1958). *Analysis of a Social Situation in Modern Zululand*. Rhodes–Livingstone Paper No. 28.

GLUCKMAN, M. (1960). 'Tribalism in modern British Central Africa', *Cahiers d'études africaines*, No. 1.

GLUCKMAN, M. (1961). 'Anthropological problems arising from the African Industrial Revolution', in Southall, A. (Ed.), *Social Change in Modern Africa*. London: Oxford University Press for International African Institute.

GRÉVISSE, F. (1951). *Le Centre extra-coutumier d'Elisabethville*. Brussels.

HELLMAN, E. (1948). *Rooiyard: A Sociological Survey of an Urban Slum Yard*, Rhodes–Livingstone Paper No. 13. (Report of a study conducted in 1934.)

LEMARCHAND, R. (1964). *Political Awakening in the Congo: The Politics of Fragmentation*. University of California Press.

MAES, J. and BOONE, O. (1935). *Les Peuplades du Congo Belge*, Vol. I, Publications du Bureau de Documentation Ethnographique, Brussels.

MAGOTTE, J. (1934). *Les Circonscriptions indigènes: Commentaire du décret du 5 décembre 1933, d'après les exposés des motifs, les travaux préparatoires et le rapport du Conseil Colonial*, Imprimerie Disonaise.

MAGOTTE, J. (1938). *Les Centres extra-coutumiers: Commentaires des décrets coordonnés*. Dijon.

MAYER, P. (1961). *Townsmen or Tribesmen*. Cape Town: Oxford University Press.

MAYER, P. (1962). 'Migrancy and the study of African towns', *American Anthropologist*, Vol. 64, No. 3, Part I.

MCCULLOCH, M. (1956a). 'Survey of recent and current field studies on the social effects of economic development in inter-tropical Africa', in Forde, D. (Ed.), *Social Implications of Industrialization and Urbanization in Africa South of the Sahara*. Unesco, Tensions and Technology Series.

MCCULLOCH, M. (1956b). *A Social Survey of the African Population of Livingstone*, Rhodes–Livingstone Paper No. 26.

MITCHELL, J. C. (1954). *African Urbanization in Ndola and Luanshya*, Rhodes–Livingstone Communication No. 6.

MITCHELL, J. C. (1957a). 'Aspects of African Marriage on the Copperbelt of Northern Rhodesia', *The Rhodes–Livingstone Journal*, No. 22.

MITCHELL, J. C. (1957b). *The Kalela Dance*, Rhodes–Livingstone Paper No. 27. Manchester University Press.

MITCHELL, J. C. (1961a). 'Wage labour and African population movements in Central Africa', in Barbour, K. M. and Prothero, R. M. (Eds.), *Essays on African Population*. London: Routledge & Kegan Paul.

MITCHELL, J. C. (1961b). 'Measures of marriage stability' in *Marriage and the Family: Report of the 1961 Conference of the Northern Rhodesia Council of Social Service*. Lusaka.

MITCHELL, J. C. (1961c). 'African marriage in a changing world', in *Marriage and the Family: Report of the 1961 Conference of the Northern Rhodesia Council of Social Service*. Lusaka.

MITCHELL, J. C. (1961d). 'Social change and the stability of African marriage in Northern Rhodesia', in Southall, A. (Ed.), *Social Change in Modern Africa*. London: Oxford University Press for International African Institute.

MITCHELL, J. C. (1965). 'Differential fertility amongst urban Africans in Zambia', *The Rhodes–Livingstone Journal*, No. 37.

MITCHELL, J. C. (1966). 'Theoretical orientations in African urban studies', in Banton, M. (Ed.), *The Social Anthropology of Complex Societies*. London: Tavistock Publications.

PERHAM, M. and SIMMONS, J. (1957). *African Discovery: An Anthology of Exploration*. London: Faber.

PONS, V. G. (1956a). 'The growth of Stanleyville and the composition of its African population', in Forde, D. (Ed.), *Social Implications of Industrialization and Urbanization in Africa South of the Sahara*. Unesco, Tensions and Technology Series.

PONS, V. G. (1956b). 'The changing significance of ethnic affiliations and of Westernization in the African settlement patterns in Stanleyville', in Forde, D. (Ed.), *Social Implications of Industrialization and Urbanization in Africa South of the Sahara*. Unesco, Tensions and Technology Series.

PONS, V. G. (1961). 'Two small groups in Avenue 21: some aspects of the system of social relations in a remote corner of Stanleyville, Belgian Congo', Chapter IX of Southall, A. (Ed.), *Social Change in Modern Africa*. London: Oxford University Press for International African Institute.

SOFER, C. and R. (1955). *Jinja Transformed*. East African Studies, No. 4.

SOUTHALL, A. W. (1956). 'Determinants of the social structure of African urban populations, with special reference to Kampala (Uganda)', in Forde, D. (Ed.), *Social Implications of Industrialization and Urbanization in Africa South of the Sahara*. Unesco, Tensions and Technology Series.

SOUTHALL, A. W. (1961a). 'Introductory Summary', in Southall, A. W. (Ed.), *Social Change in Modern Africa*. London: Oxford University Press for International African Institute.

SOUTHALL, A. W. (1961b). 'Kinship, friendship, and the network of relations in Kisenyi, Kampala', in Southall, A. W. (Ed.), *Social Change in Modern Africa*. London: Oxford University Press for International African Institute.

STEIN, M. R. (1960). *The Eclipse of Community: An Interpretation of American Studies*. Princeton University Press.

UNITED NATIONS (1957). 'Urbanization in Africa South of the Sahara', in *Report on the World Social Situation*. New York.

VAN REYN, P. (1960). *Le Congo Politique: les partis et les élections*. Bruxelles.

WILSON, G. (1941–2). *An Essay on the Economics of Detribalization in Northern Rhodesia*, Rhodes–Livingstone Papers Nos. 5 and 6 (1941 and 1942).

XYDIAS, N. (1956). 'Labour: conditions, aptitudes, training', in Forde, D. (Ed.), *Social Implications of Industrialization and Urbanization in Africa South of the Sahara*. Unesco, Tensions and Technology Series.

INDEX

Administration de la Colonie du Congo Belge, (cited), 41n.

Adultery: and divorce, 293; and *humwali*, 217; and urban residence, 212n; attitudes towards, 181, 182, 211n.

Affaires Indigènes et Main-d'oeuvre, Province Orientale, (cited), 251n.

African community: in 1952/53, 11; in 1967, xxii–xxiii.

African population: (*see also* age and sex structures, age composition, age, fertility, sex ratio, *etc.*), geographical origins of, 21, 62, 65, 100n; lengths of residence in town, 123n; occupational composition of, 25–26; numbers in 1920, 22; rise in numbers from 1920 to 1967, xxii, 22–24; tribal composition of, 63.

African residential areas: in contrast to the 'European town', 11; 'suburban' character of, 31–32.

African trade and commerce, 29–31.

Age and sex structures: three 'types' of, 83ff.; of the nine principal tribes, 276–280.

Age composition: of male title-holders of dwelling compounds, 287; of some other urban African populations, 45–46, 59n, 60n; of total African population of Stanleyville, 43–45; of immigrants, 43.

Age: and educational–occupational achievements, 57–58; and rural birth, 61n; differences between tribal colonies, 83ff.

Aketi (town), 21, 46.

Arab influence (*see also Arabisé* colony, *Arabisé* culture, *Arabisé* influence, *Arabisé* village, *and Arabisés*), 64.

Arabisé colony, early establishment of, 22, 103, 246.

Arabisé culture, assessment of individuals in relation to the ways and culture of the *Arabisés*, 148, 162, 176.

Arabisé village: administration of, 34, 100, 262; ethnic composition of, 70, 75; nature and size of population, 34; wages of inhabitants, 104.

Arabisés: age and sex structure, 83, 85, 87, 90, 280; and *humwali*, 212n; and trade, 246; areas of recruitment out-

side Stanleyville, 67, 73; circumcision among, 178, 207, 291; diviners, 181; fertility of, 84, 86, 90; historical origins of, 22; incidence of polygyny among, 87; in the C.E.C., 33; image and reputation of, 76; low rate of immigration, 89, 246; numbers in town, 62–63; marriages ending in divorce within specified periods, 243–244; residential distribution of, 67–68, 70, 75; schooling of adult men, 93; title-holders of dwelling compounds, 91; urban and rural involvement of, 24, 34, 99.

Ardener, S., 211n.

Armée Nationale Congolaise, xix–xxi.

Army, see *Armée Nationale Congolaise* and *Force Publique*.

Asians, 21.

Association des Anciens Élèves des Pères de Scheut, 124n.

Associations des Anciens Élèves de Mandombe, 124n.

Association des Babali, 266.

Association des Évolués de Stanleyville, 124n.

Associations, *see* voluntary associations.

Augustin's shop, contrasted with Mayala's tea room, 158–160.

Avenue 21: adult male attitudes to town life and 'civilization', 50–51; and 'small group' structure, 209; and the wider community, 127–128, 210, 257, 263 ff; close-knit networks of 'brothers' and 'family friends' in, 266; extra-marital associations of wives, 251n; 'fictitious' and 'semi-institutionalized' relationships in, 250, 267; reasons for intensive study of, 5, 127–128, 257–258; history and social character of, 128 ff; *humwali* in, 212n; *ikilemba* arrangements in, 211n; in 1967, xxiii–xxiv; influence of urban culture in, 263; landlords in, 133; mobility of inhabitants of, 132; occupational composition of, 250; permissive code of behaviour between the sexes, 267; recent immigrants and old-established residents in, 205–206; seeming individuality of, 263–264; social characteristics of the inhabitants, 132–133; social cohesion seen as 'communal' rather than

81–82; residential cluster of, 75, 112; residential concentration and dispersion of, 66–69, 71, 75; rural location of, 65; schooling of adult men, 93; title-holders of compounds, 91.

Bambole (tribe): age and sex structure, 85, 277; extensive networks of 'real' kin, 266; fertility of, 84, 86; likened to Lokele and Topoke, 146, 245; marriages ending in divorce within specified periods, 243–244; numbers in town, 62–63; residential cluster of, 75; residential concentration and dispersion of, 66–69; schooling of adult men, 93; title-holders of dwelling compounds, 91.

Banduku, see nduku.

Bangelima (tribe): numbers in town, 62–63; rural location of, 65.

Bangobango (tribe): numbers in town, 62–63; rural location of, 65.

Bantu, tribes of Bantu stock, 21, 62.

Barnes, J. A., 14, 17n, 251n.

Barumbi (tribe): as a proportion of households in the area of Avenue 21, 132; members seen as constituting a distinctive group in the neighbourhood of Avenue 21, 162, 178; residential cluster of, 75, 112–113, 248.

Basaiba, see under friendship.

Basendji, see musendji and also kisendji.

Basoko (tribe): numbers in town, 62–63; rural location of, 65.

Baumer, G., 35, 36, 42n.

Bayomba, see muyomba.

Belge I: (*see also under centre extra-coutumier*), general social character of, 32, 103; household size in, 39, 105; pattern of use of dwelling compounds, 103, 105–107; population in 1932, 30, 103; population in 1952/53, 33, 103; social character of one of its neighbourhoods, 109–111, 122, 247, 248; wages of inhabitants, 103–104.

Belge II: (*see also under centre extra-coutumier*), general social character of, 33–34, 107–108; household size in, 105; population in 1932, 34; population in 1952/53, 34, 107–108; wages of inhabitants, 104; use of dwelling compounds, 39, 105–106.

Bernard's compound, 154–155.

Bertrand, Monsieur le Colonel, 47, 60n, 86, 101n.

Boone, O. *See* Maes and Boone.

Bott, E., 14, 17n.

Brazzaville, 45, 211n, 250n.

Brides, recruitment from home villages, *see under* women.

Bridewealth: among *Arabisé*, Babali, and Babua, 246; among Lokele, 76–77, 245; examples of court rulings at time of divorce, 292–293; negotiating procedures, 180–181, 184–185, 198, 218, 219.

'Brothers': (*see also* 'brotherhood', *nduku*, and 'real' and 'fictitious' kinship), 'communities' or sub-communities of 'brothers' and 'friends', 160.

'Brotherhood': and fellow tribesmen, 160, 170, 268–269; flexibility of principle of, 165–167; interwoven bonds of 'brotherhood', 'neighbourhood', and 'family friendship', 262; of members of tribes with cultural affinities, 203; optative and permissive as a principle, 167, 261.

Brussels: (*see also under centre extra-coutumier and see* Kadondo), general social character of, 33–34, 103, 131–132; household size in, 105; pattern of use of dwelling compounds, 39, 103, 105–106; population in 1932, 33; population in 1952/53, 33, 106; wages of inhabitants, 104, 106–107.

Bunia (town), 21.

'Burial association' (*la réunion*) in the neighbourhood of Avenue 21, 164, 265–266.

Buta (town), 21, 46, 64, 78.

Carrington, John, xix, xx.

Case histories, use of, 171–172, 174, 176.

'Categorical' relations, *see under* social relations.

C.E.C., *see* Centre Extra-coutumier.

Centre Extra-coutumier de Stanleyville, Rapports Annuels, 1937, 1940, 1945, 1952, (cited), 37, 38, 40, 42n.

Centre Extra-coutumier of Stanleyville: (*see also* urban courts), application of regulations and controls in, 37–38, 42n; constituent townships of, 32, 33; chief and councillors of, 36; conditions of admission to, 36–37; system of accommodation in, 38–40.

Centres Extra-coutumiers: (*see also Décret sur les Centres Extra-coutumiers*), constitution of, 35–36; explained, 5; in the Belgian Congo from 1932 to 1935, 35; in the Eastern Province, 21.

For Product Safety Concerns and Information please contact our EU
representative GPSR@taylorandfrancis.com
Taylor & Francis Verlag GmbH, Kaufingerstraße 24, 80331 München, Germany

www.ingramcontent.com/pod-product-compliance
Lightning Source LLC
Chambersburg PA
CBHW070732270326
41926CB00054B/2177